THE PHILOSOPHY OF RELIGION

THE
PHILOSOPHY OF RELIGION

BY

HARALD HÖFFDING

TRANSLATED FROM THE GERMAN EDITION

BY

B. E. MEYER

BOOKS FOR LIBRARIES PRESS
FREEPORT, NEW YORK

First Published 1906
Reprinted 1971

INTERNATIONAL STANDARD BOOK NUMBER:
0-8369-5739-3

LIBRARY OF CONGRESS CATALOG CARD NUMBER:
71-152987

PRINTED IN THE UNITED STATES OF AMERICA

TRANSLATOR'S NOTE

I AM indebted to the Author for his kindness in reading through and commenting on the proof-sheets of this translation as they passed through the press. I hope by this means to have secured a faithful rendering of the original.

B. E. M.

CONTENTS

I. PROBLEM AND PROCEDURE

οὐκ ἔστι λύειν ἀγνοῦντα τὸν δεσμόν.—ARISTOTLE.

BY philosophy of religion we may understand either a mode of thinking which is prompted by religion and takes religion as its foundation, or a mode of thinking which makes religion its object. In this work the word is used in the latter sense. That mode of thinking, which springs out of religion and interprets phenomena in a religious sense, forms part of the subject-matter of the philosophy of religion, and must not itself be called by that name.

The word "religion" stands in the main for a psychical state in which feeling and need, fear and hope, enthusiasm and surrender play a greater part than do meditation and inquiry, and in which intuition and imagination have the mastery over investigation and reflection. It is of course true that within the religious life itself an instinctive need of analysing its own state and content, the value of its motives, and the validity of its thinking is for ever cropping up. But the religious thinking which thus originates does not definitely occupy itself with the religious problem proper. The problems with which it deals arise within the boundaries of religion; religion itself never becomes a problem. Religion is taken as the starting-point as a matter of course, or, at any rate, in comparison with the religious, other standpoints are so subordinated as to possess no determinative significance. This is the nature of religious thinking at those periods when religion is all in all within the spiritual sphere.   The classical ages of religion are either the periods of great beginnings, when, with all the power of originality, it attracts all forces and all interests to itself; or the great organising periods, when all existing culture is cast or bent into obedience to the highest religious ideas.   In these classical ages great unity, or at any rate great harmony, prevails in the spiritual world.   Christianity enjoyed such a golden age during the time of the primitive Christian community, and again, later, during the great periods of organisation in the flower of the Middle Ages.   A religious problem, in the strict sense of the word, can only arise when other sides of the spiritual life —science and art, moral and social life—begin to emancipate themselves and to claim free independent value. They then appraise religion from their own points of view and according to their own standards, while religion in her classical ages had either entirely ignored them—as in the inceptive periods—or—as in the organising periods—had assessed them from her own point of view and according to her own standards.   The question then arises whether two such different estimates can ever be brought into inner harmony with one another.   Certain definite historical conditions must be present before the religious problem can be definitely raised.   We may say, if we like, that it is only in unhappy periods that a religious problem can be said to exist.   For such a problem is always the expression of spiritual discord.   The different elements of the spiritual life are no longer working so closely together as formerly; they point in different directions, between which, perhaps, a choice has to be made.   Then it is that the necessity, as well as the possibility, of an investigation makes itself felt.

That religion should be treated as a problem at all

may give offence to many people; but, once awake,
thought must have the right to inquire into everything,
and its limits must be assigned by itself.   Who else
indeed can do this ?   He to whom the problem does
not present itself has of course no ground for thought,
but neither has he any ground for preventing other
people from thinking.   Let him who fears to lose his
spiritual haven of refuge stand far off.   No one wants
to rob the poor man of his ewe lamb — only let him
remember that he must not drive it along the high road
unnecessarily and then demand that the traffic should
be stopped on its account.   Experience, moreover, tends
to show that it is the rams, rather than the lambs, that,
at right and especially at wrong times, are wont to let
the world know they are being scandalised.   It is not
the really spiritually poor, but your obstinate and noisy
dogmatists who raise a hue and cry when free inquiry
demands the right to move within the religious as within
all other spheres.

The inquiry on which I here propose to embark
addresses itself neither to those already satisfied nor to
the anxious.   The former are to be found in all camps,
—not least among the so-called "free-thinkers"— a
class of men which, like that of worms in the Linnæan
system, can only be characterised by negative predicates,
since it has to embrace so many different forms.   Those
already satisfied hold in reserve a definite solution,
negative or positive, of the religious problem, and hence
have lost all taste for further thinking on the subject.
The anxious are afraid to think about it.   My inquiry,
therefore, addresses itself to the seekers.   "Ein Wer-
dender wird immer dankbar sein," in whatever direction
his quest may lead him.

Philosophy, as is well known, is richer in ideas,
points of view, and discussions than in definite results,
and the philosopher would often be in sore straits were

he not upheld by the conviction that the unceasing striving after truth forms part of those highest spiritual values, the conservation of which is the business of all true religion. Even if we learn nothing else from our study of the philosophy of religion, it may serve to enlighten us as to the nature of the struggle which rages round the religious question, and to give us some insight into the significance of this struggle in the development of the spiritual life ; while, should the religious problem prove insoluble, we may perhaps discover why it is that no solution can be found.

2. A philosophy of religion must not start from any ready-made philosophical system. In a certain sense all thinking must be systematic, for "system" means literally "that which stands together," and our thoughts must be prepared to satisfy the most rigorous test in this respect. Internal harmony and consistency are the sign-manual of truth within all spheres, and are therefore rightly demanded within the sphere of the philosophy of religion. But the work of the philosophy of religion will be most productive when religion and its manifestations are not brought into relation with an already concluded philosophical scheme, but are illuminated by a process of philosophising of which the main occupation is to decide whether or no we may expect to arrive at a conclusion. Our task is to elucidate the relation of religion to spiritual life. Religion is itself a mode or form of spiritual life, and it can only be truly estimated when it is viewed in its relation to other forms and modes of this life. The standard which is here applied to religion is not a strange one. For there is *one* service which no spiritual power, however great the name it bears, dares to withhold : it must serve to deepen and enrich the spiritual life as it develops. Hence the first task of the philosophy of religion must be to discover means by which to estimate how far religion can continue

to render this service under the conditions, present and
future, of our spiritual culture.   In the solution or better
handling of this problem, the philosophy of religion can
only employ such presuppositions as every other science
brings to the treatment of its subject-matter.   We may
expect to find it often obliged to confess that there are
questions it cannot answer, for within the spiritual sphere
relations are more complicated and more various than
dogmatists, negative or positive, are inclined to believe.
But this does not rob the discussion of problems of its
significance.   Conscious insight into the impossibility of
solution (*docta ignorantia*) naturally leads to the further
inquiry as to whether it is, after all, of the first necessity
that a solution should be found.   Moreover, our sight
will become sharpened for certain relations under which
our spiritual culture at present exists, but which we
have no reason to suppose will continue for ever, since
even at present they do not exercise equal influence
over all personalities.

Our inquiry into the philosophy of religion will be
more profitable if we divide it into three parts—the first,
epistemological ; the second, psychological ; the third,
ethical.

In its golden ages religion satisfies all the spiritual
needs of man, including his thirst for knowledge.   In
such periods religious ideas supply men with an explanation of existence as a whole, as well as in its various
parts.   But where an independent science has arisen,
there exists a mode of understanding or of explaining
other than the religious, and the question then arises as
to whether these two interpretations can be harmonised.
It is possible that the new scientific explanation may
gradually supersede the religious as regards particulars,
but that it is not applicable to existence as a whole—
to what are usually called "first" or "last" questions.
In this case we must proceed to inquire how far religion

is in a position to solve the riddles which are insoluble
for science.　Should it appear that religious ideas contribute nothing with regard either to the whole or to
the parts which deserves the name of understanding or
explanation, we must ask the further question : What
significance do these ideas possess ?

This latter question leads us over from the epistemo
logical to the psychological section of the philosophy of
religion.　For when religious ideas have lost their value
as knowledge, any value that they possess must lie in
their power of expressing some side of the spiritual life
other than the intellectual.　Hence, what we now require
is a description of the religious life of the soul, and
especially of the relation between these ideas and
religious experience and feeling.　It will thus be seen
that in its innermost essence religion is concerned not
with the comprehension, but with the valuation of
existence, and that religious ideas express the relation
in which actual existence, as we know it, stands to that
which, for us, invests life with its highest value.　For
the core of religion—at any rate according to the
hypothesis which we have been led to adopt—consists
in the conviction that no value perishes out of the world.
This faith appears in all popular religions, but especially
in the higher forms, in broad and easily recognisable
features.　And the same conviction may animate the
breasts of those who stand outside all these religions,
although in such cases it will not have assumed any
definite shape.

The transition from the psychological to the ethical
aspect of the philosophy of religion is brought about
quite naturally by the question which here necessarily
arises as to the ethical value of this belief in the conservation of value.　Ethics is concerned with the
production of value, and it cannot be denied that the
labour of producing value may leave a man neither time

nor strength to dwell on the thought of its conservation. The ethical side of the philosophy of religion presents a parallel with the epistemological side.   In its golden ages religion, directly or indirectly, determines the estimation of all actions and of all relations of life. Here, again, the religious problem arises as soon as an independent ethic has developed itself, for this will seek in its own way for a foundation and a criterion for the estimation of human conduct.   And it is at this point that the problem is most clearly and urgently raised, for the ultimate criterion by which religion must stand or fall must originate within the ethical sphere in which the final balancing of the spiritual account takes place.

Within the schema here sketched out we shall be able to find a place for the discussion of all the essential aspects of the religious problem.   I shall treat this problem not only with the intellectual interest which cannot fail to be excited by so great and comprehensive a subject-matter, but also in the frame of mind evoked by the consciousness that I here have before me a form of spiritual life in which, for centuries long, the human race has stored up its deepest and innermost experiences.

3. Before we pass on to study the different sections of the philosophy of religion, it will be worth while to pause a moment in order to define a little more closely the content of the religious problem.

It is pretty generally acknowledged in the Protestant world that knowledge and faith must be distinguished from one another.   The Catholic Church, however, does not admit this distinction in its full extent; accordingly, she recognises no religious problem within the intellectual sphere.   This church maintains that the existence of God can be demonstrated in the manner indicated by Thomas Aquinas, with the help of Aristotle; she even goes so far as to declare the acceptance of the

sufficiency of this proof to be *de fide*. The tradition
handed down from the great period of the Middle
Ages when "men did not doubt and were therefore
nearer the truth" (to borrow a phrase from a recent
biographer of Thomas Aquinas) is still held in honour,[1]
and it is not admitted that any real discord has arisen
within the spiritual life. The distinction between knowledge and faith is an avowal of the existence of such
discord—a confession that the unity of the spiritual life
has suffered interruption. Is it possible that this distinction is itself only a station on the road which evolution
is taking towards the expulsion of all religion from the
spiritual life, because that only can persist which is able
to enter into a harmonious relation with the other
elements of that life? We may believe either that the
great ages of religion will never repeat themselves, or
that its time has altogether gone by. In either case we
are bound to inquire whether in the course of this process
of dissolution any spiritual value has gone out of existence,
or whether new value can be discovered compensating
for the lost unity and completeness of the spiritual life.
This inquiry in itself suffices to show that the question
as to the conservation of value is an essential aspect of
the religious problem, whatever solution of the latter we
may be induced to adopt. It is indeed principally from
this side that the philosophy of the last century and a
half (since Rousseau, Lessing, and Kant) has approached
the religious problem. Romanticists as well as Positivists
have devoted their attention to this aspect of the question.[2]
We must remember that even if it could be conclusively
shown that the dissolution of religion involved no loss of
spiritual energy, this would not prove that, under the
new relations, this energy would be as profitably ex-
pended as it was in the great days of religion. In the
spiritual, no more than in the material, sphere can we
assume that the conservation of energy is equivalent to

the conservation of value.   Energy may persist without the continuance of value, while the converse of this is almost unthinkable, since, in and for itself, energy must be a condition of the preservation and development of the valuable.   Many free-thinkers take for granted that human life would assume richer and stronger forms did religion cease to exist ; but this view is very far from being self-evident, and rests on the presupposition that psychical equivalents are always at hand—equivalents in value as well as in energy.   In that case these equivalents would have to be demonstrated, and were this possible, the conservation of value would be proved.   But it is a great question and an essential feature of the problem of religion whether such equivalents can be shown to exist.   Moreover, the problem of the conservation of value raises its head within the Church itself, for religion and the religious life are constantly undergoing change ; and hence we have to inquire whether the values present in the golden ages of religion have passed through these changes unconsumed ; whether, for example, primitive Christianity, in terms of value as well as of energy, has maintained itself in the Christianity of to-day.   We get this problem stated in its most acute form in the assertion that " the Christianity of the New Testament no longer exists."

But the religious problem is not merely concerned with the conservation of value in the human world. Behind the psychological issue rises a cosmological one. We have to consider the relation between what seems to us men the highest value and existence as a whole. Is there any interconnexion between values and the laws of the forces of existence ?   Are these laws and forces themselves ultimately determined by the highest values ? or are we precluded from attributing validity to our concept of value beyond the sphere of human life ?

The hypothesis which I shall hope later (in my discussion of the psychological side of the philosophy of religion) to establish is based on the premiss that the conservation of value is *the characteristic axiom of religion*, and that we shall find it expressed from different religious standpoints in different ways. The question how far we are to attribute real validity to this axiom forms part of the religious problem. At the same time this axiom—in so far as it expresses the fundamental thought of all religion—can be used as a criterion of the consistency and significance of particular religions, or of particular religious standpoints.

Finally, as I have already observed, this axiom enables us to express very simply the relation between ethics and religion, viz. what is the relation between the conviction of the conservation of value and the work of discovering, producing, and preserving values?

Were we to investigate the axiom of the conservation of value in all its bearings, our discussion would never be concluded; moreover, we should soon lose all clear points of view from which to conduct it. Hence I do not hesitate to determine at the outset the limits within which I propose to restrict myself, and I must beg my readers kindly to bear them in mind throughout the discussion.

In my attempt to show that the above-mentioned axiom is the fundamental thought of all religion, I shall not regard it as an indication of failure if it should prove that no single religion formulates this axiom with clearness and consistency. I shall be content if I can point out an express desire or tendency to hold by this axiom, so that our standard of measurement in estimating the values of different religions in their mutual relations can be the degree in which they severally give utterance to and apply it. When I speak of the *conservation* of value, it might be taken to mean that value can never disappear—that existence must always contain value,

whether this latter increase or decrease, or alternate
between the two. But I use the expression " conservation
of value " in analogy with the expression "conservation
of energy," so that the axiom asserts the continuous conservation of value throughout all transformations.   It
may, therefore, perhaps, be necessary to distinguish
between potential and actual value, as physicists distinguish between potential and actual energy ; and the one
distinction is just as clear and just as valid as the other.
The conservation of value throughout all transformations, and in spite of the difference between possibility
and reality, is, however, only the minimum.   It may be
contended that the mere conservation of value is insufficient, and, indeed, that it involves a contradiction,
for, since repetition stales, value can only really be
preserved by increase ; while, on the other hand, change
can only itself be of value if it lead to an increase.
That an increase of value in no way conflicts with the
conservation of energy requires no elaborate proof; for
increase of value presupposes a new and more perfect
application of energy, not its increase.   For simplicity's
sake, however, I limit my investigation to the *conservation* of value.   And we shall soon see that the religious
consciousness has also, as a matter of fact, limited itself
to this.   The conservation of value will present us with
quite sufficient difficulties and problems, even though we
do not undertake to trace out all that inevitably follows
from the admission that value can only be retained by
being increased.   But we ought not to forget that this
does follow.   Finally, it might be asked, when we
speak of the conservation of value, what value do we
mean, and how great is it ?   I shall only attempt to
investigate this question in so far as the distinction
between different religions and religious standpoints
essentially depends on the different answers which they
give to it.   It is evident that acceptance of the axiom of

the conservation of value in no way depends on what
this answer is. The hypothesis that the conservation of
value is the fundamental axiom of religion will not be
shaken by the fact that different religions and different
religious standpoints differ from one another to a very
wide extent with regard to the nature and the extent of
the valuable in the conservation of which they believe.

Value denotes the property possessed by a thing
either of conferring immediate satisfaction or serving
as a means to procuring it. Value, therefore, may be
mediate or immediate. Where immediate value is given
we seek to preserve it ; where not given, to produce it.
We make it, that is to say, our end. Conversely, the
fact that we adopt something as an end implies that we
have an experience or a presumption of its immediate
value. Mediate value is possessed by everything which
helps to attain an end, *i.e.* an immediate value. Mediate
value need not necessarily be potential value. For that
which serves as a means for procuring an immediate value
itself acquires in our eyes a certain value, even though
we know it to be derivative. Between mediate and
immediate values there are all sorts of transitions, and
when motives are re-adjusted the former pass over into
the latter, so that finally what originally only had value
as a means becomes valuable as an end. Potential
value, on the other hand, often indicates nothing more
than the possibility that a thing will possess value as a
means—the possibility, that is, of mediate value. What
the values are which are experienced and therefore
recognised from the different standpoints will depend on
the different natures of these standpoints. The nature
of a being determines its needs, and its needs determine
what shall have value for it. The religious axiom,
therefore, shows that the character of a religion must
necessarily be determined by the nature and the needs
of the men who profess it. For no man can seriously

believe in the conservation of a value of which he has had not even approximate experience.

We are indebted to the philosophy of Kant for the independent consideration of the problem of value apart from the problem of knowledge. He taught us to distinguish between estimation and explanation.[3] But that this distinction does not involve a complete opposition becomes evident when we reflect that it must depend on the laws and forces of existence whether anything can retain value for us, and whether we can make the valuable an end which admits of realisation. The religious problem, therefore, cannot be separated from other philosophical problems, although it may be most advantageously treated in isolation. It exhibits a striking analogy with other problems. The fundamental problem of philosophy is concerned with the continuity of existence in relation to the special and individual forms of existence. And if we find substantial reasons for adopting the hypothesis that the axiom of the conservation of value is the religious axiom *par excellence*, then we shall admit that the religious problem also is concerned with the continuity of existence, although from a special point of view, and that it falls under the fundamental problem as a particular form of it.[4]

II. EPISTEMOLOGICAL PHILOSOPHY OF RELIGION

A. UNDERSTANDING

Ihm ziemt's die Welt im Innern zu bewegen.—GOETHE.

4. My assumption that the essence of religion consists in the conviction that value will be preserved, may seem contradicted by the fact that theoretical motives have always played a conspicuous part in the development of religious conceptions, and with many men still continue to do so. Moreover, as I have already remarked, religion which in its classical periods is all-sufficient for man, at such times also satisfies his thirst for knowledge, that is to say, it supplies him with means and forms by which to arrive at an understanding and explanation of existence. During these golden ages of religion there exists no separate impulse after knowledge, any more than there exists especial means and forms in which such an impulse could find satisfaction.

The divorce between knowing and believing, understanding and estimating, did not take place before the critical periods, *i.e.* the periods in which religion itself becomes a problem. It only began to be generally accepted after repeated and violent collisions between science and religion. Only against their will was it gradually borne in on the representatives of religion that it is no part of the work of religion to supply a scientific explanation of the world. What is now a commonplace in the mouth of theologians, viz. that we must not look to the Bible to teach us natural science, could not get a hearing in the days of Bruno, Galileo, and Spinoza. The persecution of heretics ran its course, and only when it was too late did men begin to perceive the truth of what these heretics had been saying. The same quarrel recurs in other spheres ; to-day it centres round the independence of mental science.

Every great religion has appeared in history with a conception of the world, into which it weaves, in its own particular fashion, all the ideas of its age. Christianity, for instance, was attractive to many during the first centuries in virtue of its intellectual content. Thus Tatian became a convert to Christianity because this " barbarian philosophy," as he called it, seemed to explain what he had not previously been able to understand, *i.e.* " the origin of the world." The standpoint adopted by all the early apologists was that Christianity offered the best solution of intellectual difficulties. If Plato and other Greek philosophers seemed to point to similar solutions, Justin Martyr explains this by saying they must either have been influenced by the Israelitish prophets, or else that the " Word " (*Logos*) had illuminated the souls of men with an inner light before it became flesh. In comparison with earlier religions, Christianity— as is always the case when higher religions are brought face to face with lower ones—bore a certain rational character, and more especially a simplicity, a quiet majesty which could not fail to attract many men who had previously only been acquainted with the earlier religions and their many coloured mythologies. Where the world-picture of the biblical writings was inadequate, the fathers and schoolmen supplemented it by the help of Greek science.

As Christianity to western mankind so Buddhism appealed to orientals. It was not only a great religion, but also a great world-conception ; its constituent ideas bore a certain rational character, and could not be understood without a knowledge of preceding Indian thinkers.

When we speak of the opposition between the religious and the scientific interpretation of existence, it is customary to lay stress on the fact that science—especially within the spheres of astronomy, geology, and biology —has led to results which contradict the traditionary doctrines of religion. Hence no small portion of the work of modern apologists consists in showing that the traditionary concepts of religion are reconcilable with such scientific results as are really firmly established. With more or less success—and with more or less taste —these modern apologists, confronted by modern science, avail themselves of the same process of accommodation as that to which the ancient apologists had recourse when confronted by Greek science. Such discussions, however, contribute very little towards the illumination of the religious problem as a whole, unless, perhaps, as offering characteristic examples of the adaptation which the concepts of the religious life—like all other living forces—undergo or tend to undergo with a change of environment. The chief point to notice, however, is that we find here two quite different kinds or types of "understanding" confronting one another. There are two ways of thinking and of explaining events—two ways which differ so widely from one another that when once we have started on either we can find no point at which it would be both justifiable and possible to cross over to the other. The whole mental outlook is so entirely different that it is not too much to say that the word "understanding" is here used in two quite different senses. Let us take a single example—a sudden storm, coinciding with high spring-tides, which destroys many fishing-boats on the open sea, is scientifically explained by the state of the air and sea during the preceding

days. The sermon preached at the grave of the
victims, however, explains the event by saying that
God wished to give those left behind a sign that they
should depart from the error of their ways.[5] At what
point in the series of natural causes are we to conceive
the divine intervention to have taken place? The
natural causes form a consecutive series, each member of
which is indispensable. We must choose between the
two explanations. The one kind of explanation proceeds
on the principle of discovering the longest possible
consecutive series of links, each member of which is
demonstrable by experience. The more the condition
of the air and of the sea at the moment of the catastrophe
can be consecutively connected with their conditions
during the preceding days, the more—according to one
type of explanation—do we "understand" the event.
According to the other type of explanation, it is to be
understood by its value in influencing the characters of
the survivors, and this value is regarded as intentionally
aimed at, as the end of a divine intervention.

The scientific type of explanation, especially in the
course of the three last centuries, has become wonderfully
clear and productive. It does not exclude a religious
evaluation, but it does exclude a confusion between
such an evaluation and explanation proper. It is the
task of the theory of knowledge to investigate the presuppositions and forms of thought which form the basis
of scientific knowledge, and it will not be without interest
for the philosophy of religion to elucidate these presuppositions and forms of thought and compare them
with the basis of the explanation offered by religion.
This will give us an opening for considering how far
religion is able to maintain its importance as a means of
satisfying our desire for knowledge.

(*a*) Causal Explanation

5. To understand means to reduce a hitherto unknown to the known. To understand a thing is not always the same as to assign its causes ; we may understand *what* a thing is without understanding *why* it is so, or why it happens to exist at all. And, again, the understanding why a thing is as it is may be of different kinds.

Understanding may mean recognition (perception). I understand a language when I know its sounds, so that I associate the correct sense with them. I understand what that patch of white behind the trees is when I have convinced myself that it is the moon shining on the mist. I understand a proposition when I recognise the association of the predicate with the subject intended by the speaker or writer. In all these examples my understanding rests on the discovery of *identity*.

But something more than this may be requisite to the understanding of a proposition. Because I understand the meaning of an individual statement, it does not necessarily follow that I understand why the assertion has been made. I can only arrive at this latter understanding when I am able to trace back the proposition in question to other propositions, until at length I arrive at some proposition which I have previously admitted to be established. "Understanding" in this case means establishing. I do not (in this sense of the word) understand the proposition A is C until I see that it follows from A = B, B = C. Here understanding depends on *rationality*.

I understand (in the former sense) an event in the psychical or material world when I know what has happened. And I understand it (in the latter sense) when I know why I believe that it has taken place. But there is room here for yet a third kind of under-

standing ; to understand an event may mean to deduce
it from preceding events, so that, given these events, we
may infer the happening of the first mentioned event.
Here understanding means a *causal explanation*, and
consists in the discovery of causes.

Identity, rationality, and causality are related to one
another. Rationality, *i.e.* the relation between ground
(premisses) and consequent (conclusion) presupposes
identity ; the proposition A is C is, to a certain extent,
already contained in the two propositions, A is B and
B is C ; it is really only another expression of the
content of these two propositions, which expression I
arrive at by substituting in place of B in the first
proposition the predicate of B (*i.e.* C) given in the
second proposition, and this I am entitled to do in virtue
of the identity of the two B's. The conclusion is the
result of combining the premisses. Causality, again, presupposes logical rationality. The relation of cause and
effect is analogous with that between ground and
consequent. Two events stand in causal relation to
one another when they not only follow one upon the
other in time, but when the first is related to the second,
as ground to consequent. Causality includes logical
rationality, but, over and above this, it presupposes that
a change, a temporal transition from one event to the
other, has taken place. The effect may be said, in a
certain sense, to reside in the cause, but it is something
more than its purely logical conversion into another
form. In the passage from cause to effect there is not
merely a passage of thought from one form to another,
but a process of transition takes place in actuality. The
great question is, whether all relations between actual
events are causal relations ?

When we assert that every event has a cause, which
is the fundamental axiom of causation, we thereby lay
down the principle that existence, as a whole, is under-

standable in the third sense of the word. This axiom
can never be more than hypothetical, because we shall
never be in a position to understand everything, to
assign causes to all events. But it contains the presupposition with which we instinctively confront events
which excite our attention. In any case, it is this
presupposition which prompts us to look about for
preceding events when some particular event has taken
place.

We can afford to neglect the question as to the
ground and origin of the causal axiom, since the conflicting views which are here possible need have no
significance for the philosophy of religion. Whether
the acceptance of this axiom be due to habit or to an
inner necessity of our nature, the need of discovering
causes is active more or less in all men, as is evidenced
by the religious as well as the scientific point of view.
Indeed, religious ideas may be said to possess epistemological interest precisely because they prove how deep
in human nature lies the need of ascertaining causes,
since it finds expression even before any independent
scientific interest can be said to have arisen. The
opposition between religion and science first discloses
itself when men begin to appreciate the different *nature*
of the causes they severally recognise as true and real
causes (*verae causae*). *Religious as well as scientific
understanding is a reduction of the unknown to the known ;
their difference consists in the nature of the known.*

Scientific explanation demands that the causes of an
event shall be reducible to other events, which, like the
event which has to be explained, are found in experience.
Its task is to analyse the series of events so as to find
as many members of the series and as close interconnexion between these members as is possible. It is a
matter of expounding nature by nature, just as a passage
in a book is expounded in such a manner as to connect

it with other passages in the same book. Religious explanation does not demand that the cause shall stand in continuous relation with the effect, or that it, like the event to be explained, shall be given in experience. It does not examine its causes in the critical manner adopted by science. It does not explain nature by nature itself, but by something differing from, or outside nature, which gives it, as it were, a push from without. So, at least, in the history of the world does religious explanation most frequently figure; whether it is inevitable that it should appear in this form, and consequently in opposition to scientific explanation, will become evident later on. In contradistinction to this religious explanation we may call the special form which empirical science, within the psychical as well as the material sphere, gives to the axiom of causation, *the principle of natural causation.* Where this is not applicable we feel that we understand nothing, that is, if the scientific type of understanding and the corresponding intellectual habit of mind are predominant with us.

6. But on what is the principle of natural causation based? Many reasons may be assigned why this principle has worked its way to the forefront, and why it becomes increasingly determinative of the attitude adopted by human consciousness in the face of events which it seeks to *understand.*

It is not sufficient to think out a causal explanation. It must also be possible to show that this explanation is confirmed by experience. Such a confirmation (verification) is attained when we see that, given the same relations, the same event recurs. It is clear from this that such a confirmation is only possible when the cause is itself an event that can be given in actual experience. If, for instance, the explanation given above (§ 4) of the storm and spring flood be correct, then this event must recur whenever the same conditions of air and sea are present, and this must be capable of demonstration. To derive events from the divine will, on the other hand, is no sort of scientific explanation, for it can never be shown that such intentions are present in any particular case, and the explanation is, therefore, not susceptible of proof. It was on this account, and not because of any dislike to religion, that Galileo, Bacon, and Descartes pronounced final causes (so-called) to be unscientific.

It follows from this that the principle of natural causation is the only one which can satisfy our need of special explanation of particular definite events. Thus Galileo pointed out that in the dispute over the conflicting astronomical hypotheses it was idle to appeal to the intervention of God, for to the divine omnipotence it were just as easy to make the sun turn round the earth as the earth round the sun. This cause, therefore, cannot help us to choose between conflicting hypotheses. It is a key which opens all locks, and science seeks for no such master-key. Science is interested in investigating the different natures of the different locks, hence she demands a special key for each lock. Were a master-key sufficient, the difference of locks would lose all significance, and thus present an unsolved problem. The appeal to the will of God affords no scientific explanation ; from the scientific point of view, indeed, it is a confession that the event is not understood.

Further, in doubtful cases we possess but one criterion by which to distinguish between imagination and reality, namely, the firm, unalterable interconnexion of the phenomenon in question with the whole of the rest of our experience. The more this phenomenon appears to be at variance with the rest of our experience, the wider the gaps between the links in the chain of events, the more dissimilar these links to one another, the less certainty we possess that we are confronted by a reality.   In doubtful cases, therefore, we search in experience for intermediate links until we have made out a continuous and unassailable interconnexion. It is evident that the application of the criterion of reality is tantamount to the application of the principle of natural causation.

To my thinking, the deepest foundation for the principle of natural causation is the need for continuity which lies in the nature of our consciousness, and finds expression in the general impulse to ascertain causes. Our consciousness instinctively strives to combine and hold in combination its elements, and to maintain this unity even when confronted by a new content. In such a case it tries to shape, modify, and arrange the new content so that the new may appear as a form of the old. The recognition of its own ego is then possible in spite of the change of content, and the unity of the personal life is mirrored in the continuity thus effected. The task of knowledge here is closely connected with that of the development of character. We can only speak of character, in any definite sense, when, throughout continuous striving, we can detect unity and continuity, not always leaps into something new. In analogy with this, knowledge seeks to discover the greatest possible unity and continuity ; it endeavours to display the new as a transformation or continuation of the old, and only where this is successfully done is perfect appropriation and perfect understanding possible. Hence the principle of natural causation, which demands the formation of the longest and most continuous series possible, is no mere accident ; it is closely bound up with the innermost essence of personality. It is, therefore, a mistake to suppose there is any sharp opposition between personality and science. Scientific work is a work of personality, and the more this work succeeds, the more does explanation through causes approximate to establishment and recognition. The differences presented in existence are reduced to the smallest number possible when with *one* glance we can view a great part of the All "from the point of view of eternity."

7. Religious explanation also, under the mythical and dogmatic forms in which it most frequently appears in history, reduces the unknown to the known. But the known in this case is generally the will of one or more personal beings. The religious consciousness believes itself to know the intentions of a divine will, and recognises in events the expression of this will. Its interest does not lie in discovering an inner connexion between events, but in regarding all events (in nature as a whole or in a particular sphere) as expressions of one and the same power. It places itself at the centre, or believes itself to do so, and surveys from there the whole circle of existence.

The difficulty which here besets the religious conception is that the radius with which this circle should be described is unknown. Many different circles may be described about the same centre. Hence every central point of view (and this is true not only of religious assumptions but also of the various speculative philosophical forms in which it has appeared) is powerless to afford an explanation of particular events. Hence a religious or speculative theory of knowledge can never be worked out. We have not even any serious attempts at it; our only theory of knowledge is that which has been developed by critical philosophy on the basis of the history of empirical science.

Scientific explanation proceeds, to continue our metaphor of centre and circle, on the principle of finding such interconnexion between the facts of the universe that they may be exhibited to our knowledge as a great curve. What kind of curve they form—that is the great problem. There is no reason to suppose at the outset that it must be a circle ; it might be an ellipse,

a parabola, or a hyperbola. It may even be that it is
not a curve at all but a straight line. To discover a
centre under these different relations will not always be
equally easy ; but that does not give us the right to
deny the existence of a centre. Were the curve an
ellipse there would be two centres, and the active
principle might have its seat in one of them. And
even were the series of events to appear to our knowledge as a straight line, the belief in a centre would
be nowise impossible, for a straight line may always be
regarded as part of a circle described with an infinite
radius.

Hence it is always possible, in spite of the radical
difference between the "explanations" of religion and
science, that they may meet and unite. The conditions
for such a harmonisation would be, on the one hand, that,
in its attempt to determine from a centre any particular
point in the curve of being, religion must not dispute or
encroach on the right of science to determine the same
point by means of its relations to other points on the
curve ; while, on the other hand, science must not regard
the problem of being as solved because the position of
single points in relation to other points has been
determined. Experience shows that the central and the
peripheral points of view often conflict, and this not
merely because the one regards the other as unauthorised,
but because they lead to different results. The determination of a point in the series of phenomena which religion,
with its undetermined radius, believes itself able to
assign from its "central" point of view, does not always
agree with the determination which science arrives at
by means of relations with other points in the series ;
and the determination of the centre which science bases
on the empirical character of the curve is not always in
harmony with that determination of the centre from which
religion proceeds. Hence there is not only a possibility

of harmony ; there is also a continual possibility of strife. On the other hand, it is improbable that, in the long run, religion and science will be able to develop independently of one another, so that religion shall continue undisturbedly to describe its circle round its centre without troubling itself how science establishes the interconnexion of the points it has discovered, or that science can continue to move in the periphery of being without bethinking itself that there may perhaps be a centre, and that this centre may conceivably be identical with that assumed by religion. Religion, as well as science, labours in a continuous evolution. The religious centre, however, does not always lie at the same point. Different centres struggle with and supersede each other; and in each new determination of the centre, scientific points of view and scientific results are more and more taken into consideration. The right and the significance of scientific explanation are increasingly recognised—although, it must be confessed, only under incessant opposition and mistrust on the part of religion ; even yet this recognition is not extended to all spheres. Moreover, it is evident that when a considerable number of points on the curve of being have been determined, we must be in a position to state in what direction the centre must be sought for, and thus faith in the central fact of the universe is being gradually but unintermittently influenced by empirical science. On the other hand, religion has exercised considerable influence on the development of science, and may still continue to exercise it ; for it is her part to keep the great limiting problems before men's minds, and to cherish the conviction not only that a centre does exist, but that it is the highest and most ideal task of thought, whether possible or impossible of accomplishment, to discover it.

But, alas! even the figure I have here employed gives too rosy a picture. In reality, religion and science

are not related to one another as are centre and periphery;
for, if that were so, they would be able to understand
one another better, and would indeed each form an
essential part of one comprehensive conception. As a
matter of fact, up to the present time each speaks its
own language. Their conception of causation is not
the same, and hence the difference between their conception of understanding and of explanation. There is
really no sense, therefore, in saying that religion should
be able to solve the riddles to which science can find no
clue. For, since they do not understand the same thing by
" cause " and " explanation," it follows that they must also
mean different things when they speak of " riddles " and
" problems." They frame their questions quite differently,
and are consequently not satisfied with the same answers.
Hence it is not so much the results at which science is
arriving, or has arrived, which bring about the quarrel
between science and religion, and condition the religious
problem, but rather the whole trend of ideas, the entire
habit of mind which empirical science has fostered in
those who have developed under its influence. The
questions of to-day are not those of yesterday. Our
problems are other. This change in the way in which
problems are raised is expressed in the principle of
natural causation. This principle is always extending
its sway, and is of more significance than the fact that
our knowledge of nature is large in comparison with that
of former times. New spiritual needs have arisen which
demand satisfaction and cannot find it in the traditional
concepts which, for earlier generations, offered a solution
of all the problems which could present themselves to
men's minds.

8. When the scientific type of explanation has begun
to get the ascendency in everyday matters, while it is
still rigorously excluded from certain selected points
which religion claims as its own, there arises a bastard

conception which is called *wonder* or *miracle*. Miracles only exist when both types of explanation are in force, and leaps are made from one to the other.   In the absence of a certain degree either of scientific under-standing or of scientific knowledge a "wonder" can mean nothing more than a deviation from the usual. The natural man "wonders" when something hitherto unseen or unheard happens.   But wonder, in the proper sense of the word, implies a certain knowledge of natural laws, a continuity which is interrupted, a rule which suffers exception ; on this account, therefore, wonders must obey the law of parsimony, for were they to occur so frequently as to become the rule, they would form a continuous interconnexion, and thus the concept of wonder would be extruded.

When the principle of natural causation is not maintained as a dogma the impossibility of miracles cannot be asserted *a priori*.   Here again the deciding element will be the way in which the problem is stated and the prevailing intellectual habit of mind.   For the man whose inquiries and problems are framed after the scientific type, a miracle can have no existence.   He may be confronted by something which he is not able to explain, because no cause (in the sense in which he uses the word cause) can be assigned, or at any rate has yet been assigned to it ; but he can never discover that there is no natural cause.   Nor—unless it claim omni-science—can the religious consciousness maintain that an event can *not* be explained by natural laws.   Before we can pronounce that something lies outside all natural laws we must be acquainted with every one of the latter, as well as with all their special applications.   Only by means of a revelation can we learn whether in any particular case a miracle has taken place.   The miracle does not confirm the revelation ; on the contrary, the revelation determines what is a miracle.   Hence the

Catholic Church, which decides what is revelation, is consistent in also claiming the right to decide what is and what is not miraculous. Nothing must be regarded as such which has not been sanctioned by "apostolic and ordained authority." [6]

In the case of miracles of which we ourselves have not been eye-witnesses, the further question arises as to the credibility of the report, and whether the eye-witness was such a close observer that it would be more rational to believe in a deviation from natural law than a mistake in his report and observations. An account given by an observer not having adequate knowledge of the natural conditions and laws in question is of no scientific significance.

Even if, in spite of all these considerations, we were to believe in any particular case that we had here before us as a real miracle, *i.e.* a deviation from the law-abiding order of nature, the concept of God which could be based on this fact would necessarily bear the stamp of imperfection ; for a miracle is a makeshift, a way out, something which has to make up for a want in the order of nature. The ordering of nature has not been so effected that by it all the divine ends can be attained. God encounters an obstacle within his own order of nature. It is as if there were two gods—one who is active during the ordinary course of things, and another who, in particular cases, corrects the work of the former. Hence the concept of miracle is dangerous from the religious as well as from the scientific standpoint. It is a bastard which neither parent can afford to own. The Church is wise in not acceding to the re-awakened desire for miracles. It is true of increasingly large circles that miracles, which in former times were a proof and support of religion, are now rather a stumbling-block which its apologists have to defend, and which in their hearts they must often wish themselves well rid of. The less we think of the relation between God and the world as a purely external one, analogous to the relation between a clockmaker and his clock, the less there is room for, or possibility of, miracles. The happenings of the world differ widely in value, and excite our admiration in very differing degrees ; the highest does not take place every day. But there is nothing to prevent all events from being subject to the same great law. It is large enough to embrace an infinite number of things and of problems. May we not assume that that which is of highest value may be reconcilable with the principle of natural causation? The concept of wonder really arises from the negative answer to this question. From whence the right to negate is derived is not easy to discover. The fact that something is of the highest value does not preclude a purely natural origin. The concept of wonder rests on an identification of estimation with explanation, an identification to which is largely due the confusion which at present characterises the religious problem.

9. Astonishment is the alpha of wisdom, and for the true philosopher it will also be its omega. But when shall we reach this omega? There are many points within our experience of which we are unable to find any complete explanation, or where we cannot exhibit a complete continuity between different phenomena. At such points investigators often betray an inclination to regard supernatural causation as the only possible explanation. For Newton (or at any rate for his immediate followers) gravitation was an elementary phenomenon which could not be reduced to other phenomena, and from which we could immediately infer back to creation by God. In recent times, Clerk Maxwell has adopted a similar standpoint with regard to the invariability and indissolubility of atoms. There is no lack of phenomena which bring inquirers to a standstill in their attempts to find an explanation.

Among such we may mention—in addition to those on which Newton and Maxwell have laid such emphasis—the direction and velocity of movement at the earliest point in time to which our thought can reach back, the actual distribution of energy at the same moment of time, the new qualities which originate in a chemical combination, organic life and consciousness.[7] Led by the principle of natural causation, investigators must leave such points with questions and problems ; there is neither necessity nor justification for accepting answers and explanations which conflict with our own principle of investigation.

It is possible that the relation between our knowledge and reality is an irrational one. Reality may possibly present differences which our knowledge will never be able to reduce to identity and continuity ; possibly there may be differences of quality which cannot be resolved into differences of quantity, and individualities which cannot be explained as the highest points or nodes in a continuous process. For our knowledge itself is a part of the whole of reality, and to assume that the whole of reality must be comprehensible by us is to assume that the whole can be perfectly represented by a particular part, an assumption which, in and for itself, we have no right to make. But even if such an irrational relation exist, a "supernatural" cause does not help us out of the difficulty ; for it is not more able to effect the desired continuity. On the contrary, it adds a new difference and a more crass opposition—namely, that between supernatural and natural working—to those with which thought was already struggling. The riddles remain when we pass over from science to religion—if, indeed, they do not become greater.

Existence is given us as a multiplicity of interconnected phenomena, that is to say, bearing the stamp of unity. But we are not able to deduce the multiplicity from the unity. The conclusion can never contain more than is in the premisses, and if we start our thinking from the concept of an absolute unity, it is impossible for the utmost agility of thought to deduce the manifold from this. The unity of being seems to our knowledge to be the condition and basis of the interconnexion between phenomena; it appears always as the collating principle of particular connexions, and is never given in and for itself alone. The same may be said of the multiplicity of being. From a manifold of absolutely isolated elements no unity can be deduced. Experience, however, shows us the multitudinous elements of being not as absolutely isolated and independent, but—and this the more we learn to know them —as united among themselves, borne by and bearing one another. Unity and manifold, then, are each in themselves an abstraction; what is really given is a totality. Every experience shows us a limited totality which is connected with other totalities. We shall never attain to a completely rounded-off concept of existence as an absolute totality, for our experience is always incomplete.

The real elementary phenomenon which, whatever be the fate of the hitherto irreducible phenomena already alluded to, can itself never be analysed, for it is the condition of all understanding of existence—the real elementary phenomenon is the inner law-abiding interconnexion which holds the world together from within. It is more reasonable to lay weight on this great fundamental fact than on the hindrances to the effectuation of a perfect continuity. For it comes into evidence wherever science has won an understanding of events, and increases in range with every increase of scientific explanation, of which, indeed, it is the presupposition. It is a presupposition to which the fact that the things and events of the world are reciprocally related to one another necessarily leads back ; for isolated, entirely independent things could not stand in a relation of reciprocal action to one another. It would be self-contradictory to attribute absolute independence to the elements of being while accepting the reality of reciprocal action. In virtue of the law of reciprocal action, the nature, working, and suffering of every individual element is determined by its relations to other elements. There must, therefore, be a principle of unity which renders reciprocal action and orderly dependence possible.[8]

For these reasons monism, which takes as its basis this reciprocal action and interconnexion, and finds in these a principle of unity, will always, from an epistemological point of view, be preferable to pluralism, which more or less definitely lays chief stress on the particular elements or things in the world, and betrays a tendency to conceive each one of these in itself as an absolute unity (atoms, monads, individuals). As a consequence of this, it follows that pluralism must either deny interconnexion and reciprocal action, or regard them as illusory. Both views have their special difficulties, and a complete solution of the problem of the unity and multiplicity of existence is unattainable. Every conception of existence —whether it appear in popular, scientific, religious, or philosophical form—will approximate to one or other of these two views, which only appear in absolute opposition when pushed to their extremest forms. But, as already said, from the epistemological point of view the chief stress must be laid on the unity, since it is this which is the presupposition of all understanding—of all identity, logical rationality, and causality. The datum presented to our knowledge is a totality ; we analyse this in order to find the uniting band and the united elements. All the qualities and forces which we attribute to individual elements or things (atoms, monads, individuals) are discovered by investigating the orderly interconnexion in which they stand to one another. The *law* must always be discovered before we can attribute to individual elements or things any faculty or power of working in a particular manner.[9] The nature of the elements is determined by the place which they occupy within the totality in which they have their being. The doctrine of atoms teaches this clearly; natural science attributes to the atoms those qualities which it is led to assume by its understanding of the law of connexion between chemical or physical phenomena. The concept of law is the primary concept of our knowledge; the concepts of particular elements and forces are derivatives from it. The "qualities" of a thing are indeed nothing more than the different forms and ways in which this thing influences that thing and is influenced by it. They are a thing's capabilities of doing and suffering. An absolutely isolated, absolutely independent thing would be able neither to work nor to suffer—and hence could neither be discovered nor known.

How far the fundamental thought which we have here reached, and which is the presupposition of the interconnexion and hence of the understanding of existence, offers an objective conclusion to thought, or whether it is not rather a point beyond which, as a matter of fact, we are not able to go, is a question which I shall take up in a subsequent section. I shall here only bring forward a consideration closely related with our previous argument which tends to show the impossibility of an objective conclusion for thought.

10. The above argument is based on the scientific conception of cause, according to which an event is explained when its interconnexion with other events, either as their continuation or as the transformation of their content into another form, can be pointed out. We next saw that the presupposition of all causal explanation

is a principle of unity which makes the interconnexion possible. We arrived at this principle by means of an analysis of the concept of causal connexion or reciprocal action. It is the bond which holds the "world" together, and makes it a totality, a something more than a chaos of elements—although a totality which we shall never be able to review in its entirety.

The principle of unity to which we thus attain brings to our remembrance the concept of God. The ordinary course of thought, however, arrives at the concept of God by a different route; it does not go back to the presupposition of the causal series, to the principle that makes such a series in any way possible, but carries the causal series back to a "first cause." This line of thought replies to the line of thought followed above as follows : " Religion, with the exception of a few supernatural events, is quite content to leave to science the discovery of finite causes, and the weaving of causal series reaching as far back as possible. But the causes which science can discover can never be more than subordinate, derivative causes (*causae secundae*). What religion asserts is that existence would be meaningless if we could not ultimately find the origin of the whole causal series in a first cause, in an absolute cause, in which our thought can come to rest, where all further questions fall away, and from whence full, clear light is shed over all."

This line of argument was adopted by Thomas Aquinas from Aristotle, and it is on the authority of the former that Catholic, as well as many Protestant, theologians hold it up to the present day.[10] We have here before us the so-called "cosmological proof," the most important of all the "proofs," of the existence of God.

This proof is grounded in the assumption that the series of motions or changes cannot be prolonged into infinity, but must be traced back to a prime mover which

is not itself in motion.   We must get back to a cause
which is not itself an effect.   Every reality has its ground
in a preceding possibility, and this again in a preceding
reality ; this series must end in an absolute reality, which
is itself not only possible but is also the fountain-head
of all possibilities and of all realities.   That the series of
causes must be limited is argued on the ground, that were
this not so no complete explanation of any member of the
series of events could ever be reached.   " Without a first
cause," said Aristotle, "there would be no other cause."
Here, too, as in the previous line of thought (§ 9), the
argument is based on the necessary condition for the
understanding of existence.   Underlying the theological
argument we can discover a rationalistic tendency.
Being must be comprehensible ; that is the underlying
postulate.   Aristotle, however, does not assume that the
first cause began to be active at any definite point in
time, so that the "world" had a beginning.   And
Aquinas also admits that it is only by faith that we can
be led to accept the doctrine that the world had a
beginning (*mundum incepisse, sola fide tenetur*).

In and for itself it is a justifiable procedure to start
Kant subjected this proof to a criticism which led
him to declare that it rested on " a false self-satisfaction
of the human reason."   In its main points his criticism
still stands.   In the following sections I shall avail
myself of his argument, supplemented by some considerations of my own.

In and for itself it is a justifiable procedure to start
from the hypothesis that existence must be comprehensible.   Were we to abandon this altogether our
knowledge would have no ground on which to make a
single step ; no event, no change however great, within
or without us, would set our thought in motion.   We
should state no problems, ask no questions, make no
experiments.   But there is a difference between an
hypothesis and an eternal verity.   The actual knowledge

that we have arrived at in no way justifies us in assuming (§ 8) the absolute rationality of the universe. Strictly speaking, not a single event has ever been entirely explained. Our causal series display many gaps, and they come to an end altogether long before we have reached any cause which we can suppose to be the "first." The proof, therefore, which is based on the assumption that unless we accept a first cause we can have no causes at all, falls to the ground, for it presupposes the existence of events of which a complete causal explanation can be given. Even if we could construct a continuous causal series, at what point should we conclude our search after finite causes in order to hang up the whole chain on a "first cause," as Zeus threatened to hang up the whole world on a peak of Olympus? What sign could we have that we had arrived at the "proximate" cause, and that we must now make the decisive leap? And why may not the causal series be infinite? To say that an infinite series is unthinkable is a dogmatic assertion. There may be series which, in virtue of the law which governs the reciprocal relation of their members, can always be carried further. We conceive such series—not, of course, by thinking through all their members, which would indeed be impossible—but by conceiving the law of their interconnexion. The causal series is of this kind. It is constructed on the strength of the causal axiom, which maintains that everything which happens has a cause. This axiom—if it is to be accepted at all—must be regarded as holding good for every member of the series; for the so-called "first" to which we can reach back as well as for all the rest. Hence the assumption of an absolute first cause would conflict with the causal axiom, although it is precisely by the absolute rationality of the universe, in other words, by the causal axiom, that it is supposed to be justified.

In answer to this it has been argued from the

theological side[11] that we are here operating with the
category of finite causes, according to which everything
in existence has a preceding cause, while what we need
here is a higher concept of cause. God as first cause
must be the cause of himself, *i.e.* at once his own effect
and his own cause. But how this is conceivable is not
explained. Martensen asserts that in God possibility
ought not to be separated from reality in such a way
as to make possibility precede reality : " God," says he,
" produces himself as his own result ; but the result is co-
eternal with the self-production." But a result which
has always existed cannot be a result. To say that
anything is the cause of itself is at once to apply and
to annul the concept of cause. The schoolmen were
more logical when they refused to predicate the concept
of possibility of God, conceiving him as pure activity in
which there is no trace of mere possibility to be found
(*actus purus, non habens aliquid de potentialitate*). But
here the difficulty arises as to how we can conceive an
activity without a continuous passage from possibility to
reality, potentiality to actuality. An activity without a
distinction in time between possibility and reality is self-
contradictory, for it would be an activity which effected
nothing, not even the consumption of force. But even
this contradiction is not so glaring as that involved in the
realisation of possibilities which have through all eternity
been realities. We cannot attribute validity to concepts
such as possibility, time, activity, when predicated of
God unless we are prepared to admit the impossibility
of completing the concept of God. I shall return to the
discussion of this side of the question in a subsequent
section.

Rather than plunge into such speculations, popular
theology prefers to abide by that form of the cosmological proof which runs as follows : " Since everything
has a cause, the world must also have a cause." Here

the concept "world" is employed in ignorance of the fact that it is open to the same or similar difficulties as those which encumber the concept of God. If by "world" we are to understand the sum total of all existing things, or at any rate of all finite existing things, then it is a concept which can never be completed. The given is never ended; new experiences are always appearing which demand a new determination of our concepts. Hence the path of scientific inquiry never brings us to a point at which we have occasion to ask for the cause of the "whole world." The given forms a totality which we analyse that we may discover its laws and elements; but every given totality refers us to other totalities; we endeavour to combine all the given totalities in a still higher totality; but however long we continue to do this, we shall still have to go on doing it. We get here a series like the causal series—a series which in obedience to its own law can never reach a conclusion. Hence the concept of "world" is in reality a false concept, although people are ready enough to operate with it; they play with it like a ball. "But," it may perhaps here be rejoined, "it cannot be denied that the world of being may be limited both in content and circumference, and thus form a finite totality—whether or not we are able to embrace this totality in thought. And this totality must therefore have a cause, for it cannot be its own cause." But the admission of this does not help to establish the validity of the cosmological proof. For we cannot conclude from a finite effect to an infinite cause, and even if we did we should not reach the concept of God for which we are seeking.

It is not by prolonging the series of causes which, after all, we shall never be able to bring to a conclusion, but by fixing our gaze on the law peculiar to the series, and on to the principle of unity to which this testifies, that we arrive at the ultimate premiss of our knowledge.

The inner motive power of the series—that which is present alike in the totality and in the individual parts—must be the determining factor. But we must note carefully here that the distinction between the series and its parts, or between the bond and the bound, can only be a provisional one. Unity and manifold are not thus externally related. Each particular member of the series—the particular event or the particular individual —is itself in its turn a totality having interconnexion between its parts. Individuality, as Leibnitz has shown us, consists in the law according to which changes in the state of a being take place. Every particular individuality is a little world, and we can only understand this little world in virtue of an inner connexion between its laws and those of the larger world, or worlds, to which it belongs. If the principle of unity is valid, there must be an inner relation between the laws obtaining within each particular member of the series and those which hold good for the reciprocal relation of the members of the series. The ideal of knowledge would be attained if we could unite continuity and individuality (or better still, universal and individual continuity), unity and multiplicity in one and the same concept, and could apply this concept within all the different spheres. And even if this task can never be completely fulfilled, yet it furnishes us with a principle by which to measure the progress of our knowledge.

Could the principle of the unity of existence coincide with the religious concept of God, a reconciliation between religion and scientific thought would at once become possible. The development of the scientific concept of cause would then be demanded in the interest of the highest concept of religion, and religious explanation and scientific explanation would no longer be mutually exclusive. The intellectual habit of mind which has developed under the influence of modern

empirical science would itself acquire religious significance ; all questions, problems, and tasks would centre
round the attempt to gain a clearer insight into the
great thought in which science and religion meet.
The view, which must always be inimical to peace, that
religious truths find their best shelter within the lacunæ
of science, and the consequent terror of these lacunæ
being filled up, would disappear.   Goethe's words, "Ihm
ziemt's die Welt im Innern zu bewegen," would be
fulfilled.   This thought must be the lode-star of every
serious attempt to discuss the religious problem.

(*b*) THE WORLD OF SPACE

11. If history shows us the religious consciousness
constantly tending to limit the series of causes, we must
remember that this is partly to be explained by the need
for clearness.   The religious consciousness desires above
all else a clear picture of its object, and such a picture
necessarily implies limitation.   This also explains its
tendency to assign to the deity a definite place in space.
Spatial ideas are our clearest ideas, and when we want
to present an idea to ourselves very clearly we are apt
to clothe it in spatial figures or schemata.   Closely
connected with this is the notion that every existing
thing has its definite place in the world, *i.e.* that it must
be localised.   That which has no definite place seems to
the childish point of view—which is nothing if not
realistic—to have no existence at all.   As it would be
the simplest *explanation* of the world if we could, by
following up the series of causes, member by member,
reach God at last, so we should have the simplest *conception* of the world if men had only to raise their eyes
to the heavens in order to find God, or at any rate his
dwelling-place.

The ancient conception of the world satisfied this

need. Its world was strictly limited. The earth stood
in the middle of the world, and the heavenly vault,
which was not conceived to be at any very great distance,
formed the outermost limit of the world. The clear
sky was, especially by the Indo-Germanic races, regarded
either as the deity or as the seat of the deity. The root
from which the word for 'god' is derived in many of
the Indo-Germanic languages really means the heavens
or the heavenly. So we have the Indian *devas*, the
Persian *deva*, the Greek *zeus*, the Latin *deus*, etc.
Herodotus tells us that the Persians called the sky *Zeus*,
and it is in keeping with this that in the more modern
history of religion we find the sky regarded as the natural
background of the god Ahura-Mazda (Ormuzd). The
Greeks of the olden time believed first that the gods
lived on Olympus, and afterwards that they had the
heavens or " the æther " as their dwelling-place. Aristotle
says : " All men believe there are gods, and all—
barbarians as well as Greeks—assign to the godhead the
highest place." Thus the opposition between heaven and
earth was identified quite naturally in antiquity with that
between the divine and the human, the eternal and the
temporal, the perfect and the imperfect. The expressions 'higher' and 'lower' were originally understood
literally ; the symbolic significance, here as everywhere,
only came into existence later. The fact that Aristotle
incorporated with his system the astronomical conception of antiquity was of great importance. For since this
conception, as well as his system in general, was capable
of being harmonised with the biblical circle of ideas, and
seemed suited to extend them still further, it was adopted
by theology and, through its influence, prevailed up to
quite recent times.[12]

Among the Jews we find the greatest significance
attributed to the opposition between heaven and earth.
In the opinion of some scholars Jahve was originally a

god of thunder ; at any rate he reveals himself with
special majesty in the heavenly phenomena. The
heavens are his seat and the earth his footstool. The
New Testament conception is here based on that of the
Old Testament. Sometimes we hear of several heavens
(2 Cor. xii. ; Eph. iv. 10), and God's dwelling-place is
then the heavenly holy of holies, which is above all
heavens, these latter forming, as it were, the outer court
and the holy place.[13] Accounts, such as that of the
visible ascension of Jesus into heaven, and of Paul's
being taken up into the third heaven, testify that the
world-picture of antiquity was still commonly accepted.
As these reports come before us they are evidently
intended to be understood literally, although modern
(even orthodox) theology, as we shall see afterwards, is
inclined to adopt a rationalistic explanation of this point.

The narrow frame in which the world-picture is here
presented ensured both clearness and certainty. Instead
of being disturbed and disquieted by infinite distances,
the religious consciousness could surrender itself entirely
to the great experiences of life, and could regard the all-
determining process of redemption, planned in heaven
and executed on earth, as the pivot round which the
whole life of the world turned. There was, as it were,
a ladder between heaven and earth ; the two worlds, the
world of the highest value and the world of conflicting
values, stood in visible reciprocal action. We learn from
the Homers and Dantes of the world what a haven of
refuge and support this limited world-picture afforded to
human imagination.

Within the religious consciousness itself, however,
at a somewhat higher stage of evolution, a conflicting
tendency begins to make itself felt. This tendency is
bent, even at the cost of clearness, on doing away with
the localisation of the content of the religious ideas. It
is now felt to denote an imperfection in the conception

of the deity to suppose that he really has his seat at any
particular place, for were that so either he would have to
move through space to come to man, or man must go a
great journey in order to meet his God.   God must be
all-present and all-embracing if he is not to be limited
and imperfect as is man himself.   However short the
distance between heaven and earth is conceived to be, it
is all too wide for religious needs.   The deity must stand
in far closer relation to man than is consistent with
localisation in a particular place.

This reaction against localisation and limitation was
also a reaction against clearness.   Expressions like "the
higher," "the lower," "the heavenly," and "the earthly,"
gradually acquired a symbolical meaning.   Plato (in the
7th book of his *Republic*) had already mocked at those
who held that astronomy "compels the soul to look
upwards and draws it from the things of this world to
the other."   "I cannot conceive," he says, "that any
science makes the soul look upwards, unless it has to do
with the real or the invisible.   It makes no difference
whether a person stares stupidly at the sky or looks with
half-bent eyes upon the ground; so long as he is trying
to study any sensible object . . . his soul is looking
downwards, not upwards."   The distinction between
above and below, then, must be understood symbolically
if it is to indicate a distinction of value.   Yet it cost a
hard struggle before the admission that spatial relations
can only have symbolic significance in religion could
be wrung from theologians.   Only very unwillingly did
they give up the clearness and definite limitation which
had characterised their conception; and we must remember
that this embodiment of religious ideas had come down
from an age and a people who had no hesitation in
attributing absolute significance to spatial relations.   So
long as the antique, and more especially the Greek world-
picture was still accepted in science, there was no reason

for sacrificing its clearness and limitation, appealing as it did so especially to the needs of the unlearned and the young. For reality divided itself so naturally into heaven, earth, and a subterranean hell; this gradated series of the *regions* of the world afforded such palpable evidence of its gradated series of *values*.

We find thus a double tendency both in the biblical writings and among Church theologians. Clearness is preserved; but where the inwardness of feeling rather than the need of clearness governs the imagination, there the significance of the spatial relation is abandoned. God dwells in heaven, but in reality he is not far from any one of us, for in him we live and move and have our being. Jesus ascends into heaven, from whence he shall come again; but he lives in the hearts of the faithful, and is with them alway.

The religious conception, then, contained during its classical ages a " both — and," which was gradually superseded by an " either — or." We will pause to illustrate this " both—and " by a few examples.

12. The theologians of earlier times were enabled to retain this " both—and " by the bold use they made of allegorical or symbolic exegesis. An allegorical interpretation did not, according to their ideas, exclude the literal sense. But the relation between these two different senses was veiled in considerable ambiguity; hence they came not infrequently into violent collision. As Adolf Harnack points out in his *History of Dogma*,[14] no definite rule was laid down as to how far the letter of the Holy Scriptures was to be respected. Has God a human shape? Has he eyes?—voice? Is Paradise situated on this earth? Will the dead arise with all their limbs, including their hair, etc.? To all these questions and a hundred similar ones there was no definite answer.

Augustine was certainly the person who did the most towards suppressing a merely literal interpretation. His study of Plato influenced him here considerably ; in conjunction with his own deep and tumultuous inner life, it gave him a clear insight into the distinction between spiritual and material, and thus led him to utter thoughts which entitle him to be regarded as the forerunner of Descartes and of Kant.   Specially interesting for us in this connexion is his rejection of all spatial determinations as predicable of the deity.   Speaking of his own earlier conception, he says : " I did not know that God was a spirit, not having limbs with length and breadth any more than corporeal mass (*moles*).   The corporeal (*moles*) is less in the part than the whole, and if it is infinite, then it is smaller in a limited part than in the infinite ; and it is not everywhere in its entirety (*tota ubique*), as is God."   " God in his entirety is present everywhere and yet is nowhere (*ubique totus, et nusquam locorum*)."   " God dwells deep in my being as my innermost ego, and is higher than the highest that I can reach (*interior intimo meo, superior summo meo*)."   " God is above my soul, but not in the same way as the heaven is above the earth." [15]

When thoughts such as these were appropriated and developed, they could not fail to come into conflict with the old world-picture and with its childish opposition between heaven and earth.   The schoolmen of the Middle Ages held firmly to the concept of a God independent of determinations of place, and from them it passed on to the mystics who were influenced in addition by neo-Platonic thought.   " Sir," Suso was asked by his pupil, " where is God ? "   And his answer was, " The Masters say : God has no where—God is like a circular ring ; the ring's central point is everywhere, and its circumference nowhere." [16]   Thus the validity of the spatial relation perished through its own inherent contradiction.

With regard to accounts such as that of the visible

ascension thinkers of the Middle Ages held that the reported events had occurred as they were described, but that they also had a spiritual meaning, which meaning was the essential one.   Hugo von St. Victor explains that by the highest we are to understand the innermost, and "to ascend to God" means to withdraw into the depths of ourselves, and there find something higher than ourselves.   Still, he does not deny that heaven and hell occupy definite places in the world. His contemporary, Abelard, asserts (in his remarkable *Dialogue between a Philosopher, a Jew, and a Christian*) that what is said of God in bodily form is not to be understood, as the laity commonly do, corporeally and literally, but mystically and allegorically.   By the height of the heaven above the earth is meant the sublimity (*sublimitas*) of the character of the future life rather than the site of any material heaven ;   and that Jesus shall sit at God's right hand does not mean that he is to occupy a definite position in space (*localis positio*), but that he will enjoy an equality of dignity (*aequalis dignitas*). The bodily ascension of Jesus did indeed take place as reported, but it signifies "a nobler kind of ascension" (*melior ascensus*), namely, that which takes place within the soul of believers.   Unlearned and simple men could not understand what was not presented in clear and pictorial form.[17]

The characteristic "both — and" here comes out plainly.   It had great advantages for educational purposes when it was not necessary to draw any sharp distinction between idea and reality, symbol and truth. With his bodily eyes a man could look up to heaven, the seat of power and grace ; but he might find that same heaven in his own heart in which God made known his wishes and imparted his consolations.   The Gospel stories might be taken literally, and yet at the same time expounded to spiritual edification.   The absolute differences between places in this world of space immediately expressed differences in degree of value.

13. But the time came when a choice had to be made. A struggle arose between an idealistic conception, which emphasised the purely spiritual interpretation of the religious ideas, and a realistic or materialistic view, which supported a clear and literal interpretation. Such a struggle occurs in many religions. In the Upanishads, which give the idealistic exposition of the religion of the Vedas, we find it stated that Brahma, the deity, is eternal ; and since " name, place, time, and body " perish, none of these can be predicated of Brahma. In Xenophanes' and Plato's criticisms of the popular religion of the Greeks we find a similar idealising tendency. We encounter it again in Mohammedanism, where, *e.g.*, the sensuous and pictorial account of the joys of Paradise are expounded allegorically as the description of spiritual pleasures.[18]

When at length it dawned on thought that there can be no absolute determinations of place, since every place is determined by its relation to other places, these again by their relation to others, and so on, the old world-picture was doomed. The gradated series of places was overtaken by the same fate as befell the series of causes ; it was found impossible to arrive at any absolute conclusion of the series, such as was necessary for the limitations of the picture. And when once Copernicus made men realise that the simplest way to conceive the world was to think of the earth as moving round the sun, our planet dropped from the centre of the universe, and the clear and certain framework, within which religious ideas had hitherto found a home, was broken in pieces. Nor was this all. Giordano Bruno took a further step, and pointed out that it was inconsistent to retain the limitations involved in the conception of the world when once the relativity of all determinations of place and the Copernican astronomy had been accepted. An infinite horizon opened up; [19] the distinction between heaven and earth disappeared, and 'either—or' necessarily superseded the old 'both—and.' If the word 'heaven' was still to be retained in use as a religious expression, it could only be in its idealistic signification.

But yet another movement of thought came into operation. Hitherto it had been possible to express spiritual distinctions of value by means of spatial distances; hence no sharp distinction between the material and spiritual had ever been drawn. But with the dawn of natural science this distinction came more and more into prominence, and spatial extension, with Kepler and Descartes, began to be regarded as the chief mark of the material. The relationship between the spiritual and the material now constituted a special problem in itself. There was also the further question as to whether the spiritual world could be as comprehensive as the material world appeared in the light of the new world-picture. The certainty with which up till now spiritual things had been expressed in terms of material forms was shattered. Formerly it had been literally possible to see spirits, but since the Cartesian reform of psychology this was no longer the case. The spiritual world had to be presented in sharp contrast to the world of space, of extension, and of visibility, however the underlying relation between the two worlds might be conceived. The significance of everything visible, in short, from a religious point of view, was now restricted to the symbolical.

But it was easier for philosophy than for theology to deduce this consequence. Thinkers such as Bruno and Spinoza deepened and widened the significance of the religious ideas in correspondence with the new world-conception, and in so doing they were only following the path already indicated by Augustine and the mystics.

E

After long opposition and hesitation theology began to take the same path. Nowadays we often see it stated that the idealistic interpretation of expressions such as ' heaven ' ' hell,' etc., is the only valid one and the only one in consonance with the teaching of the Bible and the Church. Cardinal Newman, for example, states that the Tridentine Council did not teach that the fires of purgatory cause sensible pain, although he admits that this was the tradition of the Latin Church, and that he himself had seen pictures of souls in flames in the streets of Naples. But in one of the handbooks sanctioned by the Church, in a dialogue on the doctrine of purgatory, the question is asked: " Is the flame of purgatory a physical flame ? " And the answer runs : " Cardinal Bellarmin asserts that it is generally held among theologians that the purgatorial flame is a true and real flame of the same kind as the fire of our earth." And it goes on to say that the great majority among the fathers, schoolmen, and theologians teach that, like hell, the purgatorial fire is situated in the middle of the earth ; that this doctrine is based on the Holy Scriptures and that it has always been maintained by the Church.[20] Here idealism and realism are sharply opposed to one another. It is idle to attempt by the discussion of isolated points to distract attention from the breach in the course of spiritual evolution as a whole, which took place when ' either — or ' superseded the old ' both — and ' (just as this in its turn had superseded the immediate and childish localisation in space) ; the history of the world will always force it into prominence, and it is of the greatest importance, if we are to get any right understanding of the religious problem, that it should not be forgotten.

It has been found very difficult to give a consistently spiritual interpretation of the word ' heaven ' in the account of the Ascension of Jesus given in the Acts of the Apostles. There is no doubt that in the opinion of the writer Jesus ascended into heaven as into a definite place, a place like—only more splendid than—other places. Moreover, the two angels expressly assert this. But modern theologians have become such zealous Copernicans (or Brunists) that they are not even over-awed by angels. Martensen [21] declares it to be a mediæval conception that heaven is a place which is reached by a long journey through the stars ; he main-tains that " heaven is the inner ground of the outer world ; that the visible ascent into heaven was only meant as a sign to the disciples that their Master had quitted the outer world." We need not, therefore, conceive of the Ascension as " a movement occupying some considerable time," which is as much as to say that it was only necessary for Jesus to be raised up a little distance ! In such colourless and rationalistic fashion does modern theology—in the face of the evident meaning of the text—interpret the Bible. In the old story, as it is written, there is much more clearness and consistency, and there is clear and logical sense in regarding it as a legend. But there is no sense at all in the compromise by which Martensen tries to help himself out. We show a great deal more respect to the old story by regarding it as a legend than by so expounding its content as to call to mind some stage contrivance. Moreover, by what right does Martensen assert that the conception of heaven as a definite place is ' mediæval ' ? It is so certainly, but it is also biblical. Martensen sees the untenability of the ' both—and,' but he cannot reconcile himself to the transition to ' either—or.'

The Copernican and Cartesian reforms drew a clearer line between thought and intention, between reality and symbolism, than was before possible. It is easy to see what the significance of this has been for the philosophy of religion. Especially significant is the increased extension of the world, the infinite horizon which the material world has gained, in comparison with which the spiritual world now seems so limited. How can we still—the question forces itself upon us —hold fast to the conviction that spiritual values are the highest in existence, round which all else turns? For the external world no longer moves round the home of the only spiritual life that has been revealed in experience. Thus there arises an opposition between psychology and cosmology which was unknown in an earlier age. Great minds like Jacob Boehme and Blaise Pascal were deeply stirred by the problem to which this gives rise, and which could never have arisen in the classical ages of religion. But it is not only positive religion that is here confronted by a great and perhaps insoluble problem. The same problem must present itself under one form or another to every conception of life, although there are of course no problems anywhere for those who have been induced by fear or love of ease to abandon thinking altogether. To the problem itself we shall recur later.

(c) THE COURSE OF TIME

14. The need of clearness asserted itself also in relation to the question of time; there too it effected in its own interest an abridgment and close of the series of ideas. And here we are confronted with one of the most important differences the history of religion has to offer us, for while the idea of a completed course of time is inessential for so religious a people as the Indians, it is of the utmost importance in the religions of Zarathustra and of Christ. To the Indian mind time means movement leading to no result; change and unrest which must at all costs be got rid of. Hence no value could be attributed to development in time; the

absorption of temporal existence in 'Nirvana' was regarded as the highest.   We find a similar feature in Greek thought ; Plato's doctrine of ideas may be taken as the classical example ; the stern reality is the unchangeable ; that which always is what it is ; the mutable phenomena of the world of experience, caught as they are in the grip of becoming, are in the last resort mere appearance. In the Iranian worship of Zarathustra, on the other hand, the development of the world is an historical process, which reaches its conclusion within a comparatively short space of time (12,000 years), and in which the great struggle between good and evil—in nature, in human life, and in the world of spirits—is accomplished.   Here we get the idea of a history of the world in its literal sense.   A strong cosmical light is thus thrown on all human activity, and on all the vicissitudes of human fate.   This notion of a period of time within the grasp of the imagination has been of great effect in concentrating men's minds.   Thought has an aim towards which all striving is directed, and man appears as a fellow-worker with God.   How and where this belief in the significance of history first arose we are unable to say.   It is not certain that it is Indo-Germanic in origin ; it may possibly be due to Semitic or pre-Semitic influences.[22]   It is likewise uncertain whether this belief passed from the Persians to the post-exilic Jews and from them to Christianity.[23]   But in any case, the worship of Zarathustra is the first great popular religion in which the idea of life as an historical development towards an aim determines the whole point of view. The courage of men is strengthened for the struggle of life by these great pictures of the future, by the thought of a kingdom to come, whose consummation is to be effected by means of a judgment of the world.

In the New Testament this view is especially conspicuous in the first three Gospels, in the Epistles of St.

Paul, and in the Revelation of St. John. In the Gospel of St. John, on the other hand, it is asserted most emphatically that eternal life is not a future but an already present life. He who believes has already passed from death unto life. The judgment, the great decision, is pre-eminently an inner judgment; the external judgment of the future recedes more and more into the distance as a final conclusion. Towards "the idealism which sees its ideal already realised in the present," we can find, certainly, only a very gradual approximation in the New Testament Scriptures.[24] This gradual approximation, however, is of great importance. It gives rise to two different types of doctrine, and it is a puzzle, not only for psychology but also for the history of literature, how tradition can have ascribed to one and the same author the book (i.e. the Revelation of St. John) in which the consummation of the kingdom is most often described as future, and the Gospel of St. John, in which its ideal presence is most profoundly asserted and defended. This opposition is all the more conspicuous in the New Testament, since the last judgment was expected by the then living generation; a fact which must have sharpened the tension of the relation between present and future, and must have exhibited the lively expectation which attached itself to the future in striking contrast with the calm of inner possession.

In the religion of Zarathustra the idealistic view, probably owing to the sober and practical character of the Iranians, comes out less distinctly. In the New Testament, however, we find again on this point, as on that of space, a characteristic 'both—and'; and here there is more chance of a 'both—and' being able to maintain itself. For in and for itself there is no contradiction in holding that the ideal has taken root and in so far is already in existence, and yet that it gradually unfolds to its full extent. The question—to which we shall come back by and by—is whether such a lengthy and gradual development was foreseen and taught in the New Testament. According to the New Testament conception only a short time was to elapse before the end should come, and a comparatively short time is assumed between the creation and the judgment. Between these two fixed points the whole course of time runs out ; within this interval the great events of religion find their place, and imagination rounds off this period to a natural whole. There is a beginning and an end with no dizzying distance between them. Were the two points of rest placed farther apart ; were it asked what was before the 'beginning' and what comes after the 'end,' the clearness would vanish and our heads begin to turn, as happens when it dawns on consciousness that there are no absolute limits to space.

15. It follows from the concept of time that each particular moment must lie between two other moments. Hence we can conceive neither of a first nor of a last moment. Just as the causal axiom must hold good for every link in the causal series, and the spatial relation must be valid for every place in space, so too the temporal relation must be valid for every member of the temporal series. Hence every course of time which we can conceive—including that between the 'creation' and the 'judgment'—can only be a wave in the great immeasurable sea of time. A completed course of time denotes a period which is filled out by the realisation of a certain result, of a certain aim. It is its content which divides time into periods. The temporal relation, however, continues in virtue of its own law beyond both 'beginning' and 'end'; if our thought can assign no content, and hence no periodical divisions beyond the two points hitherto regarded as fixed, we, at any rate, end with a question, a problem, as we do in the series of causes and of spatial determinations. The most

logical course would be to suppose that time was created at the 'beginning' and destroyed at the 'end'; but the only result of this would be to render the problem of the significance of time for eternity still more complicated.

With regard to time, therefore, a conclusion can only mean a station on the way, a place of rest, where energy for fresh development can be collected. At such points it may seem as though time were done away with. The goal attained is so dazzling, and so engrosses the entire consciousness, that the thought of past or future cannot effect an entrance. This concentration on the present, however, which is a kind of ecstasy, is itself, in accordance with the law of temporal relation, superseded by new processes, if, indeed, it does not with repetition and custom pass over into stupefaction.

It is not surprising that the religious consciousness should regard the time-relation as an imperfection. The misfortune of development in time is due, more or less, to the fact that one period of life is looked upon merely as a means to another. Means and end are separated, and life is divided between work without any enjoyment, and enjoyment without any work. Time is for the most part filled out with something which only has value *because of* and *in* its effects. Every advance in the art of education, in ethics and in sociology implies an attempt to annul this, the worst of all dualisms. Just as no one man ought to be treated merely as a means for other men, so no single moment in a man's life ought to be regarded merely as a means for other moments, *e.g.* the past and the present merely as a means for the future. This will be avoided if work and development themselves acquire immediate value, and can thus themselves become ends or parts of an end. The child is something more than a man in the making; childhood becomes an independent period of life, with its own special tasks and its own peculiar value. Every period of life, every piece of the course of time must thus be conceived. Then at last it will be possible in the midst of time to live in eternity, yet without sinking into mystic contemplation. The externality of the time-relation disappears. 'Eternity' no longer appears as a continuation of time or as a distant time, but as the expression of the permanence of value throughout time's changes. We shall then be able to contemplate the unendingness and infinity of time without becoming giddy, nor will it impress us with a sense of aimless restlessness. Here, too, as with causal explanation (§§ 9, 10) and the world of space (§ 12) the only possible solution of the difficulties involved in the time-relation lies in the direction of inwardness ; we must lay chief weight on the inner law and the valuable content, not on any external differences. And here we find something which can exist in independence of the limiting framework to which religion in its mythical and dogmatic forms is inclined to cling.

B. CONCLUDING THOUGHTS

What we gain from speculative philosophy is not so much answers to questions which common sense universally asks, as the knowledge that these questions themselves, since they are based on untrue concepts, must vanish away.—PAUL MÖLLER.

16. The final presupposition for the scientific understanding of existence is, as I have tried to show, a principle of unity underlying the whole inter-connected systems of the course of time, of spatial extension, and of the causal series. We have now to consider whether thought can determine more nearly, can cast into the form of a concluding concept, this principle of unity.

The question is the more important since the notion of a principle of unity opens up the possibility of a reconciliation between the religious and the scientific views of existence. I shall divide my discussion of this question into a more formal and a more real part. The discussion of it from the real side I will postpone till the next section (*C*), and pass on at once here to its formal consideration, *i.e.* I shall ask what qualities must characterise an idea which is to afford an absolute and objective conclusion for our knowledge. Such an idea must evidently be one which does not, in virtue of its own nature, lead out beyond itself; which does not itself contain new problems and postulates. It must be an idea which in virtue of the law proper to our thought rounds off knowledge so completely that no new questions can arise. The intellectual process must be so completely concluded that its reopening is an impossibility.

We are all obliged to set a bound to our knowledge. There are points beyond which, as a matter of fact, we cannot pass. But this conclusion may be the outcome of accidental circumstances. One man wearies in his pursuit sooner than another, or he has not so many intellectual needs as another. The conclusion, therefore, differs for different individuals, different ages, different peoples. Or temporal and spatial limitations may hinder knowledge from acquiring sufficient material. I am not here concerned with any conclusion of this kind; on the contrary, I am seeking after a conclusion which is based not on particular individual or historical circumstances, but upon the laws of thought itself.

But I cannot at once proceed with my inquiry as to whether the principle of unity to which our previous discussion pointed is likely to be able to afford an objective conclusion. I must first investigate the possibility whether it is not the manifold elements of existence rather than the principle of unity which form the conclusion in which thought can and must find rest. It might be suggested that the atoms of natural science, of which it is assumed that they have persisted unaltered throughout all motion and changes, must form the conclusion of all our knowledge.

Up to the present no atomic concept has been brought forward which does not attribute to atoms some of the qualities which are possessed by sensuous bodies. Atoms are conceived as extended, *i.e.* as consisting of parts, only these parts cannot be separated by means of any of the natural forces with which we are acquainted. Even when this extension has been conceived as infinitely small (a millionth, or a ten-millionth of a millimetre has been proposed), yet it suffices to make the atom a complete microcosm, about the inner relations of which questions can be asked. Their constitution may be extremely complicated, and in the opinion of some investigators electric currents exist within them. Here then we get a prospect of new riddles, for the treatment and solution of which our present scientific concepts may prove unsuited. The conclusion, therefore, is pushed further back. We are led to the same result if we ask whether atoms are absolutely hard? Absolutely hard atoms would conflict with the law of the persistence of energy, since every time they collided with each other there would be a loss of energy. Through the collision of bodies the suspended motion is transformed into motion of the particles of the body, *e.g.* when warmth is produced by rubbing. Absolute hardness, however, excludes such motion. These particles, then, must be conceived as displaccable and movable ; but then again the atom becomes a complete microcosm, a solar system, and a whole army of new questions and problems regarding the inner relations of this little world arises. Lastly, the forces which are attributed to atoms indicate that they can only afford a temporary conclusion. The atomic concept springs out of the need to localise the well-spring of force. The laws of physical and chemical phenomena are statements

of definite relations which hold good between different
kinds of elements, and we then attribute to these
elements such qualities or forces as must be assumed
in order to explain their reciprocal action. We only
know anything of matter and its elements through the
forces it exhibits. Hence, epistemologically, 'energy'
is a more fundamental concept than 'matter.' Matter
is the unknown which is more or less determined by the
forces or qualities which we attribute to it in virtue of
the particular manner in which it enters into reciprocal
relations with other matter. Plato said long ago that
the concept of 'matter' was the product of 'spurious
thinking'; probably he meant by this that men only
begin to talk about matter when they cannot find any
more real determinations for thought. That we only
know matter through the forces it manifests may be seen
most easily in the atoms of chemistry which are parts
of weight ; to 'have' weight means to weigh, to exert
gravity. Matter, then, is known through energy. But
energy is a relative concept ; it is abstracted from the
relation of reciprocal action, and presupposes a resistance
which is overcome or has to be overcome. Thus the
single atom is always determined by its relation to other
atoms. Here, again, at the end of all things, it is interconnexion, totality which is the original phenomenon,
and this brings us back to the principle of unity.

However great the differences and wide the manifold
embraced by existence, the relation of reciprocal action
between the different and manifold elements will always
constrain us to assume the existence of a bond, a common
basis, a unity which renders this reciprocal action
possible.

17. I pass on, therefore, to the investigation of this
principle of unity. Only through it, and not through
the manifold of elements, can we arrive at a conclusion—
if indeed we can ever find a conclusion at all.

The principle of unity is, as we saw, a necessary presupposition if we are to understand being. And since it may be presumed that the rationality of existence (however limited this be) must be somehow or other bound up with the nature of existence, we have a right to speak of a force or power in virtue of which everything which is and everything which happens is interconnected, is held together in a relation of continuity. If we define God as the rational principle of being, and therefore also as the principle of the unity of being, it appears possible to arrive at a concept of God capable of being harmonised with scientific knowledge. In the concepts of God developed by popular religions — at any rate in their higher stages — this determination appears as a more or less conspicuous element. But we must remember that in the formation of religious concepts interests quite other than the purely theological and intellectual have participated. Every religious standpoint gathers up in its concept of God the highest known values. Not only ethical and æsthetic interests, but also, and more especially, the enthusiasm or felt dependence excited in the struggle for life, urge thought to a deeper and deeper concentration, which disburdens itself at last in the cry of 'God!' The religious problem arises originally through a division of spiritual labour, in which the intellectual interest is separated from other interests and seeks satisfaction in the construction of special modes and forms of thought. Small wonder then that the thought constructions of science and religion do not correspond with one another. The languages of philosophy and of religion are not always so related that we can, without more ado, translate a thought from one language into the other, or find for a concept formed within one sphere an adequately corresponding concept in the other.

Not only the philosophical consciousness but also

the religious consciousness is confronted by the great
problem as to the relation between unity and multiplicity. But while philosophical thought goes no
further than the ultimate phenomenon I have so often
referred to, *i.e.* the unity as necessary presupposition
of the interconnexion according to law of the manifold of elements, the religious consciousness betrays,
in its mythical and dogmatic forms, a tendency
to display the unity and the manifold in a relation of
extreme contrast, as though they were two different
beings or powers. It thus forms two distinct concluding
concepts, which it calls respectively, 'God' and 'the
world'; the world is conceived as unity in so far as all
multiplicity is gathered up into a totality. In opposition
to this way of envisaging things, philosophical thought
takes up the position that it finds in both these concepts
one and the same difficulty, and hence sees nothing in
this so-called explanation but a reduplication of the
problem; indeed, there arises here a third problem,
i.e. as to the mutual relation of these two beings or
powers. If this be so—and I shall now try to prove it
is so—it is of the greatest significance for the discussion
of religion. For it follows from this that no one has
a right to infer, from the rejection of the religious
concept of God, that the only thing left to believe in
is what, in the language of religion, is called 'the
world.' The concept of 'world' involves philosophical
difficulties similar to those presented by the concept
'God,' if it be taken as absolutely conclusive. And it
has often happened that thinkers have been dubbed
'atheists' for rejecting the current concept of 'world'
rather than that of God. This was the case both with
Spinoza and Fichte.[25] But polemical fanaticism can
never, of course, accept correction, however often this
circumstance be pointed out.

If God and the world are to be regarded as two

different beings or powers, then they must mutually limit
one another.   One stops where the other begins.   The
watchmaker and the watch which he has made are two
different things ; such is the external relation in which,
according to the ordinary view, God and the world stand
to one another.   But, in that case, God cannot be an
infinite being.   The world with its laws and forces is
the limit of the deity.   Hence what we really have here is
a polytheistic conception ; for the world, as distinct from
' God,' becomes itself a god, and thus a certain personification of the world unconsciously creeps even into views
which are at no little pains to proclaim their monotheistic
orthodoxy.

The concept 'world,' as already remarked, is not a
validly formed concept.   If this concept denote a whole—
a totality ruled by law—it is an ideal towards which all
inquiry steers, but which, on account of the inexhaustibility of experience, it can never reach.   Our thought is
always trying to spell out reality.   The mark by which
we can distinguish between mere subjective thinking
and objective reality is the presence in the latter of
laws which can be shown to govern the relations between
its phenomena.   But two difficulties meet us here.   In
the first place, new phenomena are constantly appearing
within experience ; secondly, it becomes evident that the
relations existing between the already given phenomena
are far more complicated and mysterious than could
have been anticipated.   Hence we never come to an
end of applying our criterion to reality, and the concept of reality becomes an ideal concept.[26]   Theologians,
as a general rule, have not sufficient patience to be
satisfied with the continuous work that this ideal of
inquiry demands, *i.e.* with the discovery of deeper
and deeper interconnexions between more and more
phenomena.   They break off in the midst of their task
and treat the work as though it were completed.

Hence the concept 'world' is the expression of a half-thought. On the lowest stage of religious development this concept does not appear at all.[27] The notion of a cosmos, of an ordered whole of existing things, presupposes a certain development of thought. In virtue of an over-hasty conclusion, this pseudo-concept seems to form an absolute totality ; and once introduced into religious language it has held its place ever since, as though its validity were unimpeachable.

But suppose, for the sake of argument, we admit the validity of this concept. The question then arises as to how these two beings or powers stand to one another. Whenever there is a causal relation we are forced, as we saw above, to presuppose a principle which conditions the interconnexion between its members. Were there not a something bringing these members together the causal relation would be inexplicable. This must hold good also for the causal relation between God and the world. But then the bond, the principle of unity, which makes their mutual relation possible, is itself in reality the deity, or, as we may prefer to say, the real world consists of 'God' + 'World,' *i.e.* of the whole formed by the two together. Once more, then, we find ourselves involved in an unending series—a sign that we have been near what must be for us the ultimate thought, though we did not recognise it. This ultimate, valid thought is the principle of unity, the principle of conformity to law which characterises Being ; and if we overlook it, it revenges itself upon us, cropping up again every time we think we have made a step in advance. All limiting concepts contain a certain element of raillery, which comes to the fore whenever we are rash enough to try to knot up the thread of thought instead of following the line of interconnexion, which makes the thread a thread. Only when theologians have given us a theory of knowledge quite different from that with which we are at present obliged to work, will there be any hope of overcoming this raillery on the part of our limiting concepts. At present it follows us even into the highest theological and metaphysical speculations. Plato (in the dialogue *Parmenides*) had already recognised in it a growing obstacle to his doctrine of ideas : for if ideas underlie the things of sense, a new question with regard to the relation between the ideas and things arises, and this relation must itself have its idea, etc. With Spinoza and Lotze, this problem centres in the relation between substance and modes. I am not able to see that theology by its doctrine of ' God ' and ' world ' can help us over this fundamental difficulty, which epistemologically affords an indirect proof that we have arrived at a limiting concept. In the principle of unity we have a thought which is conclusive *for us*, but it is also a thought which demands in a never-ending series and series of series its continually renewed application. To find my concluding idea in a member of a series instead of in the principle which makes the construction of series possible would be to write myself down a fool.

We cannot, however, deduce from the uniting principle, which is for us the ultimate irreducible basis of all understanding, the manifold of phenomena (of things and events). Unity is and remains unity, and the manifold is never more than empirically given, it cannot be reached by any process of deduction. Human inquiry seeks to reduce the manifold differences given in experience to a minimum, so that the principle of unity may be traced in the identity, rationality, and causality which are exhibited in experience. A progressive reduction of this kind is possible, as the history of the empirical sciences shows us ; but a deduction is not possible. The attempts of speculative philosophers such as Plotinus, Boehme, and Schelling to deduce the manifold from the unity were unsuccessful, and come under the head of

F

mythological imaginings rather than philosophical thought. Spinoza saw more clearly on this point, for he admitted that particular phenomena (*modi*) are only known to us through experience, and that only by analysis of experience can we get back to unity. Theology, having committed itself to a twofold construction of concepts by its erection of God and the world into two different beings, tries to get over this doubleness by saying that the world is produced by God; but in reality it only gives us back—in even larger dimensions—the philosophical problem of the unity and the manifold. As it is logically impossible to deduce the manifold from the unity, since there would always be something in the conclusion which was not in the premisses, so it is logically impossible to conceive the world as produced by God. And the sting of the problem becomes all the sharper when the Godhead is conceived as perfect and immutable; for how can the imperfect spring from the perfect and the mutable from the immutable? From the logical point of view the difficulty is the same, whether with Augustine we suppose the imperfect and mutable to have been produced by an act of will, or with Plotinus, by an emanation.[28] (From the ethical point of view the former presents, of course, the greater difficulties.) Neither the doctrine of creation nor that of emanation removes the difficulty which is contained in the fact that our concept of cause is a concept of a plurality of conditions, so that a 'cause' can no more be an absolute unity than a conclusion can be drawn from a single premiss. If the dogma of creation offers an explanation of the origin of the world, we must mean by explanation something very different from what is meant by it in scientific thought. To cease thinking is not the same thing as to begin understanding.

18. The impossibility of arriving at an objective conclusion to our knowledge follows, as we saw, from

the inexhaustibility of experience, which precludes a complete verification of the first principle of knowledge. We shall never be able to solve Hume's problem as to the validity of the principle of causation. Even Kant was betrayed into dogmatising when he attempted to bring forward a proof of its validity. While new experiences are continually appearing, there is always a possibility that the ultimate basis of these experiences (what Kant called the 'thing-in-itself') does not work in a constant manner, but is itself in the grip of becoming, of evolution; it may possibly suffer changes, even though these changes are subject themselves to laws which lie deeper than any one of those which we have hitherto discovered governing the phenomena of experience. We come here to the idea of natural laws of a higher order, just as a little while ago we arrived at the possibility of atoms of a higher order. Kant was satisfied in his time with the postulate of the 'thing-in-itself' as the basis of the stuff of our knowledge; he took it for granted that this basis worked at all times in one and the same way.[29] But no proof of this assumption can be adduced; which shows that the fundamental assumptions of philosophy are more hypothetical than Kant believed them to be. The right to apply the forms of our knowledge, *e.g.* the concept of cause, to any given empirical matter, can, strictly speaking, never be established once and for ever, but must be confirmed by repeated experiments.

Kant's dogmatic assumption that the thing in itself must be unchangeable was not without influence on Herbert Spencer, for he, after having shown the validity of the concept of evolution within all spheres of experience, does not hesitate to deny that it can be predicated of the 'Unknowable' which, according to his teaching, underlies all phenomena. F. C. Sibbern, too, elsewhere an ardent evolutionist, assumed that only finite beings, not God, undergo development, or, as he expresses it, God's kingdom develops, but not God Himself.[30]   But we cannot draw the line in any such external fashion between the unknowable and the knowable, or between the unchangeable and the changeable.   The old dogmatic limiting concept of the schoolmen, which opposes the immutability of the deity to the mutability of the world, has not lost its influence on modern philosophers.   An absolutely unchangeable ground of continuous change is unthinkable.   The old difficulty returns as soon as we attempt an objective conclusion.

We have at any rate no right to reject the possibility that the inconclusiveness of experience and of knowledge may be bound up with the fact that being itself is not complete but is continually developing.   We are prone to forget that experience and knowledge themselves form part of being.   When we speak of a knowledge of being, we imply that the whole of existence can be expressed by a single part or a single side of it.   So long as this task remains unperformed, being as a totality is not complete.   And conversely, if being itself is not complete, our knowledge cannot be complete.   Further, in order to know the relation between that part or side of being which we call knowledge, and the rest of being or being as a totality, we should require a new knowledge and so on.   From this side too the problem recurs. The Indian Vedanta philosophers (the writers of the Upanishads) as well as the Neo-Platonists were aware of this.   An absolute conclusion to knowledge would involve the annulling of the distinction between knowing and being, subject and object; and it is precisely this distinction which is the condition of all knowledge.

Speaking generally, it is a fundamental law of all our concepts that they express relations, and that every concept presupposes a relation to other concepts.[31]   This is the inner law proper to all movement of thought.   It follows from this law—which we might call the law of relation—that no concept can be formed of a something which stands in no relation to any other something. All movement of thought consists in discovering simi-larity or difference, in finding ground or consequent, in deducing cause or effect. Similarity and difference, ground and consequent, cause and effect, however, can only be applied when different members can be brought into mutual relations with each other.

A thing or being can only be known by its qualities, and its qualities signify the different ways in which the thing or being is related to other things or beings. We attribute force to things or beings when they possess the capacity of overcoming resistance. The concept of force, however, does not only presuppose a relation between a thing and an encountered resistance, but also a something which is able to liberate force when this is not effected by the resistance itself. As soon as we attribute life or personality to a being, we conceive in addition an outer world with which it stands in a relation of reciprocal action, and which offers both motives for the liberation of force and also opposition for this force to overcome. And so whatever concept of whatever kind we investigate, we shall find that thought always consists in putting together and comparing one with another, in other words, relating them. This law is so generally valid that the burden of proof must lie with those who assert that there are exceptions to it. And it is this law which makes an objective conclusion to our knowledge impossible.

Every conceptual construction is a limitation which is annulled again when thought occupies itself with the larger interconnexion from which it took that which the concepts held together, and without which the content of the concepts could not be determined. The law of relation itself bears witness to the unity of thought, since under it different members of a relation are combined in a single concept. But it testifies also to the constant limitation of thought, for besides the members thus combined in the particular concept still other members have to be presupposed, the nearer determination of which must always present a fresh task. But here our thought betrays its nobility, for not only can it perceive its own limitations, but even at this limit it hears—in virtue of its own law—an Excelsior. Every concept of God, said Fichte, is the concept of an idol. But the fact that in the face of all pious attempts to formulate the divine it dares to denounce them as idolatry is itself a witness to the divine spark within human thought.

C. THOUGHT AND PICTURE

Und deines Geistes höchster Feuerflug
Hat schon am Gleichnis, hat am Bild genug.
GOETHE.

19. We do not cease forming ideas even when we have reached the limit of all knowledge, where no further clear and uncontradictory concepts can be formed. The religious need is particularly impelled to construct ideas at this limit. If we examine these ideas a little more closely we shall see that they all owe their origin to *analogy*.

The word analogy really means the same as proportion, but it is usual to make a distinction in the application of the two words, restricting proportion to a relation of quantitative similarity (*e.g.* $\frac{1}{2} = \frac{2}{4} = \frac{3}{6}$, etc.), while analogy is used to denote a relation of qualitative similarity (*e.g.* red is related to orange as orange is to yellow). Proportion enables us to discover unknown magnitudes, when we know no more than that they are members of a proportional series with the other members of which we are acquainted. Analogy, on the other hand, only offers our knowledge a most imperfect assistance. It can give us no positive knowledge concerning unknown members, but is excellent at expressing the relation between those with which we are already familiar. From conceptual relation analogy steps lightly on to poetic grouping, and may be said generally to move on the borderland between thought and imagination.

In my *History of Modern Philosophy* I have tried to show that those philosophers who refuse to admit the correctness of the limitations assigned by critical philosophy to knowledge have always, with more or less express consciousness, made use of analogies in their attempts to solve the riddle of existence. They are the only auxiliaries left to us when experience refuses its aid. In such cases, existence in its totality, or the final ground of existence, is conceived in analogy with certain elements, phenomena or relations within the sphere of existence. The character of the different systems, of the different metaphysical world-conceptions thus constructed depends essentially on which elements, phenomena or relations are taken as the basis of the analogy.[32]

In this connexion the opposition between two philosophical thought-constructions, between metaphysical idealism and materialism, is especially interesting.

Metaphysical idealism may be grounded in one of two different, though not mutually exclusive, ways. We have seen that—if existence is to be comprehensible—we must presuppose a principle of unity, a something "which holds the world together from within." If it be asked what this is, if a nearer determination be demanded, it is convenient to use the analogy with the unity which psychology discovers in the human consciousness. Just as it is evident that the different states and elements of my consciousness are united in an inner inter-relation, so that they belong to one and the same ego, so the states and elements of existence may be conceived as united in one all-embracing ego. In existence, as much as in individual consciousness, we get the relation between a unity and a multiplicity, and perhaps we may be able to get a clearer idea of the cosmological relation if we conceive it as analogous with the psychological relation. This was the path struck out by Kant's speculative successors in Germany (Fichte, Schelling, Hegel), and it has also been adopted by later thinkers in search of a solution. The other way starts from the fact that, if we want to convince ourselves that any other beings have a conscious life, analogy alone can supply us with a basis for this assumption. It is argued as follows : As our expressions, movements, and actions are related to our psychical states, so the expressions, movements, and actions of other beings are related to similar states in them. Immediate observation of the psychical states of other men will always remain without the bounds of possibility. But now may we not be justified in extending this conclusion by analogy ? Why should we stop at animals ? Since there has proved to be such close continuity on the material side of existence with regard to its elements and laws, why should we not assume that the psychical side of existence is also continuous, although beyond our own conscious life it can never be the object of immediate observation ? And since we are only in a position to make quite clear to ourselves what it is to be a psychical being, while, on the other hand, the material can never be anything but an object for us, can never become immediately one with our own subjective ego, we shall gain the most comprehensible solution of the riddle of existence if we conceive the psychical to be the innermost essence of existence, and the material as an outer, sensuous form of this inner life. This interpretation reveals to us the nature of what the 'thing-in-itself' is ; it is no longer an x but a something that is in its essence akin to that which we know immediately in our own breasts. Leibniz adopted this line of thought in his day with great clearness and of set purpose; in modern times it has been followed by Schopenhauer, Beneke, Fechner, and Lotze. But this thought made its first appearance in the history of human thought in the philosophy of the Vedantas (the Upanishads) which replied to the question : What is Brahma, the principle of being? It is Atma, it is the soul within thy breast, it is thou thyself.

Materialism, too, if it is to figure as a conclusive theory, must depend on analogy; only in this case it will be the analogy with external sensuous experience, not that with the inner states of psychical life. Materialism turns the scientific doctrine of matter and its qualities into a doctrine of the innermost essence of existence. A part of experience is here made into the whole, or, at any rate, into its fundamental element.

20. Were it necessary to choose between these two possibilities, I should find no difficulty in making my choice. All experience—both the so-called 'outer' as well as the so-called 'inner'—is spiritual activity, and the material is always given to us as the object of intuition and thought, never as identical with our own states. All experience (of the kind which is here in question) consists of feelings and ideas in mutual relation, and it is by means of these that we learn to know all other phenomena. The inner unity which embraces all the elements of our consciousness, and which underlies our concept of 'I,' becomes for us, by means of an involuntary analogy, the picture of whatever other unity and whatever other interconnexion we can discover. Idealism, then, takes as its starting-point in its reading of existence that which, from the point of view of theory of knowledge, is the most fundamental in our knowledge. But the question still remains whether

we are justified in applying the analogy, whether its application can be sufficiently established. Here it is to me perfectly clear that the idealistic conception of the world may be a justifiable faith which need not conflict at any point with scientific presuppositions, methods or results, although it can never be rigorously proved any more than it can be scientifically developed in detail.

While it is comparatively easy to exhibit the justification of the conclusion from analogy so long as this is applied to beings which stand as near to ourselves as do other men and animals, the verification becomes the more difficult the more we extend the analogy to forms of existence very different from our own, and especially so when we extend it to the principle which unites together the whole infinity of existence. A positive concept of spiritual existence cannot here be formed. In virtue of the law of continuity, we are, indeed, obliged to assume that the life of the soul is not a new departure, but arises out of elements which are related to it as are lower to higher kinds of material forms ; [33] but a wider and more definite elaboration of this hypothesis is not possible.

If the argument from analogy of metaphysical idealism be allowed, we are driven on to the narrower choice between the two possibilities as to the inner essence of existence, *i.e.* whether it is psychical or material. But the dichotomy of being into psychical and material is purely empirical. No proof can be adduced that being must necessarily come under one or other of these two forms, so that the relation between them must be that of either —or (which logicians call a relation of contradiction). Perhaps the great difficulties which have attended the search for a satisfactory hypothesis concerning the relation between the psychical and the material may be due to the fact that being is not exhausted in these two forms of

existence; but that, on the contrary, there are many—
not to say with Spinoza infinitely many—other forms of
existence.   It may be that the relation between the
two forms of existence known to us will only become
comprehensible when we know other forms of existence.
At any rate, we do not possess all the data necessary
for the solution of this problem.   Let us suppose that
we only knew two colours.   We should then be inclined
to believe that all existing colour must be one of these
two.   Now we know that light can be broken in more
than two ways; and yet the physics, physiology and
psychology of colour bristle with problems.   The light
of existence can be broken, we may be sure, in a great
many more ways than the metaphysical system-makers
have dreamed of.   This faith (and this analogy) is, at
any rate, as capable of justification as that upon which
the idealistic conception of the world is based.

If we are not too particular about the cogency of
analogies it is easy enough to speculate.   But in that
case we replace concepts by figures — philosophy by
poetry.   For the theory of knowledge it is of the first
importance that we should draw a sharp distinction
between concept and figure.   A figure may be of great
value, but when it is not an example or intuitive sign of
a concept, whatever value it possesses depends on its
relation to sides of our nature other than the cognitive.

Natural science itself uses symbols and figures.
If modern science proceeds by way of explaining all
material phenomena as phenomena of motion, it does so
because motions are the simplest and clearest of phenomena; because by conceiving all phenomena in analogy
with them we gain the clearest and most logical conception of nature.   This analogy is justified by the fact that
definite material changes can, by its help, be predicted
and calculated.   It has become evident, in increasingly
wider fields, that the changes of material nature take

place *as though* they were nothing but the motions of material particles.   In biology the concept 'analogy' means, more specifically, the similarity which is found to exist between organs of different living creatures when these organs (*e.g.* the human hand and the parrot's bill) exercise similar functions, even though they cannot be classed together anatomically.   Analogy here suggests most fertile comparisons.   One member of the analogical relation throws light on the other, and in this way thought is stimulated to ask new questions and to start on new investigations.

In *psychology*, too, analogy plays an important part, as is evident from the facts that all expressions for psychical states and activities were originally used of material phenomena.   We represent psychical relations to ourselves by means of material relations.   Language does not form entirely new words (*e.g.* new prepositions) in order to express psychical phenomena ; analogy busies itself with procuring a terminology.   Psychology, however, like natural science, can confirm its analogies by experience, for self-observation presents to us that which the symbols express.   When, for example, the consideration which precedes a determination is spoken of as 'weighing,' self-observation tells us why this figure, taken from a pair of scales, is a suitable one ; the marshalling of motives, some coming forward while others retire again, reminding us of the scales which rise and fall according to the weights laid within them.   Moreover, when we speak of motives advancing or retiring, we have no difficulty in recognising what happenings are denoted by these figurative expressions.

Finally, analogy is of great importance in the *theory of knowledge*.   Between identity, rationality, and causality there is a certain analogy (§ 5).   Rationality, the relation between ground and consequent (premisses and conclusion), offers an analogy with the relation of simple identity, as this appears in recognition. It has been called the "paradox of the logical conclusion," that there must be an identity between ground and consequent, while yet in the transition from ground to consequent something new is gained. Hence an attempt has been made to reduce as far as possible the process of strictly logical inference to the confirmation of an identity, *i.e.* to an act of recognition. Causality, again, we seek to conceive in analogy with rationality, the causal relation in analogy with that between ground and consequent. We try to conceive the relation between events as a relation between ground and consequent, so that we may be able to infer backward from a present event to its cause and forward to its effects. This analogy also, which is an analogy between logical thinking and real being, has been most fruitful. It induces us to ask questions and raise problems, instead of merely watching and describing. Whether this analogy be really valid, and if so how far it can be extended, is the most important question in the problem of knowledge. Were it entirely valid, existence would be entirely comprehensible, that is to say, the processes of existence might then be conceived *as though* they were subject to the same laws as is human thought.

The symbolism of natural science sheds light on a complex material phenomenon by means of a simple material phenomenon; psychological symbolism illustrates a psychical phenomenon by some intuitable material phenomenon; epistemological symbolism illuminates relations between events by relations of thought; the symbolism of *metaphysics* differs from all these; it seeks to shed light on existence in its totality, or in its innermost essence, by figures which are taken from a single fact or a single side of existence as it appears in our experience. Neither the totality nor the innermost essence of existence is given in our experience. The symbolism of *religion* (considered epistemologically) only differs from the metaphysical in that its figures are more concrete, richer in colour, and more tinged with emotion.

21. Only with reluctance does the human conscious-ness abandon immediate intuition, as this occurs under the forms of sensuous perception, memory, and imagina-tion, to tread the path of analysis and to form con-cepts which can hardly afford adequate compensation for that which it gained from intuition.[34] But it comes to pass that the objects of religious consciousness—where this consciousness has reached a high stage of development—can no longer be grasped by means of immediate intuition. The old naïvely constructed figures are constantly modified and improved, until at last it is recognised that they are inadequate to express the eternal, infinite and august nature of the object of religion. The religious consciousness here wavers between two tendencies. On the one hand, it scruples to use sensuous and human expressions for its infinite object, on the other, it is reluctant to rob immediate feeling of the lively and striking expressions in which it instinctively relieves itself. We may study these two tendencies at war with one another in that religious genius, Augustine, who was at once a thinker and a prince of the Church. For him (as later for Schleiermacher) the expression 'mercy' had only figurative meaning when predicated of God, because it implies suffering through the suffering of others. Nevertheless, Augustine believed himself justified in so using it in order to save the souls of the unlearned (*animae indoctorum*) from stumbling ; he employed, that is to say, a kind of educational anthropomorphism. Only those, he adds, who unite religion with study can dispense with figurative expressions.[35] But how far does the figurative extend ? Is there ever anywhere an expression for an object of religion which is not figurative ? If we study the history of religion our attention will be caught

by two interesting lines of development, both of which are intent on threshing out all that is figurative and which reach their zenith in the rejection of all definite expressions, on the ground that they are all taken from limited spheres of experience and hence finitise what they seek to define.

The first of these lines of development occurs in the Indian Upanishads. The Vedanta philosophers became convinced that no concept and no figure could express the essence of the deity—Atma as little as Brahma (§ 19). They constructed their metaphysical idealism only in the end to knock it down again. The deity is "without end, without age, without shore ; it has neither without nor within." It can best be indicated negatively (*neti, neti*) ; it is neither 'that' nor 'this.' Silence is the correct answer to the question what is it. Could it be perceived by us it would not be what it is. It is the unthinkable, and yet thought thinks itself through it. No duality, no oppositeness can be predicated of it—and hence it can never be known. Neither sight nor word nor thought can attain unto it, although it works through sight as well as through word and thought. It is neither existent nor non-existent; neither knowable nor unknowable. It can only be expressed symbolically. In order to exclude all sensuous ideas, such as are apt to be associated with symbols having definite significance, the Vedanta philosophers used as an expression for the Highest the syllable 'Om' which means 'Yes,' but which does not lead the mind in any particular direction.[36]

The other line of development is to be found in *neo-Platonism* and was propagated from this (through Dionysius the Areopagite (so-called)) into the *Christian mysticism* of the Middle Ages. Although recent inquiries have shown that the opposition between scholasticism and mysticism was by no means so complete as had previously been supposed, yet there is one point

on which these two mediæval tendencies differ widely,
and that is the question as to whether it is permissible
to employ analogies in forming our conception of God.
The scholastics were in favour of analogy, the mystics
rejected it. Thomas Aquinas, it is true, teaches that
while it is impossible to predicate a term of God in the
same sense (*univoce*) in which it is predicated of created
beings, yet there are expressions which signify more
than a play of words (*pure aequivoce*) when applied to
God. According to him there is a kind of analogy
which lies between synonymity and homonymity, namely,
that which rests on a causal relation, *e.g.* when we say
both of some remedy and of the patient healed by
it that they are 'healthy.' An analogical relation of this
kind exists between the Creator and created beings. But
there is no relation of similarity present to justify us in
tracing back Creator and creation to the same genus.
No, every determination, even the concept of being,
must be used of the Creator and creation in different
senses: God stands outside every concept of genus (*extra
omne genus*). The knowledge which we can thus get
can never, it is evident, be very distinct, and it is not
easy to represent it to ourselves. For—however much
we restrict it—analogy is a relation of similarity, and in
all comparison we must be able to apply concepts of
genus and species : when we relate things by means of
analogy we are really forming a generic concept. When
Thomas Aquinas quotes the analogy which is dependent
on the causal connexion as an example of one which is
theologically admissible, we must remember that we
understand the causal relation the less, the more the cause
differs from the effect specifically, or is even generically
different. When the causal relation is not imposed from
without on purely external and practical grounds, there is
always a certain continuity, and with that a similarity
between cause and effect, which justifies us in reducing

them to the same generic concept.   Moreover, a closer examination will show us that the same connexion exists between the remedy and the state it produces in an organism.   Hence the scholastic affirmation of the justification of analogy passes logically over into the mystical denial of this justification.   Hugo von St. Victor in his time taught that God can be better conceived under negative than under positive expressions. Later on, Suso called God "a nameless Nothingness "— "a Not of all the things which man can think or say " (although "in himself he is an all-essential somewhat "). And the author of *German Theology* teaches that if the highest and only good (*i.e.* God) were something, this or that, which the creation could understand, then it would not be all-in-all, would not be unique, and would therefore not be perfect ; hence it must be called Nothing, by which is meant that it is nothing of all which created beings understand, know, think, or name.[37] Mysticism was at once a movement of feeling, based on inwardness, and an intellectual movement from figure to thought and from thought to the limit of thought. Because the representatives of this movement, while in a state of violent emotion, lived through states in which they could form no distinct ideas, they were therefore prepared in advance to attack every attempt to express the highest under the form of a concept.   Mysticism here joins hands with critical philosophy, which asserts that our ideas are not adequate to express that which exists outside the form of our limited experience.   Even in antiquity we find this kinship between criticism and mysticism, for there is a certain similarity between the philosophies of religion developed by Carneades and Plotinus respectively in their treatment of theory of knowledge.

22. But neither scholasticism nor Protestant theology are prepared to admit with mysticism and criticism that

all religious ideas are necessarily figurative. In a certain sense this may be said to be a question of life or death. The concept of revelation (in the strictest sense), for instance, would no longer hold good did not the difference between figure and reality disappear at certain points. Moreover, the old problem of the relation between knowledge and things would crop up again and an absolute conclusion, and with it the possibility of rest, would be excluded. We must now pass on to examine the most important of the ideas which are included in the concept of God. It will be evident with regard to figurative ideas, as we have already seen it to be true of concepts, that they express *relations* and presuppose *relations*, and hence that they can never express an absolute conclusion.

When God is called 'lord' or 'king' a relation to servants or subjects must be understood, who differ from him and stand in an external relation to him. Hence Newton says of the word 'God' that it is a relative term expressing a relation to servants (*deus est vox relativa et ad servos refertur*). It would be mere childishness, however, to conceive the relation between God and man to be as external as that between a lord and his servants. It gives us a figure—but what could we have in its stead? And how could we express the thoughts which form its background, if the relation which is so essentially expressed by the figure is to disappear or at any rate to lose its externality, for, in that case, each member of the relation will lose the independence in virtue of which they limit one another? Perhaps we may with Thomas Aquinas attempt a scholastic distinction. The famous scholastic thought that he could employ the concept of 'Lord' in his theology, although this expresses a relation (*relatio dominii*): the relation, however, is only real as holding of the creation to God, not of God to creation. The creation, that is to say, stands in relation to God but not God to creation. To make this clearer, Aquinas uses a figure : God no more changes because creation (after it has been called into existence) enters into a relation with Him than a column changes because an animal lies down on one side of it.[38] But this comparison does not help us out of the difficulty. It is after all not a matter of complete indifference to the column whether an animal lies down near it or not : if we think a little more we shall see the relations of light, air, and warmth must be changed a little so that the two sides of the pillar are not exactly alike. A relation cannot be absolutely one-sided, and the religious consciousness itself would take exception at the idea of its being a matter of indifference to God whether creation existed or not. Instead of a dead column let us think of a living mother; it will be easy enough for the onlooker to say whether her tender child lies on her left or her right side.

Next to the symbol of 'lord' that of 'father' is the most common. This symbol has a history. The family relation was transferred unconsciously in polytheism to the world of the gods. The gods had fathers and mothers, and the chief god was often called 'father' by the people—even though from the standpoint of nature-religions this term had not the deeper significance it acquired at higher stages. In polytheism no one felt any drawback in accepting all the consequences of the figure thus naïvely used, and men represented to themselves the fatherly relation on all its different sides. This is not the case in monotheistic religions. The word 'father' continues in use, but it is divorced from its consequences ; the maternal relation, as also other aspects, is ignored. It is forgotten, for instance, that a human father only stands to his child in the relation of guardian for a certain time, and aims, or ought to aim, at making that child as independent as possible, so that he shall not continue to require his father's protection.

The symbols of 'lord' and 'father' are often employed side by side, so that in their special application they are liable to conflict. When *e.g.* the orthodox doctrine of the atonement demands a bloody sacrifice in order to melt God's wrath, this may pass for the relation of a stern oriental lord to his obedient servants, but it is not congruous with the relation of a father to his children. We cannot, of course, expect to arrive at any logical thought-construction by means of figures taken from such different spheres. Even the logical application of one of these figures very soon leads to absurdities; absurdities which have been held up to derision only too often by anti-theological criticism. But even those who find such mockery in bad taste cannot deny its relative justification. Dogma has hung its leaden weight round the neck of these religious symbols, dragging them down into spheres in which they are exposed both to criticism and to mockery.

As reflection develops we pass from more intuitive and concrete relations to more abstract ones. Among these abstract determinations is 'personality.' The more definite characterisation gives place to a more indefinite one, which is still, however, borrowed from human surroundings. Psychologically regarded, the determination of the content of the concept of personality can be reduced to two chief points.[39] Personality (the ego), as we know it, is characterised in the first place by its unity. All the elements of its being are gathered up and united with more or less energy, and this in more inner fashion than the elements of matter are bound together by the laws of external nature. The elements thus bound together in the unity of personality, however, are not absolutely produced by it; here it is more or less dependent on its environment. It may happen that, without its wish, although not without its own unconscious or involuntary co-operation, new elements arise within it, and all now depends on how and how far these can be brought into connexion with the already organised elements. Secondly, within the content of every personality are some elements which occupy a more central place and have a more constant character than others. Such central and constant elements are the predominant aims and interests which determine the nature and direction of the will. This is the real side of personality, that which chiefly determines the special idiosyncrasies of particular individuals. Both from the formal and the real side, personal life, as we know it, exhibits an alternation between activity and passivity. Activity is displayed in organising the content received in a predominantly passive state. During this elaboration the peripheral and changing elements are more or less energetically ruled by whatever elements in the particular personality (or during particular periods of life) are central and constant. We only know personality as it strives and struggles, asserting itself in the face of opposition and difficulties which arise partly from lack or superfluity of content, partly from internecine strife between its constituent elements. A personality which produced its entire content absolutely out of itself— which had no still unattained ends to strive after, no real opposition to overcome—would not be what we must understand by personality as long as we remain within the sphere of psychological experience.

The dispute whether the deity (as conceived from the standpoints of higher religions) is to be called a personal being or not—a dispute which is often alluded to as the point at issue between theism and pantheism— comes about because on one side the concept of personality is idealised and extended, so that we get back to the idea discussed above (§ 10) of a *causa sui*, while on the other it is declared unjustifiable to call a being personal when it produces all its own elements and hence encounters no real opposition and is not in a position either to struggle, to strive, or to hope.

Personal life is the highest form of existence revealed to us in experience. And the unity which in the end we are bound to attribute to being on account of its continuity and obedience to law reminds us of the unity of our consciousness, of the formal side of personality. Nevertheless it is an analogy which fails at the essential point ; for our idea of the finite ego, itself but a single member of the great world-order, cannot express the inexhaustible principle which comes to light in the very fact of the existence of this world-order. And it is the more difficult to maintain this analogy the greater the inclination to conceive the deity as perfect or absolute, *i.e.* as finished and complete, so that (as the scholastic Andreas Sunesen says in his didactic poem) it does not admit of extension (*natura dei cui nil accrescere posset*). The difficulties in maintaining the analogy with the concept of personality are heightened to the point of becoming obviously self-contradictory by this dogmatic assertion of absoluteness and the strong emphasis laid on immutability.

Philosophical theists, such as C. H. Weisse and H. Lotze assert, it is true, that only an infinite being can possess personality, while a limited and hence a dependent being is not really worthy to be so called. That is to say, only an absolutely active being can be a person. But to say this is to admit that the word 'personality' is used in two entirely different meanings (or, as Thomas Aquinas would say, *pure aequivoce*) when used of God and of man. Hence, strictly speaking, they are in accord with the result at which Spinoza and Kant arrived, *i.e.* that, after elimination of all that is valid of finite beings only, nothing remains of our fundamental psychological concept except the name. So-called 'pantheism' rejects the term 'personality,' not because it is too high but because it is too low a determination of the deity. The deity must be more than a person if it is the principle which unites together the whole of being. As we already saw (§ 20), we have no right to assume that we have sufficient data to determine that which is the foundation of all things, and which therefore cannot be characterised by any of the particular forms of existence which are exhibited to us in experience. Schleiermacher wrote to that zealous theist, Jacobi: "Rather than deify nature, you deify consciousness. But, my dear friend, one deification is, at any rate in my eyes, as good as another. . . . We can never get over the opposition between the ideal and the real, or however else you like to call them. . . . Does it not strike you that a personality must necessarily be *finite* when you yourself endow it with life?"[40] The difference between a theistic and a pantheistic conception does not always depend solely on epistemological arguments; other motives are unconsciously operative, and the difference for the most part depends on the varying degree of strength with which the need of forming clear figures—especially at the limits of thought—is present in different individuals. We shall have something more to say on this point later, when we come to the psychological section of our philosopy of religion. With regard to the term 'pantheism' itself, we may note that it is used in somewhat different senses. According to a manner of speech, which has the authorisation of no less a person than Eduard Zeller, pantheism denotes a conception of the world in which the relation between God and the world is conceived as immanent, whether God be conceived as a person or not. According to this usage of the term, a point of view such as Lotze's would be as deserving of the name pantheism as is that of Spinoza. According to another usage (to which I myself adhere), the concept is narrower in its range, and an immanent world-conception can only be properly called pantheistic when it does not attribute personality (unless by poetic license) to the principle which unites existence from within.

Nor will it help us to use more abstract expressions such as force, life, substance, for these, too, as we have already seen (§ 18), denote relations and hence presuppose a something with which the relation can be set up. Moreover, these expressions also, before they could be applied in the way desired by the religious consciousness in its mythical and dogmatic forms, would have to be subjected to such a process of whittling down that nothing would be left of them but the mere word.

It is therefore abundantly evident that at the critical point all analogies fail us. We stand at the limits of thought, and it is no wonder that real concepts can no longer be framed, and that the figures in which the individual mood finds satisfaction admit of no logical application. This unknowability is very strongly insisted upon by what is called *agnosticism.* But we have already (§ 18) had occasion to see that this school is inclined to assert that 'the Unknowable' is entirely different from everything that appears in experience, so that no one of the empirical laws can have any significance whatever for that which is nevertheless regarded as the principle of being. This is a dualistic conception for which there is no foundation. Although our finite points of view and forms of thought are not able to afford us a definition, still less an exhaustive formulation of this principle, yet they must stand in interconnexion with it, and we are not justified in declaring them to be without significance. Our thought, our knowledge itself forms part of existence, has arisen within it and is itself one of the facts which must be taken into consideration before we bring our inquiry into the nature of being to a conclusion. The ideas which our experience prompts us to develop are probably, in comparison with the great related whole of which we form a part as individual members, both subordinate and derivative ; devoid of all significance, however, we need not suppose them to be. Only we are not able to indicate the degree and nature of the metamorphosis our points of view will have to undergo before they can be assimilated into the highest and most all-embracing interconnexion that we are able to conceive. To use the poetical language of religion : our highest knowledge must suffer an entire transformation if—while preserving its value — it is to be absorbed into the highest most all-embracing totality that we can conceive. A nearer determination of the relation between the part and the whole is of course as out of our reach here as we already saw a nearer determination of the whole itself to be.

The expression 'agnosticism' was coined by Huxley in order that he too might have a term, like all other proper terms for opinions, ending in 'ism.' Were I in search of a name for the conception I am here trying to develop, I should call it *Critical Monism.*

23. Before concepts, analogies, and images can be used to express the object of religion at the higher stages of its development, they have to undergo a process of idealisation and sublimation which is apt to seem cold and strange to religious feeling. The religious consciousness itself tends, it is true, to conceive its object as exalted far above all finite relations. But where it yields unreservedly to this tendency it works against itself, for then the inner living relation to its object becomes impossible. Many nations believe the highest god to be an infinite spirit, but in their meditation and in their need they turn to divine beings who stand nearer to human nature and human circumstances. So we hear

of the South American Indians : " The intelligence of
the Indians is certainly capable of conceiving the idea
of an all-wise and all-powerful spirit, of a highest ruler
of the world ; but it does not always rise to the level
of this being, who appears to them so great, so far,
and so incomprehensible.   When danger threatens him,
when his hope is crushed, when sorrow overwhelms him,
the Indian likes to turn to a more subordinate being, who
is more within the grasp of his comprehension.   He has
a guardian spirit to whom he looks for help and guidance.
The whole of nature is for him full of mysterious
happenings.   He studies the nature which surrounds
him, as the astrologer studies the stars."   And of the
Hindus an observer tells us : " We have frequently
asked : ' Where is the temple of the Supreme ? '   And
the answer given, with evident surprise at a question so
unexpected, has always been : ' Temple of the Supreme ?
What do you mean ?   There is no such temple.'
' Why ? '   ' Because He can have none.   He is formless,
nameless, inconceivable, and we cannot worship Him.'
' And therefore you worship idols ? '   ' Certainly, an
idol is indispensable.   We need some visible object in
which our minds can find rest.' "[41]   We find both
these tendencies in Christianity.   The Catholic Church
fosters belief in a whole series of beings to which
the worshipper can turn in order to satisfy his need
for a finite limited object of prayer and meditation,
when the highest member of the series seems too
distant and too exalted.   Beginning with God, the series
passes down through Jesus and the Madonna to special
saints, who are active in special sorts of cases or who
take charge of special individuals.   In the Protestant
Church this tendency is limited, but it still exists.   As
a Copenhagen preacher once said in a funeral discourse,
" God cannot help us in our great sorrow because He is
so infinitely far away ; we must therefore look to Jesus."

As the religious consciousness hesitates between the literal and the figurative interpretation of the expressions it employs, so, too, it vacillates between the tendency to exalt and infinitise its object, and the tendency to bring it down into this finite world as fellow-worker and sufferer.   Often the strongest feeling, the deepest meditation centres in the struggling and suffering rather than the eternal and perfect God.   When these tendencies are retained together in their extreme form we get the *religious paradox*:—God is unchangeable and changeable, eternal and becoming, victorious and vanquished, blessed and suffering.   Religious minds often take a special delight in multiplying such oppositions, partly in ecstatic admiration of the Almighty, partly in contempt of the thought which tries in vain to grasp them.   But the chief contrast—to which all these can be reduced— is, as we shall see presently, that between mutability and immutability.   The typical difference between the two greatest popular religions is determined by their relation to this opposition.   But we even find it appearing within one and the same religion.   The believer in a God "in whom is no variableness neither shadow of turning" may also reach the conclusion that "God is the most changeable of all beings." [42]   The paradox did not originally appear in the shape of any special dogma, *e.g.* that of the incarnation, as S. Kierkegaard in his *Philosophical Fragments* tries to make out.   In reality it is already present in every anthropomorphism, every image which claims to be more than an image. The assertion that any image whatsoever can suffice is in fact an assertion that the unlimited is limited, the infinite finite.   The power of habit makes men blind to this paradox, their imagination makes itself at home among the imagery which has gradually established itself and become consecrated by tradition.   But whenever the wave of feeling or the movement of thought rises

higher, this limited form is rent asunder, and if it is to
be retained, or rather if men *are determined* it shall be
retained, it can only be by a *credo quia absurdum.*

24. Once again, a 'both — and' appears as a
characteristic of the religious consciousness. But when
this 'both—and' is carried to the point of paradox, it
is clear that the interest which has led to the development of the religious ideas in their distinctive form can
be no purely intellectual interest, no mere need of the
understanding. For every religious standpoint, and
especially for the great popular religions, knowledge
is certainly not without importance. During its classical
ages, as we have seen, religion is everything to man,
satisfying also his thirst for knowledge. But the thirst
for knowledge is here subordinate to the impulse of
self-preservation, to the need to develop and maintain
life. "I seek Thee in order that my soul may live,"
says Augustine to his God. Only by remembering this
can we understand how it is that certain ideas are
developed and retained in defiance of the intellectual
interest in clear and consistent thinking. We are thus
led to realise that the basis of religion must be sought
in other sides of the spiritual life than that of pure
thought.

Religion cannot be made or constructed. It grows
up out of life itself, springs out of the basal mood of
man in his struggle for life, out of his resolution to hold
fast, under all circumstances, to the validity of that which
he has learnt from experience to be of the highest value.
The hypothesis that religion consists essentially in faith
in the conservation of value here naturally recurs. Now
that we have seen that it cannot be of the essence of
religion to afford an understanding or explanation of
existence such as the intellectual interest demands, the
hypothesis that it consists in faith in the conservation
of value naturally presents itself. The riddle which

science is unable to read proves equally insoluble from
the religious point of view.   We have seen that religion
can give no explanation of special events (Section A)—
that its ideas are not capable of affording a conclusion
for scientific thought (Section B)—and that these ideas
exhibit the character of figures rather than of concepts
(Section C).   If the religious ideas are to have any
significance at all, therefore, it can only be in serving as
symbolical expressions for the feeling, the aspirations,
and the wishes of men in their struggle for existence ;
thus they are secondary not primary both in significance
and origin.   The philosophy of religion is here at odds
with dogmatism, just as the history of art is with the
mythology of art.   That which, according to the history
of art,[43] impels the artist to activity is the lively joy
in the forms which life exhibits to him ; he wishes to
reproduce them, though it may be in ideal form.   But
what name he gives to the figure he has shaped is a
subordinate question, which is often left till afterwards to
be decided.

Once developed, however, it is, of course, inevitable
that the intellectual interest should influence the religious
interest.   If religion essentially consists in the conviction
that value is preserved, yet this conviction must always
require ideas by which to make clear to itself its own
meaning ; and these ideas—slowly, perhaps, but continuously—are wrought into greater consistency and greater
harmony with the ideas which men have arrived at by
other routes and under the influence of other motives ;
the question then arises as to how the two interests
are related to one another.   The intellectual interest
prompts us to conceive existence as a great immeasurable
system of causal groups and causal series ; the religious
interest moves us to a conception of being as the home
of the development and conservation of value.   Can
these two points of view be harmonised ?   What is the

relation between value and causality, the riddle of life and the riddle of the world ? This problem is perhaps insoluble, and to solve it would be to find the philosopher's stone. But our epistemological study of the philosophy of religion has perhaps taught us to see more clearly wherein the problem consists. It is no doubt true that the theory of knowledge can throw light for the most part only indirectly and negatively on the religious problem ; nevertheless we cannot hope to arrive at any clear results if we neglect it. We pass on now, with the assistance of psychology, to the direct study of the nature of religion. The question now before us is how far the hypothesis that religion consists essentially in the conviction that value is preserved, to which I have more than once made allusion, can find adequate foundation and confirmation.

III. PSYCHOLOGICAL PHILOSOPHY OF RELIGION

25. STRICTLY speaking we have already, in the preceding sections, made use of psychology ; for theory of knowledge and psychology are constantly crossing each other's borders. Theory of knowledge examines the forms and elements of our knowledge to find out whether they can be relied on for procuring us an understanding of what is ; while psychology examines them in respect of their actual constitution and their actual origin, irrespective of their use or validity. We have seen that the significance of the religious ideas cannot consist in making existence comprehensible (in the sense in which our intellectual interest understands the word 'comprehensible'). There remains, therefore, nothing but the purely psychological investigation. This may possibly show us what positive significance actually attaches to the religious ideas.

The psychology of religion is a part of general psychology, a specialised form of it. It stands in reciprocal relation with general psychology. It serves as a means for the latter, for within its own particular sphere it collects and elaborates stuff of the greatest psychological interest. For it is within the religious sphere that men have made their deepest and most intense psychical experiences. In religion (when it is real and original) all the elements of psychical life work together with an energy and harmony which is hardly to be found within any other sphere. It is on this account that the study of the religious life of the soul is of such great importance for general psychology. The attention of psychologists is claimed not only by the history of religion but also—and in a still higher degree—by the religious life of individuals. The history of religion cannot so easily trace the psychical powers in their original activities. It is occupied, for the most part, with great types ; with those forms of religion which are common to large groups of men. Good biographies, especially autobiographies of religious persons, are more instructive than the most learned works on great popular religions. Thus—to name a few examples—the Confessions of Augustine, the Autobiographies of Suso and Saint Theresa, are some of the most important materials for the psychology of religion. The history of individual piety, too, forms a natural part of the history of religion ; but up till now the latter has occupied itself almost exclusively with great types. The psychology of religion, however, does not only collect material for general psychology ; within its special sphere it employs the points of view and laws of the latter. It tries to understand psychologically the phenomena of the religious life. Here general psychology appears as a means for the psychology of religion. And it is from the latter side especially that we shall be occupied with the psychology of religion here, where it appears as part of the philosophy of religion. It applies the general methods of psychology so far as the material admits, and starts from the same presuppositions as does general psychology.[44]

A. RELIGIOUS EXPERIENCE AND RELIGIOUS FAITH

Quid est, quod amo, quum te amo ?
AUGUSTINE.

(*a*) RELIGIOUS EXPERIENCE

26. I take the word experience here in the sense of the happening, the coming to pass of states of mind, in opposition to their elaboration by means of thought. We shall be chiefly concerned with trying to decide what and how much must be reckoned as religious experience, and what are the limitations to which this experience, in virtue of its own nature, is subjected. My aim in the following pages will be to describe religious experience from a strictly psychological point of view.

27. Experience, in the sense of that which we live through, is never concluded as long as life lasts. Hence it may present a series of particular states but never a completed totality, and no general axiom can emerge as the crystallised result of experience. Totalities and generalisations spring either from an elaboration by thought of that which has been experienced, or by an unconscious emphasis of one particular experience or one particular kind of experience as that which decides and determines all else. Before the stage of conscious reflection we shall find this unconscious emphasis forming the basis of all which afterwards comes to be regarded as the result of religious experience. It lies in the nature of feeling that once aroused by any particular event, it tends to spread over the whole life of consciousness and seeks to impart its own colouring to all other elements of this life, indifferent as to whether they are or are not connected with the event in question. In virtue of this *expansion of feeling* (as I have called this phenomenon in my psychology), inner states, which in

H

and for themselves have nothing to do with one another, may acquire a common character, and out of the series of inner happenings a whole may arise, although the series in itself had reached no real conclusion. The experiences which thus determine the whole colouring of the inner life may vary very widely with different individuals and circumstances. Inevitable and significant though this expansion of feeling may be, yet it contains sources of error which we must not forget in estimating the contributions of experience. Such an expansion of feeling is, of course, itself an experience ; in comparison, however, with those inner happenings whose results we are trying to trace, it is only a secondary one.

In the conflict between optimism and pessimism, for instance, we shall find that single experiences are regarded as typical, and are allowed to determine the chosen point of view. Although the adherents of both views appeal to observation and thought, the result attained is determined much less by logical generalisation and induction than by an expansion of feeling. They have only to preserve the experiences taken as a basis in their freshness, and to let them maintain their place in the centre of consciousness, so as to rivet attention on themselves, and the rest follows of itself.

If faith in the conservation of value be the core of all religion, it follows that no religion can be constructed on the basis of immediate experience. We can only immediately learn to know the particular and definite values which are conditioned by our human and individual nature and our special conditions of life ; no experience can immediately teach us anything about the conservation of these values any more than it can show us that that which possesses the highest value for us is the central fact of existence. What we have experienced and lived through may supply us with *a motive* for believing in the conservation of value, but it can never supply

the *content* of this faith.   Personal life—more especially
as it expresses itself in great crises, when new paths
are struck out and new forms of life produced—is the
highest value we know.   Hence we involuntarily employ
the experiences we have of this life to illuminate the
whole of existence ; it appears to us as though in such
crises existence reveals to us its hidden powers.   An
expansion of feeling is here in operation.   If we try
to translate this into the form of thought, we get a
conclusion by analogy, and an analogy which lies on
the other side of the line at which thought passes over
into poetry (§§ 19, 20).

28. In every experience we must distinguish between
the immediately given and that which serves to explain
and to express it.   These three moments, the state itself,
its cause, and its expression, may lie so near together that
they can only be separated by means of a more close
and exact after-scrutiny.   The relation here is similar
to that between a discovery, its verification and its
formulation.   These three moments may also approach
one another very nearly, though it may be of great
importance to keep them apart.

If we appeal to our individual experience, the *experienced state itself* can only afford us a temporary foot-
hold.   The fact that this state has *a definite cause*
cannot be experienced as immediately as the state itself.
For when something has deeply stirred our psychical
life and produced in it great effects, we are so absorbed
in these effects—for they are what we are immediately
living through—that it becomes impossible for us to
form a clear and adequate idea of their cause.   The real
cause consists in a plurality of conditions and can only
be discovered by means of a critical investigation.   We
are under an illusion if we think we experience the ' cause
as cause.'   The existence of a causal relation can never
be immediately perceived ; immediate observation only

shows us that one thing comes *after* another, never that
it comes *out* of it.   The presence of a causal relation is
not proved until we can show that only after this particular
preceding event does this particular state *inevitably*
follow.   But neither an 'only' nor an 'inevitably' can
be known purely immediately ; they must be ascertained
by comparison or by experiment.   In doubtful cases,
therefore, we appeal to comparisons and experiments, and
it is especially in doubtful cases that the appeal to
experience is most frequently made.   We do not begin
with doubt within the sphere either of inner or outer
experience.   Every element of consciousness as it
emerges is at first instinctively accepted as valid, as the
expression of reality.   It presents itself, so to say,
clothed in an existential quality, which is only dispelled
when contradictory elements present themselves with
the same existential quality.   Where no such conflict
occurs no doubt arises, and in such case there is no need
for a criterion of reality or of validity.   But if there
is conflict the question inevitably follows : which of
these elements possesses true reality ? and can only be
decided when there is found to be inevitable connexion
between one of the conflicting elements and other
elements, the validity of which has previously been
established.   This is what we do when we are in doubt
as to something in our surroundings.   The difference
between an hallucination and a real event is recognisable
by the fact that the latter, but not the former, can be
shown to be a member of a long consecutive causal
series, composed of elements of undoubted validity.
The more consecutive our dream, the more it seems to
us a reality, and the more isolated any real event remains
in our experience, the more apt we are to take it for a
dream.[45]   What is true in this respect of outer experience
is also true of inner experience.   Here again immediate
experience of a causal relation is impossible.   In any

discussion of the significance of religious experience which is more than merely superficial, it will at any rate be helpful—when not absolutely necessary—to treat the immediately experienced in as great abstraction as possible from the supposed cause. That which is strongly and immediately experienced cannot itself be an illusion. The illusory only arises through a false causal explanation which is confounded with immediate observation. We shall have occasion later on to explain the procedure followed by causal explanation.

In the case of a violently excited state of mind or a violently exciting experience, the first need to be felt will not be to ascertain its cause but *to give vent to it in gestures or ejaculations, in words or in actions.* The individual then seeks for thoughts or images wherewith to satisfy this need or guide it in a certain direction. We have here the need for reaction—and reaction in fear or in thanks, in love or in anger and hatred, according to circumstances. The manner of this reaction will be determined by earlier experiences and by whatever traditions the subject is influenced by. Only in particularly original natures does a new construction take place. From such natures the prophets and founders of religions are recruited.

By means of a natural shifting that which satisfies the need for expression and reaction is apt to coincide with that which satisfies the need for a causal explanation when this latter need arises. During distinctly religious states of consciousness the thirst after knowledge does not make itself felt independently and certainly not critically; the need to express and react, which is identical with the need for symbolisation, is distinctly predominant and therefore determines the content of the religious idea.

If immediate experience can give us no sure indication of the cause of that which we have experienced, still less is it able to give us reliable information as to whether the experience is due to a 'natural' or 'supernatural' cause. In detailed descriptions of religious states we often find that the subject only jumps to the conclusion that the cause must be 'supernatural,' because he is not able to assign a natural cause and does not think that he himself has taken any part in it. Thus St. Theresa says: "I felt my soul inflamed by ardent love to God; this love was evidently supernatural, for *I knew not* what had set it alight in me and *I myself had done nothing in the matter*." It is a constantly recurring trait with mystics and pietists that the more they withhold (or believe themselves to withhold) their own thinking and willing, the more they attribute a divine origin to their inner experiences.[46] Here we get the same underlying dualistic conception which we found in the concept of wonder in general. Psychological wonders belong to the same category as physical wonders, although belief in the former persists longer than in the latter.

29. Religious ideas may stand in various relations to immediate experiences. It may be that the experience develops as a series of psychical states, and that only afterwards is an idea sought for which can indicate (*i.e.* explain or express—or both together) this experience. Such ideas may, under the impression of extraordinary experiences and in original creative personalities, be original. Generally speaking, however, they have their source in the circle of traditional ideas with which the subject was already familiar, but which he had previously disregarded. Examples are not wanting of persons who first became convinced that they were 'converted' or 'born again,' by the fact that their experiences tallied with those recounted by accredited believers.[47] The change which is noticed is interpreted by means of traditions, which now for the first time are brought into practical use and are transformed from a dead to a living treasure. But very often it happens that it is the

traditional ideas themselves which evoke the experiences.
Religious experience consists for most men in strivings
and states which are described and inculcated by tradition.
The ideas, then, are ready made in advance and have
only to be translated into experience.   Most men make
their religious experiences in company with believers
who have a more or less developed creed.   By this
means the range of experience is restricted in advance.
Experiences which cannot find expression in the traditional
circle of religious ideas appear uncertain, dangerous, or
even pernicious.   In theological expositions this confessional character, so frequent in religious experiences,
comes out clearly and often with express consciousness.

The older pietism—in opposition to the orthodoxy
which it combated—attached great importance to inner
experiences.   But since the Protestant Church regards
the Bible as the highest norm, the Church pietists
expressly asserted that inner experience must be
subordinated to the teachings of the Bible.   In
that remarkable work *Theologia Experimentalis* (1715),
Gottfried Arnold teaches that religious experience ranks
below Scripture and denotes no particular principle
beyond this.   The whole significance of experience, in
his eyes, lies in the fact that it affords a field for the
practice of the doctrines of Scripture.   Experience, then,
is not a ground but a consequent and fruit, and must
be judged "according to the Word of God."   With the
clearness which distinguishes him, Arnold goes on to
draw from this the conclusion that experience must
occupy a different place in religion from that which it
holds in science ; in religion it follows after belief, in
science it precedes it.   Modern theologians have, on the
contrary, attempted to draw a parallel between religious
and scientific experience, without recognising the for-
midable consequences to which such a procedure must
lead.   It will, at any rate, oblige them to acknowledge

that the individual can never learn by way of experience
all which, according to the teachings of the Church,
he ought to believe. And what significance has the
"common experience of the congregation " for individuals,
and can it rightly be called a 'common experience' if
every one does not or cannot share it? Moreover, the
teaching of the Church includes a great deal, *e.g.* the
creation, the last judgment, which it is impossible that
any one can have experienced at all.

The limitation imposed by creeds has made religious
experience—and, indeed, inner experience in general—
one-sided and imperfect. It has left unnoticed aspects
of the inner life which have well-established grounds for
consideration. And, what is of paramount importance
for the philosophy of religion, it has rendered the
origin of the religious ideas psychologically inexplicable.
For religious experience must surely sometimes lead to
the formation of new ideas, or, at any rate, to the
appreciation of ideas other than those which are
traditionally sanctioned. It must be as possible to make
discoveries within the sphere of the inner life as within
that of the outer. The conditions of the inner life
change just as much as do those of the outer—and this
must necessarily be the case, since the inner and outer
life are constantly acting and re-acting upon one
another. We have no right to assume dogmatically
that all essential psychical experiences have already
been made, so that future generations have but to
exercise themselves in the forms and thoughts which
were established at a certain definite point in time. It
will never be possible to prove that the world of spirit
has attained its conclusion.

30. The practical value of an idea is proved in one
of two ways; either experience moves us to form or to
choose it as an expression of what we have lived through,
or it helps us, when we hold fast to it and absorb our-

selves in it, to keep up our courage in the battle of
life, to remain faithful to the best that we know, and to
impose tasks on ourselves which advance our personal
development. It matters not, then, whether an idea be
the cause or the effect of experience, it must be tested in
experience. But at the same time we must never forget
that a complete, empirical proof of the practical value
of an idea can only be adduced when there has been
opportunity of trying whether the same experiences may
not be expressed differently, or whether the same or
equally valuable experiences cannot clothe themselves in
other ideas than the one in question. Not only a test
but also a counter-test is necessary ; and for this the life
of the individual seldom affords opportunity. As a
rule, the individual is restricted to the experience that
certain ideas have or have not helped him under
certain circumstances. He will not be able to prove
that ideas other than those which have actually helped
him could not have helped him. Immediate experience,
at any rate, can tell him nothing on this point. No
more can it tell him whether that which has not
helped him might not help other men—or himself—under
different circumstances. Experience will always retain
the stamp of individual personality; 'common experience'
is more or less an illusion, because, as a matter of fact,
different individuals interpret and apply this 'common'
experience each in his own way. But now that we have
recognised the difficulties involved in the transition from
individual to confessional experience, we shall be on our
guard when confessional experience claims that it is
accessible to all men if they 'will' only accept it.
Here again the underlying assumption is that all
possibilities are known, *i.e.* all personal relations and
conditions.

31. So far (§§ 26-30) we have been investigating
religious experience as experience, *i.e.* according to the

conditions and qualities which it has in common with other experience. We will now pass on to discuss that which is peculiar to religious experience and which distinguishes it from other psychological experience. Religious experience is essentially religious feeling. Its immediate object is the inner state of mind which persists throughout the course of inner and outer happenings. But there are other experiences of feeling besides religious feeling. Hence our description of the nature of religious feeling will not be complete without a study of the similarities or dissimilarities which obtain between it and the feelings most akin to it.

All feeling, *i.e.* all pleasure and pain, of whatever kind, expresses the value that an event in the inner or outer world has for us. And conversely : that has value which is the object of immediate satisfaction or affords a means for such (cf. § 3). The concept of ' end ' and ' means ' presupposes the concept of ' value,' and value in its turn presupposes a subject which is capable of feeling pleasure and pain. When we attribute value to things and states, this quality, like all other qualities, denotes a definite relation to a subject, in this case to a subject capable of feeling pleasure and pain. This quality of value, in comparison with other qualities possessed by things and states, is secondary only, for that which makes things and states valuable must be these qualities. Hence value is a quality at its second degree.

Different kinds of value correspond to different kinds of feeling. One group of values is connected with self-assertion, from its most elementary up to its most idealistic form. Another group of values is connected with the surrender to beings, circumstances, and tasks which point beyond the conditions of isolated self-assertion—among these belong the ethical, æsthetic, and intellectual feelings. The possibility of a third group of values—the religious values—depends on whether the first two groups of values, those of self-assertion and surrender, are both attained and retained in existence as it presents itself to us. Hence existence appears in the light of a battle-field, on which the fate of values is decided. A great drama is being played in which man is actor as well as spectator. Were he actor only, all his energy and all his interest would be absorbed in the rôle which he himself is called on to fill, and he would have neither time, strength, nor interest left to let the course of the drama, as a whole, work its deeper effects upon him. Were he spectator only, his mood through-out the course of the drama would be purely intellectual or æsthetic. But since he is both, he himself possesses values which are at stake in the struggle, and in addition to his sympathy with these the picture which he forms to himself of the whole drama affects him deeply and determines his frame of mind. He will in his innermost being, and for the sake of the highest values which he knows, feel so drawn into the whole great order and course of things that, according to the fate of these values, a lively feeling of pain or of pleasure will arise in him. In its immediate form this feeling disburdens itself in expressions of hope and fear, of admiration and detestation, of joy and of sorrow. Such expressions arise within all spheres ; they are estimations of value in their simplest form. *The feeling which is determined by the fate of values in the struggle for existence is the religious feeling.* It is determined, then, by the relation of values to reality. This relation, as it manifests itself to men, determines the value which they assign to existence. Religious judgments, therefore, are secondary judgments of value ; in comparison with the primary judgments of value in which the first two groups of values find expression they are derivative.

In spite of their derivative character, the religious

feelings may be experienced as immediately and as ardently as the primary feelings. They may even themselves become the central value for man ; for the relation of value to reality is the most tense relation in which man is involved, and hence it may bespeak his entire energies ; for is it not a question of life or death for everything which has shown itself to possess value for him ? In the religious problem the concept of value occurs in the second degree ; it is secondary, however, in the same sense in which a concentration is secondary in comparison to the forces concentrated at one and the same point. Throughout the golden ages of religion, when religions are being founded or organised, such a concentration of all interests and powers at a single point is its most characteristic feature.

And as the religious feeling, notwithstanding its secondary character as compared with other feelings, can be experienced as immediately and as keenly as they, so it may occur independently of them and react upon them. At any rate it can never be merely passively related to them. Action and reaction are continually going on, and the degree of independence on both sides may differ very much. The first two groups are likely to be more independent at the more developed stages of culture, when the division of spiritual labour has become a *fait accompli*. As we saw above, the religious problem arises first when specialised values begin to attain a greater degree of self-dependence over against that concentration of all values which is the characteristic of religion, and which finds its psychological explanation in the fact that in religion the really determining factor is the fundamental relation between value and reality.

The psychological description and analysis of a feeling must not, of course, be confounded with the peculiar reality of the feeling itself. In order to be able to describe and analyse we require an apparatus of concepts and points of view of which the actual state of feeling itself need know nothing.   This latter appears with the stamp of a completed totality or may so appear : it grows up in the same way as an instinct forms itself, under the influence of impressions and happenings which we often cannot ourselves understand, and which first cause us to have conscious recourse to a comparative investigation.   The feeling, the possibility and general character of what we have been describing is the essential element in all religions and all religious standpoints.   In comparison with it all ideas are subordinate and conditioned.

It may here be objected that in the great historical forms of religion the presence of personal beings on whom man feels himself dependent and who are conceived as presiding over existence is always an essential feature ; hence that the concept of religion presupposes myth, dogma, and cult.   How religion is defined will in the last result always be a matter of taste.   As in all definitions of fundamental concepts, considerations of the end to be advanced will always turn the scale.   But it furthers no end to define a concept in such a manner as to shear it of all important questions and problems.   The religious problem would no doubt be much simplified were we to restrict our discussion to religions in which myth, dogma, and cult can be exhibited.   But what if myth, dogma, and cult only possess religious significance because they are supported by the feeling described above ?   If this be so we must not ignore the possibility that this underlying element of religion may exist and operate without expressing itself either in myth, dogma, or cult. It is then natural to lay greatest weight on this feeling, and the wider range of the concept of religion is the natural one.   But the question is not one of great importance, and the dispute may easily degenerate into a purely verbal one.   If we prefer to avoid the use of the word religion altogether rather than take it in this wider sense we may, as I have indicated in my psychology, call the feeling which is determined by the relation between value and reality the *cosmical vital feeling*. For the organic vital feeling immediately corresponds with the course of life within our organism, and is determined by it, taking on a different character according as our organic life is checked or furthered ; so, too, in the feeling we have been describing we have a symptom of how life (so far as we know it and attach our weal and woe to it) is going in the world as a whole (so far as we can form to ourselves a picture of the latter). Those who do not care to use the word religion in the wider sense can call religion (in the narrower sense) a special kind of cosmical vital feeling. To use the word religion in the wider sense would only then be unseemly when this manner of speaking is employed as an unworthy adaptation to existing forms of religion. The criticism of existing forms of religion, on the other hand, will become all the more stringent if it should prove that they conflict in many ways with the true nature of religion and hence point to something beyond themselves. For those who wish to take refuge in compromise there are always other ways open, and the fact that a certain terminology may be misapplied in unscientific uses is no sufficient ground for abandoning it if it has proved useful scientifically.

In his brilliant work *De l'irreligion de l'avenir* (1887) Guyau abides by the narrower meaning of the word religion, for he refuses to recognise any religion as such that is lacking in myth, dogma, and cult. But he distinguishes between *irreligion* and *anti-religion* and tries to show that "the irreligion of the future will know how to retain all that is purest in religious feeling." But it seems to me a question whether "the purest in religious feeling" is not itself the essentially religious. J. Royce, an American writer on the philosophy of religion, whose standpoint is not the same as Guyau's, says in an interesting article on the young French philosopher who was cut off so early by death, " If Guyau's opinions were my own, I should unhesitatingly call them religious, for the reason that I should see in them, as he himself sees, the fulfilment, in reasonable form, of what the religious instinct of humanity has been seeking. "[48]   We are here within the region of fine *nuances*.   I, for my part, should have less hesitation than Guyau in taking the concept of religion in its wider sense, although I should not be quite so positive on the matter as is Royce.

32. The description of the religious feeling given above finds confirmation not only in the fact that it enables us to distinguish clearly between the religious feeling and other feelings, but also that it explains the different forms which the religious feeling may assume.

The more men are absorbed in the business of self-maintenance, or the more they are given up to intellectual, æsthetic, and ethical interests, the more the strictly religious interest falls into the background—if indeed it does not entirely disappear.   The world of existence, under such circumstances, is either an obstacle to be overcome, or an object to be understood or contemplated, or else a basis for efforts of will.   The difference between the intellectual and the religious attitude towards existence is especially illuminating in this connexion.   Existence presents to cognition unfathomable riches and an immeasurable manifold ; it contains a great deal more than men can ever grasp from the point of view of that which they call value.   For it realises forms and degrees of existence which extend far beyond and are often in sharp opposition to that which from a human standpoint would be regarded as value.   Intellectually considered, this super-abundant fulness is a good : the world-conception which our knowledge labours to construct becomes thereby

more comprehensive, and it stimulates our efforts to
understand the particular forms and stages which occur
in their peculiar idiosyncrasies, as well as the definite
interconnexion between these and the great whole.   The
religious interest, on the other hand, regards this richness
of form and degree merely as a means of expression for
the realisation of great values in existence.   For the
religious interest this great manifold is a source of danger
and anxiety, since the reality of values is not so easily
demonstrable as it would be were existence less rich in
content.   The immeasurable world seems too vast to be
summed up in terms of human values.   Hence a collision
is apt to arise here between the intellectual interest
which, rejoicing in the fulness of things, is always searching for new variations and new interconnexions, and the
religious interest which, in order that it may be able
to establish the point of view of values, has a natural
tendency to limit the world-conception (when we come
to our ethical section we shall see that this becomes a
leading point).

This opposition comes out very clearly if we compare
two such natures as Pascal and Spinoza.   The infinity
of nature which appals the one rejoices and inspires the
other.   And yet Spinoza's, too, was in its way a religious
nature.   For intellectual interest may unconsciously bring
about an evaluation of existence.   If existence in all
its fulness yet prove to be comprehensible, it becomes,
from the intellectual point of view also, a *home of values.*
It affords us the great joy of knowledge, and the effect of
this will be all the greater if we recognise ourselves to be
particular members of the great whole.   There arises the
intellectual love which was for Spinoza the Highest,—the
quiet, yet enthusiastic contemplation in which he gradually
came to view all things as forming a great harmonious
whole.   In analogy with this it will be easy to trace the
relation between the religious feeling and those feelings

which are related to it in the same way as is the intellectual
feeling. The religious relation is always characterised by
the effort to hold fast to the conservation of whatever is
valuable in existence, apart from any considerations as to
what value man esteems most highly or what his conception of existence may be. But the existence of the religious feeling is only possible on the presupposition that
men have experienced life, truth, beauty and goodness.
The religious feeling comes into operation when these
values are compared with actual reality. We may see
here both the opposition and the connexion between the
religious feeling and other feelings. But here I must warn
my readers that what I have described as two different
acts of experience, *i.e.* the experience of life, truth, beauty
and goodness, and the experience of the relation of these
values to actual reality need not arise at different points
of time but may be combined in a single act, so that the
subject experiencing is not himself conscious of any
distinction between them (cf. § 31). We draw this
distinction for purposes of psychological description, but
it is not necessarily drawn in life itself. The real sting
of the religious quarrel lies in the fact that during the
classical ages of religion no valuable life, no truth, no
beauty and no goodness could exist outside its pale ;
religion in its concentrated form had absorbed into
itself all elements of value, hence these were never
able to present themselves with their independent characteristics. This only happens, as has already several
times been stated, when — as a result of the dawning
division of labour within the spiritual sphere — the
religious problem makes its appearance.

The differences between religious standpoints depend
partly on the different values which are presupposed
as experienced, partly on the different conceptions
of existence which are taken as a basis, and partly
on the degree of energy which is applied to the

I

comparison of value with reality with a view to making this relation the object of a more penetrating experience. These three sources of difference all spring from the description of religion already given, *i.e.* a feeling determined by the relation between value and reality. Every exhaustive characterisation of any given religion or religious standpoint will be based on these three points of view.   Both in the preceding as well as in our subsequent discussion examples occur of their importance.

33. If our conception of the world immediately presented us with the realisation of the highest values, or if it even showed us existence as the assured home of values, no specialised religious feeling would come into existence.   There would be immediate harmony between the explanation and the evaluation of existence ; whatever could be shown to be an operative cause in the world would at the same time be shown to be a means to the realisation of a value.   There would, in fact, to borrow an expression from economics, be no marginal uses.   But as things are, since the connexion between values and actual reality presents so great a problem, special exertion is needed in order to hold fast to the conviction that values are preserved.

Again, no peculiarly religious feeling would arise, were man's power of working on behalf of the valuable (in himself and in existence) limitless.   Religious feeling presupposes a striving to maintain values both within and without us—a striving that has to encounter opposition.   It is precisely within this innermost region that man feels himself dependent and divided.   The feeling of dependence can only really arise where there is a striving to advance.   The tethered animal only begins to feel its dependence when it tries to stray further than the length of its chain permits.   When this feeling of dependence is something other and something more than

a sort of fatigue which might arise from dulness, it indicates that man has come to the limits of his will. The
lion in his cage, walking up and down between the bars,
has reached his limits and feels his dependence; were he
to remain lying quietly at the back of the cage he would
feel no dependence, and would find existence much
simpler and more harmonious. But the fact that the
limits of will have been reached is not in itself sufficient
to create a religious relation. At these limits, and in spite
of them, the wish for the preservation of values must
be maintained. We must be able to form ideas of a
world of values, the reality of which is not abandoned
because human capacity has reached its limit. The
presentiment must arise that the principle of the world
of values is in the end identical with the principle of
causal connexion within existence — that it is one and
the same thing which enables us to find values in
existence and which makes this existence comprehensible to us.

In Schleiermacher's famous reduction of religion to
the feeling of dependence, he does not sufficiently
emphasise the point that this dependence is conditioned
by an activity, and that it appears at the limits of
this activity. Nor does he make it sufficiently obvious
that this dependence makes itself felt in the struggle for
those values which appear to man to be the highest.

The rôle which the consciousness of sin plays in
several religions exemplifies the character of the religious
feeling of dependence. In the consciousness of sin man
feels the misfit between the ideal of the will which his
estimation of value has led him to form and the reality of
his own will. Sometimes it is sloth and dulness, sometimes division or want of concentration, sometimes one-
sided or impatient concentration, which makes the reality
of his inner life so different from his ideal. In the consciousness of redemption or atonement the conviction

arises—often suddenly—that in spite of all this values persist, and persist within the breasts of men and will conquer there. This inner psychological drama is recognised in the highest popular religions—in Buddhism and Christianity—to be the real world-drama, and to the development of this within the soul of man the great cosmical processes are in the long run subservient.

(*b*) Religious Faith

34. Like all other experiences religious experience clothes itself in more or less definite ideas, the contents of which depend on the stage of development and knowledge which has been attained. The harmonious or inharmonious relation of value to reality finds its more immediate expression in an exclamation. When man is master of a large circle of ideas he instinctively puts together and compares the feeling aroused in him by the relation between value and reality and his other feelings and experiences, and thus, either by similarity (especially analogy) or contrast with these other experiences, religious experience acquires more precise expression and terminology. Thus, in the language of religion, terms such as life and death, health and disease, light and darkness, truth and falsehood, beauty and ugliness, justice and injustice, are used to denote certain oppositions experienced within the religious life. These terms are borrowed from the spheres of the first two groups of values, *i.e.* those of preservation of life, and of truth, beauty and goodness.

Like all other feelings, the religious feeling oscillates between pleasure and pain, violence and exhaustion, inwardness and exteriority. But since in every personal being there is always a certain striving after unity and interconnexion, so—in spite of these oscillations—there must always be certain main ideas to which the soul

turns, and in which it finds the expression of all that
is essential in its experience.   In clouded and weak
moments the spirit seeks to hold fast to that which it
experienced and thought in its bright and powerful
moments.   In spite of the oscillations, and throughout
them, it strives to maintain continuity.   Religious faith
is the expression not only of the utterances of the
individual's religious feeling, but also and more particularly, of the striving to hold fast to the relation between
value and reality, which relation men are impelled by
their deepest experiences to recognise.

The concept of faith implies the conviction of a
continuity, of a persistence beyond the horizon
revealed by experience and leading on through the
interruptions and gaps which characterise the latter.
We believe in a man when we feel convinced that,
even though his life lies before us unconcluded and
incompletely known, he will remain consistent with
himself throughout all changes.   We believe in
ourselves when we have confidence that we shall
not be faithless to the best that is in us, but shall
abide by our solemn resolves in spite of all hindrances.   And so, too, religious faith is the conviction
of a steadfastness, a certainty, an uninterrupted interconnexion in the fundamental relation between value
and reality, however great may be the changes to which
the conditions of reality and hence the empirical
appearances of value are subjected.   Faith is akin to
faithfulness and presupposes faithfulness in its object.
Faith is a subjective continuity of disposition and will,
which seeks to hold firmly to an objective continuity in
existence.   The object of faith is the conservation of
values, but the existence of faith is in itself a witness
to the conservation of value in the particular personality.

In its simplest and soundest forms faith arises
involuntarily.   But this does not prevent its being

an affair of the will if (as I have done in my *Psychology*) we use the word 'will' in an extended sense.   If an expression or an explanation is to retain permanent validity throughout the oscillation of conditions, throughout all that is inconclusive and frequently contradictory in experience, there must be a development of activity.   In its simplest form this activity may appear as instinctive confidence or sure expectation.   It is not till the opposition between value and reality assumes sharper and harsher forms that faith appears as desire, wish, purpose or resolve, for only then can all the forces of the soul be concentrated round this guiding and reasoning thought with a clear consciousness of what is at stake.   Moreover, in faith we often experience, as though it were present, what perhaps can only be realised at some subsequent time ; just as in the moment of resolve we regard ourselves as acting, although we may still have far to travel before we can perform the act.   By such anticipations the distinction between means and end is annulled ; the time of preparation and expectation is no longer merely a means to a future time, for the fruits of our labour are reaped while the labour is being carried on, since the labour itself is the highest reward.   To use the language of religion, in the midst of time we *have* eternal life ; we have not to wait a long time for it.

There is therefore a close kinship between faith and will.   In the description of any utterance of will which is more than merely instinctive the chief point to be brought out is the holding fast to the idea of an end which has to be reached, whether or not this end is in its turn to serve as a means to a still further end.[49] In this element, *i.e.* in the holding fast to a more or less distant idea, and under more or less opposition, the concepts of faith and will intermingle so that they

might even be called names of one and the same
psychical phenomenon.   If any distinction can be drawn,
it is that faith connotes a rest and a surrender, the
rest and the surrender involved in concentration on
a single idea.   We can speak of a 'will to believe'
just in so far as the definite striving to arrive at such
a concentration can express itself.   Conversely, we might
speak of a 'faith to will,' since a trusting surrender to
the striving of the will and confidence in its energy may
be a necessary condition for the performance of the work
of the will.

35. Important differences in the nature of religious
faith are conditioned—like the differences in the nature
of religious feeling (§ 32)—by differences of value and of
motives of evaluation, by differences of knowledge of
reality, and by differences in the energy with which
value and reality are brought together and compared.
These differences are not all of equal significance.   The
last-named is evidently the most important.

The motive of evaluation which decides what it is that
shall appear valuable to men may vary from individual
to individual, from nation to nation, and from time to
time, both in nature and range.   It may be hope or
fear ; it may be egoistic, or at any rate individualistic,
or sympathetic ; it may be simple or composite, and,
if the latter, it may have different colouring according
to the differing relations between the constituent elements.   With regard to range, the determining difference will be that between egoism, individualism, and
sympathy ; the circle of values to be preserved may
either be attached with more or less conscious isolation
to the individual himself or to groups of men and of
efforts, within which the preservation and striving of
the individual only appears as a single member.

A world-conception acquires its significance for
religious faith by the fact that it indicates the lines

along which values develop and maintain themselves. It alone supplies the stage for the great drama in which the fate of values is to be decided, and the stage determines in many ways the nature and course of the play.

But the religious moment proper does not, if the above description be correct, arise until a comparison is made between the estimation of value and the conception of the world. It is on this account that the most important group of differences which influence religious faith is that which has its origin in the difference in inwardness and energy with which value and reality are placed side by side in consciousness. We may call these 'differences of religious synthesis.' Of course all these differences co-operate, but the last is the central difference. In the sequel I shall discuss some of the most typical differences which are pre-eminently determined by the variation of the last-named relation.

36. A characteristic and very frequent type of religious faith is determined by the need of rest. The main cause of fatigue and exhaustion in life is chiefly unrest and distraction of mind. We are influenced on so many sides that it is difficult for us to collect our thoughts; we are drawn in so many directions that we find it difficult to focus our will on any one aim; so many different and changing feelings are aroused that the inner harmony of the mind is exposed to the danger of dissolution. Owing to this feeling of misfit with our ideal we experience an inner need, while our outer needs are borne in upon us in the guise of pain, frailty, and dependence on the elementary wants of life.

In the Upanishads we find: "The Self (Atma), the sinless one, who redeems from old age, death, suffering, hunger, and thirst, whose wishes are the right ones and whose decree is the right one—I am that self which men must inquire after and seek to know. He who has found and known this Self has attained all worlds and all wishes.' And in another place : " Save me, for I feel in this world's life like a frog in a sealed fountain." Jesus of Nazareth says : " Come unto me, all ye that labour and are heavy laden, and I will refresh you. Learn of me, and ye shall find rest for your souls." " Unquiet is our heart," says Augustine to his God, "until it find rest in Thee." This need for rest rises to a passion in natures such as St. Theresa, Pascal, and Sören Kierkegaard. There is no doubt an element of deep pathos in Augustine also, but in his case we have the Platonist and the prince of the church combined with the earnest seeker, and it is the combination of all these elements which renders him such a unique figure in the history of the religious life. St. Theresa felt the need of union with God so powerfully that death alone could satisfy it : " I knew not where else to seek this life but in death. The fish, drawn out of the water, sees at any rate the end of its torment ; but what death can compare with the life in which I languish ? "

With Kierkegaard, too, his great desire was to be released from the struggle of life. The lines which he desired should be inscribed on his gravestone express this longing :—" A little while the search is o'er | The din of battle sounds no more."

In this life the believer finds himself in an alien element ; between the inner and the outer, between life and its conditions there is a want of harmony. In Kierkegaard's case, too, we get the metaphor of the fish out of water ; it is characteristic of this type that the same figure should be employed by the ancient Indians in the Upanishads, by the Spanish nun of the sixteenth century, and by the northern thinker of the nineteenth century. This trait sheds a light on the psychology of religion. The aim of man is infinite, but he is condemned to spend his life in the world of finitude, and hence it follows that his existence acquires a sort of spasmodic character. In Kierkegaard, and even in Pascal, this opposition is more sharply brought out than in St. Theresa. In the latter it evokes longing and inner aspiration, but her will is occupied entirely by the highest object, and only her memory and her imagination are free to analyse her experiences. But both Pascal and Kierkegaard have constantly to summon the will to their aid ; in their case they have a desperate struggle to keep themselves upright in face of the harsh discord between the true life and the conditions of actual life ; to hold fast to the thought of the object of faith and to resist the onslaughts of doubt. In virtue of this trait these two figures belong to a type which we shall presently describe.[50]

37. In contradistinction to this type, in which a felt lack of harmony is the leading characteristic and awakens the religious need, is a type whose leading idiosyncrasy is an inner need of self-development and surrender which passes over oppositions and limitations, almost without noticing them. The religious feeling here is really not any specialised feeling but merely an increase and extension of the feeling with which the valuable was already regarded. The religious feeling in such cases arises out of the further development of the impulse towards self-preservation. There is no room for opposition here between self-assertion and self-surrender, for self-surrender is engendered by the fact that the subject has at his disposal more force and more feeling than he can employ in his purely individual interests. In his overflowing joy and enthusiasm he embraces the life of other men, and finally of all existence. Religion here arises out of the power of life and the joy in life. Here too the subject seeks rest, not rest after pain and distraction, however, but rest from his own aspirations, which no finite object can satisfy.

The happy man, as Aristotle said long ago, wishes to see life around him, a life in which he can share and which he can support.

In modern times this type is interestingly exemplified in Campanella, Joseph Butler, and Rousseau. Particularly characteristic is the following passage from a sermon of Butler on the love of God : "As we cannot remove from this earth or change our general business on it, so neither can we alter our real nature. Therefore no exercise of the mind can be recommended, but only the exercise of those faculties you are conscious of. *Religion does not demand new affections but only claims the direction of those you already have,* those affections you daily feel, though unhappily confined to objects not altogether unsuitable but altogether unequal to them." Goethe takes this type as fundamental (in Faust's confession of faith and in the Marienbad Elegy) and so also does Schleiermacher (in his Addresses on Religion). We get it again, in a guise which reminds us of the gospel of St. John, in F. D. Maurice, for whom hell consisted in separation from God, and who, in contradistinction from those "who base all theology on sin," says in one of his letters : "How I long to be telling myself and telling every one that the hell we have to fly is ignorance of the perfect goodness and separation from it, and the heaven we have to seek is the knowledge of it, and participation in it." [51]

38. Yet a third type is characterised by the rôle played by the intellectual and æsthetic element. Contemplative natures are bent on gaining a *conception of the whole* in the light of which the relation between value and reality shall be made clear. Sometimes it is the need of thought for comprehension, sometimes the need of the imagination for intuitive images which is the predominating factor. In Plato's doctrine of Ideas he found satisfaction for both these needs ; his spirit found rest in the

contemplation of the eternal ideas which alone had true reality ; in comparison with them the ever-changing world of science was finally regarded as mere illusion. We may discover a tendency in the same direction in the Upanishads. This type passed *via* Platonism into Christian theology, where it may be recognised in Augustine, in the mediæval mystics, and (although in a weaker form) in modern speculative theologians such as B. Martensen. Spinoza is a distinguished representative of this type (cf. § 32). Although as long as he remains on empirical ground his thought is distinctly realistic, yet he finds the highest perfection in the contemplation of things *sub specie aeternitatis* : a point of view which could assuredly only be reached by means of strenuous intellectual labour, but which, nevertheless, is artistic rather than scientific. The attainment of this point of view seemed to Spinoza the highest good, the only one which is able to afford lasting and deep satisfaction. In this contemplation the innermost life is bound up with the most strenuous thought as to the nature of existence, and the joy in knowledge thus awaked illumines the entire world-picture, blotting out the inharmonious traits, which are so conspicuous from the finite and limited standpoint. Every feeling and every experience may contribute to this highest spiritual state, and access to this good is open to every seeker. The struggle between men which finite goods so often occasion here disappears, for the joy in this good only grows the more men are able to participate in it.

Many of the representatives of this type believe that in this highest idea, or in the intellectual contemplation which they regard as the Highest, they have the result of the highest science. This rests on an illusion, based on an insufficient inquiry into the conditions and limits of knowledge. When such spirits finally come to rest in philosophy, it is not philosophy as science but as art.[52] Nevertheless, the great merit of this type is that they have asserted the importance of thought for life, even where thought moves at its extreme limit. The art of thinking is of the greatest importance for the art of living, and we should lapse into spiritual barbarism were this type to fail in representatives.

39. While the form of religious faith we have just been describing approaches the speculative or artistic standpoint, we get deeper into the domain of the will when we meet faith under the guise of *confident boldness*. Luther and Zwingli—often in sharp opposition to the scholastic doctrine that faith and knowledge differ in degree only—lay great stress on the point that cheerful trust (*fiducia*) is the essence of faith. Luther has brought out this thought with special energy in his major catechism, and even uses it as the basis for his definition of God. " A god is that whereat a man can provide himself with all good and find a refuge in all need ; to have a god therefore is nothing else but to believe in him and trust him from the heart. As I have often said, it is nothing but the trust and faith of the heart which makes god, whether true or false. When faith and trust are right then is thy god right, and contrariwise, when trust is false and wrong then the right god is not."[53] In this sturdy confidence, which, it is true, presupposes a feeling of discord and need (reminding us of our first type, § 36) but which yet takes for granted that this need can be overcome—is indeed overcome—we get Luther's main idea ; it was the fundamental idea of the new religion which he founded without knowing it. If the movement from discord to harmony has, as with the first type, to be continually repeated, there is neither time nor strength left to share in the interests and labours of human life. The cheerful faith that man is well provided for, as far as essentials are concerned, makes it, on the other hand, possible to place oneself in a more positive relation to actual human life and to take part whole-

heartedly in the development of culture.   In his small
work entitled *Von der Freiheit eines Christen Menschen*
("On the Freedom of a Christian Man"), Luther remarks
that by making himself the servant of all men the Christian
gains the right to rule over all things.   Freedom and
great strength have their source in cheerful trust in the
underlying basis of life.   This trust is won through
struggle (or it is presupposed that it is won through
struggle); here this fourth type reminds us of our first
and presents a contrast to the second (§ 37) and the third
(§ 38), which are mainly characterised by the direct
development of the psychical forces.

40. A more important difference in the nature of
religious faith is conditioned by the significance and
intensity of the part played by resignation.   In the second
type (§ 37) this element falls almost entirely into the background; in the others it has more or less significance.
But it is not only a question of the degree but also of the
nature of the resignation.   The feeling of resignation
may arise in very different ways, and it takes on different
colouring according to the different relations which may
exist between its constituent parts or its motives.   It
may bear the stamp of sadness and longing, of coldness
and disappointment, of humour, or of an intellectual
satisfaction gained through a comprehension of human
limitations which carries with it the comprehension of the
connexion of man with the great interconnected whole
of existence.   It may also originate in the exhaustion
produced by kicking against the pricks, when feeling is
blunted by the fact that one after another our wishes
prove unattainable.   But when there is an active consciousness that the world of values extends far beyond
the span of our thoughts and wishes, resignation assumes
a positive form.[54]   Value may continue to exist even
though that which man calls and is forced to call value
does not continue; our power of estimation has its limits,

as has our comprehension of the way in which value may realise itself and remain in existence.

But we get the deepest form of faith when the will asserts itself, unblunted and unexhausted, precisely at its own limit, in a lively wish that the highest value may be realised. The deepest religious word ever spoken is the prayer of Jesus : " Not my will, but Thine be done." The will is surrendered, but this surrender is itself a positive wish or, at any rate, is but the negative side of a positive wish.

41. It is one thing to acknowledge that our power of estimation, like our understanding, must have its limits, but quite another to attribute positive value to a something which conflicts with the only criterion of value we can apply. If this is to be a characteristic of the highest religious faith, then faith can only arise *by means of an arbitrary act, more or less spasmodic in form.* We cling to a postulate which seems the only means of safety, and which bears the stamp of a paradox (cf. §§ 23, 24). We make a leap into the absurd. Cheerful surrender and anticipation are replaced by arbitrary and passionate postulate-making. The greater the contradiction between that which is to be believed and the results of human estimation and human understanding, the higher, according to this criterion, the point of view.[55]

Tension and strife may occur in the course of every development, and may be symptomatic of health and vigour of life, especially during those periods in which a new content is being absorbed or new problems recognised. But we must not take these states of conflict for our standard of measurement ; we must estimate them according to their significance in furthering the development of life as a whole, and not, conversely, the life development according to the conflicts to which it gives rise. Convulsive postulation can only be a last effort of the religious life—a symptom that religious development no longer bases itself on the same assumptions as formerly. Kant's postulates bear witness to the fact that the age of 'natural theology' has gone by, while those of Pascal and Kierkegaard show that the dogmatism of the Church found itself in irreconcilable conflict with the whole basis of men's spiritual life.

Were the standpoint here characterised really the religious standpoint, the hypothesis that the essence of religion consists in faith in the conservation of value would be invalid, for, according to this standpoint, there could be no connexion between human values and the divine values we are called on to believe.

42. One type (amongst the many, in addition to those already described, possible types) still remains to be noticed. The characteristic of this type is that while, like the resigned type (§ 40) and the spasmodic type (§ 41), it surrenders its own standard of measurement, yet in other respects it approximates most nearly to the type of cheerful boldness (§ 39). It is determined by *adherence to an example, an authority*; faith is here an echo, a reflex—an echo, however, which is made possible by inner surrender to the example. Faith is not here based on direct and independent experience, but on confidence in the experience of other men. Personal experience is not entirely excluded; for we must discover by experience that we can base our life on confiding trust in our example, that we can find light by letting ourselves be guided by the light of our example. Under this relation to an example, which is, of course, also a relation involving the exercise of faith, many widely differing types, including all those already described, may be subsumed.

We shall nowhere be likely to find a man whose conception of life, whether or not it bears the impress of religious faith, is entirely based on his own experiences. Types and traditions determine all of us, and they more especially determine what experiences we shall have and the way in which we shall absorb these experiences into our life. But where decisive importance is attributed to one particular content and one particular form of religious ideas, and these are put forward as the only valid object of faith, then dependence on the example and on authority comes to be unconditional, and is regarded as the only virtue.

When, following the path of theological speculation, the Church had developed a number of doctrines which could not but be beyond the comprehension of the majority of men, she was kind enough to announce that in the case of the majority of speculative doctrines (*e.g.* that of the Trinity) it is not necessary for every man to believe for himself; it suffices "to believe in something because one believes that the Church believes in it." This willingness to be satisfied with the Church's belief was said to be deserving because it arose in the "love which believes all things." Innocent III. and subsequent Popes recognised this 'implicit faith' (*fides implicita*) because it prevented the laity from falling into heresy through innocent misunderstanding of theological specialisms. This kind of faith was dubbed "charcoal-burner's faith," after a charcoal-burner (the story is told somewhat differently by Luther and Erasmus Rotterdamus) whose only reply to the question, "What do you believe?" was, "What Holy Church believes," although he could not state what it was that Holy Church *did* believe.[56]

Luther's Protestant zeal led him to declare that the man who had no better faith than that of this charcoal-burner would go to hell. But the Protestant Church is no more able to dispense with this kind of implicit faith than is any other Church. If she wishes to distinguish between the experiences of individual believers and "the common experience of Church members," and if much which, owing to the nature of its subject-matter cannot

K

be an object of personal experience, must yet be believed (see §§ 29, 30), then the recognition of mediate or implicit faith is inevitable. It is to the credit of Protestantism that it so eagerly defended the duty of the individual to make his own experiences and draw his own conclusions; but it brought a great deal with it from the old Church, *e.g.* the doctrine of the Trinity, the very doctrine which caused the mediæval Church to institute the concept of 'implicit faith'; hence it is under an illusion if it thinks to dispense with this concept. Moreover, this concept plays a great part in the education of the individual. All men begin their development with a childlike trust in authorities and examples. Their first assertions of freedom arise when their experience moves them to choose other examples than those they started with, instead of strengthening them in their adherence to the latter. The course of development may lead to an increasing predominance of the results of independent experience, and with a very few—the heroes in the world of spirit—creative self-activity may go so far in depth and range that they themselves become patterns to other men.

The spirit of Protestantism demands that the door to the free investigation of religious experience, its basis and its results, shall always remain open. Its traditions and examples must be subjected to an historical and critical inquiry; psychology must examine whether its constituent experiences are natural and immediate; logic has to investigate the consistency of its postulates; while it is for ethics to discuss the integrity of its values. Were this process of testing to be abandoned, we should relapse into barbarism or into spasmodic attempts to hold fast to that which is absurd. The religious consciousness is always inclined to drag about with it traditions which have neither religious, intellectual, nor ethical significance; dead values which no human being can really experience, but which it does not dare to throw away for fear lest in their fall they should tear away something more with them. As Rudolph Eucken says: " Men hold fast to the impossible lest they lose the necessary." This leads us back to the spasmodic type described in § 41, for, as we have seen, the chief characteristic of that type was the union of the impossible and the necessary effected by the uncritical retention of tradition—'implicit faith' in the bad sense of the word.

43. Hitherto (§§ 36-42) we have been occupied with individualistic types. I now pass on to discuss the great differences which have found expression in the highest popular religions. Such types develop under the reciprocal action which takes place between older religious traditions, racial characteristics, and the experiences of centuries. We may notice especially here two leading types which are of deep and lasting significance for spiritual development.

One of these types is characterised by the need to rise above the struggle for existence, to be freed from all change and opposition, from all 'doubleness' and difference. Difference entails suffering, change, unrest, and this suffering and unrest cause men to aim at attaining better conditions ; but, these attained, still more cruel disappointments await them. This whole process of oscillation, therefore, must be checked and suspended. Only in the eternal and immutable can rest be found. But since all ideas arise in that world of experience, so unrestful and so much at the mercy of difference, no expression of ours can characterise positively the eternal and immutable state after which we long. And since all change and movement, when once we have attained this state, is seen to be an illusion, we shall see that the longing for it is also an illusion. We must strive to be freed from all striving.

This type reminds us in some respects of the first

(§ 36), in others of the third (§ 38) of the individualistic types. *The religious life of the Hindus*, particularly as presented in the Buddhist doctrine of Nirvana, is the most characteristic example of this type. Nirvana is not a state of pure nothingness. It is a form of existence of which none of the qualities presented in the constant flux of experience can be predicated, and which there-fore appears as nothingness to us in comparison with the states with which existence has familiarised us. It is deliverance from all needs and sorrows, from hate and passion, from birth and death. It is only to be attained by the highest possible concentration of thought and will.[57] Similar traits may be found in *Neo-Platonism* and in the *mysticism of the Middle Ages*. In all religiosity the opposition between the changeable and the unchange-able plays an essential part, but in this main type it is all-important.

In the other leading type it is again a question of de-liverance from struggle, but the opponents are no longer regarded as of equal value. Men attach themselves to one or other of the struggling powers, and deliverance is won by the conquest of this power, not by passing beyond the sphere in which there can be any possi-bility of struggle. Life is a battle between the powers of good and evil. This battle shall and must be carried on to the end; it has positive reality, and the all-important point is the side on which men range themselves in the course of the struggle. The *Persian* and *Christian* religions are the leading representatives of this type, the chief characteristic of which is the great importance attributed to historical development and ethical striving. Time and life in time have here undoubted reality (cf. § 14).

There are, of course, many intermediary forms between these two main types, as also many com-binations, if for no other reason than that one type

influenced the other historically.   The Indo-Greek type
influenced the Christian type by way of Neo-Platonism,
and we can trace the collision and the reciprocal action
between the two in Augustine, whose thought has
exercised such enormous influence on the entire current
of European development.   The opposition between
the mutable and the immutable tends to supplant that
between good and evil.   The assertion that God is the
most mutable of beings—an assertion made by a distinguished Christian religionist—could never have been
uttered by an Indian or a Greek, hardly even by
Augustine.

Common to both these great types is the experience of the contrast between times when the goal (be
this the deliverance from struggle or victory in struggle)
appears to be attained, or at any rate assured and
present, and other times in which darkness, apathy, and
hopelessness prevail.   And in virtue of the effect of
contrast, the one state is heightened by the other ; he
who has tasted the high sublimity of felt union with the
highest will find the fall into gloom and depression
doubly painful and insupportable, while, conversely, the
former state acquires double brilliance through contrast
with the latter.   Here faith (as faithfulness, § 34) is
needed to maintain the continuity of the personal life.
In moments of darkness the happy moments are apt to
appear illusory.   It then becomes of first importance to
hold fast to the underlying connexion between the two,
in the firm conviction that our weakness will become
strength and our darkness light, and that even though
all comfort be removed from us, value is not extinguished.
That the oscillation between these two poles should be
more violent and more frequent in the second than in
the first leading type follows from their respective
characteristics.   In the second type, when the time-
relation is of vital importance, there will be far greater

difference between the different moments ; perhaps there may even arise a need to experience these extremes again and again, to hover between these alternate moods, in order that the consciousness of victory may be the more glorious. This need finds its chief expression in religious worship.

44. The concept of faith corresponds with the concept of God. From a purely theoretical (epistemological and metaphysical) standpoint the concept of God can mean nothing other than the principle of the continuity, and hence of the comprehensibility, of existence. From the religious point of view, God, as the object of faith, means the principle of the conservation of value throughout all oscillations and all struggles, or, if we like to call it so, the principle of fidelity in existence. If the religious problem is ever to be completely solved, the coincidence of these two principles must be demonstrable (cf. §§ 11, 24). The analogy between them is clear; but it is a wide step from this to their identity, and the great question is whether this step can be so taken as to lead to a self-consistent concept. We shall return to this question in another connexion.

Religious experience may be called an experience of God, in as far as it leads to a faith in the preservation of value in spite of all things and throughout all things. He who will experience God must exercise himself in discerning the kernel of value beneath the hard husk of reality ; so too he must train his mind in the patient hope that such a kernel is always there to be found. He who will labour for the kingdom of God must labour to discover, to produce, and to maintain the valuable—

> In that thou seek'st thou hast the treasure found,
> Close with thy question is the answer bound.

For the justification of this use of the word 'God' we may remind our readers of what we have already said

(§ 31) with reference to the word 'religion.' The kinship between different standpoints often appears closer when they are considered psychologically than might have appeared possible from a strictly dogmatic point of view.

So far as we have yet gone our psychological investigation of the philosophy of religion tends to confirm our hypothesis that faith in the conservation of value constitutes the essence of religion, since our discussion of the nature both of religious experience and of religious faith inclines us to admit its probability. Religious experience acquires its peculiar characteristics as experience of the relation between value and reality, while the characteristics peculiar to religious faith are due not only to the stable and continuous direction of the mind which it implies, but also to its assertion of the persistence of value throughout all the oscillations of existence. In a subsequent section (D), however, we shall return to the consideration of faith in the conservation of value in order to see whether the most important forms of positive religion can be reduced to it.

B. THE DEVELOPMENT OF RELIGIOUS IDEAS

Various enough have been the religious symbols, as men stood in this stage
of culture or the other, and could worse or better body forth the
godlike.   CARLYLE.

(*a*) RELIGION AS DESIRE

45. It falls neither within the province nor the capacity of the philosophy of religion to inquire after the historical beginnings of religion. It is the duty of such philosophy to handle the religious problem as it presents itself to us to-day, under the present conditions of enlightenment. To do this we must, it is true, appeal *inter alia* to the history of religion, but our interest will be in the question whether, in spite of the continual change of religious forms, an underlying principle in constant

operation can be discerned, rather than in the historical origin of religion. And even should it prove possible to point to the historical beginning of all religion, this fact would have small significance for the philosophy of religion. We cannot always glean much as to the real nature of a being from its first beginnings, for the trans- formations and rearrangements which take place in the course of its development may produce qualities of which, in its initial stages, we could discern no trace. The real nature of a being consists in the law of its development from its orignal to its later forms. It is improbable that the history of religion will ever succeed in solving the problem of the first dawn of religion in the human race. Even the lowest savages with which we are acquainted have passed through a long process of development. To say that any one among existing religions is the primitive religion is merely to cut the knots. And in any case, even could it be found, this primitive religion would not necessarily be the 'real' religion. We could not e.g. say that all religions are 'really' fetichism if it could be proved that the religious development of the human race started from fetichism. We might just as well say that according to the Darwinian theory man is 'really' an ape. Such con- clusions have been drawn from the theological as well as from the anti-theological side, but they are based on an entire misunderstanding of the nature of all development. Theologians have, for the most part, postulated an original revelation to the first men, a perfect religion to which men have been disloyal, and they then proceed to con- struct this original revelation in terms of their own religion, which they maintain to be the original revelation restored. In comparison with this the fetichism theory is far more natural. For of the two it is far easier to understand that the more perfect may have developed out of the less than that the imperfect should have had its origin in the perfect. If the perfect contain within itself the possibility or the seed of the imperfect it is not perfect (this is readily granted in the case of God, while it is not admitted to hold good in the case of man) ; while the imperfect may by completion or transformation develop in the direction of perfection.   History nowhere shows us the first beginning of religion.   What we find is a series of different lower or higher forms of religion, a series which does not advance at an equal pace but leans to one side or the other ; throughout all oscillations, however, a general tendency may be discerned, especially in the religious ideas, the side of religion most open to investigation.

If we work on the lines sketched out in our preceding description of religious phenomena we shall always expect to find the development of religion based on a certain conception of reality.   Man can have no religious feeling until he can to a certain extent systematise his observations of the world.   For religious feeling is evoked by the experience of the relation between value and reality, and hence presupposes a known reality.   In my inquiry into the development of the religious ideas I shall begin with their simplest forms, and shall then pass on to the more complex, while my constant endeavour will be to explain the transition from one stage to another by means of purely psychological laws.

46. The conception of the world which we find amongst men at the lowest stage of development known to us is usually termed, after Tylor,[58] animism.   Animism is a conception of the world, and is not, in and for itself, a religion.   But it is interesting to the philosophy of religion because it is the most elementary world-conception, the simplest circle of ideas which religion has pressed into her service.   Its peculiar characteristic is that it explains events—especially remarkable events— through the interpolation of spirits, of personal beings. Its origin may be traced chiefly to the influence of ideas taken from dreams ; in dreams the savage meets

with experiences which must seem to him as real as those of his waking life, and in these dream experiences he himself and other beings—men and animals, the living and the dead—appear to be freer and more independent of space, time, and material relations, than he could have supposed possible judging from the experiences of his waking life. The world of dreams, the reality of which is never called in question, then, is consistently used to explain and fill out the world of the waking life. Consciousness is especially occupied with the spirits of the departed ; in their lifetime these beings took a more or less leading part in whatever happened ; it is but natural, therefore, that it should be believed possible to trace their doings and strivings, since dreams have revealed not only their continued existence but also their existence under more perfect relations. Man's instinctive tendency to personify, to conceive things as similar to himself and hence to explain natural processes as personal actions, would find encouragement in these ideas, even were they not sufficient in themselves to form a basis for animism.

Animism appears amongst all peoples in the world at a certain low stage of development. It is the most elementary of human philosophies, and even in the highest and most enlightened religions, exhibiting idealistic conceptions of God, a close and unprejudiced scrutiny will discover many traces of this circle of ideas.

Within the limits of animism we may, with Tiele,[59] distinguish between fetichism and spiritism. Fetichism contents itself with particular objects in which it is supposed a spirit has for a longer or shorter time taken up its abode. In spiritism spirits are not bound up with certain objects but may—partly according to their own discretion, partly under the influence of magic—change their mode of revelation. Fetichism thus distinguishes itself from spiritism by the special weight that it attributes to certain definite objects as media of psychical activity.

47. The simplest psychical act here involved is the choice of a fetich.   There must be some particular definite object, some special occasion, which induces men to believe in a power which cares whether he has or has not experiences which he values.   This process of choice involves the simplest conceivable construction of religious ideas.   The choice is entirely elementary and involuntary, as elementary and involuntary as the exclamation which is the simplest form of a judgment of worth.   The object chosen must be something or other which is closely bound up with whatever engrosses the mind.   It perhaps awakens memories of earlier events in which it was present or co-operative.   Or else it presents a certain— perhaps a very distant — similarity to objects which helped in previous times of need.   Or it may be merely the first object which presents itself in a moment of strained expectation.   It attracts attention, and is therefore involuntarily associated with what is about to happen, with the possibility of attaining the desired end.   Hope as well as fear may influence the choice ; indeed in the beginning hope is probably predominant, for man is by nature sanguine.   It is true that it seems to be the rule that evil rather than good beings are prayed to, but it may be that this is done in the hopes of winning their favour.

In such phenomena as these we encounter religion under the guise of desire.   At first ideas (as distinct from sensations) appear as elements of desire (I here follow the usage which distinguishes between desire and mere instinct).   Desire contains the idea of a something which is able to satisfy a need or to occasion some sort of pleasure, hence the idea is here of immediate practical significance.   The thirsty man's idea of water is thoroughly practical ; it expresses the end towards which he is striving, and is sustained by his need and expectation. His idea of water, therefore, is very different from that of a theoretical chemist or of a painter. Religious ideas are only religious in virtue of this connexion between need and expectation, *i.e.* as elements of desire. Hence one and the same idea may present an entirely different aspect according to whether it is viewed from the religious, from the theoretical and psychological, or from the critical and historical point of view; and we shall only be able fully to understand the significance of religious ideas so long as we keep in mind the close connexion with desire in which they really originate. Fetichism especially can only be understood when thus regarded. When the Indian youth is about to choose his 'medicine' (as he calls his fetich or talisman), he retires into solitude and gives himself up to fasting; the first animal which knocks against him when he quits his retreat becomes his 'medicine.' The negro as he starts off from his hut one morning on an expedition sees a stone glistening in the sunshine, he picks it up almost unconsciously and relies upon its help. In these examples the religious idea is formed or chosen by a kind of *improvisation.*

We need not expect to find any connexion between the different religious improvisations, although custom and tradition soon begin to exert their influence. The fetich is only the provisional and momentary dwelling-place of a spirit. As Hermann Usener has strikingly called it, it is "the god of a moment." "The individual thing is deified in absolute immediacy without room for the intervention of even the simplest generic concept; the thing which thou seest before thee—that and nothing further is God." In illustration of this Usener quotes the custom among the old Prussians and Lithuanians of treating the first or last sheaf from the field as the habitation of a god, to which honours must be paid in

order to secure a good harvest, also the bunch of St.
John's wort, which the young girls in Lithuania gather
and fasten to a pole at the entrance to their houses,
where it is worshipped with reverence.   Both sheaf and
bunch of flowers were originally fetiches.   We find the
same thing among the Greeks, *e.g.* when Æschylus
makes a hero swear by his sword.[60]

The tendency to create such momentary gods may
be traced even now in the unconscious personification
and symbolisation which is apt to take place when men
stand in any very lively and interesting relation to
external things.   For instance, it may be taken as a
good omen for some new enterprise that the fire on the
hearth is easily set alight ; the momentary expectation
which springs up during the struggle with the refractory
firewood is extended by means of an expansion of feeling
to the larger undertaking with which consciousness is
all the time occupied.   This expansion is accompanied
by the idea of the successfully produced fire as by a
kind of assistant and encouraging genius.   If we study
such momentary, and by no means rare, mythologisings,
we shall find them a finger-post to guide us to the
understanding of how the most elementary religious
ideas are formed.   But that which from the standpoint
of animism is taken for a guiding star we shall recognise to be but a fleeting meteor on the horizon of
consciousness.

48. Such momentary divinities can only be approximately indicated in history.   For, on the recurrence of the
occasion, men naturally turn to the idea of god that had
served them before, so that the god is not created anew
on every recurring occasion, *e.g.* in every harvest.   Thus
each god gradually becomes invested with certain constant
qualities, and with lordship over certain definite regions.
Owing to these constant qualities and definite sove-
reignties the individual god acquires a sharper outline in

consciousness. As a process of development is necessary
before we can rise above the passing moment, so development is necessary if we are to rise above any one
particular form of expression and any one special
sphere. Still it is an advance when the constancy of
quality and sphere leads beyond the momentariness of
the simplest ideas of God. And it is for this reason that
the specialised divinities (A. Lang's 'departmental gods,'
Usener's *Sondergötter*) constitute an advance on gods of
the moment. Thought does not yet rise above the manifold and all its differences, but assumes a principle, a
ruling power for each different sphere. A New Zealand
chieftain once said to a European : " Is it true that in
Europe there is only one God who produces all things ?
But there must be one man who is a carpenter, another
a smith, a third a ship-builder. And so it was in the
beginning. One produced this and another that. Tane
made the trees, Ru the hills, Tangaroa the fish," etc. etc.

Usener points out religious ideas at this stage of
development in the religion of the ancient Romans
before they came under Greek influences. The liturgical books (the so-called *indigitamenta*) of the Roman
priests contained lists of specialised gods, which from
antiquity onwards had been worshipped on special occasions and in virtue of special qualities (*dii proprii, dii
certi*). "Special gods were created, to whom distinctive
appellations were given, for all actions and conditions
which could be of importance to the men of those days ;
and not only were actions and conditions, as a whole,
thus deified, but also every conspicuous feature, act,
or movement of the same." Thus the husbandmen
invoked not only the earth (Tellus) and the goddess
of fruitfulness (Ceres), but also twelve special deities :
one when first ploughing fallow ground ; another for the
second ploughing ; a third on making the last furrow ;
a fourth when sowing ; a fifth when ploughing in the

seed, etc. etc. Amongst the Lithuanians and Greeks
also we can trace gods of this kind, limited to one
particular quality and to a very restricted sphere ; indeed,
it would be safe to say that they are to be found among
uncivilised races all the world over.[61]

Such specialised gods, like the momentary gods,
correspond to a need of the religious consciousness to
feel near at hand a power which is exclusively occupied
in affording whatever help is needed. The old specialised
gods often pass over into new religions under changed
names. The saints of Christendom not infrequently
appear with qualities and functions which prove them
to be the heirs of these special gods ; a saint is often
worshipped on the very spot where in antiquity a
corresponding special god was worshipped. The saints,
like their predecessors, have their own departments, and,
like them, they satisfy the need for departmental gods.
In one of his Italian poems, Ludwig Bödtcher takes
from life the reply of a young Roman woman in answer
to the question whether she was afraid of earthquakes : " Our gracious Lady will our home protect,
if dangers come, Emidius' help's direct." St. Emidius
is the special protector from earthquakes. Usener
quotes as an interesting example of the continuity of the
development of religious ideas that of the mother with
her child. She was originally worshipped as a special
goddess under the name of Kurotrophos, foster-mother,
without any proper name. Later on this name (Kurotrophos) became the surname of various goddesses
(Leto, Demeter), and her worship passed over into the
mediæval cult of the Madonna and child. The continuity
of this development shows that this particular form of
deity, representing maternal love, evoked an especial
need of worship.

In the view of several thinkers, the most ancient
god of the Jewish nation should be regarded as a special

god. "The Jahvism of ancient times was a power inimical to culture. We encounter Jahve as the destroyer of all things, as the god of storms in nature, as the god of war in the life of nations, as the god to whom, after a victory gained by means of the divine ban, all living things are sacrificed in death." Not until the Jews had become familiarised with other nations' ideas of God did their own acquire its universal sense, and receive into itself elements which qualified Jahve to be the god of a civilised people.[62]

(*b*) POLYTHEISM AND MONOTHEISM

49. The kind of instinctive personification which characterises the religious consciousness in its most elementary form does not produce ideas of personal beings in the proper sense of the word. A personal being possesses several different qualities at once ; personal life develops as the nexus which unites not only these different qualities, but also the different moments of time through which they persist. The formation of ideas of such beings implies a certain spiritual development, which is absent from the more childlike stages. For it is characteristic of the ideas of children and savages alike that they seize upon a single aspect or quality of a thing, and recognise the thing by means of this quality ; hence the quaint juxtapositions and the many confusions to which the speech of children and of savages testifies.[63] There must be the capacity to rise above the momentary and the special, and to construct a whole out of particular experiences ; for a personal being is not exhausted in a single situation or a single quality. In other words, there must be the capacity of forming ideas which are recognised as typical of some one individual. By an idea which is typical of an individual I mean an idea which is applicable to an individual being in all the many different states into

which it may enter.   No small skill is requisite to form
such ideas, for the individuals in question are often not
only of complex nature, but this nature is in process of
continual development, so that the ideas are necessarily
incomplete.   Our ideas of personal beings have, for the
most part, an artificial rounding off, which is not altogether
verifiable by observation, and our knowledge of the
idiosyncrasies of any personal being partakes of the nature
of faith rather than of knowledge.[64]

As the transition from particular observation and
particular ideas to typical ideas of any individual is,
psychologically speaking, one of the most important
transitions in the life of ideas, so the transition from
momentary and special gods to gods which can properly
be called personal is one of the most important transitions
in the history of religion.   It denotes the transition from
animism to polytheism.   A sharper distinction is now
drawn between the divine beings and the natural
phenomena with which they are associated.   The figures
of the gods themselves are endowed with richer and
deeper qualities, and now, for the first time, it is possible
for faith, in the true sense of the word, to arise ; for
between the object and its revelation there exists a
relation of distance which could not exist on the lower
stages which we have hitherto been considering.   We
are here face to face with one of those rare advances in
the history of religion which are favourable at once to
science and to faith.   In virtue of the clear distinction
now drawn between the gods themselves and the
particular natural phenomena with which they had
hitherto been inextricably associated, the latter become
more open to objective observation and investigation.
If science owes anything to religion it is at this juncture,
i.e. at the transition from fetichism to polytheism, and
not, as has been thought, at that from polytheism to
monotheism.   Above all else, however, this transition

tended to foster religious faith, for, as we have seen, the gods were endowed with deeper and richer qualities, and could therefore be more intimately united with the life of feeling than was possible when certain natural phenomena were regarded as their immediately correspondent expressions.   Men began now for the first time to live in an invisible world.

The significance of this epoch of the history of religion was sharply emphasised by Auguste Comte. Hermann Usener has recently been led by a series of interesting historical and philological investigations to renewed emphasis of its importance.   But when this distinguished historian of religion reproaches philosophers of religion with taking polytheism as the starting-point of religious development, we have only to quote Comte to show that this reproof is unmerited.   And no less unjustifiable is his remark that philosophers "treat the formation of concepts and the gathering together of particulars into genus and species as the self-evident and necessary procedure of the human mind."   For Plato and Aristotle recognised the problem involved in the formation of concepts, and in modern philosophy, since the time of John Locke, it has been discussed again and again. While psychology distinguishes between particular ideas (corresponding to a particular feature or quality), concrete individual ideas (corresponding to a composite observation, to a group of qualities), typical individual ideas (corresponding to a series of different complex observations of the same phenomenon), and common ideas (generic and specific concepts, corresponding to a series of observations of kindred phenomena), we shall have a sufficiently wide frame for the phenomena in religious history on which Usener lays such weight to find their place. The transition from one kind of idea to another does not, of course, take place uninterruptedly, and is always dependent on favourable inner and outer conditions.

Usener has pointed out with special emphasis that only at a certain stage of evolution, *i.e.* on the appearance of polytheism, do the gods acquire proper names. The special gods were only alluded to adjectivally, according to the particular quality with which they were associated. He quotes as an example—in addition to Kurotrophos which we have already mentioned (§ 48)—Apollo, whose name really means 'averter of evil,' but who afterwards united in his personality the attributes of the god of song, the god of light, the cleanser, the mediator, and the god of healing.

Usener attributes great importance to the appearance of proper names for the gods, for he regards this as the necessary condition for the transition from the momentary and special to personal gods. Here as everywhere, however, there is a constant relation of action and re-action between idea and word. The proper name is only comprehensible when several qualities and states can be bound together in a single idea. The word serves to help and support, to retain and to develop the results won within the realm of ideas, but it cannot be their exclusive cause. Moreover, Usener himself is somewhat uncertain on this point, and, as a matter of fact, admits that words and ideas modify each other in the course of construction. No important period in the history of religion can begin with an empty word. The word can neither be the beginning nor exist at the beginning.[65]

History cannot, of course, point out with any approach to precision the moment when polytheism came into being. As we have already seen, even the momentary and special gods implied the existence of a personifying tendency and faculty, and it is almost impossible—chiefly on account of custom and tradition—to point to any pure examples of such gods ; hence it follows that between the stages which, for theoretical purposes, we have described in sharp contrast to one another, there are many transi-

tional members. We shall see later on that the same
may be said of the relation between polytheism and
monotheism.

50. Neither the development of ideas nor the formation
of words affords in itself an exhaustive explanation of
the transition to polytheism. There is always a concur-
rent movement of feeling. The historians of religion
dwell with emphasis on *the conservative and restraining influence of worship*, and this involves the life of
feeling, for in worship feeling finds a sure refuge. If in
any particular region or among any particular people
worship centres round a special god, this god will be
an obstacle to the formation and acceptance of a more
complex idea of god. The influence exerted by worship
on the life of religious ideas can find no more striking
exemplification than in the word 'god' itself; when we
study those etymologies of this word which from the
philological point of view appear most likely to be
correct, we find the word really means " he to whom
sacrifice is made," or " he who is worshipped." [66] Owing
to the connexion between the idea of god and the form of
worship, any radical change in the latter must cause a
modification of the former, and it is at this point, according
to the experience of all ages, that organised worship so
often offers strong, sometimes violent, resistance. Old
ideas maintain themselves longer when they are bound up
with old customs, and old customs often maintain themselves longer than the ideas correspondent with them.
In a Danish village church the custom of bowing when
passing a certain spot in the church wall was maintained into the nineteenth century, but no one knew the
reason for this until, on the whitewash being scraped
away, a picture of the Madonna was found on the wall;
thus the custom had outlived the Catholicism which
prompted it by three hundred years; it was a part of the
old cult which had maintained itself. In this instance

we have a habit only. But the stream of feeling is in
general reluctant to quit the bed that it has worn for
itself. It has accommodated itself to the traditional
ideas, and a time of unrest and discord must be passed
through before it can reaccommodate itself to the new
ideas. During such a time of transition the two streams
of feeling, the one tending to flow on in the old bed, the
other to expand (cf. §§ 27 and 47), have a hard struggle
with one another. Or, to express it more correctly, the
tendency of the old feeling to spread itself over and to
colour the whole of consciousness struggles against the
same tendency on the part of the new feeling, for the
feelings which are bound up with tradition have also an
expansive tendency and will always try, if they cannot
altogether crowd out the new feeling, at any rate to
colour and transform it ; in extreme cases, where they
can maintain themselves in no other way, the old ideas
become transformed in correspondence with the new.

This restraining and inhibitive influence of feeling on
the life of ideas is, however, only one side of the matter.
The new experiences may have such a penetrating effect
that a modification of ideas through *selection, idealisation*
and *combination* takes place. Usener, who is for the
most part inclined to lay chief stress on the development of word and idea, admits that the different special
gods cannot be all equally valuable to consciousness.
" The god of blessing and of the life-giving light of heaven,
the tutelary god of the home and of domestic peace, the
saviour, the warder-off of evil, must have an incomparably
higher importance than a god who blesses the harrow or
the clearing of weeds, or who chases away the flies."
Those special gods who excite the strongest and most
lasting feelings will be given greater sovereignty than
others. As objects of particular attention they will
obtain a special place; a comparison with other divinities
will be avoided, and the mind will not dwell upon any-

thing which may seem to imply a limitation of their
powers.   An unconscious idealisation is here going on.
Naturally connected with this selection and idealisation is
a process of combination, for all valuable qualities and
effects which offer even the slightest similarity or contact
with the original attribute of the god are gathered round
this idealised god.   He is now regarded as the bearer of
some particular value, and any new value which is experienced is involuntarily attributed to him.   In the conception
of every great god the processes of selecting, of idealising,
and of combining are co-operative.   Ideas and words are
secondary compared with the experiences of feeling.

The history of the god of light is an interesting
example of this evolution.   The great importance of
light for all living things, since it furthers the vigorous
and healthy prosecution of all vital processes and makes
activity and safety possible, and its ideal significance as
the symbol of truth and justice, have led to all kinds of
modifications of ideas ; nevertheless they can all be traced
back to immediate experiences of the value of light and
of the forces symbolised by light.

Those gods who play the part of protectors of
common goods—as protectors of the family, of the tribe,
or of the nation—are especially liable to be the object of
these different processes.   When man in company with
other men, or within his own breast, experiences the
opposition between good and evil, and when this opposition occupies the chief place in his consciousness, he will
transfer these ideas, in an idealised form, to his gods.
This idealising personification is of great ethical significance, for it is to it that we owe those luminous and
divine examples which men have set themselves to follow.
The transition from nature religion to ethical religion is
thus effectuated, a transition which has rightly been said
to be the most important in the whole history of religion,
but which proceeds in accordance with the same laws as

those which govern all other transitions.   In the absence
of experience of the power of thunder, no one would ever
have believed in a god of thunder, so in the absence of
experience of good as one of the realities of life, no one
would ever have believed in the goodness of the gods.
The conception of the gods as bearers of the ethical values
of existence presupposes that man has himself learnt to
know these values (cf. § 31).

In addition to the inhibitive, selective, idealising, and
combining influences which feeling exercises on the
development of ideas, we have still to notice the significance of the *effects of contrast* within the sphere of
feeling (cf. § 43).   The contrast of two moods will react
upon the ideas in which each finds expression or by
which it is motivated.   If, *e.g.*, an ideal has been formed,
this ideal will be raised to a still higher power through
the contrast between the imagined perfection and the
thinker's own limited humanity ; while, conversely, this
limitation will be seen the more clearly the brighter the
mood evoked by the contemplation of the ideal.   This
moment of contrast, therefore, is important not only in
the evolution of the idea of god, but also in that of the
consciousness of sin which plays so great a part in many
religions (cf. § 33).

51. Outside the circle of ideas relating exclusively to
deities the belief in the transmigration of souls offers a
good example of the selective and transforming influence
of the feelings.   The idea that after death souls pass
into another body can hardly be said to have had its
origin in religion.   It is connected with the ordinary
animism, and is to be found amongst different races all
over the world at a very early stage of their development.   It is frequent amongst the races of eastern Asia ;
we find it amongst the inhabitants of Guinea and the
Zulus ; among the Greenlanders and the tribes of North
America.

But we note that after the Vedic age this belief began to play an important part in the religion of India. It is prominent in the Upanishads, whereas we find no trace of it in the earlier religion of India as this is presented in the Vedistic poems. Hence it has been thought that the doctrine of transmigration may be traced to the desire of religious thought to explain the great ethical inequalities which obtain among men, even under the earliest circumstances and conditions. Whatever they could not trace to the effect of a man's actions in this life, so the theory runs, the old Vedanta thinkers explained as the effect of his actions in earlier existences. The Pythagoreans and Plato were brought by the same considerations to the mythical idea of the transmigration of souls. According to the theory which is embraced by Deussen,[67] the need of deliverance experienced by the Hindus led them on the one hand to the idea of the transmigration of souls, in explanation of the inequality of inner and outer conditions ; on the other to that of absorption in Brahma (afterwards to that of Nirvana), so that these two ideas originally arose independently of one another.

The view of this distinguished student of Indian philosophy must be taken in connexion with the fact that he overlooks the continuous after-effects of animism which may be traced even in the exalted teaching of the Vedantas. In the prominence given by the Upanishads to dream-states we may recognise one of the fundamental and characteristic ideas of animism. " In sleep," it is said, " the spirit rejects all that is corporeal and hovers up and down, creating for itself, like a god, all sorts of forms." Not even the naïve animistic conclusion is wanting, viz., that a sleeper should not be too hastily aroused, since " it is impossible to heal a man if his spirit has not found its way back to him." [68] Since, then, we find unmistakable traces of elementary ideas in the teaching

of the Vedanta, ought we not to take these into
account in explaining the importance attached at this
particular point of time to the doctrine of transmigration? Is it not more natural to suppose that this doctrine
is the outcome of older ideas (perhaps emanating from
subjugated peoples), rather than of ingenious speculation? Such ideas may up till the moment under
consideration have possessed no religious significance,
but some modification in the life of religious feeling
may have led to their adoption into the circle of
religious ideas, where they would be interpreted as
expressions of religious experience. Under the overpowering impression of the suffering and restless striving
of life, an unfavourable environment could only be explained as the result of previous existences which were
vouched for by popular belief. Moreover, the view
of this world taken by the Hindus was so pessimistic
that, in the absence of the certainty that no new life in
endless forms lay behind it, not even death was supposed
to bring peace. Thus Richard Garbe (in his work on
the Sankhya Philosophy) connects the significance which
the old doctrine of transmigration now acquired with a
remarkable change in the whole trend of feeling among
the ancient Hindus. " In the old Vedic days there
obtained in India a cheerful conception of life in which
we can discover no germ of the later conception which
dominated and oppressed the thought of the whole
nation : life was not yet felt as a burden but as the
greatest of goods, and an eternal continuance after death
was hoped for as the reward of a pious life. All of a
sudden—without any intermediate steps that we can
discover—in the place of this harmless joy in life stood
the conviction that the existence of the individual is a
tormented wandering from death to death." [69] If this
explanation be the correct one, we have before us a
classic example of the way in which a change of feeling

exerts a selective, idealising and heightening influence on ideas ; while at the same time we have a notable instance of the effect of contrast : for in contrast to the continuous life-process with its unrest and anxiety, which even death did not interrupt, the aim now set before men is the entire annulling of temporal and final existence. The Vedantic and Buddhistic doctrine of deliverance develops in distinct opposition to that of the transmigration of souls.

A striking analogy to the course of development we have just been describing is presented by the Greek religion in the period between Homer and Plato.   Here, too, under the influence of a new and darker conception of life, the belief in the migration of souls was adopted into the circle of religious ideas and practically applied ; whilst anxiety for the fate of souls in another world, an anxiety unknown to Homer, prevailed in extended circles.[70]   The idea of personal immortality could hardly have had religious significance originally ; it springs from the same circle of ideas which gave birth to animism, and only later and under the combined influence of a change in the trend of feeling and of ethical ideas did it supply motives for the development of religious ideas.

An illuminative counterpart of the significance which the doctrine of transmigration attained at a certain point of development both among the Hindus and Greeks is afforded by the appearance of this doctrine among the Egyptians.   They indeed assumed that after death souls might enter into the bodies of different animals, but this transmigration was in no way associated with religious ideas.[71]   They had no use for the motive which was of such effect in the religions of the Greeks and Hindus.

52. I now go back to polytheism.   Its development presents to our view a web of psychological and historical happenings, for the elucidation of which the history of religion affords no sufficient material and which psycho-

logical analysis—even were it more perfect than it is—
could hardly hope to disentangle. As far as we can
follow, however, we have reason to believe that within
the sphere of religion the same psychological and logical
laws are in operation as those which we discover in other
spheres of mental life. Polytheism seems to present us
with a psychological absurdity, for how could men feel
themselves dependent on many different divine beings?
One divinity seems to stand in the way of another; it
appears as though thoughts of one must drive out thoughts
of the other. Indeed even the religion of desire with its
momentary and special gods might call forth this objection. The solution of the difficulty is to be found in the
fact that, at the moment of experience and of movement
of feeling, the subject is so much occupied with the idea
before him that there is no room for collating and comparing, perhaps hardly even for remembering, other gods.
Speaking generally, psychical life presents us with a
rhythmical interchange between immediate attention and
reflection. It is during the subsequent moments of contemplation that we can collate and compare the ideas
which operate during the moments of strong and deep
feeling. Contradictions may thus be discovered ; these
contradictions have to be resolved, and we try to resolve
them as long as new experiences do not make such calls
upon us as to lead us to neglect the difficulties and
problems revealed by reflection. This holds good of all
stages of religious development and of all religious standpoints. But during this rhythmical pulsation one wave
may react upon another. If the difficulties laid bare by
reflection are real ones, experiences may gradually change
in character while, conversely, reflection is modified by the
experiences of the moments it is analysing. There will
always be an involuntary tendency to harmonise the
different ideas which express the differing experiences of
the object of feeling. Within the sphere of polytheism

the difficulty is overcome by the notion of a race of divinities or of a world of gods in which each individual divinity has his proper place. It is easy to find a solution here, since we can make use of the analogies from human relations which lie to our hand. The family as well as the State can show examples of the harmonious co-operation of personal beings, and it is mainly by means of such analogies that the effects of ethical and social development penetrate to the conceptions of the gods. The relation between gods and men is also exhibited by means of these analogies, *e.g.* when God is called the ' father ' and ' ruler ' of men, and when the world is pictured as a great State peopled by gods and men.

We nowhere find that the development of religious ideas is determined exclusively by a nation's own experiences.   There is always an intermingling of ideas borrowed from the nations with whom it has intercourse or whom it has subjugated.   The different worlds of divinities come into contact when the nations come into contact ; indeed one historian of religion has gone so far as to maintain that there has never been religious development except when different religions have been brought into contact with one another.[72]   This renders the course of development followed by religious ideas exceedingly obscure and perplexing.   The possible number of combinations and assimilations, effects of contrast and expansion, increases to infinity.   A host of problems awaits the religious history and religious psychology of the future.

53. The conception of a world of gods, of a divine kingdom, is a station on the way from polytheism to monotheism.   If the transition from polytheism to monotheism has presented peculiar difficulty, this is because the matter has been treated too much from the outside.   Even in polytheism the need of practical and theoretical concentration, the logical consequence of

which is monotheism, expresses itself in a thousand ways. And the same psychological laws which lead from the religion of desire to polytheism, lead from polytheism to monotheism, in so far as a real monotheism, in the strict sense of the word, can be said to exist outside dogmatic speculation (if there !).

The transition to monotheism may take place under one of two forms, which, however, merge into one another through many *nuances*. One particular god may become pre-eminent in the world of gods, so that he stands high above all other gods and above the gods of other nations, and finally comes to be regarded as the only god. This is generally followed by a purifying and deepening of the conception of God, or, conversely, a purifying and deepening of the conception of God leads in a monotheistic direction. Or an idea of the deity may develop itself which is not specially based on a deepened and enriched conception of any particular god but on the divine element common to all gods, *i.e.* that which first made gods gods and which is presented by the different gods under different aspects. The stream of development followed the first of these directions among the Assyrians, Babylonians, Egyptians, and Israelites. The Jewish prophets exhibit the best-known, the most thorough-going, and the most historically important example of monotheistic development.

The evolution of the Judaic monotheism is identical with the evolution of Jahve from a special and national god to a universal god. It is to be traced to the deep influence exerted on the minds of the prophets by historical events. The prophet stands in the midst of his people and of their traditions : the object of his care, however, is not his people and their spiritual and temporal rulers, but the ideal nature and the continued existence of his people beyond the temporal relations of the moment. He unites in his person ecstatic emotion, produced by the

great happenings of the world, with the faculty of
asserting in bold outlines the ideal conception of his
nation and of its significance which he has gathered
from history. We may distinguish two different views
which together form the basis of the development of
the Jewish monotheism; of these one is predominantly
coloured by the great events in the history of the world,
the other by ethical considerations ; but in both it was
the striving to hold fast to the traditional religious ideas
under a new environment which led to their development into higher ideal forms. Only because he had
ceased to be a national god and had become god of the
world did Jahve escape participation in the fate of his
people when they lost their national independence ; and
only when he was regarded as the guardian of higher
ethical ideas than those which had previously been
associated with him, only when his nature was less
superficially conceived, was that pre-eminence possible
which presented such a striking contrast to the fate of
the people whose national god he had been.

The historical view appears first in Hosea and Amos
(*circa* 760 B.C.).   They taught that the Assyrians did not
conquer by the help of their own gods, but because Jahve
wished to make their armies the instrument of punishment to a disobedient people.   The great unknown
prophet, who is usually called Deuteroisaiah (*circa* 540
B.C.), goes a step farther.   The people of Israel suffers
not only for its own sins, but in order that it may be
purified and fitted to bring peace and salvation to all
peoples.   To the longing gaze of the prophet appears
the figure of him who through deepest abasement and
humility was to win and bring the highest ; he saw that
inwardness and sympathy are of more intrinsic value
than the violent acquisition of power after which the
all-conquering, world-ruling nations lusted.   Here the
historical and ethical views merge into one another.

Jeremiah (*circa* 620 B.C.) is the chief representative of the ethical view, although it was not unfamiliar to Amos. As the god of justice Jahve must rule wherever justice prevails or ought to prevail—hence he must be the god of the whole world, unbounded by national limitations. And since the true relation to Jahve is an inner relation of the heart, external forms and their differences finally lose all significance. The time will come when every man will have the law in his heart; and even in his own day the prophet praised the fidelity of other nations to their gods in contradistinction to Israel's unfaithfulness to Jahve. The universality of the ethical ideas as well as the inwardness which they demand transcend all national limitations.

In comparison with the concepts of God enunciated by the great prophets in their struggle upwards, Jesus of Nazareth taught nothing new. But he testified in his own person that the time had come to which the prophets had looked forward in longing visions and aspirations—the time when men could enter into an inner and infinite relation to God. The deep emotion stirred in men's breasts by the personality of Jesus, which deprived all outer relations and distinctions of their value, made it possible for monotheism to become a national religion on a larger scale. The one true God was a god to whom a Jesus of Nazareth could testify and whose messenger he could be.

Development with the Hindus and Greeks took the other direction. With the Hindus there was no god who claimed sole sway; they went back to the power which makes all gods what they are: to the inner aspirations and needs which find vent for themselves in prayer and sacrifice. Following an extremely remarkable line of thought, that which drives men to worship gods was itself regarded as the true divine power. Brahma meant originally the magical, creative word of

prayer, but it afterwards came to denote the principle of
existence itself, so that we have a transition from the
idea of motion towards to that of its goal, from prayer to
the object addressed in prayer.　If we ask more definitely
(as do the gods themselves in the Upanishads) what
Brahma really is, no other answer can be given but that he
is one with Atman, with the soul which each man knows
within himself.　We get here (*i.e. circa* 800 B.C.), as we
saw above (§ 19), the first attempt at a metaphysical
idealism.　The divinities of the popular religion rank
below Brahma, for they are but forms of his manifestations.　This relation of subordination was only recognised
after violent struggle.　The monotheistic tendency first
appeared as an esoteric doctrine (which is what the word
Upanishad signifies), and in Deussen's opinion it was
originally developed by thinkers who belonged to the
caste of warriors, while the Brahmins (the priests) long
adhered to the literal interpretation of the traditional
ritual, and only after a struggle admitted an allegorical
interpretation such as made it possible to unite the new
doctrine with the old worship.　Among the Greeks the
monotheistic tendency was developed mainly by their
philosophers.　Xenophanes' (*circa* 500 B.C.) attack on
polytheism took the form partly of a comparison of the
Greek gods with the gods of other peoples, partly of a
critcism of anthropomorphism.　Every people makes its
gods in its own image: the gods of the negroes are black,
those of the Thracians fair, and had oxen gods they would
picture them under the image of an ox.　In his zeal
against all finite and unworthy conceptions, Xenophanes
rises to that of a principle of unity, which cannot be the
object of any sensuous imagination.　But he criticised
the polytheism of the people on ethical grounds also, and
it was from this side more particularly that Plato carried
on his work.　In India the strivings after unity of the
thinkers was overpowered by the need of the people for

a manifold representation of the divine ; and in Greece too philosophic thought was not able to supply the material for a popular religion. This only became possible when, as in the prophetic dispensation of the Jews and its continuation in Jesus of Nazareth, thought was developed through the nation's own experience and its own fate ; when a person appeared who was himself a revelation of the deepest inwardness and love, and hence could be taken as a symbol of the value of the ideas for which he strove.

Religious psychology can here, as at many other points, do no more than indicate points of view which enable us to understand how the transition from polytheism to monotheism took place. But we have here no special psychological mystery, as has sometimes, rather rhetorically, been asserted. Even admitting this, however, neither history nor psychology need complain of any lack of problems to solve.

But when was the transition from polytheism to monotheism completed ? When was a pure monotheism arrived at, or indeed is such a thing really possible ? If the deity is conceived as differentiated into several 'persons' and in opposition to a 'world' which is its limit and hindrance, can this really be said to be a purely monotheistic conception of God ? If the 'world,' the 'other' which exists outside God, is a reality, and not a nothing, then it has a power which is not infinitesimal in comparison with the divine power ; it is indeed it-self a god within its own boundaries, just as 'God' is within his. This holds good whether we assume a 'free' will (in the metaphysical, not in the psychological or ethical, sense of the word) or a devil. And since assumptions such as these are to be found in all popular religions, there is no justification for asserting, as is often done, that there is any very great opposition between polytheism and monotheism. As there are monotheistic

M

tendencies within polytheism, so there are polytheistic tendencies within monotheism.

The most vigorous efforts to conceive a monotheistic system have been made by philosophers, *i.e.* the Vedantists, the Eleatics and Spinoza. But it is precisely these attempts which have shown us most clearly that the problem of the relation between the unity and the manifold which together make up existence is not to be solved by exalting one of the two members of the relation at the expense of the other. For if we start from either alone, nothing less than the wand of a magician could produce the other.

Whether the ' re-born ' knowledge of which some theologians have spoken is here more favourably situated than natural knowledge can only be known when the logic of this ' higher ' knowledge has been given us— a work for which we are still waiting. A further discussion of this matter, however, would lead us back to the epistemology of religious philosophy.

54. The two tendencies which appear with varying distinctness and in varying proportions in every system of religious ideas—in polytheism as well as in monotheism —point back to the two tendencies in the nature of religious feeling on which we have already had occasion to touch (§ 23).

On the one hand there is the need to collect and concentrate ourselves, to resign ourselves, to feel ourselves supported and carried by a power raised above all struggle and opposition and beyond all change. This need finds its development in mysticism and monotheism ; it coincides with the intellectual need to find a conclusion in an absolute principle of unity.

But within the religious consciousness another need makes itself felt, more or less energetically and in rhythmical interchange with the first need, *i.e.* the need of feeling that in the midst of the struggle we have a fellow-struggler at our side, a fellow-struggler who knows from his own experience what it is to suffer and to meet resistance. This need hinders the development of a complete monotheism and is supported by various other motives. A need for intuitive ideas, a need for figures will be active, and this need will lead to the formation of limited ideas of the deity—or rather to ideas of the deity as limited—for it is only the limited that can be presented in a figure. We have here the so-called 'antinomy of religious feeling,' which is not content until the infinite and exalted is presented in the form of the finite. This need of forms may become so strong as to take fright at the thought of the infinite and thus come into direct opposition to the first need.

We have already (§ 52) seen the reason why this opposition is not always remarked. The religious consciousness is absorbed by the one trend of feeling and allows this to develop and express itself as fully and completely as possible. Only when recollection, collation and comparison are possible do we discover the opposition or the contradiction between the two tendencies. Religious experience fares no better on the soil of monotheism than on that of the religion of desire and of polytheism. The best—and often the only—weapon of religious faith against all the criticism brought to bear on it is the command to abstain from all collating and comparing. Back, it cries, to the complete, full moments of feeling, to the moments of religious emotion! He, for example, who never reads the Bible, as has been demanded, but 'upon his knees' will be spared all the difficulties of criticism. He will be possessed by one view only, by one content, and even here he will unconsciously select and take only what he can use. He will never, for instance, inquire as to whether the different accounts of the resurrection of Jesus are in accordance with one another. The problem as to how the omnipotence of God can be reconciled with man's 'free will' can of course never occur to the mind which when thinking of one of two things can never think of the other. Rasmus Nielsen and Henry Mansel attempted to draw a sharp distinction between religion and theology, and the possibility of this distinction lies in the opposition above described between the states in which the greatest differences are forgotten and those in which they are put side by side and compared. Only by way of intellectual asceticism can this opposition be maintained. At any rate there will always be men who will prefer to stand upright rather than to kneel, who claim the right to look round freely in the world, and who hold that the highest known to them suffers no hurt thereby. Orientalism might bring us to our knees, but as heirs of the ancient Greeks we hold fast to the conviction that even in the most important questions of life it is possible to maintain an upright posture.

This opposition between different states sometimes occasions tragic conflicts. The comparison of the ideas in which the opposing tendencies find expression in their extreme forms may lead, in the case of natures which are at once passionate and intellectually developed, to a convulsive clinging to the paradoxical. It appears in a mitigated form and as it were more unconsciously in what I will call 'religious shame.' For this religious shame springs not only from a natural shyness in expressing one's innermost feelings, but also from a certain vague presentiment that every figure and every word by means of which we seek to express the highest can give us no more than the finite and limited, and hence not only challenges the criticism of other men, which is of comparatively small importance, but also excites in our own minds doubts as to the validity and value of what has hitherto appeared to us to be the highest. It costs many natures the

greatest pain to balance their account on this point,
especially when they are also moved by a certain piety
towards the traditional forms, for this disinclines them to
collate and compare as they would otherwise do.

When we take all these circumstances into consideration, we shall understand at once the inevitableness of
criticism and the slowness of its influence.   Perhaps the
eternal struggle awaits us here.   But this battle must
be waged, and, even though it should never end, it will
not always be fought over the same ground and with
the same weapons.   For the unendingness of the struggle
does not exclude progress.   The struggle among Odin's
heroes was always the same, but the struggle of
which we here speak is never the same ; hence it ranks
higher than that in Walhalla.   The reason of this
constant renewal of the struggle is that change in the
life of ideas takes place more quickly than change in the
life of feeling ; hence a purely theoretical critique of
religious ideas can never probe to the heart of the
problem : the point must always be decided by the value
of the feelings which form the basis of the religious
ideas and which enable religious idealism to throw out
new shoots after every critical onslaught.   An unceasing
oscillation and a reciprocal action between the different
poles of the spiritual life is everlastingly going on.
The evaluation of religious feeling must be reserved for
the ethical section of the philosophy of religion.

55. The serious and logical recognition of this
ceaseless reciprocal action, which makes any definite
solution impossible, is in itself a step forward.   Let us
try to include this experience in our religious reckoning.
It makes the conception of a completed deity impossible.
Can then the religious consciousness resign itself to a
conception of a god who is not completed and rounded
off, but is always involved in a state of becoming, of
development—like the religious consciousness itself,

only on a larger scale? If so, we may have a religion
of hope, which assumes that new problems must always
arise but that new possibilities of handling them will
arise with them. Every state is then seen to be
provisional, a station on the path—on the path of
existence in general, on the path of the individual in
particular—and we shall be neither astonished nor dis-
mayed to find ourselves still questioning, for old problems
will recur under new forms, and the new question in
which our inquiry finds shape may perhaps denote an
advance on the last. Why should we be concerned
at this constant process of change? It expresses a
law of our thought (see § 18), perhaps also a law of
existence. It may be that divine immutability consists in or expresses itself in the fact that all change
takes place according to definite laws, and that this
very law of development is itself one of the primary
laws of existence; in which case the contradiction
between invariability and variability vanishes. The
invariable, in that case, is the law of change itself, and
where any particular law undergoes modification this
change will always take place in obedience to a higher
law. Our thought can only climb a few rungs of the
ladder, of the possibility of which we here catch a glimpse,
but the capacity for mounting even thus far suffices to
evoke a definite hope, a faith in the conservation of the
valuable, a fidelity to the great Excelsior, which is the
noblest element of all the higher religions. Pity that
it should so often be checked in its development by
dogmatic formulæ! Were the conclusion at which we
have here arrived more than a concluding *hope*, more
than a *subjective* motive, we should lose our recurrent
Excelsior. But if neither our experience nor our
thought lead to an objective conclusion, the reason
for this may be that existence itself is never finished.
This would afford us the most thorough-going explana-

tion of the failure to find any dogma or figure sufficient
to the fulness of reality. If it be objected that this
thought (which must be taken in conjunction with
what has been said in §§ 10, 15, 22, 31, 44) surpasses
the limit of what can rightly be called religion, I will
not dispute it, but will give up the word as soon as
any one will provide me with a substitute for it. We
are free men and must not make ourselves the slaves
of a word.

(c) RELIGIOUS EXPERIENCE AND TRADITION

56. The form and content of religious faith can
never be explained from the religious experience of any
individual. Our previous investigation has already shown
us this ; the evolution from the religion of desire through
polytheism to monotheism occupied long ages and many
generations, and every individual stands at a certain
point in this line of evolution, a point which is
determined alike by that which goes before and that
which follows after. Even when a man has had the
deepest and most independent experiences of the relation
between value and reality, yet the manner in which he
expresses and interprets these experiences will itself be
conditioned both by the circle of ideas with which he
is familiar, and also, to a greater or less degree, by
tradition, although he himself need not necessarily be
aware of this. Ideas may be so unconsciously inter-
woven with that which he has felt and experienced that
it may seem to him that he has immediately experienced
their content. Only on closer inspection can the difference
between the elements which were immediately given and
those which have been inwoven with them be discovered.
In illustration of this point I will adduce a few historical
examples.

57. Even among uncivilised peoples the relation

between the experiences of the individual (especially
during states of ecstasy) and tradition comes out clearly.
There is a Siberian race amongst whom it is customary
for a young man when he wishes to become a Shaman
or priest to retire into solitude, and to wander about at
night amid hills and forests, where he sees strange
sights in which the gods of his tribe and the spirits
of his ancestors reveal themselves to him. He now
sees what hitherto he had only known by hearsay.
He repeats this experience in the loss of consciousness
which supervenes on turning violently round and round ;
during the ecstatic state thus produced he sees before
him what he had otherwise only known by tradition.

And what is said here of the raw material of vision
and ecstasy holds good in principle of the higher stages
also. The visions of the ecstatic and inspired dreamer
are determined in detail by the ideas he has previously
entertained. It is even possible to produce hallucinations of a definite kind by telling hypnotised subjects
beforehand that they will see a certain object ;
or they may be induced by sense-stimuli (colours,
tones, tastes, etc.). Charcot and Pierre Janet were able
to predetermine in this manner the visions of their
patients. This state of things finds support in the fact
that the hallucinations on which the visions are based are
often very indefinite and elementary, so that they only
become definite and significant when united with ideas
and interpreted by ideas which the subject unconsciously
supplies from his own memory ;—the subject, *e.g.*, has
hallucinations of points of light or of a shimmer of light,
and he unconsciously builds up out of this a white
figure, which was perhaps the last thing he heard
mentioned. A good example of an indefinite vision
becoming definite and articulate is afforded by that of
the peasant-girl Bernadette, in which the cult of the
Madonna at Lourdes originated. This characteristic

comes out still more clearly in the visions of Swedenborg. One morning as he sat, sunk in religious contemplation, he raised his eyes and saw in the sky above him a brilliant light : as he gazed at it it withdrew to one side, the heavens opened before him and, amongst many other wonders, he saw the angels in converse one with another ; inflamed by the ardent wish to hear what they were saying, this too was granted him ; at first he heard only a noise (*sonus*) which expressed heavenly love, but afterwards articulate speech (*loquela*) full of heavenly wisdom. We have in this case hallucinations of sight as well as of hearing, both of which, as the vision developed, became more and more articulate. And although the angels talked of 'unspeakable things,' the greater part of which could not be expressed by speech of man, yet by the help of earlier visions Swedenborg was able partially to understand them ; the angels discoursed a kind of unitarian theology. The angelic dogmas would no doubt have differed had the privilege of hearing them been granted to an orthodox theologian.

Purely elementary hallucinations are no doubt more frequent than is usually believed ; but they only become what we call visions under special circumstances, *i.e.* under strong excitement and tension of consciousness and under the influence of dominant ideas charged with emotion. Such visions may differ widely in value, although their psychological explanation is identical in essentials. We only call an hallucination a vision when it possesses a certain value, but from a psychological point of view there is no difference in principle. All visions are stamped with the character, the memories, and the stage of culture of the visionary. As an example of how ideas, which have previously been active in consciousness, are able to determine an elementary hallucination and invest it with their own significance, I will quote (in addition to that of Swedenborg's already mentioned) a vision of Vincent de Paul, which appeared to him as his friend Madame de Chantal breathed her last. He saw a shining ball mount upwards and, high in the air, unite itself with another ball of light, after which both together were taken up into a still more radiant globe of light, while an inner voice told him that he gazed on the soul of his pious friend, who in conjunction with the soul of the previously deceased François de Sales, had become one with God.[73] We see, therefore, how largely visions are determined by precedingly predominant ideas; if these ideas are formulated and organised they will be able both to interpret and to assuage violent visionary and ecstatic crises within the religious sphere. This phenomenon recurs throughout the history of the religious life.

When the ecstatic cult of Dionysus found its way from Thrace to Greece the oracle at Delphi was able to organise this wild movement by associating it with the already existing cult of Apollo. While hitherto the Bacchic votaries had known no other rule than the impulses of fanatical feeling, they were now subjected to the influence of a harmonious and clearly formulated cult. The Delphic oracle or, in other words, the Delphic priesthood, seems to have been a kind of authority which interpreted and organised the movements of the religious life. Plato speaks of the god at Delphi as 'the interpreter'—an office which went down from father to son. Since the oracle was consulted by all the Greek states on points of ritual, the Delphic tradition acquired great influence over the development of the Grecian religion.[74]

58. In the history of the Jewish religion the finding of the book of the law (Deuteronomy) in the temple in the reign of King Josiah (*circa* 620 B.C.) was an event of no small significance. Free individual action within

the sphere of the life of worship and of prophecy found itself confronted by an established organisation. An exclusive priesthood now wielded authority over the religious life, while formerly fathers of families had led their own and their children's devotions. The line between priests and people grew more defined,— the prophets were soon superseded by the priesthood. Judaism acquired a canonical book, a codification of tradition : it became the religion of a book, and as such was afterwards imitated by Christianity and Mohammedanism.[75]

59. In the inception of Christianity the religious traditions of the people and of the age in the midst of which the founder of Christianity lived were co-operative. It is not granted to us to know anything of the inner life of Jesus of Nazareth before his public appearance. But however his life of feeling may have developed, he must have used the traditions of his nation to interpret and formulate it. In his sermon on the mount he presented his ethical teaching as a deeper and more spiritual rendering of the Mosaic law. In the Messianic idea he found the expression of his work and of his place in history. In the expectations of the millennium, in the hopes, which had perhaps been transplanted from Parseeism into Judaism, of a future kingdom of perfection, he found forms and images for the great hope which he instilled into the human race. Thus even the greatest religious personality known to history influenced and was influenced by tradition, alike in his work and his development. This did not diminish his originality, for the old becomes new when appropriated and applied by a deep and original genius.

The position of Jesus when formulating his religious ideas was similar to that of his disciples when they had to interpret and express the effect which the personality, the life and the death of the Master had made upon

them.   They conceived him either, in close adherence to
his own interpretation, as the expected Messiah (the first
three Gospels), or as the Logos, the eternal Word (the
Gospel of St. John), or as the sacrifice for sin (St. Paul),
or as a spiritual high priest (Epistle to the Hebrews).
These are all different ways in which they sought to make
clear what the Master was to them.

60. The picture given us in the apostolic letters of
the first Christian Churches shows us no fixed organisation.   Enthusiasm and ecstasy found free vent.   But if
communal life was to develop, it no longer sufficed
that individuals should abandon themselves to inner
experiences, especially as, owing to the violent excitement these experiences occasioned, it was found impossible to formulate them either in thoughts or words,
so that such outbreaks were incomprehensible to other
men.   The 'gift of tongues' consisted in inarticulate, and
hence incomprehensible, cries.   The 'spirit' worked
so powerfully that the 'understanding' could not
play its part.   Hence Paul exhorts the Corinthians
to limit these ecstatic states during the times of their
assemblies to such as could be tested and interpreted
by one specially appointed for the purpose, so that
others might profit by these experiences.   The
fourteenth chapter of the first Epistle to the Corinthians gives us an insight into the state of things
(see also 2 Cor. v. 13).   The interpreter was probably
able to so identify himself with the state of him who
'spake with tongues' that he could find thoughts
and words which expressed what was going on in
his mind while he was in this state.   An immediate
sympathy, a power of analogy guided by unerring tact, is
the necessary presupposition of such interpretation, as in
all cases where we have to infer from the looks and
movements of other men to what is going on within their
minds.   But, at the same time, we may be sure that

models for such interpretations were taken partly from
the Old Testament Scriptures and partly from the
apostolic teachings.   Perhaps this is the explanation of
the command in the Epistle to the Romans (xii. 6) that
the gift of prophecy should be exercised ' in proportion ' to
faith, where ' faith ' refers to the subject-matter of faith.
Thus the inner experiences of the individual were early
brought into subjection to traditional models.

Later, as the Church became progressively organised,
the stream of individual inspiration was gradually
choked up.   In apostolic times the chief reason for this
was the edification of others.   But later it became all
important to preserve harmony with tradition so as to
exclude heresy.   All free individual motions were checked
as dangerous—when they did not cease from exhaustion.   The faculty of seeing visions and speaking with
tongues ceased first, as was only natural, among the laity,
but afterwards it failed among monks and priests also.
Men began to compare and to reflect.   They no longer
put their faith in immediate inspiration, but tested this
inspiration according to norms which became increasingly
precise.   In the so-called pastoral epistles (to Timothy
and Titus) 'sound doctrine' is already inculcated in contradistinction to heretical errors.   The history of the Church
shows how the organisation and establishment of dogmas
proceeded down the course of the centuries.   Expansion
gave place to organisation and articulation.   The establishment of the canon (the collection of the New Testament
Scriptures) was the most important moment in this
course of development.   The Church here, at a certain
point of her development, decided once and for ever
what books were to be regarded as genuine witnesses to
the true doctrine.

Hereafter only the authorities of the Church were
competent to decide whether or not a religious idea
were valid, while formerly revelation had been un-

ceasingly testifying within the hearts of individuals.
The Church now became the guardian of the gift of
grace. We have seen how the same thing happened
in the case of miracles (§ 8) ; as the Church alone decided
whether a miracle was genuine or not, so the Church
alone could decide as to the validity of a religious truth.
Even in the ordering of the religious life the Church
demanded that her traditions should be followed : when
Francis of Assisi wanted to restore the apostolic life
(according to the tenth chapter of the Gospel of St.
Matthew), the Church insisted that all new Orders must
be founded on the pattern of previous ones (*exempla
antiquorum*). The Church here, as so often elsewhere,
opposed the restoration of the primitive where this
collided with the traditions which had grown up in the
interval.

But the Catholic Church reserved to herself the
right of promulgating new doctrines. Where religious
need has led to the formulation of certain ideas, the
Head of the Church may declare the content of such
ideas to be a doctrine of the Church. The new dogma
then appears as the valid expression of a something
that the Church had really always believed, but of
which she has only now become fully aware. Before
the promulgation of the dogma of the immaculate
conception of the Virgin Mary, Pius IX. sent round an
encyclical with the object of finding out whether such a
dogma would be agreeable to the faithful. This step
justified the inscription subsequently put up on the
walls of the Cathedral of St. Peter to the effect that in
promulgating this dogma the Pope had carried out the
wishes of the entire Catholic world (*totius orbis catholici
desideria explevit*).[76] Catholic authors sometimes write
as though all the dogmas promulgated by the Church—
even in the nineteenth century—are but a further unfolding of that which Jesus talked with his disciples[77]

during the forty days between the resurrection and the
ascension.   The history of the said dogmas provides an
interesting contribution to the psychology of religion, for
in it we can clearly trace the relation between the needs
of feeling (*desideria*) and ideas.   Men felt the need of
an intermediary between the deified Jesus and humanity
(cf. §§ 23 and 54).   And they also felt a desire to have
a representative of the element of femininity, more
especially of maternal love (cf. the idea of Kurotrophos,
see § 48) included in the circle of religious ideas.

As in every other psychological process, many factors
co-operated here.   No dogma can be adequately explained
by reference to any one immediate religious need.   The
inner and outer relations of the Church play an essential
part.   The Church feels herself bound by her traditions
(as she understands these), whether she follow them in
blind habit, or in analogy with ideas already formed, or
in the search for new ideas wherewith to complete old
ones.   She fights against a 'heresy' and therefore
seeks after a formula which shall give it the lie in the
sharpest possible form, or she seeks to unite and reconcile
conflicting tendencies by a prudent compromise or an even
more prudent indefiniteness or ambiguity.   Or perhaps
she exerts herself to formulate ideas which correspond
to her ritual as this has gradually developed.   In his
History of Dogma Harnack has pointed out eleven
different factors—*i.e.* ten others in addition to the
religious need proper—which co-operated in the development of the dogmas of the Church (*i.e.* the content of the
orthodox dogmatism of the present day) during the first
centuries.[78]

61. What is thus apparent in the history of a
religious community comes out still more clearly in the
religious life of a particular person, when such an one
feels at once the power and the need of describing his
inner development.   We have a great example of this

in the *Confessions* of Augustine. When Augustine
wrote this work his feet were firmly planted on the soil
of ecclesiastical tradition. He himself has told us he
only believed in the gospel because it formed part
of the Church's tradition. The central religious process
—the feeling that yearned for ideas in which to find
expression can however be discerned. The tenth book
of the *Confessions* is especially revealing. Augustine
seeks here to get clear with himself as to what the
object of his innermost need really is. "What do I
love when I love Thee?" he asks of his God. He goes
through a long list of things and forms which experience
has presented to him—but none of these satisfy the need
of his heart. Only in his own breast, in his own spirit
does he find a possible analogy. In a deep and, for the
history of the fundamental concepts of psychology, a
most extraordinarily interesting argument, he points out
that memory is the peculiar characteristic of the spiritual
life. God must be a being who works as does the
power of memory within us. And he works in our
innermost souls—in that which lies far deeper than
the innermost self known to me! In this innermost
man truth dwells. But yet (and here we get the transition from the psychological to the ecclesiastical point of
view) God is not only that which thus works within;
before all things he is himself the object of a memory—
the memory of the preaching of the Church (*ministerium
praedicationis*) through which alone we really know him.[79]

In no other man have deep personal experience,
energetic thought, and absolute faith in authority entered
into such close and characteristic union as in this great
doctor of the Church. But even with him we see clearly
the opposition between absorption in the ego and
dependence on external tradition. "Go not outside
thyself, for truth dwells within thy breast," he exclaims.
And yet he believed he owed everything to the Church's

tradition. As if this did not come from without! This strict dependence on tradition, however, is not able to obscure the fundamental psychological relation between feeling and idea which is peculiar to the religious sphere. This fundamental relation is brought out very strongly in the words which I have taken as a motto for the first chapter of this section : Augustine is here seeking for a predicate which may serve to determine that which reveals itself to feeling. The doubt which had so tormented him during the spiritual struggles of his youth led him now to cling to the authority of the Church ; still later, when he had come forward as one of the Church's apologists, he was dominated by the need of maintaining her authority in the face of disintegrating elements ; otherwise the stirrings of his inner life might have led him to freer and more universal results. In addition to this we must remember that he lived in an age when—to use his own expression—the world had grown old (*senuisse jam mundum*) : it is not in such times that we find the boldness which is necessary for the free and independent unfolding of the inner life.

We may trace a certain analogy between the argument developed in the tenth book of the *Confessions* of Augustine and the line of thought followed in the Upanishads. As Augustine asked "What do I love in loving Thee ? " so it is asked in the Upanishads : What is Brahma ? And the answer runs : Brahma is Atma (breath, spirit, soul) (cf. § 19). Thus we see that the principle which supports the whole world of existence, which is itself (for Brahma really denotes the power of prayer, see § 53) a projection of the needs of feeling, finds (at any rate provisionally, see § 21) its most appropriate expression in ideas which are taken from the life of the soul.[80] The old Indian thinkers sat more loosely to tradition than did Augustine : hence in their case the psychological process can be traced more clearly.

N

62. Amongst the mystics of the Middle Ages we find interesting examples of the reciprocal influence between feeling, ideation and tradition. According to a terminology in frequent use among the mystics, 'will' or love is regarded as the opposite of memory and understanding (cf. § 36). In the highest states all these faculties slumber, for the will is overpowered by overflowing blessedness ; all suffering is forgotten ; no search for the cause of this state nor comparison with other states is possible. Not even a vision is possible during the highest moment of ecstasy. And during this state the subject cannot communicate with other men. The 'will' persists longer in this state than do the memory and the understanding, and as soon as these latter can work, ideation and communication again become possible. The subject is now able to dictate an account of what he believes himself to have experienced. But all mystics agree in emphasising the difference between their actual experiences and the thoughts and words in which they try to express them : " It can be felt but not expressed," says Hugo von St. Victor ; and employing the figure used in the Song of Solomon, he goes on, " Thy Beloved comes invisibly, he comes concealed, he comes incomprehensibly ; he comes to embrace thee, not to be seen of thee." Angela di Foligno describes a vision as follows : "What did I see? God Himself. I can say no more about it. It was a fulness, an inner all-satisfying light for which neither words nor comparisons suffice. It was the highest beauty which locks all lips and contains the highest good." When she read the account of her experiences which had been written down at her dictation she often failed to recognise them.[81]

Although the mystics strongly emphasise the difference between their experiences and their descriptions of them, yet they assert with no less emphasis that these experiences were in harmony with the teachings of the

Bible and of the Church. It remains a psychological riddle how they could convince themselves of this harmony between the content of their experiences and the teaching of the Church if the experiences were so different from the description : for a comparison with the Church's teaching could only be effected by means of the description. We see here clearly that the harmony with Church teaching is expressly willed and not found to exist. In their interpretation and description of what they had gone through, great care was taken that nothing should be included which could be in contradiction to the teaching of the Bible and the Church. We have express explanations on this point from some of the greatest of the mediæval mystics. Thus Suso says of himself : " In writing his chief work (*i.e.* the *Book of Eternal Wisdom*) his state was not that of one actively dictating, but of one overpowered by God (*divina patiens*). When what was thus given him had been reduced to writing he came to himself (*ad se revertens*) and looked diligently (*diligenter rimatus est*) to see that there was nothing in it which differed from the teachings of the holy Fathers." The difference between the overpowering, the return to self-consciousness and the anxious submission to authority here comes out very clearly. The return to self-consciousness did not lead Suso as it did Augustine to try by means of his own powers of reflection to find expression for that which he had experienced : his one care was to avoid any dissent from the teaching of the Church. In the case of women mystics this obedience to the authority of the Church is still more prominent than among the men. The Apostle Paul had indeed forbidden women to speak in the Churches, and had bidden them consult the men in religious matters. And since they were lacking in the scholastic education of the men mystics, they must have been keenly alive to the insecurity of their position.

Hence, convinced though they were that their highest experiences were of divine origin, yet they submitted themselves entirely to the authority of the Church. The visions and experiences of Angela di Foligno were written down by a monk, who explained that, though he had added nothing, he had left out many things which were too exalted to be grasped by his miserable understanding, and even after this the book was 'edited' by more than one learned monk. St. Theresa describes how in order to avoid erroneous opinions she inquired of every one who could teach her, and so firmly did she hold to her creed, she tells us, that her faith in the most insignificant point taught by the Church could not be shaken, even though all possible revelations were permitted to her. Yes, even if she saw the heavens open! And if for one moment the thought occurs to her that that which she had heard might be just as true as that which the Fathers had heard, she is sure that the devil is tempting her. She left it to a learned and pious Dominican [82] to decide whether or not her book was in agreement with the doctrines of the Church.

Here again we find a relation of reciprocity. For as experiences were expounded and tested by the aid of tradition, so they were often evoked by absorption in the traditional conceptions. For it is by reading that the mystical trances and visions are induced. Hugo and Theresa both emphasise the importance of reading. We may perhaps remember that the figures in the religious pictures of Van Eyck and Memling are depicted as so absorbed in their books as to be oblivious of all and everything around them. [83]

And yet the mystics possessed a purely subjective criterion of the validity of their experiences, *i.e.* the peace and rest which arose within their hearts. So long as the need to subject themselves to the Bible and the

Church was strong and lively, peace and rest could hardly be attained except by bringing their ideas into harmony with traditional doctrine.   But there remained another possibility ; immediate trust in the experiences of the inner life and in the intellectual activity employed in finding ideas in which to formulate these, might become so powerful as to render subjection to tradition an impossibility ; the new wine might burst the old bottles. Many great religious conflicts have thus originated, and this is the path that has been trodden by all reformers and founders of religion, generally after an honest attempt to find peace in the old forms.   It is then discovered that a new and living garment must be woven for the Godhead.

63. With the reformers, too, we may trace the psychological process in which immediate experiences of the personal life encounter the traditions of Church and are at once formed and limited by them.

In the case of Luther we have already seen (§ 39) how he sought — in a manner recalling Augustine's line of thought (§ 61) — to find expression for that which stirred within him.   But in his first development of the concept of God he accepted the old teaching of the Church in all simplicity.   He left the scholastic doctrine of the Trinity untouched, while he stamped with the mark of his personality those religious conceptions which were immediately connected with his personal experiences, *e.g.* justification by faith and the Holy Communion, the latter in a form closely akin to the Catholic conception of it.   Luther's inclusion of some things which did not correspond with his personal experiences was an inconsistency which can be explained by his faith in the Church, but it was unfortunate for the subsequent development of Protestantism.   Protestantism only arrived at a clear principle—admitting of logical development—when it learned to base itself

on freedom of conscience and on personal and individual
experiences of the relation of value to reality.

Still more clearly than with Luther can we trace
the psychological basis of Zwingli's religious views.
While Luther suspended his independent line of thought
after he had defined God as the object of the highest
trust, Zwingli went a step further and arrived at his
doctrine of absolute predestination. Zwingli laid more
weight than Luther did on the unconditional certainty of
his own salvation which may be enjoyed by the individual;
this subjective but unshakable certainty corresponds to
the belief in divine election. And if this election is to
attain its end it must proceed from a power which can
disarm all resistance—from an absolute, infinite, exalted
power. Zwingli, too, was no doubt influenced in the
development of his line of thought by his philosophical
studies (of Plato and the Stoics), but it was his personal
experience which set his thought in motion. Only an
experience won as was Zwingli's could usher in such a
line of thought as his.[84]

Protestantism can show us even more emphatic
attempts than those of the reformers to reduce all
religion to the experience of the heart, to make all
religion a cult of the heart. Rousseau and Schleiermacher
are the most important representatives of this movement.
But they, too, in their effort to clothe their experiences
in thoughts and words, are driven to ideas borrowed
from the spiritual atmosphere in which they lived, and
are inclined to regard these ideas as equally immediate as
the experiences themselves. Rousseau " directly felt the
truths of natural religion " and although Schleiermacher
was gifted with greater psychological insight and greater
powers of critical reflection, yet he too is not innocent
of the all too common confusion between the expression of a feeling and its cause.

As a general rule, personal experience receives

naïvely and immediately the conceptions and forms
handed down by tradition, and believes itself to accept
these as they are.   Only a closer inspection reveals the
continual readjustments that have really taken place.   The
very fact that other elements of the ideational life are
emphasised than were emphasised before produces a
shade of difference.   The same thing takes place here
as happens in the history of art when a pictorial type is
adopted by a younger generation of artists.   Speaking of
the relation of the older Italian painters to the Madonna
of the traditional Byzantine type, Julius Lange remarks
that they did not assume a revolutionary attitude towards
it, but gradually modified it in a new direction.   " They
began to invest the leading features of the traditional life-
less mask with their personal notions of the pure beauty
which should adorn the Mother of God.   Thus, *e.g.*, Guido
of Siena.   Here we still have the almost circular contour
of the head, the long-drawn oval of the face . . . but how
fresh, how living, and how amiable is the glance of this
Madonna!"[85]   In the history of religion the readjustments
cannot be so easily demonstrated.   They may be brought
about in two ways ; either the traditionary elements,
in which feeling finds a special support, are pressed into
the foreground, or else certain elements are unconsciously
reinterpreted ; they are conceived poetically, symbolically,
or rationalistically, or perhaps omitted altogether : this
may be done in unconsciousness that any deviation from
the original interpretation is thereby involved.   It was a
great relief to Augustine in his youth when he was told
that the corporeal expressions used of God in the Bible
might be understood metaphorically and not literally ;
later in life he had no scruples in stretching allegorical interpretation as far as it would go, whenever
he found something in the teaching of the Church from
which he could otherwise derive no sort of religious
value.   That the spirit of God brooded on the face of

the waters at creation meant, according to Augustine, that through the gift of the spirit, which is love to God, men rise above the corporeal; that "God created Heaven as well as Earth" had for him the symbolic significance that within the Church we may distinguish between a more spiritual (*serena intelligentia veritatis*) and a more literal understanding (*fides simplex parvulorum*). The mystics continued on this path, for, as has strikingly been said, they annulled every barrier between themselves and the content of Scripture, and strove to realise everything set down in Scripture as an eternal Now. Meister Eckhart, for example, in a sermon on the story of the resuscitation of the widow of Nain's son, explains that the widow is the soul, the dead son the reason. All religious speech and exhortation moves more or less on the same lines to the present day, for it is guided by the desire to find in the account of that which happened centuries ago something which shall afford immediate nourishment for the spiritual life of the present. A double sense is thus attributed to the old stories, without, as a general rule, any clear idea as to the relation of these two senses to one another. Even among the religious philosophers of the nineteenth century—amongst men such as Schleiermacher, Hegel and Coleridge— we find no recognition of the fact that the transformation of the traditionary doctrines into forms which harmonised with their own life of feeling and thought changed the original sense of the content of these dogmas. Sören Kierkegaard, too, who was particularly anxious to free dogmatic content from speculative subtilisations, was obliged to restrict the objective content of dogma; at any rate, he only appropriated what could nourish his passionate, tense life of feeling, and even that only in such sense (often a very transformed one) as he could turn to account.[86]

When an accommodation of this kind is no longer

possible, the old forms are burst asunder, and if religious
life is to go on at all, new forms must be forthcoming.
Here we reach the crisis of which I have already spoken
—the crisis which ushers in the birth of something new.
We have next to consider the attitude of the psychology
of religion towards these crises and the prophetic personalities in which the new element originates.

But before entering on this question, I should like
to make a few general remarks on the relation of feeling
to ideation within the sphere of religion.

64. Like æsthetic and ethical judgments, religious
judgments arc distinguished from others by the element
of feeling which, never entirely absent in any act of
judgment, yet in their case is particularly prominent.
Religious judgments are judgments of value.   According
to the hypothesis on which I build, they express men's
experiences of the relation of value to reality (see § 31),
which relation may itself have immediate value.   In
their simplest forms religious judgments occur as exclama-
tions in which an inner state of admiration, love, hope
or fear finds vent.   We get a more articulate form of
the religious judgment when consciousness tries to make
clear to itself what it is it is experiencing—what it
admires, loves, hopes or fears (cf. § 61).   What, for
example, it may be asked, is the meaning of this
wonderful event?   Who is this man who has taken such
hold on our inner lives (cf. §§ 57-60)?   Now comes the
more deliberate formation of a judgment.   Every judgment is a union of concepts; these concepts have been
brought together by the attention which, starting from a
conception given in a more indefinite form, has been
seeking its nearer determination.   The concept from
which we start is the subject of the judgment, and it
finds its nearer determination in the concluding concept,
which is the predicate of the judgment.   The psychological process which takes place in the formation of a

judgment is the passage from the former to the latter of
these ideas.

In judgments of value the concept with which we
start is more obscure than in other judgments because
the element of feeling predominates. Indeed, when the
underlying feeling is fresh and original, or when, for
other reasons, it is especially strong, the cognitive
element may be entirely lacking. It is characteristic of
every violent movement of feeling that concepts fall
more and more into the background. In the preceding
discussion I adduced cases in which all articulation and
analysis, and consequently all power of forming a judgment, were impossible ; such were the 'gift of tongues'
amongst the primitive Christians and the ecstasy of the
mystics. But the formation of a judgment is only possible
when we have a concept to start from, however obscure
it may be. We must therefore assume that such religious
judgments as express what has been experienced in
moments of agitated feeling are really formed in subsequent moments, when the agitation is abating and the
subject 'comes to himself' again ; he is then able to
characterise his experience from memory by collating
it with other experiences, and reflecting on its significance for his personal life.

Great religious personalities have called the object
of their highest trust and love 'God,' and we can comprehend this if we understand by 'God' the principle of the
conservation of value in reality. That which supports
and comprehends within itself all values, that which is
seen to be the origin and consummation of all values must
be the object of the deepest feeling. All instinctive and
spontaneous religious judgments imply this. "What I am
here experiencing is only a single expression of a single
witness to the power which is the bearer of all values
in the world of reality. It must be this power, then,
which I am here experiencing!" The concept of God is

the fundamental predicate of all religious judgments, the predicate for which religious thought is in search when it starts from experiences of the relation between value and reality. Religious thought would reach its close in a complete determination of this fundamental predicate, for, could this be attained, the relation between value and reality would be perfectly clear and transparent. This would be more likely to happen if the principles of the conservation of value and of interconnexion according to law throughout existence could both be subsumed under a single higher principle. Such a conclusion is, we fear, impossible in any form which would be acceptable to scientific thought. But the religious problem remains in existence so long as there is any effort to hold fast to the predicate of the religious judgment, *i.e.* so long as a religious question is psychologically possible.

The history of religion and of philosophy shows that a closer determination of the predicative concept of the religious judgment (or, to borrow an expression from Kant, of the religious category) generally takes place by the help of traditional forms and figures. Only when some individual possesses the capacity and the courage to form images and to speculate for himself does development take a new direction, and this happens for the most part when religious development has arrived at a crisis.

It is, however, of the greatest psychological importance to remember that the predicate concept, or the category, is not the first—not the originally given; it is precisely that which we are striving to find. What we are in search of is a comprehensible determination of the religious category ('God'), by which I mean a determination which will allow us to regard particular experiences as particular examples of its validity, or, to employ a poetical personification, to regard such experiences as

actions of God.   The primary religious judgments have
'God' as their predicate, not their subject.   The concept
of God, the religious category, is subject to the same
rule as all other concepts and categories ; it must serve
as a predicate before it can figure as a subject.   The
simplest judgments are predicative judgments.   Both
during the formation of a judgment, as well as in the more
exact formulation of judgments already framed, however,
there is a relation of reciprocity between subject and
predicate ; for not only is the subject determined by the
predicate which is combined with it, but the predicate in
virtue of its reduction to this subject also increases in
determination.   Let us take an example which I have
used elsewhere : [87] when I learn that the amphioxus is a
vertebrate, I learn not only something about the amphioxus but also something about the concept of vertebrate, *e.g.* that the possession of a brain is not an essential
characteristic.   Just so the religious category (the concept
of God) acquires nearer determination by its applications,
which really means by the different occasions which induce
us to apply this concept.   But will this concept ever be
completely determined so that we shall be able to operate
with it as with a clear and distinct concept ?   This is the
great question.

Orthodox and speculative dogmatism alike believed
that they had in the religious predicates a key not only
to the understanding of the essence of religion but also
to the understanding of the whole of existence ; they
sought by means of these uncompleted and uncomplet-
able conceptions to construct a higher science.   But the
nature of the religious predicates has been misunderstood
from other sides also.   A certain school of religious
historians, who for some time took the lead in the science
of religion, thought that in the purely etymological
inquiry into religious designations—especially the names
of gods—they possessed an adequate method of studying

the essence of religion.   Etymology then was to be the
correct philosophy of religion.   By this path we may, it
is true, reach interesting conclusions.   Thus it is of no
small interest to learn that the word 'god' itself seems
to show us that the primary religious predicate was
formed under the influence of an act of worship, and that
it denoted him to whom that action referred (cf. § 50).
But this example shows us the inadequacy of the method,
for the primary religious predicate had, as a matter of
fact, a far wider range than was afforded by acts of worship.   At any rate the concept of worship must be considerably widened if it is to make clear to us what is
involved in the name 'God.'   The development of
religion is far deeper, far more complex and manifold than
is the development of language pure and simple, and the
relation of inner states to their expressions is even more
complicated within the religious sphere than the relation
of psychical phenomena to their linguistic expression
usually is.   Nor has language proved itself a safe guide,
for it appears that different nations' conceptions of God,
expressed by words having quite different roots, are
sometimes intimately related to one another, both inter-
nally and externally ; while, conversely, the names of God
which, from a purely linguistic point of view, fall into the
same class may denote gods differing widely in nature.[88]
The verbal designation is only a support which is gained
at a certain point of religious development ; afterwards it
may be attached to ideas far remote from the stage of
development which the ideational life of religion had
reached when the expression was framed.

As long as religion lives, new processes of thought
will always be starting out in search of a predicative
concept in which religion may find rest ; hence this concept will be constantly receiving new determinations.

Is there not here a something which the human spirit
has at all times been seeking more or less energetically,

but which it has never found, or never been able to reduce to form and expression ?   Have we not here a riddle, a mystery, over which the human mind must ever be poring, and which, in accordance with modifications of experience and personal differences, is always being posited in a different manner ?

(*d*) SCIENTIFIC CONCLUSION ·FOR THE PSYCHOLOGY OF RELIGION

65. The previous chapter brought us to a point at which the psychological method was subjected to a crucial test.   As long as the inception of religious feeling and the ideas in which it finds expression are clearly and distinctly determined by historical circumstances, the psychological method can work as well as any other scientific method within the sphere of mental science.   But when something qualitatively new arises, when a radical deepening or extension of feeling takes place, when the latter takes on a new complexion, or when new ideas are constructed for its expression, is it still possible to give an exhaustive psychological explanation ?   This question forces itself upon us when we find ourselves confronted with one of the crises above mentioned, where uninterrupted action and reaction between personal experience and tradition fails to afford an adequate ex-planation.   The appearance of prophetic personalities, who have new experiences and create new symbols, seems at first insusceptible of explanation by the psychological method which worked well enough as long as the said reciprocal action remained in force.   But such personalities as these seem to go off at a tangent instead of moving in a closed curve round a given point ; they lead us into entirely new regions in the spiritual world.

This point is of all the greater interest because the tendency of the most recent theology—the theology which most closely approximates to the scientific way of looking at things—is to lay great stress on the point that all revelation takes place within the breasts of prophetic personalities ; it consists, according to these writers, in the liveliness and originality which characterises the religious experience of such persons, leading them to the discovery of thoughts and symbols which are able to spread light and peace in the hearts of many. While the older theologians presented faith and the object of faith as confronting one another in an external sort of fashion, the tendency now is to find (or, at any rate, to emphasise as greatest) the wonder, the true revelation in the springing up of faith within the soul of man ; they maintain that the fact of this springing up itself forms part of the revelation. Theology is thus brought into a more intimate connexion with psychology than has been the case since Schleiermacher. All the more pressing, then, is the question whether it is possible to find a concluding concept, recognised as such by science, for the psychology of religion.

Before I attempt to determine the position of psychology with regard to this problem, I will discuss the standpoint adopted by earlier psychologists of religion with reference to this point.

66. In his *Esquisse d'une philosophie de la religion d'après la psychologie et l'histoire*, Auguste Sabatier, as the title of his work announces, tries to place himself at a purely scientific point of view. His intention is to make use of the ordinary psychological and historical methods, and his results are therefore akin in several respects to the fundamental ideas which I have brought forward. For him dogma is never the original and fundamental element in religion. It arises comparatively late in the history of religion. Prophets always precede rabbis. Dogmas, like all ecclesiastical uses and forms, are derivative in comparison with religious feeling, and

it is the task of the psychology of religion to show how this derivation takes place. The concept of God is to be regarded as a symbol in which religious feeling finds expression.

In carrying out his psychological and historical method, Sabatier remains true to the conviction that we can never explain any individual and particular phenomenon by appealing to the intervention of God. " Since God," he says, " is the final cause of all things, He is not the scientific explanation of any one thing." This is the same thought that we found (see § 5) in operation at the birth of modern science, determining the latter's relation to the concept of God. It is as valid and as necessary in psychology as in physics.

Nevertheless, whenever Sabatier is in difficulties in his psychology of religion, he has recourse to theological explanation. According to him, God creates religious feeling, which, in its turn, sets in motion the ideational life, and by this means creates symbols and dogmas. " God," he says, " comes into commerce and contact with a human soul, and lets it make a certain religious experience, which, when reflected upon, gives rise to a dogma. What constitutes revelation and what ought to be the norm of our life is the creative and fruitful religious experience which was first made in the souls of the prophets, of the Saviour, and of the apostles." Here I can come to no other conclusion but that the French philosopher is at odds with his own scientific principle ; for he here explains a special psychical phenomenon by an appeal to God, although, according to his own express avowal, such an appeal can never explain a particular phenomenon. And if the concept of God is itself a symbolic idea, founded on the experiences of the life of feeling, any 'explanation' of the religious feeling which we reach by its means can only be a symbolic explanation, and the gap in the psychology of religion (if there

be a gap) is certainly not filled up. Every dogma presupposes a religious feeling; hence no dogma can be
employed in explanation of the latter.[89]

If we assume that there is a gap in the series of
psychological (and the corresponding physiological)
phenomena which can only be filled up by employing
theological concepts, it is our duty to state definitely
where this gap occurs. At what point are we to assume
supernatural intervention? The more we know about
psychical development, the more we see that it is characterised by such close interconnexion and rests on such a
co-operation of elements that it is as difficult to discover
a gap at which we may suppose the new influence
to intervene as it is to follow all its transitions and
disentangle all its different threads. The assumption of
an interruption of continuity involves no fewer difficulties
than does the assumption of perfect continuity. As a
rule, those who assert a breach of continuity do not state
the problem sufficiently sharply. It is rare to find such an
energetic search for the point at which the intervention
might occur as we get in Sören Kierkegaard's *Begrebet
Angst* (Conception of Anguish), where he tries to discover at what point in the life of the will 'freedom'
must be supposed to operate; or in older Catholic
theologians who—with perfect logic but with rather
questionable taste—inquired whether the supernatural act
which effectuated the sinlessness of the Virgin Mary
took place at the moment of conception or not till some
moment in the life of the embryo, and, if so, at what
moment. This question has never yet been decided,
and an attempt to do so would doubtless be fruitless:
but for the standpoint we are discussing its solution is a
necessity.

Theological philosophy of religion involves itself in
the same epistemological circle as does materialism.
The conception of matter is built up by thought on the

basis of sense-impressions; whereupon materialism proceeds in dogmatic fashion to use this conception in explaining the origin alike of sense-impressions and of thought. Just as sense-impressions and logical principles, being the presuppositions involved in our conception of existence, cannot be explained by the latter, so, in the psychology of religion, the religious feeling is a presupposition which cannot in its turn be explained by ideas, the formulation of which it has itself brought about. Perhaps it is in virtue of this analogy between theology and materialism that they so often seem to understand one another better than either of them understands critical philosophy.

67. Fifty years before the appearance of Sabatier's work, Ludwig Feuerbach had maintained that the psychological method is fully adequate within the religious sphere: that religion is in fact nothing else but a psychological product — that all theology is psychology. The psychology of the philosophy of religion owes a great debt to Feuerbach, and his most excellent analyses and characterisations are still in many respects unequalled. But his method and the critical limitation of his results are both open to question.[90]

Feuerbach loved short and striking formulæ: perhaps this was because in his case the psychologist had so often to make way for the agitator. Whenever he discovered an essential factor in the psychology of religion he was inclined to regard this as the all in all: thus, *e.g.*, he erected the wish into the theogonic principle because it produced the concept of god "out of itself and only out of itself." Feuerbach here ignores the complex conditions under which the formation of religious ideas takes place. However great the influence that must be ascribed to feeling, yet even within the religious sphere and its relation to knowledge feeling is not purely active; it is in its turn dependent on knowledge. An important side of religious development consists precisely in the quiet influence exerted on feeling by knowledge. As I have tried to show in my preceding argument, action and reaction are constantly going on between them, even though the element of feeling is predominant. Without a reciprocal relation of this kind religion could have no practical significance for men. On the other hand, myths and legends may be the forms under which the conception of nature and the memory of great persons may exert their influence on the life of the race ; the symbolical language of dogmas may present the content of the weightiest and most important experiences of life to later generations in poetical and concentrated form.

Even with these modifications, the axiom that all theology is psychology could never be susceptible of definite proof, any more than is the axiom that all material phenomena have material causes within the sphere of external nature. Still the combined psychological and historical method proves to be the only one which we can employ, the only one which, when it can be applied in detail, is able to give us a real explanation. Where it is not applicable, there we get no explanation at all. What we are not able to explain by means of this method remains as pure fact—something which we can describe but cannot explain,—hence we must be careful that we do not smuggle in ' description ' as a substitute for explanation. The assertion that all religious phenomena are subject to psychological laws would be just as dogmatic as the assertion that there are phenomena which can never be explained psychologically. Psychology gives us working hypotheses, and we shall not give up these hypotheses until we have been shown better methods. Nevertheless we do not confound them with demonstrable truths. It is in this spirit that I have tried to work at the above investigation of the development

of religious ideas. Following this view we shall find ourselves forced at many points to the confession that we
are confronted by 'pure facts.' But we shall add: every
'pure fact' (when rightly apprehended and described) is
a problem so long as it is not brought into close and
law-abiding connexion with our other experiences.

68. Returning to the problem of new constructions
within the religious sphere, especially in connexion with
prophetic personalities, we must notice that this is not
really a separate problem, but only the special form of a
problem which recurs in different degrees and *nuances*
within all spheres of experience. The more individualistic and the more qualitatively novel a phenomenon is,
the more difficult it is to bring it into that continuity
with other phenomena which is the necessary condition
of scientific understanding. It is this opposition between
continuity and qualitativeness or individuality that presents
so many difficulties to knowledge within all spheres.
The religious problem, therefore, is not peculiar; on the
contrary, it offers a distinct analogy with other problems
of thought.

The concept of personality sets a double task to
inquiry : viz. to find the law of continuity within the
particular microcosm constituted by every personality
(for without inner continuity there is no personality),
and to find the law of continuity between individual personalities, with their particular idiosyncrasies, and the rest
of existence. Natural science has a task not unlike
this in its search for the qualitative characteristics of
force and stuff: but there is no denying that the concept
of personality offers far greater difficulties to mental
science than does the concept of quality to natural
science. Personality is really the most distinctive
quality known to us. Hence mental science encounters
more difficulties than does natural science [91] in attempting
to solve its problem.

The problem is notably intensified when we are considering personalities in which, in a special sense, something new arises—the 'genial' man in the widest sense of the word, in whom a genius peculiar to himself is at work, *i.e.* in whom the involuntary and half-unconscious mental life produces effects which surpass everything that clear consciousness and steady work could have produced. The prophets belong to this genus in virtue of the vigour and originality of their religious experiences. Here we get the problem of life in a special form. It makes no difference whether we are studying a Buddha, a Socrates or a Jesus ; the same great problem confronts us in each case.

But the fact that the difficulty of the problem is intensified does not warrant our treating it by methods altogether different from those we have elsewhere applied. In that case, at any rate, we must demand not only a new method but also an entirely new theory of knowledge (cf. §§ 5-7, 53 fin.). To lose ourselves in astonishment will not help us ; moreover astonishment and admiration may be at least equally great in him who sets quietly to work to discover within the world of personality the greatest possible psychological and historical interconnexion, as in the theologising romantic who thinks himself obliged at this point to assume an entirely different principle of knowledge from any he has elsewhere applied. That we are brought up short at the limits of our knowledge more often within the sphere of mental science than within that of natural science is taught us not only by religious inquiry. This limitation is due not only to our imperfection but, first and foremost, to the fulness of existence, to the revelation of the inner richness of the world of being. We find here not only limits for our investigation, but also stuff and field for it. The appearance of a new element is a witness that there are more hidden forces in existence than experience had hitherto revealed to us ;

and even if we do not succeed in incorporating this new
element into a continuous series, such as is demanded by
our cognitive ideal, yet it retains its value as a witness
—all the better perhaps when we attach no dogmatic
label to it.   It will be seen that in a certain sense the
psychology of religion may be said to take the concept of
' revelation ' more seriously than does orthodox theology,
which is ever confusing its dogmatic concepts with the
immediately and actually given (cf. §§ 28, 29).   So long
as existence itself is in the toils of becoming (and that it
is so we are bound to conclude from the fact that neither
in the world of mind nor in that of nature can we find
anything absolutely immutable and at rest), so long something new may arise presenting, at any rate provisionally,
a kind of paradox.   But this does not involve any radical
change in the attitude of our knowledge towards existence, any more than it changes the method of our knowledge or the conduct of our individual lives.   Who dares
to say that we ought to be able to explain everything, or
that it would be impossible to live if we could not explain
everything?

    But the value of these crises and of these prophetic
personalities is not exhausted in their novelty ; it is also
apparent in the influence on the whole spiritual life which
is exercised by the content of the new ideas.   And it is
not easy to see how this value could be endangered were
we to succeed in showing that these new ideas have their
roots in previous psychological and historical development.   Our ideal demands that all that is of value shall
be brought into the closest possible connexion with that
" which moves the world within."   And religious feeling
will be obliged, in virtue of its own nature, to recognise
this ideal more and more.   Such an ideal is the un-
spoken presupposition of all striving after a psychological
and historical understanding of the phenomena of the
religious life.

C. DOGMAS AND SYMBOLS

Du kerkerst den Geist in ein tönend Wort,
Doch der Freie wandelt im Sturme fort.

SCHILLER.

69. In our account of the development of religious ideas we have laid most weight on the selective, heightening or inhibitive influence of feeling. The religious consciousness acquires its content by means of a continuous process of qualitative choice. In this process, however, the mutual relations between ideas play a part; moreover, the reality attributed to the ideas thus gained may differ in kind. Thus myths differ from legends and both from dogma, which again is not the same as symbol. At the present day it is the difference between dogma and symbol which is of most importance for the religious problem; but the psychology of religion has also to consider the relation of both these to myths and legends.

Mythology and religion do not coincide with one another. A mythology may develop on the soil of religion; but religion—at least if we accept the psychological analysis of it given above—need not lead to the construction of a mythology. On the other hand, there are myths which have no religious significance, or only acquire such subsequently. The myth is built up unconsciously, as a form under which men intuit the relations and events of the world, chiefly of the external world. The myth is animistic in character, for it converts an event into a history of what has taken place between personal beings. Mythology may be of service to religion. When once religious feeling is aroused, it may emphasise some elements of the myth, and by so doing more or less transform them. Mythology may also, independently of any religious motive, be serviceable to art; imagination may take its originally rude or naïve figures and features and transform them into beings and actions invested with distinct individuality, or it may retell its stories so as to exhibit a definite and motivated interconnexion.

Legends stand nearer religion than myths generally do. The legend is the religious saga. Its essence consists in the idea of a wonderful personality who has made a deep impression on human life—who excited admiration, furnished an example, and opened new paths. Under the influence of memory, a strong expansion of feeling takes place (§ 27) : this in its turn gives rise to a need for intuition and explanation, to satisfy which a process of picture-making is set in motion. At individual points in this process historical tradition and mythological figures co-operate, sometimes in very intricate fashion.

The predominant tendency in myths is to create images by means of the union of as many possible individual features. The construction of myths bears the stamp of luxuriant growth ; they expand according to the laws of association by contiguity. In legends, on the contrary, the central interest is in the subject-matter, in the centripetal power, which depends on an intensification of memory rather than on any naïve personification and colouring. Analogy plays a larger part than does combination. In myths things and relations are personified ; in legends the idea of a personality is the starting-point ; light is thrown on this personality by features and relations taken from other spheres, without which no adequate expression of its value could be found.[92] While in mysticism the feeling of immediate unity with the highest is the predominant feature, in myth and legend imagination is predominant. And the legend again stands in closer relation to the feeling of unity than does the myth, which frequently follows paths and takes directions which concern the periphery rather than the

centre of life. But as legends may become myths
(although it would not be correct to say that all myths
arise in this manner), so myths too may be pressed into
the service of legends, especially when they help to fill
out certain traits of character or incidents in the fate of
legendary persons.

In both myth and legend immediate intuition prevails
and the association of ideas works unconsciously, though
always within the limitation imposed by interest in the
subject-matter; in legends, as we have seen, this subject-
matter is the individual round whom the legend grows up.
Dogma is related to myth and legend as thought proper
to intuition and the association of ideas.[93] Dogma presupposes analysis, comparison, and, above all, distinction.
Images are collated and their separate traits considered
and evaluated. One image has to be harmonised with
another in such a manner that either one coincides with
the other, or that they can be reconciled without contradiction. This process of thought is at work in the development of personal gods—in the proper sense of the term—
out of momentary and special gods, in the transition
from polytheism to monotheism, and in the development
of the ideas of the different qualities and the different
revelations of the deity. In this process of thought
philosophical ideas and reflections are made use of more or
less consciously. It is here we must seek for the points
at which religious and philosophical elements are inter-
woven, often so closely that it is only with the greatest
difficulty that subsequent critical inquiry can disentangle
the various elements. During the interval religious consciousness has often so steeped itself in the results of the
thinking process that it believes itself to be considering
the immediate results of experience: it confuses the
feelings which may be evoked by the finished dogma
(especially in its conjunction with acts of worship) with
those feelings which in their turn set the dogmatising

process in motion; while in its definite dogmatic experiences it believes itself to be living through again
that which took place at the first dawn of religion.

Dogma is analogous to the *artistic* application and
elaboration of myths and legends. But, as we have
already had occasion to remark (§ 60), no purely theoretical interest presides over the birth of dogma. For
dogma arises from a need for fixed ideas in contrast to
the changing forms and manifold readjustments of the
myth and the legend. And this need is not experienced
by individuals alone. It is especially prominent when
a community has formed itself with the object of
protecting certain religious ideas and rebutting 'heresy.'
Distinctions are then demanded which were previously
neither necessary nor comprehensible. Dilemmas are
stated which could not hitherto have presented themselves, and men try to meet these dilemmas by applying
logical thought to the interpretation of tradition. When
this interpretation is approved by the religious head
of the community the dogma is completed. Thus the
concept of dogma presupposes the concept of a Church,
and rests on a peculiar admixture of reflection and
authority.

As long as a dogma lives we can always trace
the affective interest which was astir at the inception
of the myths or legends which lie behind it. The
conclusions drawn when a dogma is formulated and
promulgated, or when it is derived from another dogma,
are by no means disinterested. There will always
be a more or less decided religious, or, at any rate,
ecclesiastical, interest at work. The ideal dogmatic
would be one in which every individual dogma sprang
immediately out of religious feeling, and where the relation
between the individual dogmas was characterised by a
felicitous logical harmony. This was the ideal set up in
the nineteenth century by Schleiermacher and Newman.

But it is an ideal which was not possible in this definite form until a sharp distinction had been drawn and emphasised by modern psychology between knowing and feeling. The history of dogma shows us that strict logical thought and pure religious feeling were not the only forces in operation. Association of ideas pure and simple, as well as ecclesiastical interest in obtaining and instituting homogeneity in doctrine and cult, played their part in deciding the direction of dogmatic development, not to mention more 'human' motives which also co-operated. Dogma, then, is a product of very manifold elements (cf. § 60).

A striking distinction has been drawn between dogmas of the first grade, which express as immediately as possible a religious experience, and dogmas of the second grade, which serve partly to unite together those of the first grade, partly to bring these into touch with the external environment.[94] In the dogmatic theology of Christianity, the dogma of the Trinity may be quoted as an example of a dogma of the second grade; it associates ideas which have been formed of God, of Jesus, and of the spirit prevailing in the community. We might even go on to speak of dogmas of the third grade. These would be such as guaranteed the truth of the first two groups of dogmas. Amongst such would rank the dogma of the Church, and those of the infallibility of the Pope and of the Bible. These dogmas of the third grade exhibit a tendency, easily explicable by psychology, to extend themselves at the cost of the first two groups, or at any rate to press more and more into the foreground, so that men can only come into contact with the first two degrees by means of the third.

70. The difference between dogma on one side and myth and legend on the other rests, according to our preceding argument, mainly on the fact that dogma presupposes reflection and authority. But this distinction

is by no means absolute.   Even in myth and legend we
often find traces of reflection, although it expresses itself
in a more subordinate, naïve and sporadic manner.
Neither is the element of authority altogether absent
from myth and legend.   For myths and legends only
flourish in a community in which the need of communication finds vent, and can invest imagination with
life and power to produce intuitable forms.   And they
are carried on by tradition from generation to generation,
a fact which invests them, in addition to the importance
they owe to their subject-matter, with a special stamp of
venerability.   This venerability procures for them immediate adoption, and is the secret of the strength of
the resistance which historical criticism encounters when
trying to get back to the origin of the whole psychical
process.

On the other hand, dogma is not altogether lacking in the characteristic of intuitableness, which is so
prominent a feature of legends and myths.   The need
for images lies deep in the nature of all religion, although
it is not necessarily favourable to the production of external and artistic images.   In dogma this need works side
by side with the need for the definiteness and limitation
which only concepts can ensure.   Every image (logically
considered) points beyond itself and has (psychologically
considered) a tendency to bring other images in its
train ; moreover, every image is at fault when it tries to
express a content which is in itself not intuitable, for then
every likeness limps.   Hence the content of legends
and myths preserves itself in the form of dogma.   But
the figurative element does not thereby vanish away, as
a closer examination of any dogmatic concept will
convince us (cf. § 22).

From the point of view of the philosophy of religion,
therefore, we cannot admit any distinction in principle
between myth, legend and dogma, although the assertion

of such a distinction is imposed on every confessional theology in the interest of its creed. But the legend will be increasingly recognised in the future as the most important of these three forms. In essence it is the effect which has been produced on mankind by the sincerity and depth of the spiritual life of prominent and typical persons. Long after dogma has died out and myths have been made over to the literature of fairy-tale, legends will preserve their value for all serious pilgrims through life. The gospels will live long after the dogmas which are now believed to be based upon them have been thrown on one side.

It is quite comprehensible that when its ideas have once crystallised into dogmas, and these—in virtue of the prestige of tradition and the results they have achieved, —have taken firm root, the religious consciousness should be averse to abandoning them. For when dogma is abandoned or regarded as nothing more than a symbol, there is no longer an absolute conclusion, nor clear-cut definiteness nor fixed haven, and men are confronted by the indefinite and the vanishing. Symbol is distinguished from dogma by the fact that it sets forth more clearly than does the latter the difference between the original actual religious experience and the ideas through which this experience expresses itself. From the philosophical point of view this is a great advantage—an advantage, it is true, which the religious consciousness does not usually admit. We might perhaps say that the difference between dogma and symbol is not so great as it often seems, and this the religious consciousness would be prepared to admit. For the religious consciousness involuntarily attributes to dogmatic truths a different kind of validity from that of scientific truths or the experiences of everyday life. We are too often led to believe that Sunday thoughts belong to another region than work-a-day thoughts, and are too apt to live in the prose of the week-day, as though Sunday thoughts were 'only' poetry. Moreover, an examination of the manner in which dogmatic ideas are applied in practical piety will show us that the application is always symbolic—this comes out especially in sermons on miracles. But however far the religious consciousness is able—either in more prosaic and ignoble, or in more idealistic form—to recognise the symbolic character of dogma, yet it always feels astonishment and vexation when this symbolical character is distinctly asserted. The definite limited horizon fades; the distinction made between the experience itself and its expression excites doubt, division and unrest; certainty is no more; it is as though a man were bidden to sew with an unknotted thread. The conception of revelation itself seems shaken, for does not this conception presuppose that there is a larger or smaller sphere in which the image and the thing in itself attain to absolute coincidence.

There is no denying, therefore, that it is an open question whether, in the absence of dogmas, symbols would suffice to maintain a religious point of view. And by symbols I do not mean only those which have become historically traditional, but also freely chosen ones, through which personal experience, liberated from the fetters of dogma, can express its new experiences— new bottles for the new wine. This is a great question, but sometimes even great questions receive an affirmative answer. The answer to this one will depend on what result we reach as to the hypothesis that the essence of all religion consists not in the solution of riddles but in the conviction that value will be preserved.

Symbols arise by a sort of analogy of feeling. A feeling which is determined by the experienced relation of value to reality seeks expression and finds it in ideas which exist as the expression of analogous experiences.

An analogy between secondary and primary judgments of value is much in evidence here (see § 31). Religious experiences are expressed by means of ideas taken from the spheres of self-preservation and surrender. A man draws his circle of ideas from his practical relations in the struggle for the primary values of life, and his religious experiences find expression in these without the formation of entirely new ideas, which would probably be an impossibility. Thus the idea of 'father' is a symbol, the use of which rests on the influence of experiences of the aid and protection which existence can grant to that which is of value to men; the idea of 'devil' is a symbol which is employed under the influence of the contrary experiences. In all symbolisation, ideas taken from narrow although more intuitable relations are used as expressions for relations which, on account of their exaltedness and ideality, cannot be directly expressed. In religious symbolism the analogy rests on the relation to feeling. But a direct and positive determination can never be reached by this kind of analogising. It can 'only' bring us as far as poetry, never to objective doctrine. I use the word 'only' advisedly, for this is how the matter is generally presented from the dogmatic point of view. I myself occupy a standpoint from which the fact that the poetic form is the only possible one is a sign that we are in the presence of the highest.

If the symbol be genuine, it springs out of immediate experience and out of the needs which this excites. Symbols are taken from all accessible spheres of human experience, but it is chiefly from the great fundamental relations of nature and of human life—light and darkness, power and weakness, life and death, spirit and matter, good and evil—that the material for symbol-making is drawn. A particular element of existence is promoted to be the most characteristic mark of the

whole of existence; it is treated as though it entirely
summed up the relation between value and reality given
in experience.

The symbolic way of looking at things regards
existence *as though* its essence were exhausted in the
one element, the one experience of a harmonious or
inharmonious relation between value and reality. There is
kinship here between the poetic symbolism of religion
and the scientific use of analogy, side by side with the
difference which I have already (§ 20) pointed out.

The need which gives rise to free symbol-making
has always lived in the heart of man. It forms the basis
of animism, and is active in myths, legends and dogmas,
in all fairy-tales, and in all art. In recognising the
symbolic element in all religious ideas, the religious
consciousness approximates to the æsthetic point of
view from which the particular individual phenomenon
also appears as typical—as a nutshell, in which the
content of a world lies hid. But it approximates still
more closely to the more primitive expressions of the
religious life in myth and legend. It shares in common
with them the immediate relation to experience and to
feeling, while it is distinguished from them through the
reflective and authoritative character of dogma. Unlike
dogmatism, the religious consciousness entertains no
mistrust of the instinctive formation of religious ideas.
If immediacy and personal sincerity are to be the sole
factors in the determination of images, the symbolic way
of looking at things sees no danger in the construction
of myths and legends. These are forms natural to the
spiritual life of man at certain definite stages of development—nay, more, they are perhaps the forms under
which the most intense spiritual production of which
man is capable outside the strictly scientific sphere is
carried on. All conscious art and speculation feed on
the content which arose originally under the form of

myths; they analyse this content and re-combine its constituent elements in new forms. Hence we may be sure that religious symbolism, if it ever succeed in breaking down the barriers of creed and dogma, will continue to borrow from the treasure contained in myths and legends. In any case, this treasure will maintain its position, even when the work of creating new symbols—a work the possibility of which cannot be denied —is being freely carried on. That the faculty of forming new symbols is to-day so weak finds its explanation partly in the fact that it has been enslaved by dogmatism, and partly that dogmatic criticism has developed analysis and doubt at the cost of free and positive production. The struggle for and against dogmas has for so long absorbed the most important spiritual forces that it may perhaps take a long time before sufficient spiritual freedom and power have developed, not only to preserve an upright posture (§ 54) in the highest questions of life, but also to perform great spiritual work in that posture—*i.e.* to shape our innermost and most essential experiences into images so powerful that we shall never be able to consign them to oblivion. The power which worked in childish fashion in myth and legend will now, having become a man, do the work of a man. This is the great hope of him whose faith is in the conservation of value, and who finds in religious phenomena values which must be preserved under new forms, when those forms under which they have hitherto usually appeared vanish away. Faith in the conservation of value rests on the conviction that, in spite of the division of labour within the spiritual sphere which has given rise to the religious problem, the real values which were possessed by the spiritual life before the division of labour took place will never be lost. This faith is analogous to the faith we put in a friend of our youth; we believe that, in spite of the disorganising and dis-

P

organised experiences of maturity, he will remain "true to the plan which pleased his childish thought," whatever metamorphoses this plan may undergo in the fires of experience.

71. To illustrate still further the way in which dogmas arise and how they pass over into symbols, we will consider some religious thought-constructions which were indeed built up under the unremitting influence of feeling, but which it is equally clear were determined by the laws peculiar to ideas. These examples will show us more particularly how ideas which at first occur in narrower and lower forms are able to suffer change, extension and transference, and to acquire ethical and cosmological significance.

But such a change, as the history of religion shows us, cannot take place under all circumstances. We get here a characteristic difference between the Romans and the Greeks. The Romans held obstinately to their special gods as they had always conceived and worshipped them. They were content as long as they had an authentic list of the gods to be worshipped, and their religious imagination was not sufficiently lively or productive to cause them to feel any need of rising above the forms which had been handed down by tradition or established as a part of their ritual. Not until they had come under Greek influence did the Romans acquire a richer mythology. Among the Greeks religious imagination attained a luxuriant growth. It had its roots in the worship of the gods and was regulated by this worship (cf. § 57). But the usages of worship were themselves taken by the imagination as motives for new ideational constructions— especially when old customs, or perhaps the lapse of old customs, seemed to need explanation. In the myth of Prometheus guilefully inducing Zeus to choose the bones of the sacrificial animal and leave him the flesh, it was felt that some explanation was necessary as to why the best part of the sacrificial animal should fall to the share of the sacrificer. A vast number of the myths of the Greeks, Romans, Hindus and Jews explain the discontinuance of an earlier human sacrifice by saying that the gods themselves preferred the sacrifice of animals. The worship of animals expresses the feeling that the nature of the gods differs from that of men and must therefore be represented under non-human forms. And the animal form becomes gradually so depreciated that it is no longer taken for a real picture of the god but represents a companion of the god only. We find a remnant of animal-worship wherever a god is represented with organs or qualities (few or many) of an animal; in such cases, of course, the significance of these organs or qualities is purely symbolic. The worship of the light of heaven and, at a later stage, of the sun is motivated by the symbolic significance of light, as the expression of purity, truth and salvation.[95]

An interesting example—perhaps the most interesting in the history of religion—of the transition from liturgy to *cosmology* occurs in the already mentioned (§ 53) conception of Brahma as the principle of all existence. For Brahma signifies the magical power of prayer, of the lively wish. Here the motive of the transition from liturgy to cosmology lies in the magical power ascribed to prayer : who can rightly pray receives power over the gods ; hence prayer, or the power which finds expression in prayer, must be the real world-power. Even the gods know this : they fear the man who is powerful in prayer, and they pray themselves. The power of prayer, therefore, becomes the god of gods. Later (in the Upanishads) there is a fresh transition (cf. § 61) from cosmology to *psychology*, for Brahma is here identified with the soul which each man knows in his own breast. In both these transitions, in that from liturgy to cosmology as well as that from cosmology to psychology, the force in operation is the need of assurance that the innermost ground of the world is one with the highest goal of all striving or that it is itself a striving.[96]   When the last step was finally taken in the Hindu religion, *i.e.* when every name and every thought were declared inadequate, free religious symbolisation lay so extra-ordinarily near at hand that we can only explain the fact that it never came into force by circumstances peculiar to the state of culture at that time in India.   At this point of Indian evolution we find either mere repetition of what had been before, or stagnation, or else a relapse into fetichism and polytheism.   There is no necessity to suppose that this need be the case under all circumstances.

In the opinion of some inquirers, the idea of a final judgment and a future kingdom of God as presented in post-exilic Judaism can only be explained through the influence of Persian ideas.   But even if we are inclined to embrace this view, which has recently been ex-haustively defended by Erik Stave, yet we must remember that the adopted ideas suffered a change, both in form and meaning, in virtue of the deeper con-ception of the evil of the world and of the attitude of men thereto which had already formed itself in the Jewish mind.   The Persian dualism no doubt possessed an ethical character, but this had grown up together with more external elements.   The struggle with evil in Parseeism was indeed partly a liturgical or magical battle, for it was carried on by means of prayer, sacrifice, and purification, but to a great extent it was a work of agriculture, for the evil in nature had to be driven out by husbandry, breeding of cattle, and the extinction of beasts of prey.   The ethical element does not yet come out as clearly as it did—even before the adoption of the Persian ideas—in the best of the Israelitish people.   For the dreamers in the land of Israel the whole question was essentially one of the inner life, and their expectation increasingly turned towards a purely spiritual deliverance.[97] The conception of the kingdom of God became more and more ethical in character.

This conception gradually developed until it became the basis of an entire world-conception ; that is to say, it was no longer of national and ethical significance only, it had also cosmological significance. This was only possible under the influence of rabbinistic and Greek speculation, and when the dogmas of the Christian Church were definitely established, Greek speculation did, as a matter of fact (together, as Harnack has pointed out, with Roman jurisprudence), supply the conceptual forms employed. Plato and Aristotle would hardly have recognised their own concepts as they were applied by the scholastics and fathers of the Church. The intellectual needs of the Christian Church, under the given conditions, however, were satisfied with this 'heathen' thought, or what was then regarded as such. In this dogmatic evolution, interesting as it is from many points of view, we look in vain for the power and inward energy of thought which led the Hindus from liturgy to cosmology, from cosmology to psychology, and from psychology to the very limits of all thought. In 'Christian thought' it is only too evident that the forms employed are alien. Nor does this thought challenge criticism only by its eclecticism, its external choosing and piecing together, the weakness of which has been exposed to light by the history of dogma. The critical history of dogma presses its inquiry back to the idea which the theologians of the day hoped to complete and establish by means of classical ideas ; the idea, namely, of a necessary connexion between faith in the historical personality of the Saviour on the one hand, and certain speculative theories as to the essence and working of the deity in time and in eternity on the other. This connexion is disputed by modern critical theology, which maintains that a great work of redaction is needed in order to disengage the ethical and religious elements of Christianity. I shall revert to this point in a future context.

As a last example of the construction of religious ideas and their relation to dogma, I will take the history of 'natural' religion so-called.

'Natural religion' is the result of attempts at a redaction of positive religion. Such attempts have been made at various times by the Stoics and popular philosophers of antiquity and by the so-called deists of the sixteenth, seventeenth and eighteenth centuries. It retains certain dogmatically constructed ideas (especially those of a personal god and of personal immortality) and regards them as 'reasonable' or else as immediate experiences. Even where—as with Kant and his disciples —the important step is taken of considering all religious ideas as symbolical, yet the dogmatic tendency can still be traced in the conviction that certain definite symbols— generally indeed those which 'natural' religion furnishes —are the only ones that are valid, 'necessary' and 'right.'[98] In principle, however, natural religion is confronted by the same problem that positive religion has to face, *i.e.* the problem as to the connexion between ethical and psychological ideas and cosmical reality, or between value and reality. When it is said that certain symbols are truer than others, this can logically only mean that they have greater value for us because they rest on analogies which lie nearer us.

The transition from dogma to symbol is closely bound up with the distinct recognition of the difference between feeling and idea. This distinction again (which in a less definite form was familiar to the Neo-Platonists, Augustine and the mystics) is connected with the differentiation of the intellectual life of man, which everywhere appears as the exciting cause of the religious problem. Evaluation and explanation of existence no longer simply coincide ; explanation does not necessarily follow on evaluation, nor evaluation on explanation.

This differentiation again is mainly conditioned by the appearance of the modern scientific conception of the world. The extension to infinity of the world-system which followed as a necessary result from the Copernican astronomy made it impossible to continue to regard human life and ideas as the pivot of existence, while the clearer apprehension of the difference between the spiritual and material which the Cartesian philosophy effected led to a criticism of animism on which religion had always leant. Then came critical philosophy with its examination of the nature and limits of knowledge, and this, as far as the intellectual element of religion is concerned, marked a distinct turning-point.

All the more pressingly, therefore, does the question recur : what is the really essential element in religion, and how far can this maintain itself in existence under the conditions of modern spiritual life?

D. THE AXIOM OF THE CONSERVATION OF VALUE

> Das Sein ist ewig, denn Gesetze
> Bewahren die lebendigen Schätze,
> Aus welchen sich das All geschmückt.
>
> GOETHE.

72. I have already in the preceding sections referred in several places to a definite hypothesis as to the essential content of all religious myths, legends, dogmas and symbols. I maintained that the fundamental axiom of religion, that which expresses the innermost tendency of all religions, is the axiom of the conservation of value. If this view be correct, the religious problem presents an interesting analogy with all other fundamental problems.

That which within the different spheres of human thought
is always setting thought in motion is the relation between
the unity and the manifold, or between continuity and
difference or change. If the possibility of asserting the
conservation of value forms its essence, the religious
problem is only a special form of a great riddle which
splits up into different forms within the special spheres.
The axiom of the conservation of value is likewise a
form of the principle of the continuity of existence. It
is analogous to the axiom of causality, for it too, in its
own way, asserts an inner continuity of existence in spite
of all differences and changes. But it presents a still
more striking analogy with the axiom of the persistence
of energy, which asserts an interconnexion of nature
underlying the inter-play of natural forces. This
analogy with other axioms and problems is of course
not enough in itself to prove that the axiom in question
is really the religious axiom. It favours this view, however, since we are entitled to suppose—on the ground of
the identity of human consciousness with itself in all
spheres—that all the problems which present themselves
to men have features in common. The considerations
which I have already brought forward in the preceding
sections might seem sufficient to maintain the assertion
that the axiom of the conservation of value is the religious
axiom, but its proof does not rest only on these ; it is
specially psychological in character. I have attempted
to show, by a description and analysis of religious experiences and of religious faith, that this axiom meets religious
need, since this need consists in the desire to hold fast to
the conservation of the highest values beyond the limits
which experience exhibits and in spite of all the transformations which experience reveals. Or, in other words,
faith is fidelity, and the content of faith is that fidelity
prevails throughout existence. Fidelity is conservation,
continuity throughout all changes (cf. §§ 34 and 44). In

this proof it is taken for granted that the description and analysis of religious experience given above is correct. But even if this were admitted, the proof given above would still be inconclusive. We need an objective, historical confirmation, a demonstration that the actually occurring forms of religion, especially the great positive religions in their essential content, are based on the axiom of the conservation of value as their ultimate presupposition. Such an historical verification of the axiom I shall now attempt to give, but first (to complete what was said in Section A on religious experience and religious faith) I must determine my axiom more nearly. If it should prove that history confirms what our purely psychological inquiry led us to assume, I shall then go on to discuss the possibility of holding fast to the axiom of the conservation of value from a standpoint which lies outside all positive religion.

(*a*) Nearer Determination of the Axiom of the Conservation of Value and its Relation to Experience

73. Religion presupposes that men have discovered by experience that there is something valuable. Whatever a man may mean by religion, he must admit that it did not itself from the very beginning create all values. If, for example, he believes in a future life of good or evil, he must know from his own experience that good and evil exist ; otherwise his faith would have no meaning for him. And before a man can attribute certain excellent qualities to his god, he must have learnt to know both the qualities and their value in his own experience, for in the absence of such knowledge there would be no connexion between a man's religious state and his other states, or, in other words, between his religion and the whole of the rest of his life.

The content of religion is always dependent on the experience of man, and more especially on what he has found valuable. *What* values a man finds depends again on what motives prompt him in estimating existence. This motive may be a merely momentary need, which is soon pressed into the background by another need ; or it may lie in a deep and ceaseless striving, which is one with the instinct of self-preservation. It may be conditioned by man as a single isolated being, in which case it is stamped with an individualistic or even egoistic character, or it may arise because a man cannot separate his own fate, his individual weal and woe, from the great web of things, in which he feels himself a member of a great group of men, a partaker in wide and common interests. The values in the conservation of which a man believes will be those which he regards as the highest. These, however, differ widely in different cases, among different men living under different historical conditions. The Greenlander's belief in the conservation of value differs widely from the Greek's, the Hindu's from the Christian's. The egoist and the voluptuary may have their heaven as well as the ethical idealist, or he whose life is spent in the worship of the beautiful ; these heavens, however, will be very different. Strictly speaking, such differences do not here concern us, for our task is to discover the element which is common to all religions—to pierce to that which makes us attribute a religion to the Greenlander as well as to the Greek, to the Hindu as well as to the Christian. The opposition between ‘lower’ and ‘higher’ values is, no doubt, of great importance for religion ; it is in virtue of it that we distinguish between nature religions and ethical religions, and between higher and lower forms of the latter (cf. §§ 32 and 35). But it cannot decide the question as to the fundamental religious axiom.

Since all religion presupposes the experience of values, religious values must themselves in a certain sense (cf. § 31) be derived, *i.e.* conditioned, by interest in the primary values which our experience of life has taught us to know and to maintain. Religion presupposes the special experience that the fate of values is at stake in the battle of existence. A psychical life of the most elementary kind cannot know religious values; it is limited to the simplest forms of self-assertion and self-surrender. An animal cannot (probably) be religious because it cannot (probably) have experiences of the fate of its values in the world.

As I have already had occasion to remark, however, it does not follow that because religious values are secondary in comparison with other values, there must always be an interval of time between the experiences in which they manifest themselves and those in which the primary values assert themselves. Primary values often arise in a religious form from the outset, so that the two kinds of experience are made simultaneously. The distinction is reached by an abstraction or differentiation which need not necessarily occur. It is quite conceivable that I may immediately apprehend some new beauty in nature as a testimony to the splendour of existence; primary value and religious value—beauty as such, and existence as making beauty possible—are then revealed to me at one blow. And even when the difference between primary and religious values makes itself felt, the religious value may still retain its immediacy and independence. It is not necessary that the object of faith should only appear as a means to maintaining the primary values in existence. It may itself appear as the highest good, as the object of immediate admiration, enthusiastic worship, confidence and love. The distinction between lower and higher religions will depend on whether the religious values appear as mediate only, or whether they are given immediately (cf. § 3). The transition from lower to higher forms sometimes, as in other spheres, takes place by means of a readjustment of motives and values. A thing which at first had value only as a means may afterwards acquire value as an end, and that which was originally taken as an end may produce effects which far surpass itself in value. Such readjustments are of the utmost importance not only within the ethical,[99] but also within the religious sphere. The continuity of the religious development of mankind is largely due to them. The transition from the most ancient Judaic worship of Jahve to the belief in God as a Father was effected by a great process of readjustment, reinforced by important historical and personal events. The religious consciousness often wavers between mediate and immediate values. When Augustine says to his God, " I seek thee *in order that* my soul may live," he attributes in this utterance only mediate value to the object of his faith ; but when in other utterances he speaks of God as the highest or only good, as goodness and truth itself, the object of his faith appears invested with immediate values. According to Spinoza, ' the intellectual love of God ' arises when the full understanding of our own ego and of its unity with the whole of existence gives rise to deep intellectual joy, which is united with the idea of God (the unitary principle of existence) as its cause ; but if we steep ourselves in this thought we shall see that in understanding, in intellectual joy and in intellectual love, God himself is active, so that the merely mediate relation vanishes. All mysticism asserts, in contradistinction from the external, mechanical and dualistic character of ordinary orthodoxy, the immediate character of religious values. The principle of the conservation of value within existence is at length seen to contain the highest value. And it is in virtue of this that religion reacts on the other sides of spiritual life,

and can take up a position of more or less opposition
to them.   Reciprocal action takes place between the
primary and secondary values, which makes the religious
problem especially involved.   It is often difficult, in any
given case, to decide what is original and what secondary.
Further, when the form under which the conservation of
value appears itself possesses immediate value, it increases
the sum of values the conservation of which is under
discussion, and thus the conservation of religion becomes
a part of the religious problem.   It is not sufficient to
show that the primary values would suffer no loss through
the disappearance of positive religions ; for in their fall
they would take with them other immediate values, and
we should have to be prepared to point out equivalents
for these before we could assert that positive religion
might vanish from the spiritual life of man without
causing any loss.   If it were possible to demonstrate
these equivalents, we should have a confirmation of
the validity of the religious axiom.   The continuity
of value would be preserved, so that if this be
the essential element of religion, 'the purest element
of religion' would continue to exist even if positive
religion were to disappear (cf. end of § 31).   This
reflection reveals to us alike the inevitableness and the
deep significance of the religious problem, irrespective
of the attitude adopted towards the existing forms of
religion.

74. We possess much that is valuable which we do
not enjoy uninterruptedly.   A state which makes us
happy need not exist uninterruptedly at its full strength.
There are pauses which do not necessarily signify that
the melody has ceased ; they may be only temporary
cessations, or stages of rest or of preparation.   The
pause is itself a member of the melodic series and produces therein the effect peculiar to itself.   Such a pause
can only be appreciated by a consciousness which pre-

serves continuity with what has preceded and goes on to experience that which follows. The man who only comes at the beginning of the pause experiences nothing; for him the pause is a cipher. Similarly, the man who goes away before the pause is resolved into the succeeding tones gets the impression of an absolute conclusion. The pauses in the world-course may last very long, and only he who is able to weave them into their inner connexion with what went before and what follows after can understand their value and rest assured that they are something more than mere interruptions. Whether, in any particular case, we have a pause or an absolute ending is perhaps an insoluble problem. If continuity is to be asserted it can only be by the help of faith. It may seem as if we have a case of absolute loss of value.

If we are to assert continuity in such cases, we must avail ourselves of the distinction between potential and actual value (cf. § 3). Faith in the conservation of value does not presuppose that there must always be an equal amount of actual value in existence, but only that there must always be the same possibility for the coming into being of value. But were all values to become potential the result would be indistinguishable from a state of dead equilibrium. Possibilities would become impossibilities. The special forms of religious faith acquire their distinctive character in virtue of the relation between the actual and potential values in existence which they presuppose. Thus, where men assume that potential values will be realised without any very bitter struggle, their faith takes on a cheerful and optimistic character; when, on the other hand, they incline to the belief that existence is woven of such tragi-comic stuff that the riches of potential values which, in and for itself, it contains can never be realised, or that every particular process of realisation will involve a disproportionate destruction of values at other points, it becomes dark and pessimistic.

In order completely to establish and verify the axiom of the conservation of value, it would be necessary to show that nothing in the course of the world is merely a means or a possibility, still less a mere hindrance, but that, on the contrary, that which possesses mediate worth has always immediate value also, and that all hindrances are also means. We cannot expect to find any historical religion which has ever either formulated or even tacitly understood the axiom in this absolute form. But were we entitled to assert that the religion which took this idea as its basis would be the ideal religion, we should obtain a confirmation of our hypothesis. And if it should prove that we must make this ideal our criterion in estimating the value of different religions, if it should prove that prominent religious personalities thought the greatest reproof that could be brought against their religion was that it did not satisfy this ideal, our hypothesis would certainly obtain confirmation. More than a striving towards the carrying out of this ideal we must not expect to find in any of the religions presented to us in history. But when it is claimed for any one of these religions that it is the absolute religion, *i.e.* the complete expression of all which makes up the essence of religion, we must inquire whether this claim is not based on the fact that this religion professes completely to fulfil the axiom of the conservation of value, to carry out this axiom not merely more perfectly than any other religion but in such a manner that nothing is to be found at any point within it which does not harmonise with the axiom or is not demanded by it.

It is particularly interesting to note that the ideal form of the axiom of the conservation of value presents an analogy with the highest ethical principle and may even be regarded as a kind of extension of it. The ethical ideal—where this is based on universal sympathy —appears in the guise of a kingdom of humanity in which every particular personality appears as an end and never merely as a means,[100] *i.e.* always as possessing immediate value, never mediate or potential value only. Just as this ethical ideal may be traced with more or less clearness as a presupposition or, at any rate, as a tendency in the special ethical rules and laws and at different stages of development, so this ideal form of the axiom of the conservation of value within existence appears with more or less clearness as presupposition or as tendency in the special forms of religion. And should it subsequently prove that the final measure of value for all religions is of an ethical nature, the importance of this analogy between the religious axiom and the highest ethical principle would be vindicated, for it gives us, even here, a hint that religion tends to appear as a projection of the ethical.

Each particular religion will, of course, attribute especial importance to the form under which the religious axiom appears in its own teaching and worship. It will be inclined to confuse the garment with the person, or at any rate to regard the garment as part of the person. It is no contradiction of the assertion that the axiom of the conservation of value is the fundamental axiom of religion, to find some particular religion refusing to admit that other religions, after their own manner, revere and express the same axiom. For this axiom may be thrown into many different forms, and can be expressed by myths, legends, dogmas or symbols of widely different character. But, from the philosophical point of view, we have to distinguish between the axiom itself and the different modes in which it is expressed. The burden of proof, at any rate, lies with those who assert that the axiom admits of only a single definite expression.

The axiom which is to express the essence of religion under all its different forms must necessarily be abstract in character. Hence it is important not to confuse the axiom as framed by the philosophy of religion with ideas which arise and make themselves felt immediately and clearly within the religious consciousness. It is not necessary for the religious consciousness to be acquainted with the axiom in its abstract form ; it may perhaps even reject it in this form. The ordinary human consciousness may be unaware of the laws of the association of ideas, but this fact is quite compatible with the assertion that these laws underlie every association of ideas which takes place within that same consciousness. So we breathe without necessarily having the slightest acquaintance with the physiological laws of respiration.

It may be a characteristic of some particular positive religion that it acknowledges no other form of the conservation of value than that maintained by itself. The philosopher of religion makes a note of this trait, and it helps him to evaluate the said religion. But this fact does not shake the conviction to which he has been led by other considerations with regard to the fundamental axiom of all religion.

75. From the conviction that value will be preserved, the conviction that all existence, in respect of its conservation and its special forms, is conditioned by the highest value does not necessarily follow. This conviction springs from reflection on the relation between value and reality, not from the immediate experience of their actual relation. The values in whose preservation we believe may be given in actuality without prompting at the moment any speculation as to whether reality *produces* the value or whether it exists *for the sake of* the values.

Wherever an attempt is made to deduce reality from value the religious problem is intensified. For even if it could be shown that all hindrances and all

Q

opposition are necessary means to the development and preservation of the valuable, still the questions would always arise, why any means at all should be necessary ; why the valuable should not exist and prevail immediately ; why there should be difference or strife between value and reality. In the problem of evil the religious consciousness has always to contend against this difficulty, and it is round this point, too, as we shall see, that difficulties thicken for the philosopher of religion in his attempt to show that the fundamental axiom of the conservation of value is the presupposition or tendency of all religion.

It might seem as though the hypothesis of the conservation of value were irreconcilable with a pessimistic conception of life. And were pessimism a form of religion, it would no doubt be a stumbling-block in the path of the hypothesis we are trying to establish.

Pessimism assumes a fundamental misfit between value and reality. But even a misfit is a relation, and if, according to the description given above, religious experience is concerned with the relation between value and reality, then pessimism too is based on religious experience, only this experience leads to a faith other than that which most frequently obtains in the history of religion. And yet even in pessimism there must be an underlying faith in the conservation of value, for were all value to disappear, the relation between value and reality must necessarily disappear also. The pessimist is compelled to admit that there is something valuable in the world, but he asserts that this value can only be preserved at the cost of hard struggle and unceasing suffering, and he devotes his attention entirely to this struggle and suffering. Struggle and suffering presuppose life and the need of self-assertion. Could all life and all need be excluded from existence there would no longer be room for pessimism. In Leopardi's poem

La Ginestra the relation between man and pitiless nature is described under the relation of the plant to the lava on which it grows If the lava were one day to burn or overwhelm the plant the struggle would be over.   The life of the plant is the value, the opposition of which to rude reality evoked or expressed the mood of the poet.   And since Leopardi, notwithstanding his strong emphasis of the want of harmony between value and reality, does not propose (any more than Schopenhauer and Buddha) to meet the difficulty by the destruction of life, *i.e.* by destroying the valuable in order to get rid of the discord, there must be an underlying faith in the possibility of the valuable being preserved in spite of the constant struggle and suffering.   An absolute pessimism has never yet been developed either in religion or philosophy.   Buddha points to the possibility of attaining Nirvana (which must not be confounded with extinction), and Schopenhauer looks for the solution of the discord to artistic and scientific activity, sympathy and religious asceticism.[101] In all pessimism there is a value which exists, which can assert itself and even perhaps increase.   An absolute pessimism would only hold good for those whom some religions condemn to an eternity of pain.   But in no religion is this eternal pain the only content, and, as we shall see later, characteristic attempts have been made to show that the highest value persists not merely in spite of but precisely in virtue of this eternal pain in a part of existence.   Such attempts, which are the outcome of the meditations of distinctly religious natures, testify to the historical validity of our religious axiom.

We can conceive a pessimism which should believe in a continual diminution of value within existence.   This view too would be determined by religious experience (see § 31), although it might be lacking in religious faith (see § 34).   If we wanted to emphasise the continual tendency to the shrinkage of values we might call such a pessimism ' religion with negative signs.' The complete opposite of all religion would be neither pessimism nor optimism, but neutralism ; all valuation within the sphere of human action would fall away, and in the conviction of its infinite indifference towards everything which they call ' value,' men would be mere spectators of the great process of the world. In my opinion, it is very difficult to decide if such a neutralism can really exist. Even in a mere spectator a mood tinged by religion would arise during every intellectual or æsthetic (to say nothing of ethical) state of mind ; existence is invested with a peculiar value by the fact that the comprehension or sight of it causes us joy, and our conception of the world is involuntarily coloured by the progress or decay of such intellectual or æsthetic values.

(b) Psychological and Historical Discussion of the Axiom of the Conservation of Value

76. In historical religions we find faith in the conservation of value appearing in two different forms. We meet here with the same leading forms that we have already encountered (§ 43) in our description of religious experience and religious faith. In essence they are not altogether antagonistic, and historically we find them influencing each other at many points ; but still they may be taken as typical forms of religion, since the different religious standpoints and specialised forms approximate more or less decidedly to one or other of them. As it would be impossible to investigate all specialised forms of religion and all religious standpoints, we must restrict ourselves to these two types, in the confidence that the religious life has expressed itself through them in all its most characteristic features. Before I discuss each one in detail, I will give a brief characterisation of both of them.

According to one type the highest value is always actually present. It is hidden from men's sight by the many-coloured manifold and the continual flux of the empirical world, as also by illusions of the reality of the sensuous, in which illusions men become entangled. With the disappearance of these illusions—which is the presupposition of all serious activity of thought and will —men become clear as to the eternal reality, and as to their immediate unity with it. The manifold (at any rate the external, sensuous manifold) entirely vanishes ; the temporal relation loses its significance, and the valuable reveals itself as the only thing that exists always and has always existed, as the one true reality.

According to the other type the valuable only maintains itself by means of continual struggle with forces which try to check and to destroy it. In addition to this it must pass through an evolution before it exists in all its fulness ; it has a history. Only when the historical development of the world has run its course will the valuable be all in all to all men. The temporal relation here acquires real and decisive significance ; it is no illusion, as it was for the first type, to vanish away on a true understanding. New values actually arise, and the work necessary to participation in existing values is just as much a reality as the goal which is reached by means of the work.

77. The first type is represented historically in the Vedantist doctrines of the Hindus, in Buddhism, in Platonism, in mediæval mysticism and in the system of Spinoza. The conservation of value is here asserted in the statement that that which is given in time in a scattered manifold and in gradual evolution is concentrated in eternity into an absolute unity. Eternity is not here conceived as lying *beyond* time, but *in* time, and it unveils itself within the consciousness of man when he attains to the deepest self-absorption. This

type is logically driven to assume that between time and eternity there is a relation of equivalence; but this relation of equivalence could itself have no history, since all temporal distinctions lose their significance; hence the struggle to participate in the eternal must also be unreal.

We might think that this type could never lend itself to a popular religion. And yet the Greek religion of Homer's day may be traced back in its essential features to this type, although it there appears in a very childish form. To the Homeric Greek, Olympus stood amid the pains and struggles of this life in eternal clarity, unmoving and unmoved. Olympus is the eternal and fixed abode of the gods, ringed about with light, raised high above the regions visited by storms and rain. In this brilliant picture the Greeks saw the expression of the eternal reality of the valuable, and in its splendour they forgot the shadow of their own life; or they accepted in sadness and resignation the contrast between the Olympian and the terrestrial as something that had to be.

Here we have a naïve but unconquerable opposition between time and eternity. In the Buddhist doctrine of Nirvana we get a more interior and more deeply conceived relation. As we have already several times remarked, Nirvana is not to be confounded with pure non-existence. It is a state of peace and exaltation, the antithesis of all desire, hate and disappointment which flourish in the world of sensuous illusion. It is a state in which holiness is brought to perfection; the work is done, and 'this world' no longer exists. In order to reach this state, the individual must cut himself loose from ordinary human relations; but this is done with the deepest interior joy:

> As swans fly far from muddy mere,
> E'en so whate'er the spirit cloys
> In house and home, its cares and joys,
> The wise man, spurning, comes not near.

> Calm in the freedom of his cell,
> The monk, with sight undimmed by care,
> Securely sees all truth laid bare ;
> Beyond all earth-born he fares well.
>
> Ever with greater joy his eye
> This changing life-in-death sees through,
> Till flashes on his raptured view
> The splendour of eternity.[102]

We find a kindred line of thought in the Greek world, viz. in Plato. The world of ideas is the only true reality, and everything depends on the knowledge of these ideas (of the essence of things and their archetypes) being disclosed to men ; not till then can they be free from all division and all imperfection. This type appears most characteristically in the *Phaedo*. Through Platonism it has also influenced Christianity, which belongs for the most part to the other type. In the Gospel of St. John we get indications of a tendency in the direction of the first, the Indo-Greek type, but it is not certain that this is due to any direct influence from the latter. On the other hand, in the case of Augustine such an influence is as clear as it is certain. We find in him the Platonic concept of the eternal as the unchangeable (*semper stans aeternitas*), which exists at all times in an equally high degree, and in which nothing arises or passes away. This concept meets us again in mediæval mysticism, for we find, *e.g.*, Meister Eckhart saying " What is eternity? Eternity is a present now, that knows nothing of time. The day of a thousand years ago is not further from eternity than this hour in which I stand here, and the day which is to come a thousand years hence is no further from eternity than the hour in which I now speak." This idea, too, underlies Jacob Boehme's motto : " He for whom time is as eternity and eternity as time is freed from all struggle " ; and Spinoza's deep counsel to consider things *sub specie aeternitatis*.[108]

It cannot be denied that these different standpoints, each in its own way, proclaim the imperishability of all true value. Nevertheless a difficulty arises on a nearer investigation of the relation between 'time' and 'eternity.' If the axiom of the conservation of value is to be strictly interpreted, 'time' and 'eternity' must stand to one another in a relation of equivalence, must be two forms of value between which an exchange can take place without loss. But this is not the case. For from all these standpoints 'time' is regarded as resting on an illusion, on an illusion which must dissolve into nothingness when the true value—not arises, but—discloses itself. For this reason work and evolution in time, however necessary they may be, can have no real significance, no reality, but must be regarded as the efforts we make in dreams. Even the labour employed in destroying the illusion, in making the dream-picture sink into the nothing which it is in order that we may live in the true reality, is itself an illusion. At the best such work can only be regarded as a means to be forgotten when the end is attained, as a ladder which we push away when we have climbed up. Hence from these standpoints no immediate and independent value can be attributed either to work and development, or to the goods and the tasks which the world of time offers to us.

We look in vain, too, for any natural motive which would induce an individual to set other aims before himself than his own personal deliverance from illusion. If an individual has himself reached perfection, has torn away the veil of illusion, why should he linger longer in this illusory world, even though by so doing he could help other men to attain a perfection similar to that which he has himself won? Why should the swan return to the 'muddy mere'? When Buddha attained perfection in spite of all the hindrances laid in his way by the spirit of evil (Mara, the devil of

Buddhism), the latter begged him at any rate not to show to other men the way to perfection which he had discovered. Buddha did not obey, partly 'out of sympathy with the world'; but partly also because it did no violence to his perfection to impart it to other men.   In and for itself, however, the inevitable inference, as is admitted both by Buddha himself and in the Buddhistic poem *Dhammapadan* (The Way to Truth), is that he who will attain the highest, *i.e.* deliverance from trouble and fear, dare love no man, since separation from loved ones causes pain.[104]

In addition to this dualism of time and eternity, a second dualism besets these standpoints. For not all men attain Nirvana; hence Buddhism was constrained either to develop a doctrine of hell for itself or to borrow it from the popular faith.   Nor is it given to every man to know the Platonic eternal ideas, or, with Spinoza, to be able to view all things *sub specie aeternitatis.*   Under one form or another there reappears the old Greek opposition between the ever-shining Olympus (which corresponds to Nirvana, to the world of ideas, and to the point of view of the eternal) and the gloomy world of men.   Only a few, the darlings of the gods, can rise above this opposition. For the most part, there is a loss in values along the whole line.

Hence, with regard to this first type, we reach the result that the axiom of the conservation of value is a tacit presupposition; but that, when the different standpoints are more specifically developed, it is not unfolded with complete consistency. The reproach which therefore attaches to this type, *i.e.* that the axiom of the conservation of value is only partially carried out, is, however, no external reproach.   It is the result of the application of a standard of measurement which is acknowleged by this type of religion itself.   Human life outside Olympus and Nirvana is, after all, not

absolutely worthless : the Greek has his childlike joy in
life ; the Buddhist must at least attribute real value to
the striving to transcend time which leads to Nirvana.
Hence Olympus and Nirvana cannot logically assume
the attitude of the sole privileged, uplifted above the
happenings of this finite world, for without a living and
positive union with this world their significance as the
highest value would fall to the ground.   We are here
measuring religion by religion, for we are taking the
particular traits of a religious standpoint and comparing
them with the goal which it has itself adopted.   Religion
is open to attacks from without, from standpoints which
are alien to its innermost aims, its deepest tendencies ;
but such a criticism would not help us to discover the
religious axiom, the fundamental axiom which religion
cannot deny without denying itself.   If the axiom of
the conservation of value is an axiom which no religion
can deny without denying itself, then this axiom is the
fundamental axiom of religion.

78. The other leading type is distinguished by its
historical character.   It believes in a world - history.
This historical character appeared in distinctive form
first in Parseeism.   The struggle between good and evil
pervades all nature as well as human life, and the
attention is concentrated on a great world-struggle, on
the expiration of which perfection will ensue.   Among
the Jewish prophets we find an independent historical
belief, which had grown up under the influence of their
innermost need to hold fast to the hope of the future
of their nation and the conviction of the faithfulness of
God throughout all change.   Out of the stress of time they
looked forward to a day when they would be able to
shout, " Lo this is our God ; we have waited for him,
and he will save us " (Is. xxv. 9).   " The Lord Jehovah
is everlasting strength " (Is. xxvi. 4).   In the Messianic
expectations of post-exilic Judaism and in the Christian

doctrine of the kingdom of God and its speedy coming, the same historical faith is expressed. It is this which has imparted to the whole trend of European thought its peculiar character. Augustine's *Civitas Dei* and Bossuet's *Discours sur l'histoire universelle* form the religious prolegomena to what has been called in later times philosophy of history, sociology, or the history of culture.

The temporal relation here acquires positive and determinative significance. The distinction between past, present, and future is no longer based on an illusion, and definite tasks are set which can only be carried out by means of labour and development. There is a real 'not yet,' as there is also a 'no longer.' The highest is realised in the flux of time and at different stages of development. A comparison between the Upanishads and the New Testament is most instructive in this respect. While there could here be no question of equivalence between time and eternity, there is an equivalence between past and future; life is gained when it is lost; that which has been sacrificed will be repaid a thousandfold; Jesus is not come to destroy but to fulfil; the kingdom was prepared from the beginning of the world, but is an inheritance only just entered upon. Not even suffering and death militate against the conservation of value; for it is precisely by suffering in the service of the highest, with the eye fixed upon it, that we can witness to its power. "Victor because victim" (*victor quia victima*), cries Augustine to his Redeemer.

And the idea of the kingdom to come includes not only the significance of history, but also that of solidarity, of life in common, and the possibility of a more positive form of brotherly love than any which Buddhism could logically include within itself. The perfection of the individual is bound up with the perfection of others.

Hence the prevailing character of this type is more

realistic than that of the first ; and this involves a greater possibility of carrying out the principle of the conservation of value, since the empirical world and its relations no longer appear as mere dross from which all valuable ore is absent. The advantage which the second type possesses over the first is associated with the fact that it admits of a more complete carrying out of the axiom of the conservation of value.

If the proof of this axiom is even here still attended with difficulties, they are summed up in the fact that, though labour and development in time appear as realities, as a matter of fact they are only means. They have only mediate, no immediate value. They are only a preparation for what is to come ; and that which is to come—the kingdom of God—does not come as a natural and necessary result of development and of labour, but is suddenly and supernaturally intercalated in time, so that the bond between past and future is broken. Nor can there be said to be any relation of inner equivalence between them, for, in comparison with that great thing which is to come, human labour is of vanishing importance ; it may, indeed, be merely a hindrance. Labour becomes negative. We must not become absorbed in human relations, in the goods and business of human life, but must watch and pray so as to be ready when the time of fulfilment comes. Life in time becomes a life of expectation, and that alone has value which can serve as a preparation for the future life. Here we get a certain similarity between Christianity (the primitive Christianity, that is to say) and Buddhism, for to deny the essential continuity between past and future, and to regard the temporal relation as altogether illusory, may lead in practice to the same results.

But there are other points in this type at which the proof of the axiom of the conservation of value encounters difficulties ; and they are of particular interest because the religious consciousness has itself drawn attention to the fact, and has tried to get over the difficulties. It is of the greatest interest for the philosophy of religion to observe that the attempt to conquer these difficulties is made by means of the axiom of the conservation of value. It is Augustine, the greatest theologian in the history of Christianity, who makes this attempt.

The first point is the dogma of eternal punishment. It is not necessary to discuss whether this dogma can or can not be deduced from the New Testament scriptures,[105] suffice it that the orthodox teaching of the Church, protestant as well as catholic, maintains it. It would no doubt be easier to prove that Christianity is based on the presumptive truth of the axiom of the conservation of value if we could show that the teaching of the New Testament is that all men will finally be saved. But what interests us here is that this very dualism between the blessed and the damned can appear to the thinking religious consciousness as the necessary consequence of the conservation of value—the conservation, of course, of that value which is for this consciousness the highest value. Whatever fate may await the course of this world, the Christian consciousness holds fast to the conviction that it will be to the honour and glory of God. Augustine tries to establish this more definitely. Divine justice is satisfied because the evil are rewarded according to their deserts and are brought to their own place. Indeed Augustine goes so far as to defend this dualism, not only as as ethically but also as æsthetically necessary. If the world's history is to conclude with the eternal damnation of the many, it might seem as though this involved an imperfection in the final state of existence ; " But," says Augustine, " that which seen from the standpoint of a single part may appear imperfect and even excite horror, may from

the standpoint of the whole be a perfection ; since all that
is necessary for harmony is that everything should be in
its right place, and it may be that this very contrast
between the blessed and the damned may seem to increase the beauty of the whole " (*omnes ita ordinantur . . .
in pulchritudinem universitatis, ut quod horremus in
parte, si cum toto consideremus, plurimum placeat*).[106]
Thus the dualism which has so often been brought as a
reproach against Christianity is for Augustine a pre-
eminent witness to the conservation of the highest
ethical and æsthetic values.   There is no doubt that his
line of thought reveals an effort to hold fast to the
fundamental axiom of the conservation of value, even
against an objection which is based on the same axiom.
He tries to transform the considerations on which the
reproof was based into a confirmation of the doctrine he
is defending.   How far the concepts of value applied by
Augustine are valid is another question.   In Augustine's
own mind there was no doubt that God's blessedness
and honour were reconcilable with this dualism, indeed
even demanded it.   The deduction which has been
drawn in modern times from Augustine's premisses, viz.
that God cannot be blessed if the course of the world is
of the kind Augustine assumed it to be, was altogether
strange to Augustine himself.   Nor did it occur to him
that the knowledge that all men have not attained
blessedness could impair the blessedness of those who
had.   As far as I know, he has never touched on this
objection.   Thomas Aquinas, however, dealt with it
afterwards.   It is true, says this great scholastic, that
Aristotle teaches that no one can be happy without
having those he loves around him, but this refers only to
the earthly life ; in the eternal life the individual stands
before his God, and love to the infinite object so fills his
breast that he feels no need of loving finite beings ; only
love to God, not love to our neighbour, is necessary in a

state of blessedness, and were there but a single soul which entertained the joy of God's presence, that soul would be blessed even though it had no neighbour to love.[107]

In following such a line of thought as this we must be careful to remember that the significance which the belief in the conservation of value possesses in certain cases depends upon what values are known and presupposed. Human love cannot be reckoned among the highest values from the standpoint here under discussion, hence it is not included when the content of faith is determined. Thus we here get a confirmation of that conception of the essence of religion which I am endeavouring to establish (cf. § 73 and the preceding sections to which I there referred). Moreover, Thomas Aquinas goes on to show that there is a great difference between the feelings which a man must entertain in this life when he is still a pilgrim (*viator*) and those that will be his in a state of blessedness, when he understands the whole connexion of things (as *comprehensor*). Amongst men on earth compassion for the damned is praiseworthy, but such a feeling could not arise in the minds of the blessed, who understand God's judgments.[108] Unfortunately neither Thomas Aquinas nor any other theologian has succeeded in giving us the 'higher' psychology and ethic here implied, any more than they have been able to give us the 'higher' theory of knowledge which we saw in a previous connexion to be necessary to their point of view. They have not even succeeded in showing how a pilgrim, a viator, can attach any real sense to the 'higher' standpoint here referred to—ethical sense can certainly not be attached to it. But, as already said, all this is beside the mark for the religious axiom in its general form.

The other point at which the theological standpoint we are here considering encounters difficulties is the

dogma of creation.   While Buddhism does not commit
itself to any explanation of the origin of the 'world,'
Christian theology offers one which seems as if it might
involve the assumption of a shrinkage of value.   For
creation is less than the creator : it is finite and limited,
and there is always the possibility of a fall which does
not exist for the Creator in his eternal and ideal reality.
But here, too, Augustine finds in his concept of justice
a means of saving the conservation of value : " Who is
so mad as to dare to demand that the work shall be
equal to the producer, that which is grounded to him
who grounds? "   " It would be blasphemous levity to set
up the nothing as equal to God, which is implied by
demanding that that which God has created out of
nothing shall be of the same nature as that which has
sprung out of God's own essence ! " [109]   The shrinkage of
value involved in creation disappears for Augustine in
the satisfaction of justice ; by means of this continuity is
preserved.   We see clearly underlying the conception of
this religious thinker the axiom which, in my opinion, is
the axiom of religion.   Logically carried out, Augustine's
line of thought would lead us to a similar result as that
in which Buddhism (and the first type in general)
concludes.   God is conceived as unchangeable ; he is as
untouched by creation and the fall as by the opposition
between the blessed and the damned.   God does not
require the world, and does not change with the world's
changes.   Nor does the goodness of God imply need
and dependence, for since he is a perfect being whose
perfection can suffer no augmentation, his goodness
exists without the need of other beings.   This deduction
is drawn by Aquinas : " *Bonitas eius potest esse sine
aliis.*" [110]   With what right it can still be called ' goodness '
is another question.   We have only here to point out
that both types of religion, in spite of their indubitable
efforts to hold fast to the conservation of value, become

involved in difficulties which they are not able to overcome—difficulties in which they reveal themselves as
imperfect expressions of their own acknowledged religious
ideals.

79. To sum up—the result, up to this point, of our
inquiry into the two leading forms of religion is that
in both there is a distinct tendency to assert the conservation of value, which tendency comes out more
especially in their efforts to rebut objections which are
based on an apparent shrinkage of values.

That neither of the two leading forms succeed in
abiding strictly by the conservation of value is due in
part to the fact that historical forms of life never
completely express their own peculiar essence or idea,
because elements and relations which are not germane
to the subject are always present.   But it is also due
to a circumstance which must always be closely connected
with the essence of religion, at least if faith in the conservation of value constitutes its essence.   For it is clear
that faith in the conservation of values must requisition
forces and interests which are thus withdrawn from the
task of finding and producing values in the given world.
Hence there is always a more or less oppositional relation
between religion and the other spiritual spheres.   Since
the religious relation itself supplies a motive of valuation
and can establish values, this oppositional relation may
be regarded as an oppositional relation between primary
and secondary values (cf. §§ 31 and 73).   This comes out
with peculiar emphasis in the relation between religion
and ethics, a topic we shall discuss more nearly in the
ethical section of this work.   But in order to be able
to understand why the carrying out of the religious
axiom must always remain imperfect, it was necessary
to point out here and now that faith in the conservation
of values may easily assume a certain opposition to the
labour of the discovery and realisation of values.   In the

two leading types of religion this is illustrated in the relation to the temporal environment, the full, positive and inner validity of which is never acknowledged. For life in time appears, as we have seen, either as an illusion or as a reality of vanishing significance.

And in connexion with this we must remember that religion is inclined to proceed from far too narrow a concept of value, or from the assumption that the content of values has been discovered once and for all, so that all we now have to do is to preserve the same or to live in the conviction that it will be preserved. But so long as new experiences arise, so long new values may arise, although religion always offers a certain resistance to them, and can only gradually be induced to include them in the content which she believes will be preserved.

This is not the only way in which the inconclusiveness of experience hinders the carrying out of the religious axiom. There will always be new experiences by which this axiom must test itself. Even if we could suppose the content of value to have been completed once and for all, yet even this completed content might find itself confronted with changed relations, and the religious ideas which sufficed to express its conservation throughout the changes of earlier experiences might not, as they stand, be adequate when experiences assume another character. The religious axiom here shares the fate of all other axioms.

A last consideration of great importance in this connexion is the fact that the religious consciousness expresses itself by means of more or less figurative ideas. Only the philosophy of religion reflects on and states the axiom in the form under which we are here discussing it. In the religious consciousness it appears in concrete, figurative forms which are drawn from analogies with more or less limited relations. A glance at the different conceptions of God, theories of incarnation, theories of atonement and ideas of immortality show us that they originate in combinations of figures taken from certain special spheres of experience (*e.g.* family relations and relations of right). Small wonder that no logical line of thought can impose itself, since these images are raised above their original context and combined with others taken from quite a different context. In the attempt to erect a system of thought, the original poetical significance and influence of the figures is lost without any compensation in consistency of thought.

The hypothesis that faith in the conservation of value is the essential element of all religion has, then, sustained a critical examination as well as could have been expected.

The way for this hypothesis was already indirectly prepared in the epistemological section of this work, where it was pointed out that the meaning of religion could not be to afford a scientific explanation of existence. If religious ideas are to possess any value, it must be because they serve to give figurative form and expression to other sides of the soul's life than those which are served by intellectual ideas.

The hypothesis was justified on positive grounds by a psychological investigation of religious experience and religious faith. We saw that the relation between value and reality was the sphere in which religious experience finds its home, in distinction from other experiences which are concerned only with values or only with reality. And we saw too that religious faith is driven by its own nature to hold fast to the assumption of a constant relation between value and reality ; it is itself faithful, and it presupposes something analogous to faithfulness in existence. Thus there is an inner connexion between religious experience and religious faith on the one hand, and the assumption of the conservation of value on the other.

These purely psychological considerations appear to have been confirmed by our analysis of the two leading types of historical religions.

(c) General Philosophical Discussion of the Axiom of the Conservation of Value

80. If faith in the conservation of value is the essence of all religion, more especially of all positive religion, it will be of interest to inquire how far such a faith is reconcilable with a strictly scientific conception of the world. We must distinguish between whether it can be *reconciled* with scientific inquiry and the further question as to whether it may not even be *deduced* from this. As I have tried to show, it is not the pure need for knowledge, but the need to establish a harmony between knowledge (understanding in the scientific sense) and valuation and hence between reality and value, which leads to faith in the conservation of value. Although the motives of knowledge differ from those of valuation, yet their results may be reconcilable. If we could and ought to uphold no other views of existence than those which scientific inquiry can construct and prove, then the axiom of the conservation of value must fall to the ground. Science is not in a position to produce out of itself a religious faith. Science has worked up to the view that all changes in existence are transformations from one form of life to another, transformations which take place according to definite quantitative relations. This is the direction in which scientific inquiry advances ; it recognises with increasing facility the new to be a form of the old ; the new is deduced from the old ; and for every new phenomenon a preceding one is pointed out to which it corresponds as effect to cause. Identity as well as rationality and causality are discovered more and more often in particular

cases (cf. §§ 5-6).   Existence is unrolled before us as
a great web of inter-related and continuous elements.
But even if we could suppose this ideal of science to
be completely realised, the question as to the persistence
of value would still remain open.   The processes of
existence might be continuous without any continuity of
value.   The valuable might be a rare guest to be met at
particular stations of the great process of evolution, but
who had vanished from all other places without leaving
a trace of his presence.   If it be supposed that the
innermost essence of existence is exhausted when its
empirical content has been reduced to relations of
identity, rationality and causality then there is no room
left for faith.   But such a view is insusceptible of proof.
There always remains the possibility that the great
rational and causal web of inter-relations which science
is gradually exposing to view may be the framework or
the foundation for the unfolding, in accordance with the
very laws and forms discovered by scientific inquiry, of a
valuable content.   The axiom of the conservation of value
need assert nothing more and nothing other than this.

81. Although the axiom of the conservation of value
differs in its nature from the fundamental axioms of
science (without, however, being irreconcilable with them),
yet in its relation to experience it presents a certain
analogy with them.   The fundamental axioms of science
can never be strictly proved.   They appear as fundamental hypotheses, as principles which guide our
searchings and inquiries by directing us how to ask and
how state our problems.   Nay, more, the very fact that
we ask at all, that there are such things as problems for
us, arises from a more or less conscious recognition of
the fundamental scientific axioms of identity, rationality
and causality.   The causal axiom, for example, owes its
great importance to the fact that it is in virtue of it
that we ask of every event what other events form

the presupposition for its occurrence. Did not the causal axiom unconsciously underlie all our thought, we should content ourselves with noting and describing what takes place, with taking an inventory of the changes which occur within existence. The appearance in science of the causal axiom under the special form which we have called the principle of natural causation (§§ 5, 6) indicates that we do not believe ourselves to have understood an event until we have discovered its necessary connexion with preceding events, which are as certain and indubitable experiences as is the new event. The same holds good of the less general axioms, *e.g.* of the axiom of the conservation of energy. In obedience to this axiom the inquirer asks, on the occasion of every new expression of energy, of what kind of energy it forms the equivalent, and what quantum of this other kind corresponds to a definite quantum of the new kind. Our scientific axioms are at once hypotheses and anticipations,[111] we anticipate by our questions and presumptions the course of nature, and our knowledge advances by means of the testing and verification of these presumptions. One philosophical school (the *a prioristic*, idealistic school) attributes the greater importance to anticipation, another (the empirical, realistic school) to verification ; but in and for themselves these two sides of our knowledge do not conflict with one another.

The verification of the axioms, of the fundamental anticipations, can never be complete. It consists in the fact that closer inquiry shows that all new experiences satisfy the expectations which the fundamental axioms led us to entertain. But as long as experience continues, this investigation can never be ended ; and the significance of this fact is all the deeper since the firm, causally determined interconnexion between changes is our ultimate criterion, by which alone we can distinguish between dream and reality (cf. § 6). If we doubt the reality of a matter presented to us, we try if it can be brought into necessary connexion with other matters, the reality of which is established for us ; if this is impossible, we regard the appearance as an illusion or an hallucination, or it may be that doubt arises as to the other things which we had regarded as real. In the latter case we must test the connexion between these other things and things of which we have (up to the present) no reason to doubt the reality, and so on. Since the criterion of reality can never be more than approximately applied, so too the concept of reality is itself really an ideal concept (cf. § 17). We work unhesitatingly with it, as with various other concepts, in spite of their inevitable incompleteness. Existence is not presented to us as completed, and who knows if indeed it really is completed? Perhaps it is for ever in the toils of becoming, so that the continual appearance of new empirical content is no mere accident. If this be so, we understand why existence always remains incommensurable with our knowledge, however great the advances of the latter.

As with the axioms underlying our reading of existence, so too with the principles underlying our ethical judgments. The ethical principles lay down rules according to which we must regulate our estimation of human action, if we wish to remain in harmony with that which is deepest and most central in our nature. Hence these rules change as this core of our being changes, and their application and confirmation in experience must always remain imperfect, since the great web of inter-relations in which human actions arise, and in which they intervene, is itself in a continuous and immeasurable process of evolution. From an ethical standpoint the unfinished character of existence has a peculiar significance. For were existence in and for itself complete, there would be no room and no ground left for ethics. There can only be ethical striving as long as the course of the world is uncompleted, and as long as its continuance is partly effected by means of human will and action.[112]   One of the chief reasons why religion and ethics are so apt to fall out with one another is because religion cherishes a belief in a completed principle of existence, absolutely perfect once and for all (cf. § 79).

In analogy with the fundamental axioms of science and ethics the religious consciousness too may regard its fundamental axiom of the conservation of value as an anticipation, although verification in this case will be much more difficult and imperfect than within the theoretical and ethical spheres.   The motive for assuming this position will be a practical, personal need, evoked by the experience of the relation between value and reality.   The axiom will express the expectation that throughout the flux of time and the course of change a valuable kernel of existence will persist, and this expectation will in its turn give rise to the effort to find in the new forms and phenomena under which existence occurs new garments for old values. This is an expectation and a striving which can never let itself be trammelled by any dogmatic authority, any more than it can collide with any scientific presupposition or with any scientific result.

The life of experience encroaches upon all spheres. Life begins with a superfluity of force.   It is, for example, characteristic that the metabolic changes in the embryo of the fowl are as intensive as are those in the adult fowl.   Growth makes larger demands than does mere preservation.   Life must begin with a large balance of force, in order that it may overcome obstacles to its development and maintenance.   This is as true of psychical as it is of purely physical life.   Connected with this is the unconscious appropriation, the bold ideation, which is so characteristic of the life of thought. We live in expectation before we live in retrospection; we look forward before we look backward. We were born into faith, and began with confident anticipation. It is the task of experience to show us, through confirmations and disappointments, how to check and determine our original anticipations. If there prove to be a contradiction between our experience and the ideas we have acquired, it is due either to our experience being too limited or to our ideas being false. The discovery of such a contradiction is apt to bring about great crises in all spheres. It then remains to be seen whether there is sufficient spiritual elasticity either to extend experience so that it shall fit the ideal anticipation, or to transform the ideas so that they are brought into agreement with the evidences of indubitable experience. In this consists the great art of living.

The axiom of the conservation of value can often only be maintained by means of a change in values, or by their realisation in a fresh empirical content. Faith in the conservation of value, therefore, can only maintain itself on the assumption that an uninterrupted spiritual work is going on in which the grain is distinguished from the chaff, not merely as long as existence produces nothing but old and familiar fruits, but also when it brings forth new fruits. It may happen that what was originally regarded as chaff may afterwards be recognised to be grain and vice versa.

But can experience take us no further than limitation and more definite determination? May it not lead us on until the need which led to the establishment of the axiom of the conservation of value may entirely disappear? Let us suppose that the need of discovering the causes of events were for ever baulked and that the causal principle nowhere found corroboration; in such a case would not the need itself disappear? All spiritual needs are only active under certain conditions, and disappear with these. Every personal need, like life in general, must struggle for its existence. And the religious need is no exception to this rule. Moreover, the history of religion teaches us that a belief only dies from want of the necessary conditions of life, never because it is condemned theoretically. As Auguste Comte says: Apollo and Minerva have never been refuted. The whole soil has been transformed on which alone the need to hold fast to the existence of these deities could flourish. The gods die for want of nourishment, and nourishment comes from living spiritual need. But so far the experience of religious history has only shown us the disappearance of special forms or objects of religious faith—never the sealing up of the well-spring from which faith springs. Whether such a sealing up of the spring will take place in the distant future we cannot say. But at present we have no ground for expecting it. The religious crisis, in the midst of which we find ourselves, may be a process of transformation only; it need not be a mortal struggle.

82. As happens so often in similar cases, this crisis was prepared by changes, no one of which, taken alone, seemed to indicate any change in principle. In the course of the last century it became increasingly clear that the significance of religion could not lie in any scientific explanation of existence which she is in a position to impart to us. The negative ground for saying this is that science arrives at understanding by other paths and under other forms than religion. It finds positive confirmation in increasing psychological insight into the nature of religion; for this leads to the accentuation of the elements of feeling and will, while the ideational element is relegated to a proportionately subordinate position. The upshot of this series of modi-

fications can only be the presumption that all religious
ideas are symbolic or poetic in character.

If the need to hold fast to the conservation of value
persists after the poetical character of all mythical and
dogmatic ideas has been recognised, the continuity of the
development of the human spirit receives support at a
very essential point. It is no philosophy which here steps
into the place of religion. It is a kind of faith which
replaces other kinds of faith. Faith must always be the
object, never the *product*, of philosophy; it can only be
the latter in so far as philosophy is able to prove the
psychological possibility of a certain faith under certain
spiritual conditions of life. The philosophy of religion
investigates the epistemological, the psychological and the
ethical conditions to which this kind of faith is subjected.
But it cannot construct a faith; it can only describe,
analyse and evaluate the faith which is evolved by life
itself from different standpoints. The philosophy of
religion is a comparative science; it investigates the
standpoints and forms of faith in relation to their
spiritual environment and in their struggle with this;
just as comparative biology investigates organic beings
in their relation to the material conditions of life and
their struggle with them.

And it discovers, so far as I am able to see, not only
the possibility but also the progressive development of
a religious standpoint free from myth, dogma and cult;
—a result of personal experience which finds expression
in a poetry of life, which assumes a different complexion in
accordance with the varying idiosyncrasies of different
individuals. The retention of figures and symbols from
the classical ages of positive religion—where such are
retained—can be justified from this standpoint on historical
and psychological grounds. In the first place, a transformation such as is here assumed will be continuously
in progress within the positive religions. And secondly,

the great poetry stored up in myths and dogmas is not the exclusive property of any one people, or of any one church or sect, but belongs to humanity ; it is at the command of every one whose experience of life tends in the same or in an analogous direction as the experience to which those figures owed their first origin or moulding into shape.   But there are men in whom the process of forming symbols or figures goes on independently, whether the results of this process have significance for themselves alone or for others as well as themselves.

83. The expression 'positive' religion, of which I have made such constant use in my preceding discussion, requires a little explanation.   It is to be understood in the same sense as the expression 'positive' law.   We understand by it, that is to say, a religion which has taken shape in definite traditions, in common forms and customs ; thus it presupposes a social community having established ideals.   'Positive' religion forms the antithesis to 'natural' religion, to which the single individual may attain by way of his own conviction ; just as 'positive' right forms the antithesis to natural right, which is reached by reflection on the conditions of social life and on the relations of the individual to society.   The word 'positive' then means that which is laid down in definite forms (*quod positum est*).

All the positive religions which history shows us have one feature in common ; the content of all of them consists in myths, legends and dogmas which are regarded as valid expressions of absolute truth.   And running through all these myths and dogmas we find the belief in (one or more) personal beings as creators of the world, or at any rate as creators of the most remarkable things that happen in the world.   From a purely historical point of view, therefore, we should be justified in including this feature in our definition of positive religion.   In my *Ethik* (chap. xxxii.) I started with this historical definition. But (as I have also pointed out in that work) it cannot be denied that a religious community might possibly come into existence whose faith found poetic and symbolic expression, free from all dogmatic conclusions. There might conceivably be a common symbolism, or men might unite round great experiences of life, common to them all; the exact form of such symbolisation would be freely left to each individual to fashion for himself, so that it would depend on the originality and the productive capacity of each person how far his symbols would be recognised as significant in wider circles. It would be idle trouble to attempt a more definite determination of such a standpoint; but if such a standpoint ever does come into existence, life will produce it in her own way just as she produced the old positive religions. The concept of positive religion would thus acquire greater denotation (and hence less connotation) than purely historical considerations would lead us to assign to it. The positive religions known to history may be regarded psychologically as concentrations, as syntheses, in which human ideas of existence are conjoined and woven together with the deepest experiences of human life. The fact that the present age is one of criticism and analysis does not prove that the time for such spiritual concentrations has passed away for ever. Nor can we prove that the syntheses of the future (if such arise) will necessarily retain the mythological or dogmatic character of the positive religions with which we are at present acquainted. Great spiritual freedom and force will be requisite before we can base life on the conviction that our highest ideas are but figurative expressions. Hitherto the conditions for the development of this capacity have not been propitious, but who shall dare to set a limit to the freedom and power which may yet be developed by the human race?

It seems to me, therefore, unjustifiable so to narrow
down the concept of positive religion that mythical and
dogmatic personifications form a necessary part of it.
And it would be the more unjustifiable should the
psychological inquiry which led us to recognise the
secondary significance of ideas within the religious
sphere prove to be correct.   Moreover, this feature has
generally been included in the concept of 'natural' religion.
It would be still more unjustifiable, however, to regard
such personifications as necessary elements of all religion,
whether the latter appear as 'positive' or not.   The
question cannot fail to arise : What is the value of the
existence of the personal beings in whom men believe and
of men's faith in their existence ?   And there will then
be no further doubt that the idea of the conservation of
value is the fundamental religious idea, since the ideas
of personal gods owe all their real content and real significance to it.   Nor would this idea lose its significance
though the concept of a personal god were admitted to
have symbolic validity only, and though religious symbols
should no longer be taken exclusively from human life
and the human form.   The continuity of human spiritual
life would thus be preserved, even if the standpoint of
positive religions were altogether abandoned.   Whether
the standpoint which would supersede that of positive
religion is really a higher one is a question apart.   It is
not necessarily a higher one because myths, legends
and dogmas are laid on one side.   As I have elsewhere
remarked : that a man does *not* believe something is
about the least that can be said of him.   The negation,
the abandonment of a standpoint, says nothing as to the
value of the new standpoint, or even whether a new
standpoint has been attained.   The criterion by which
we decide what is 'higher' or 'lower' in the transition
from positive religion to a free religious standpoint must
be the same as that which is applied in comparing

existing religions when one is said to be higher than
another.   We shall return to this point in our discussion
of the ethical philosophy of religion.

As already several times remarked, I attribute no
great importance to the name ' religion.'   The danger of
using this word in a wider sense may be that it
encourages a dishonest accommodation.   On the other
hand, the religious life of the present—and not least in
circles which believe themselves to enjoy a monopoly of
religious life—often assumes forms of such a kind that it
does not require much resignation to forgo the use of
the term religion altogether.

But before we can decide on the name to be given to
a standpoint which should preserve the faith in the conservation of values without clothing it in dogmatic forms,
the philosophy of religion must inquire more closely
whether the attainment of such a standpoint is within
the bounds of possibility, and what are the difficulties it
will have to encounter.

84. All estimation of value—as all understanding and
all explanation—is undertaken from the place occupied
by humanity in existence, and is determined by the
conditions of human life.   But this standing-ground and
these conditions of life are limited, and we cannot obtain
a view of their connexion with the rest of existence.
We only get over this difficulty by conceiving the
human race and its planet as the centre of existence ;
but the Copernican conception of the world has enlarged
our horizon and thereby rendered the problem of the conservation of value far more complex than it was before.
The fact that the history of our highest values is inter-
woven into a great whole of which we can never catch
sight not only makes it impossible to find an objective
foundation for it, but also makes it impossible to give the
faith in the conservation of value a definite and still more
an intuitive form.   Beyond the general notion that that

which possesses real value stands in such close connexion
with the forces moving in existence that it must persist
under one form or another we cannot pass.   This is a
difficulty common to all religions.   Positive religions,
however, for the most part, take it for granted that
existence is strictly limited, and not one of them has
offered a solution of the doubts which arise when this
narrow limitation is annulled.

The extension of our horizon must, at any rate, lead
to the firm conviction that our concepts of value cannot
be conclusive.   A highest value is no more demonstrable
than a first cause.   We are often obliged to pause at
causes, the causes of which we are not in a position to
discover ; and so, in our estimation of values, we are
forced to halt at values which are for us the highest
values, and which must therefore be those which directly
or indirectly underlie all values which we are able to
discover.   But if our faith is so strong as to prompt us
to extend the significance of our concept of value beyond
the borders of human existence, we must familiarise
ourselves with the thought that *our* highest values may
themselves be only elements of a still more comprehensive order of things, of a kingdom of values whose
scope and fundamental laws we are no more able to
conceive than we are able to conceive the comprehensive
order of nature, of which the law-abidingness of nature
revealed to us by science is but a fragment.   Thus faith
in the conservation of value presupposes a courageous
resignation ; for we must be both courageous and resigned
if we are to retain this faith when, with our experience,
our capacity of estimating value has reached its limit.

But even if we do not transcend the purely human
sphere, it is not difficult to see that we cannot form any
definite and intuitive ideas of future forms of value.   Experience shows us a continual readjustment of values, as
has already been mentioned in an earlier connexion (§ 73).

That which originally had value only as a means may
afterwards acquire value as an end ; while that which
at first had value as an end, may reveal itself later as the
introduction and preparation for new, hitherto unknown,
and more comprehensive values. Thus there may be
subjective readjustments in which the motive governing
the estimation of value changes, as well as objective
readjustments, when entirely new values arise. And
such readjustments are the only forms under which
experience exhibits a conservation of values. They
form the real content of human history. But they show
us at once that it is not any particular definite value
which is preserved. If a value is to maintain itself it
must suffer change, just as the seed-corn changes in
order to be able to grow into a plant. Within the
sphere of values, then, we find an analogy with what is
known in anatomy as *epigenesis,* in antithesis to *pre-
formation.* Just as during growth such radical changes
take place that the germ cannot be said to be merely
a plant or an animal on a reduced scale, so too in earlier
values we cannot expect to find the later ones pre-formed.
Only experience can show us what new forms values
will assume, and this experience extends far beyond the
grasp of single individuals or generations. A second
scientific analogy lies to our hand here. We can no
more deduce from the idea of the conservation of value
the new forms in which values will clothe themselves
than we can deduce from the general idea of the conservation of energy the actual specific transformations
of energy which take place. In both cases experience
alone can teach us the character of the new forms, and
experience goes on for ever. Were we not previously
sufficiently warned against attempting a dogmatic
formularisation of the axiom of the conservation of
value, the law of readjustment or accommodation would
contain warning enough. There are no definite

S

empirical values in the conservation of which we can believe.

We must even go a step further. It follows from the psychological law of relation, in obedience to which the nature (*i.e.* the quality and degree of intensity) of every feeling is conditioned by a certain opposition to preceding and contemporaneous states and elements, that every value changes when its relations change, and that an unchangeable value would be no value at all. If the background of a feeling changes, the feeling must change with it ; and where the background is monotoned and unchangeable, the feeling will weaken and gradually disappear.[113] Value can only be preserved by means of changes and transformations. This state of things depends on the reality of the temporal relation and the reality of differences in general. Only by way of pure mysticism, the logical outcome of which is ecstasy, can we (sometimes) attain to a disregard of this order of things. But it is not difficult to see that the law of relation invests changes and differences with great importance, for they are the conditions for the origin of value. Positive religions are inclined to overlook this fact altogether, even when they recognise the significance of the temporal relation (cf. §§ 77, 78). They fail to appreciate change and difference as that in which values originate, and by which they are conditioned. The thought of change seems to inspire them with a kind of terror ; only by ignoring this most essential side of reality do they think they can maintain the conservation of the valuable. This is a point on which there are still important experiences to be made and new spiritual territories to be discovered.

The confusion of particular definite values with eternal values is irreligious. Nevertheless, few religions are innocent of it. The religious postulate, in such case, runs as follows :—" If the kinds and forms of value with which I am acquainted do not persist, then the conservation of value is nothing to me, or rather I do not admit that that which persists is value or has value." This egoistic form of religiosity is by no means rare. The belief in personal immortality is often based on this ground,—as though existence might not still have a meaning even if I were *not* immortal! Of the relation of the individual to the great kingdom of values we can form no clear idea; hence we can assign no grounds either for affirmation or negation. The ideas formed by any individual on this question fall within the sphere of poetry and symbolism so soon as they pass beyond the general thought that that which possesses real value must persist under one form or another. Such a poetical garment (it matters not whether a positive or negative decision clothe the question of personal immortality) may have its great significance, and even be indispensable; but it is not true that clothes make the man, even though he cannot do without them. The evangelical exhortation, "Take no thought for the morrow," can be applied with far greater justification to the life after death than to our attitude towards the actual morrow of this earthly life. Whether the precise forms of value known to us will persist, experience alone can decide.

85. Our discussion so far has moved within the limits of the concept of value. But a further question demands a hearing: Does the distinction which we make, and are obliged to make, between value and reality hold good beyond the purely human standpoint? or is it nothing more than a purely human distinction? In answer to which we might suggest that this distinction is perhaps bound up with the fact that neither our concept of value nor our concept of reality is complete or can be completed. Our concept of value is empirical, while our concept of reality is ideal (cf.

§§ 81, 84). And we can neither deduce reality from value nor value from reality. No one of the ways in which dogmatism and speculation have attempted such a deduction stands the test of a close investigation. Our thought is here thrown back on the possibility of a principle from which the origin and preservation of the world, and with this the interconnexion of reality, might spring. But this thought could never be cast into scientific form.

Nevertheless the mere possibility of the conservation of value extending beyond the sphere of human life seems to assume the continued existence of mental life (this again may or may not be effected by the conservation of individual psychical beings). For value presupposes a relation to psychical life. Were we acquainted with a form of existence in which the distinction between value and reality was annulled, we should not here be confronted with so great a problem ; but if we are to remain within the bounds of experience, we must see how the matter stands under the given conditions, *i.e.* when value and reality are not coincident, and when, within reality, there is a difference between spirit (psychical life) and matter.

We must remind ourselves at this point that it is not possible to deduce the psychical from the material. Criticism of materialism in its different forms has already sufficiently demonstrated this. Psychical life stands as a special, irreducible side of existence, however we may conceive its relations to other sides of existence. The common and to us inaccessible ground in which the spiritual as well as the material takes its rise (for the latter can no more be deduced from the former than the former from the latter) may contain the possibility of a continuity beyond the limited range within which alone our experience in this world exhibits psychical life ; although we may not be able to conceive the special forms under which this continuity may be realised. The chief point is that psychical life remains as an independent element of existence, although not as a superfluous corollary or without inner connexion with the other elements of existence. Nevertheless even a materialistic conception of the world could afford to retain a belief in the conservation of values provided it be assumed that matter contains within itself the necessary conditions for the existence of a psychical life in which the earlier course of development followed by that life could be carried on.

But we must not at this point let ourselves forget the limitation of our experience. We have no guarantee that existence has no other sides or attributes than the two—the psychical and the material—exhibited in our experience. Neither an idealistic nor a materialistic world - conception can therefore ever be completely established (cf. §§ 19, 20) With regard to the problem of value, the conclusion to be drawn from this circumstance (*i.e.* that our knowledge of the fundamental forms [attributes] of existence is incomplete) is that, with the extension of our horizon, the ways and kinds of readjustment of value and of the conservation of value by means of these readjustments must be conceived to be more numerous than would be possible when we assume that the relation between the psychical and the material is a relation of contradiction, for in that case our choice is limited to a single alternative. Such an extended horizon is a warning against narrow doubt as well as narrow dogma.

Perhaps I may be allowed to illustrate this point by means of an analogy. When sulphur changes its state from a solid to a liquid, and from this again into a gaseous state, it changes its colour at the same time. But the colour cannot be explained by its state, nor *vice versa.* Did we know nothing more about sulphur than its states and colours the problem of the inner connexion between form and colour would remain insoluble. But we also know the differences in temperature of the sulphur, and are aware that the change of states as well as of colour is due to a rise in temperature. In considering existence as a whole, however, we have no third alternative to fall back on. And in its absence the problem of psychical life, and more especially the problem of value, remain unsolved. As a matter of fact, values seem to us to share the fate of psychical life in general, only in a more fragmentary form ; this does not indeed make faith in the conservation of values an impossibility, but it prevents it from ever becoming more than a faith.

86. When speaking of the scientific conception of the world too much weight is often laid on the general laws of nature, and they are certainly what most take the eye, when we compare the modern with the ancient conception of the world. But these laws are in reality abstractions. They denote the forms and rules according to which the movement and the development of existence proceed. But the essential thing to notice is that movement and development within the spiritual as well as within the material sphere have a definite direction and a certain definite individual character. Existence is like a great individuality, it appears to us as one among innumerable possibilities : we must accept it as we accept the individual man who is always more than the particular case of a general law. An individuality arises through an inter-play of laws : it is (to borrow H. C. Örsted's expression) a 'collectifold' (in antithesis both to a 'unifold' and a 'manifold') which we must take as experience gives it us. However far back the boldest hypotheses may take us, we always find certain definite forces working in certain definite directions. Even if we could deduce all future

forces and directions from those which were for us the original ones, yet these original forces and tendencies are for us absolute data which we have to accept as such, just as we must conceive the original dispositions with which a human life begins in its individual definiteness to be posited in actuality. Existence is unique, and if we have the right to compare it to a drama, it is a drama with its own particular prologue and *mise-en-scène* which we must take as they are.

The inquirer into natural science, like the student of history, seeks to unravel the course of this drama. But since only a single act, perhaps even only a single scene, of this great drama comes within our experience, we are not in a position to construct the whole of it. And were we to attempt this it would become evident that the drama we had built up was in its turn a part of a still greater drama. Every mythology, every dogmatism, and every metaphysic—apart from any defects of internal structure and consistency—leave unanswered questions both as to that which preceded what is described as the beginning in their drama and that which follows after its close. Neither basis nor consequences are exhausted.

A human individuality is also inexhaustible in its idiosyncrasy. It is impossible for us to discover all its elements and to explain them so as to bring out the 'collectifold' in its special character. But this is still more true of existence in general, where we cannot, as in the case of a limited individuality, observe its action and reaction on an external world. The sting of the problem of existence lies in this, that, when we try to conceive existence as a totality, it must be conceived as having a special and individual character, while yet the individuality we attribute to it cannot be supposed to be conditioned by its relation to something other than itself, as is the case with all other individual forms of existence.

This fact is of great significance for our general theoretical and practical principles. To give a complete demonstration of their validity we must be able to exhibit existence as an individual whole, of which these principles are the inner laws. Thus the causal axiom could only be stringently proved if all phenomena could be assigned to their definite place in a great totality; the same is true of the axiom of the conservation of energy, which only admits of proof with regard to closed and isolated totalities. This insusceptibility of proof of the fundamental axioms is connected, as we have already seen (§ 81), with the incompleteness—at any rate for us, and perhaps in itself (§ 18)—of existence. The axiom of the conservation of value shares the fate of the other fundamental axioms. Only if we could grasp existence in its whole 'collectifold' could we clearly know the precise nature of the validity attributable to this axiom. And at every attempt to apply it we must remember that, like every general axiom, it is only an attack on or an insight into the reality of a single aspect of existence; it can supply no exhaustive determination. Both individual character as well as the infinity of existence bar the way for us here.

87. While the concept of 'natural law' is often treated as though it revealed to us a mystical power hovering over the stream of phenomena, the concept of 'atom' is as often regarded as the expression of an absolutely indissoluble constituent of the stream over which this mystical power presides. Were such a conception valid the axiom of the conservation of value would encounter insurmountable difficulties. For if, as is generally believed, a time is coming when our world-system will be resolved into a chaos of atoms—into exactly as many atoms as were used at the creation of the world in its composition—these atoms would, according to the said presumption, retain exactly the same nature after the dissolution that they had when they entered into our

world - system : they would, therefore, have learnt
nothing and forgotten nothing.   What sense is there,
then, in the whole self-originated world-process ?   Something, it is true, still remains in existence ; but has this
something any value ?   and what value was involved in
the development of a world at all ?

In elucidation of this point we must first of all call
to mind that 'our world' is not identical with 'the
whole world.'

The presumption that the life and motion of our
world-system will come to an end at some time or
other does not justify us in believing that the life and
motion of the countless world-systems which make up
the sum of existence will come to an end with it.   For
all we know, the action and reaction between the different
world-systems, which are probably at different stages of
development, may draw a world whose motion has come
to an end into the evolutionary process of the rest of
existence.

Further, the concept of atoms must not be taken
dogmatically any more than the religious ideas.   The
fact on which the atomic concept was built up is that the
different elements combine in composite matter in such a
manner that the weight of this composite is equal to the
combined weights of the constituent elements, while
these weights, on the resolution of the composite, are the
same as they were before they entered into it.   But it
does not necessarily follow from this that the atoms are
absolutely indissoluble.   They are indissoluble by means
of any of the forces of nature known to us ; but this does
not prevent them from being composite ; and indeed they
must be so if they possess extension, even though this,
in comparison with sensuous extension, be infinitely
small (cf. § 16).   The single atom is therefore in reality
a complete microcosm in which all the problems with
which we are occupied in our macrocosm—in comparison

with the unfathomable world-all itself but an atom—
probably recur. Nothing forbids us, therefore, to suppose
that within the atoms, effects and results of earlier world-
processes in which they have participated may be stored
up. In this case no dissolutions would be absolute, not
even the dissolution of a world-system ending in a 'chaos'
of atoms; this 'chaos,' however, is not a necessary
assumption, for the final conclusion might be a more
elementary world-order than that which existed while the
system was at the height of its development. Even in a
'chaos' the atoms might perhaps have learnt as well as
have forgotten. Thus we get a possibility of a continuity
between different world-periods, even on a purely
materialistic view. Preceding world-periods would then
form the foundation and the starting-point for succeeding ones.

88. There are thus more possibilities of the validity
of the fundamental religious axiom than is often assumed.
Empiricism no less than dogmatism may hold thought in
bondage. The real difficulty in holding fast to this axiom
arises from the fact that existence offers too many rather
than too few possibilities. Within existence a continual
struggle and battle between elements and individuals is
going on. Innumerable seed-corns fall to the ground,
but only a few take root and pass on to renewed life
and development. And when development does take
place it is under mutual restraints, supplantings and
eliminations. Development starts from a mass of
different starting-points, and the evolutionary tendencies
possessed by these different starting-points are by no
means in harmonious relations with one another originally.
For the most part a result at any one point is only
reached because at other points nothing was aimed at.
Opposition and inhibition may certainly be of great
value, for they may be the powers liberating an energy
which would otherwise have remained dormant, but as

far as we can judge from experience, they are by no
means restricted to this purpose.

It follows from the sporadic character of all development that it may appear as though the working expenses
of existence were greater than its receipts.   Existence
shows itself wasteful, and therefore unsparing.   And
this wastefulness, to judge by all appearances, produces a
loss of value.

The problem of the discord within existence leads
us back to the problem of the unity and the manifold
(§§ 16-18).   We saw that it was impossible to deduce
the manifold from the unity, and, even were it possible,
the problem of discord would only appear in still more
glaring colours ; for if the manifold—the many sporadic
starting-points—really originated in a principle of unity,
how could we explain the fact that the relation between
the different evolutionary tendencies of the manifold
elements and individuals is more frequently inharmonious
than harmonious.   Friction there might certainly be,
but not more than would be requisite for the liberation
of energy.[114]   It is idle to appeal to the legend of the
Fall here ; that would only be to substitute several riddles
for one.   For how is a fall possible if all the elements
and individuals in existence were originally rooted in an
harmonious principle ?   Moreover, a fall into sin explains
at most the want of harmony in the human world ; it
sheds no light on the other discords of existence.   If it
be urged that the possibility of a fall must exist if man
is to be a personality, since personality can only develop
through the exercise of choice between possibilities, then
we shall find ourselves involved in serious self-contra-
diction ; for we shall not be able to attribute personality
to the deity and at the same time decline to admit the
possibility of a fall into sin on the part of this deity.
Moreover, the very possibility of a fall is itself the expression of a discord : if I am capable of an act of knavery

to-morrow, I *am* a knave to-day.   If it be admitted that
the original possibility of a fall was given with creation,
this is a confession that the discord was produced by
creation, and this, as we have seen from another standpoint (§ 78), must logically be regarded as a diminution of
value.   No scholasticism is able to refute this conclusion.

There is one side of the matter which is generally
overlooked in the discussion of this problem.   People
are generally inclined to take for granted that the totality
of existence, the principle of totality, must have 'right'
on its side, and that the particular element or individual
whose evolutionary tendency leads to the interruption
of this totality must be 'wrong.'   But we are making a
great abstraction when we thus erect the principle of
totality into the antithesis of the particular elements or
individuals.   The force which moves in each one of
them is, after all, but a part of the force of the totality,
and the laws which work collectively in individual beings
are the individualised interplay of the general laws of
existence.   Every particular element of existence has so
far the same 'right' as the totality, and is not rebellious
merely because it obeys its own law, its own tendency to
develop.   The inclination to assume from the first
that the ground of the discord must lie in the elements
and not in the principle of totality is somewhat oriental
in character.   It was against this tendency that Goethe
was combating in his great *Prometheus*; he wanted to
assert the inner divine disposition of the particular finite
being against the ordinary external concept of God.
Only from a dualistic religious standpoint could this
poem be regarded as irreligious.   The deeper religious
view, according to which God himself suffers, has, as
a matter of fact (whatever mythological or dogmatic
explanation of the matter may be adduced), and without
wishing or intending it, given the death-blow to dualism.
The final balance of the account is naturally more difficult

when we have to consider not only the possibility of a total harmony which might arise through the interplay of the finite harmonies and disharmonies, but also those regions of existence in which discord prevails, and where we cannot hear how it is resolved into an all-embracing harmony. For such regions are independent parts of existence, and their claims cannot be met by saying that they represent only subordinate parts in the great world-concept. Only an oriental 'overman' (from which the 'overman' of modern times is a feeble plagiary) could, under these conditions, sit in his heaven and find his existence harmonious. Herein lies the great justi-fication, as well as the usefulness, of the protests raised by Voltaire and Schopenhauer.

If existence, even from a purely theoretical and intellectual standpoint, which asks only for scientific understanding (§ 18), seems irrational or incomplete, this is no less true from the standpoint of the estimation of worth. Here, too, it appears that religion does not solve the riddles which science is unable to solve. But religion has a certain advantage over science here, for it can more easily distract thought from these insoluble riddles, so that their sting is less acutely felt : this is an advantage when it comes to willing and doing, for here we must do battle, and our courage needs support. To escape the sting contained in this problem we must—to borrow a figure of Bayle's—prevent thought from seeing its own shadow, just as Bucephalus could only be ridden when he was not terrified by the sight of his own shadow falling on the ground. Consciousness must be absorbed in an ideal content, must be concentrated round some illuminating thought, if its striving is not to be checked and beaten back by the thought of the dark and inhar-monious side of existence ; this is a necessary condition for the continuance of the struggle with darkness and discord. But to avert our glance from a problem is not

to solve it ; and the most consistent course open to us
under such circumstances is to admit its insolubility,
especially when there is no reason why we should not
lead a great and beautiful life, even though there are
many unanswered riddles.   What concerns us practically
as striving beings is not the actual constitution of all
existence, but the conditions it offers for further development.   The strength of the opposition and the degree
of discord we encounter will inevitably determine the
character of our experience of the relation between value
and reality.   But the axiom of the conservation of value
is in itself independent of the greatness or smallness of
the value contained in existence ; it merely states that
whatever value there is remains in existence.   Only
when we deduce reality from value does the sting of the
problem become insupportable (cf. § 75).   As long as
there is a possibility of maintaining, and perhaps even
of increasing, the value which there is in existence, there
is a field for the religious axiom.

Two thoughts must always be of paramount importance
in determining our attitude to the problem presented by
the world's discords.

Firstly, in comparison with the vast whole of existence
our experience is strictly limited ; hence it remains to be
proved whether an extension of experience might not
bring about another result.   Even in purely theoretical
problems this thought is of essential importance.   If
strict inference from our experience leads to internal
contradiction, we do not therefore deny the validity of
the logical principle, but we try whether the ground
of the contradiction may not lie in the fact that our
experience is all too limited.   We then often find
that with the extension of our experience the apparent
contradiction vanishes.   So, too, objections to the conservation of value will often disappear when our horizon
becomes extended by the discovery or production of

values where hitherto no possibility for such had been
seen to exist. The most important and almost the only
valid thought contained in Leibniz's famous attempt to
establish an optimistic conception of the world was that,
owing to our familiarity with the idea of the infinity of
existence, we are more favourably situated when confronted by the problem of discord than were the thinkers
of antiquity (Plotinus, Augustine).

Secondly, life is always renewing itself. Every year
has its May, every generation its youth. Hence new
dispositions are always springing up, and there are no
signs of the world's getting old. A new chapter in the
history of existence is for ever opening, for which the
series of earlier experiences on which we based our
judgments on the value of reality is only a prologue :
the whole of the previous drama is only the prologue
of a greater drama to come. Existence is not only
immeasurable, it is also inexhaustible.

Faith in the conservation of value is therefore, in
spite of all difficulties, psychologically possible. Whether
it really exists, and, if so, under what form and with
how great a range, we can only learn from experience.

89. The lively feeling of the discord contained in
existence (both within us and in the external world)
depends, to a great extent, on the effect of contrast.
The ideal is the judge. The antithesis between reality
and the great aims which we are able to set before ourselves is the secret of the depreciatory judgments which
men pass on reality as it is. The youth who, for the
first time, encounters the tough and defiant opposition
of reality, ignorant of the value that such a resistance
may in itself possess, asks astonished : " Is this life ? "
And the greater the demands which we make, not only
in our own name but also in that of the Highest known
to us, the greater the darkness that we discover round
about us. We could avoid the discovery of discord

easily enough by fettering and starving our sense of harmony and ideality. He is spared many pains whose happiness is not bound up with great things and wide circles of interest.

It is, therefore, a token of the nobility of man that he can feel grief and pain. They are a sign of the great contrasts which human life can embrace, and witness to the deep and strong unity of human nature. Pain is in itself a symptom of dissolution, and only that the nature of which is unity can be dissolved ; pain is the feeling that this unity is threatened.[115] And that the spiritual life can not only sustain but also concentrate itself in spite of pain, is a clear indication that it has great energy at its disposal.

The fact that a discord is felt is also itself a proof that existence contains value. Pessimism has an optimistic element as its background. The effect of contrast may indeed be so strong that the sense of the value of the background may be altogether lost, but this would only happen were we to allow ourselves to sink into a purely passive state.

The last standpoint which may be occupied in considering the problem we have been discussing lies on the margin between religion and ethics. Value is not absolutely dependent on its own conservation. That which we treasure as beautiful and good may retain its value, whatever fate be its lot, and whatever shadows may darken its fall. A thought is not necessarily less true, or a feeling less pure and noble, because it must pay its debt to time. Value is not always estimated by dates. And should it be the fate of the good and beautiful to perish, would it therefore be less good and beautiful ? The more full of content life is, the more we forget time. The work of finding and producing value itself implies a faith in the conservation of value, in so far as this work presupposes the possibility that values may be redeemed and find their place in existence, whatever and however vast the latter may be. If faith in the conservation of value is the core of all religion, then the standpoint which occupies itself exclusively with finding and producing values contains a concealed religion. A man can *be* religious, may live in a state of religion, without *having* religion, while, conversely, the religion which a man merely *has* is very loosely connected with his personality. If God be defined as the principle of the conservation of value within existence, then every man, whatever be his creed, who labours for the maintenance of value within existence is a child of God.

90. It is the task of mental science to understand and to estimate psychical phenomena ; hence it must not only study their completely developed forms, but must inquire into the forces which gave them birth, and it must then pass on to the further inquiry as to whether the necessary conditions are present for the continuance of the activity of these forces under new relations and new forms.[116] As in external nature we find inner connexion persisting throughout a change of external forms, so we shall find the same holding good in the psychical sphere the more completely we immerse ourselves in it. If the results of our investigation are correct, we must regard ideas within the religious sphere as belonging to the changing forms and not to the essential kernel ; although, so long as they correspond to the general level of spiritual life, they will naturally exercise great influence on the condition of the kernel. Religious life, according to the results we have reached, presents greater continuity than do the religious ideas. As an attempt to understand existence, to solve the riddle of the world, religion has lost the battle. But she lives in human feelings and needs, and from thence will always impel the will to the discovery and production of

T

values, while, with the help of imagination, she will be able to shape figures and symbols through which to express the highest poetry of life.

The problem of the conservation of value here recurs, however, in a specialised form. Must there not necessarily be a loss of value when the transition from dogma to symbol is made? The spiritual life must at any rate be able to include and concentrate itself upon a very different content, when the highest ideas known to it—or rather the ideas of the highest known to it—occur under intuitive forms, the reality and validity of which are accepted with unqualified faith, and which, moreover, are common to all individuals, or at any rate to large circles. The many reservations and critical objections which have led us to abandon the standpoint of dogmatism for that of the poetry of life, seem as though they must weaken the concentration indispensable to the continuance of life. Such an essential change in the significance of ideas will have far-reaching effects on the life of feeling and of will.[117]

In modern developments of the spiritual life there is much to justify this question. Not without reason has the figure of Hamlet held its place in literature up to the present day as typical of a certain character, even though it has gradually dwindled in proportions, and though the painful process of dissolution in which Shakespeare's hero finds himself on the borderland between instinct and reflection has gradually yielded to a self-complacent decadence, which, pleased with the glitter of the foam, ignores the strength of the wave which begets it. Foam is not without its beauty, but true culture is no mere foam, it is also the wave which produces it—it is not only effect but cause.

The first remark to be made here is that the dissolution, if dissolution there be, began in positive religion itself with the decay of its golden ages. Religious

life has lost its unity within the Church.   She has gradually been forced to admit that religion sheds no light
either on astronomy, physics, or natural history.   Higher
criticism (or, to call it by a more appropriate name, the
literary history of the books of the Bible) is showing us
more and more clearly every day that we must not go to
the Bible to learn history.   While in practice, *e.g.* in the
theological reinterpretations of the   clear message of
the sermon on the mount, it is assumed that it has no
ethical message for us.   The snake has already entered
Paradise.   The rift is proclaimed aloud, and the problem
is there for any one who cares to think.   Religion, which
in its classical ages was all in all, is fast becoming a last
consolation.   Clear-seeing men can now only adhere
to it, in its classical form, by means of a convulsive effort ;
which shows that the forces of the spiritual life no longer
concentrate naturally in it as they did of yore.   If the
Old Testament fares no better than the New has done,
from the orthodox point of view, at the hands of modern
research, the Church had better make up her mind to
go through a course of exercises in the use of symbolic
ideas.   The figures of the patriarchs will then pass
over from history to fable or legend, and the most
pressing task will be to ensure the retention of their
religious significance under this new form.   But the
Church advances by small steps.   It took two centuries
for her to accept the independence of natural science.
Time will show how long it will take before she accepts
the independence of scientific historical investigation.
And then it will be the turn of psychology and of ethics.

Immediate certainty vanishes as soon as independent
research becomes of essential importance.   At its first
appearance Protestantism signified a dissolution, although
afterwards it attained a position of security.   Only where
religion surrounds men on all sides as an objective
power independent of human conviction, only then is there

complete certainty.   Where self-activity can be clearly
traced, and where private choice finds utterance, there
complete certainty is unattainable.   There is, therefore, a
certain amount of justification for the view that religion
is something which a man can neither attain nor produce
himself.   The Russian peasant took it as a matter of
course that his Tartar fellow-villagers should have a
different religion from his own, but he was disgusted at
the seceders from his own religion.   As he explained :
" The Tartars have received their religion from God,
like the colour of their skins, but the Molokanians
[the Russian protestants] are Russians who have invented
their own faith." [118]   Most men find God more easily in
fixed traditional ordinances than in inner searchings
and strivings ; for these may lead a man beyond his
external historical environment into paths where, to the
eye of a spectator, he seems to wander unguided and
alone.

A conception of life won by the individual's own
efforts does not acquire fixity so easily as a traditional
belief which, though its most important work is long
since over, yet has stored up within it the collective
experience of centuries, under the form of figures, suited
both in execution and application to the spiritual
needs of generations.   The unrest and hesitation which
characterises a state of transition involving new thought-
constructions are due to the crudeness and untriedness of
the new forms.   Only gradually can inner absorption in
the new spiritual relations rid us of the sense of dizziness
which is apt to follow an estrangement from the narrow
but secure forms within which our life has hitherto moved.

With many men, through one of those readjustments so important in the life of the soul, criticism and
negation becomes an end in itself instead of merely a
means of liberation.   The nut-crackers become more
important to such men than the kernel, for the sake of

which the nut-crackers exist. An ironical, *blasé* attitude is the result, and is perhaps mistaken for a sign of the most advanced point of view. But it is not such a form as this—one of the many forms of Philistinism—which makes a transition to a new stage of life possible. The spring of development has run dry here, and we must turn to another region for the really new. Nor will it help us any better to cling to the old forms when they have lost nearly all life ; for this will leave us homeless in the new world which is rising up around us. From fear of becoming a Hamlet we shall become a Don Quixote.

91. There have been masters of the art of living and thinking who, passing through the fires of doubt undaunted, have attained and realised in a harmonious life the standpoint of the free man. Spinoza and Goethe, Fichte and Stuart Mill, may be quoted as examples, and there is no ground for supposing that the number of such is decreasing. Even with minds who are not energetic enough to reach such a harmony, indications and presentiments of a new ideal of personality, tending in the same direction as that followed by the earlier thinkers, are not wanting. We have much to learn from Carlyle as well as from Eugen Dühring and Friedrich Nietzsche. Even where individual capacity, owing to unfavourable inner and outer relations, is inadequate, the need may be active, testifying to the tendency of the life.

There is no reason to doubt that new forms will aim at harmonious concentration when the effects, both simultaneous and subsequent, of dogmatic narrowness and critical exhaustion shall have disappeared. Imagination, which developed such power within the mythical and dogmatic framework of the earlier positive religions, will thus be free to create her own forms, for men will be penetrated anew with the wonder of life, of the contrasts it embraces, and of the struggle it demands.

The great examples of the past have not perished, though their footsteps no longer seem to guide us on our way. It is only that what was able to fill the life of an earlier generation becomes for later generations one element in a totality; and this fact, *i.e.* the fact that what was originally a totality may afterwards become an element of a larger whole, is one of the most important forms in which the conservation of value is secured. It was thus that the spiritual life of the Jews and Hellenes became absorbed in the Christian view of life, and it is in this way that a new conception of life will absorb the Christian. The uniting bond of the new conception is not yet ready; but may we not hope that it is being prepared in silence? Every earnest effort may be a contribution towards it.

E. THE PRINCIPLE OF PERSONALITY

La seule chose universelle doit être l'entière liberté donnée aux individus de se représenter à leur manière l'éternel énigme.   GUYAU.

(*a*) SIGNIFICANCE AND JUSTIFICATION OF THE PRINCIPLE OF PERSONALITY

92. The discussion of the ground and significance of the principle of personality, by which we understand in this connexion the fundamental axiom of the justification and value of personal differences within the religious sphere, falls between the psychological and the ethical sections of our philosophy of religion. The principle of personality is also of great ethical and judicial significance, and its basis and signification present a certain analogy within the different spheres. Its necessity within the religious sphere depends partly on assumptions common

to religion and ethics, partly on assumptions peculiar to religion.

A personal being must never be treated as a mere means, but is always and first of all to be regarded as an end. The ground for this is that in our experience personal beings appear in existence as centres of value, by which I mean as the living central points in which value can be felt and acknowledged. It is personality which in the world of our experience invests all other things with value. The religious problem owes its sting largely to the fact that the religious concept of value claims not only psychological, but also cosmical validity. Whether this sting will ever be eliminated may be left uncertain ; it has already been discussed in the preceding pages. Here I am concerned only with the sphere of experience, where human personalities appear as centres of evaluation, and must therefore possess independent and immediate value. The inhibition of a centre of value must necessarily involve a decrease of value. Hence there is no justification for any inhibition, any constraint, or any pain, except as a means of education, as a means the time for which will one day be over. All authority inhibits, forces, or pains. Hence authority can never be anything but a means, and the principle of authority is subordinate to the principle of personality, as mediate value must always be subordinate to immediate value. The burden of proof must always lie with those who wish to inhibit, limit, force, or pain.[119] Authority pleads as its justification that it is the necessary condition for the complete carrying out of the principle of personality. Personality, on the other hand, does not seek its justification in any authority. Positive religion, as it has hitherto appeared, has always shown a more or less decided tendency to make authority absolute. In Catholicism especially the principle of authority consistently appears as an absolute principle. Here authority assigns its own limits, decides what shall and what shall not appertain, directly or indirectly, to religion, decrees, *e.g.*, that the proofs of the existence of God are scientifically valid. "Complete intellectual subordination to the Church" is demanded, and to attempt to instruct the Church instead of passively receiving instruction at her hands is to court a breach of all relations.[120] Here we find an irreconcilable conflict between the principles of authority and of personality.

Constraint is exercised whenever the individual personality is not allowed to work according to its complete idiosyncrasy. When religious belief is mainly due to tradition, imitation, or habit there may always lie in the nature of any individual forces and elements which do not participate in his activity. Only when the individual has won and developed his religious conviction for himself can he throw his whole nature into it. Hence the ideal to be arrived at is the greatest possible activity of the self; all tradition and authority should be restricted to the work of stimulating, guiding, and educating. All deeply penetrative religious tendencies have recognised this principle on a larger or smaller scale. It is the principle of inwardness. A misconception of this offends the principle of the conservation of value and is therefore irreligious. Within the religious sphere we must claim room for the greatest possible play of individual differences. It is homogeneity and schematism, not differences and peculiarities which have to justify themselves.

Ethics and the philosophy of religion alike base themselves on this principle. But there is another fundamental principle which belongs especially to the philosophy of religion, and which we are led to formulate by the investigation of the psychology of religion we undertook above.

Individual personalities are not only centres of value,

they are also centres of experience. For it is within the realm of personality that the relation of value to reality is experienced, and such experience forms the foundation of all religion. Hence it is of the utmost importance that this experience should be as comprehensive and unconstrained as possible. But this can only be so when every individual has the right to work armed with all his capacities and all sides of his nature. There are many values, and reality is immeasurable not only in its range but also in virtue of the manifoldness of its qualitative relations. No two individuals are situated precisely alike, either in the world of values or of reality. Every man must start from his own personality ; he must grasp its peculiarities, and the more he is himself the more he will make experiences which no other can make. Hence the art of life must be one-sided, as Julius Lange has shown of plastic art. " A work of art," says Lange,[121] " can never impart an all-sided conception of the human figure ; such a conception can only be gained by following history through all stages of its career. Art is precisely that form of intuition which is determined by a warm feeling towards its object and is carried out consistently with one particular form of intuition—hence it is one-sided in its very essence. . . . The individual artist in an individual work of art can get no farther than saying something definite of his object in conformity with the relation of the subject to him ; the more warmly, freshly, and finely the matter is apprehended the better." This principle of the plastic art holds good also for the art of life. All art has as its basis the principle of personal truth, and personal truth is only to be found when the entire personality of the individual impresses its stamp on the work, whether that work be an external picture or the shaping of one's own life of feeling and will, a work of art, this latter, to the creation of which every man is called. Afterwards comparative and classificatory thought can set to work, taking notes, carrying out reductions and combinations, establishing types and forms. This is all work of secondary importance. All dogmatism and all criticism are secondary within the religious sphere. When a definite religious idea establishes itself it can only be as a form, expression or explanation of immediate experience, and here the question will always arise : With what right does this particular idea get itself established, and with what right does it claim to be anything other or more than the expression of the experience of the particular individual ? Criticism and dogmatism come into collision at the outset. Only in virtue of the absolute principle of authority can certain forms of ideas be declared as generally valid and as the necessary expression of all religious experience.

From the point of view of the psychology of religion Schleiermacher hit the nail on the head when he said, " Everything immediate in religion is true, for otherwise how could it have come into existence? but only that is immediate which has not gone through the conceptual mill but has grown up on the soil of pure feeling." [122]

Dogmatism is the index to the book of life ; not the book itself. A Nemesis which often overtakes religion is that while she thinks she is fighting for life she is really only fighting for the preservation of this index. And criticism has often imitated her by believing itself to have dealt religion a mortal blow, when it has really only shown the untenability of the index. No index can take the place of the book, and only in the book itself, and not in any sort of index, can all *nuances* and peculiarities be set forth in their natural truth.

93. Historically, then, we find an increasing acknowledgment of the principle of personality within the sphere of religion.

Criminal law is withdrawing itself more and more

from this sphere. Religious crimes play a smaller part in the Greek and Roman codes than in the Jewish law, the same is true of modern times as compared with mediæval. According to the antique and mediæval conception, the province of the Church and of the State coincided partly or altogether, and he who broke with the Church was looked upon as an enemy to the State.[123] The legal and ethical acknowledgments of the principle of personality have not been without influence on religion: but this would hardly have been possible had there not been within religion itself a development in the direction of inwardness and of personal truth. Such a development may be traced in the religion of India, if we compare Brahmanism with Buddhism ; in the course of Greek religiosity after Æschylus and Socrates; within Christianity when we compare the Catholic with the Protestant world. In recent times we must notice the increasing emphasis of the significance of great personalities as founders and exemplars. The example is more and more taking the place of the dogma. And we shall follow our example most faithfully by developing into personalities according to the laws of our own nature as did our example in accordance with those of his own.

(*b*) Main Groups of Personal Differences

94. Having sketched the general grounds on which the principle of personality is based, I will now pass on to discuss the most important personal differences which are of significance within the religious sphere. Such differences have already been touched upon in another connexion (§§ 35-47). But there they were considered as results, as given phenomena. Here, on the contrary, I propose to consider them as dispositions. Although the forms I am about to describe will remind

us of those already dealt with, yet I shall here consider
them from another aspect.

The differences which are of interest for the
psychology of religion are concerned either with the
life of feeling and will or with the intellectual faculties.
Let us first occupy ourselves with those which relate to
the life of feeling and will.

One group of differences is determined by the rôle
played by opposition. In some natures the life of feeling
and will is spurred on by a continual feeling of inner
resistance which causes a discord in the mind and urges
to a restless striving after harmony and unity. Inner
division is the prevailing condition; compared with
this unity seems an exalted ideal. As a result of
this we get a number of contrast effects, sometimes one,
sometimes the other member of the conflicting opposites
will prevail, and the prevailing element at any moment
will produce a disposition towards its opposite. A series
of oscillations will set in, and since there is a fundamental
want of harmony between the constituent elements of
the mind, this series of oscillations is hardly likely to
pass over into continuous motion. While in such natures
it is discord which acts as the stimulating power, other
natures possess in their soul's life a fulness of unity
which, on account of its overwhelming power, moves
them to activity and communicativeness. These are the
expansive natures, as the others were the *discordant*
ones. The strength of both may be equal, but it differs
in its source and application. Religious feeling and
religious ideas will assume very different forms and
nuances in these two types, hence they will always find
it difficult to understand one another. Expansive natures,
even in moments of the deepest surrender, live entirely
and immediately from themselves; they seek for the
supreme in the inner power and source, which gives
them more than they themselves can clearly understand,

and gives it without any conscious co-operation on their part. They speak of the highest as "the force which sustains them, as the deep spiritual voice, whose sound gave them thoughts." The discordant natures, on the other hand, will be inclined to seek for the source of their spiritual self-preservation outside their own ego ; they are conscious of such violent inner opposition that only a force different from any of those at work within them can help them to surmount the obstacles which confront them. They are therefore natural dualists, while the expansive natures are natural monists. For the determined monist the difference between value and reality may finally vanish altogether, so unable are such natures to discern distinctions within the great, collective stream of life. The expansive natures may be acquainted with the feeling of sinfulness, but with them it bears the character of restriction ; there are forces which have not yet been liberated, and help may be necessary in order to unlock this inner source. Their saviour is a liberator rather than a redeemer. The discordant natures, tortured by the opposition offered within their own breasts to their ideal, the effect of which is heightened by the close proximity of the ideal, turn to juristic analogies ; they feel like criminals in the presence of the judge : the judge, it is true, becomes transformed into a mediator, but the play of contrasting effects soon breaks out again, and the mediator, in his turn, takes his seat on the judge's bench. The different forms which the feeling of sin-fulness may assume are brought out clearly in the characterisation of this feeling drawn by the American psychologist, Leuba, from a mass of materials collected by him for the purpose.[124] Leuba, however, deduces the difference between the two types from the different religious ideas which different individuals take as their basis. The influence of those ideas cannot of course be denied. And not only the accepted ideas but also the original intellectual dispositions are participatory. But it is to the emotional and volitional dispositions that we must look for an explanation of the fact that individuals, brought up for the most part in one and the same religious tradition (Protestantism of a more or less strong Methodistical tendency), present such different and characteristic types. The difference between the two types—on the one hand, those in whom discord, contrast, fear and division predominate, on the other, those in whom an inner aspiration prevails, which only requires help to develop—lies so deep that the influence which ideas may exercise is conditioned by this difference and not *vice versa*. A nature such as John Bunyan, who has given us the story of his own conversion, evidently belongs to the first type. Deep melancholy, uncontrollable motor tendencies, restless reflection here form the psychological foundation for a series of spiritual struggles which only came to an end when a stage of despair had ushered in a state of complete passivity, in which his forces were collected for a new and higher life. In his later vigorous activity, after he had conquered, in its essentials, the inner opposition, Bunyan approximated to the expansive type; still he had constantly to summon up all his energy of self-control to keep in bounds the old chaos within his breast.[125] The unconscious development of the expansive natures does not always take place easily, however : often it can only happen by fits and starts, just as a spring often only gives its water in jets ; but the expansive natures have to fight against restriction, not against the chaotic.

Another group of differences is characterised by the opposition between activity and passivity. Active natures (whether the activity be brought about by the sting of discord or by the need of expansion) may be so much absorbed in finding and producing values that they have neither time, sense, nor strength to develop a special

religious life. Faith in the conservation of value finds
immediate vent in their activities, and they do not feel the
need of any special formulation or symbolisation of it ;
moreover, the moods which are bound up with this faith,
either as causes or effects, acquire in their case peculiar
significance.   Their faith in value is one with their own
life.   Passive natures are rather inclined to a life of
special moods and reflections.   They look forwards and
backwards.   Recollection and repentance, hope and faith,
are their prevailing moods, and each of these moods
tends to expand, while the active natures have neither
time nor inclination to remember or hope, to feel repentance or to cherish convictions.   The passive natures
often regard the active as irreligious, as the discordant
spirits do the expansive.

A third group of differences within the sphere of
the life of feeling and will rests on the distinction
between emotion and sentiment.   Some natures are
inclined to vehement fermentations.   The transitions
from one state to another, or one period of life to
another, take place for the most part by sudden crises
and visible leaps.   They differ from the discordant
natures already described, in that the oppositions succeed
one another in time, while with the discordant ones
the conflicting tendencies are contemporaneous.   There
are, of course, many intermediate and mixed forms, for
successive discords and simultaneous discords are not
mutually exclusive.   Since, however, other circumstances
being equal, simultaneous discord is more powerful in
its effects than successive, we are justified in giving
the name ' discordant ' to that particular type in which
the opposing elements appear simultaneously.   Where
development proceeds by leaps, and where there is a
tendency to emotional states, we get a type which might
be called the *affective*.   The peculiarity of other natures
causes their development to proceed by small steps, and

hence it presents the character of continuity. The life of feeling and will has, in such cases, a more divided, more interior character, while in affective natures there are momentary concentrations, and they are characterised by the stamp of violence rather than of inwardness. The *continuous* type (as we will call this type) has a certain kinship with the expansive type. The life of expansive natures may, however, express itself in momentary and violent forms of emotion, and this will naturally happen when energy is suddenly liberated. The difference between the affective and the continuous types is perhaps the most striking of all. It corresponds to the two kinds of strength which the life of feeling and will can possess; the strength of violence and the strength of inwardness.

A fourth group of differences rests on the kind of feeling, and in this type either self-assertion or self-surrender may be the prevailing disposition. There are natures to whom their own individual salvation and surety is everything, and who would therefore have no objection to finding themselves the unique recipients of salvation. Such an *idiopathic* religiosity may occur in all religions, not least in the higher forms of it, in which the difference between self-assertion and self-surrender is clearly grasped. The motivation—if indeed it is possible to assign any—may be very different in different individuals. Thomas Aquinas, *e.g.*, justifies his statement that the fact that a man knew himself, alone of mankind, to be blessed, would not necessarily impair the perfection of his blessedness on the grounds that such an one would be so absorbed in the contemplation of an un-ending fulness of glory that all other feelings would disappear. When a similar thought is brought forward by Kierkegaard, his explanation is that in matters of the highest welfare no man can save his brother, hence each need concern himself about his own salvation only. In contrast to this we have the strongly *sympathetic*

susceptibility of other natures.   In sharp contradistinction
to the tendency to limit the need of salvation to one's
own, is the wish which broke from St. Paul at the thought
of the spiritual fate of his Jewish fellow-countrymen
(Romans ix.): " I have great heaviness and continual
sorrow in my heart.   For I could wish that I myself
were accursed from Christ for my brethren, my kinsmen
according to the flesh." The sympathetic element is
also prominent in men like Stuart Mill and Buckle, for
whom the whole value of immortality consisted in its
affording the possibility of reunion with lost loved ones.
Sympathy, again, may move in larger or narrower circles.
Just as there may be a family ethic, a national ethic, and
an ethic of humanity, so there may be family religions,
national religions, and religions of humanity.   The
Frisian chieftain who withdrew his foot from the
baptismal stream, saying he would rather be in the place
where his forefathers were than in the paradise of the
new religion, did homage to a family and national religion.
We need not go back to antiquity to find examples to
show that, even after it has once broken through national
limitations, religion tends to renationalise itself. Primitive
Christianity (as before it Buddhism in India and Stoicism
in Greece) tried to transcend national limits.   In modern
days, Auguste Comte's 'positive religion' is distinctly
a religion of humanity—the faith in and resignation to
humanity as 'the great being' which develops in the
course of time, and in comparison with which the
individual man is only an abstraction.[126]   But for many
the sympathetic tendency of their religious life will not be
limited to humanity, as to a single plant in the wilderness
of existence. The religious problem only dawns upon
them with the question as to the relation of human life
and the human ideal to the whole of existence ; the
religion of humanity widens into a cosmological religion.
Such natures feel that their own fate is bound up, not

only with that of humanity, but also with that of the greater totality which makes up existence.   Here, again, St. Paul has expressed the fundamental mood of the sympathetic type, and in words of the most exalted poetry : " The whole creation groaneth and travaileth in pain together until now.   And not only they, but ourselves also, which have the firstfruits of the Spirit, even we ourselves groan within ourselves " (Romans viii. 22, 23).   Within each of these types, the idiopathic as well as the sympathetic, other qualitative differences of feeling may be conspicuous, *e.g.* the difference between fear and hope ; resignation and expectation ; between ethical, intellectual and æsthetic feeling, etc.

The main groups here characterised divide themselves into more specialised subgroups, if we take into consideration not only the predominant disposition but also temperamental differences.   For temperament also indicates dispositions—dispositions, however, of a more formal kind, for here differences depend on variations in the strength and *tempo* of the life of feeling and will, as well as on whether feelings of pleasure or of pain tend to predominate.   The attempt to co-ordinate these different dispositions and to discover the forms under which they appear in experience when inter-related can only be successfully conducted by the comparative individualistic psychology of the future.   The diversity of *nuances* will, of course, be very great, and will require the art of description, as distinct from psychological analysis in its elementary and abstract form, to do them full justice.

95. Within the sphere of knowledge the distinction between intuition and reflection is the most important. For the significance of this distinction in general, and for the transition from one of these forms to another, I refer my readers to my article entitled " La base psychologique des jugements " in the *Revue philosophique* of 1901.

Some men feel a great need of, and have a great

capacity for forming intuitive and permanent figures. In opposition to these *intuitive* natures are the *reflective* natures, with whom the process of thought itself, and not its close in the construction of a figure, is the main thing; indeed they may even be wanting altogether in the faculty and need of forming and holding fast to definite figures. Recent psychological inquiries have shown that there is a great difference between different people in this respect.[127] Within the religious sphere these differences are of great significance, since the need to personify the content of ideas differs widely with different individuals. Examples are not wanting of cases where this need, prompted by an affective interest in the object of the ideas, has led to the concrete personification of all surrounding things, *e.g.* numbers, letters, etc., and has even gone so far as to invest each one of these with sex.[128] Among men at this stage of development important differences may exist in this and similar relations, but the proper study of this question is of quite recent date. It is evident that this difference in the need for figures, especially for personification (which must in all consistency lead to the attribution of a definite sex to the object of the idea in question, since personality in and for itself is an abstraction), must be of the greatest significance in the controversy as to the personality of God, although it is a controversy which is generally carried on in abstract terms. Schleiermacher, who belonged decidedly to the reflective type, recognised this clearly : "Which of the two concepts (the theistic or the pantheistic), in so far as he will still need one or other, a man will appropriate to himself, will depend entirely on what he needs and to which side his imagination principally turns. . . . By imagination I do not understand something subordinate and confused, but that which is highest and most original in man ; outside it there can be nothing but reflection upon it, which is therefore dependent upon it. . . . Starting back in fear from the darkness of indefinite thoughts is one tendency of imagination, and starting back in terror from the apparent contradiction involved when we invest the infinite with the form of the finite is the other. May we not suppose that the same religious inwardness may be bound up with one as with the other?" Perhaps the opposition between the intuitive and the reflective types admits of a somewhat nearer determination. We must not assume that the reflective man has no faculty for forming definite and concrete images. But such an image only momentarily fills the whole horizon of his consciousness, and he will feel impelled to collate and compare these different figures and to push each one to its limits. He discovers that every figure has a limit, and that even within its own limits it is determined in various respects by its relation to what lies outside these limits. With intuitive natures a single figure is more apt to establish itself, and they are apt to forget that every figure has limits. Their thought moves between certain definite figures, and any impulses to reflexion that they experience are satisfied by this movement. Characteristic in this connexion is a conversation with Schleiermacher which Martensen, who was distinctly intuitive, reports in his *Autobiography*. The conversation turned on the possibility of forming a concept of the nature of God. Schleiermacher denied this possibility on the ground that we are only able to think in opposites, so that God, when he is conceived, must be placed in opposition to something else which would limit, and thus render him finite. Martensen, on the other hand, maintained that there must be inner oppositions within God himself, for without them he would not be 'the living God.'[129] He did not reflect that if 'inner oppositions' are to have real significance they must be determined by outer relations or correspond to such.

There is no life, either personal or impersonal, which is
not, at bottom, grounded on the relation of tension
between the inner and the outer. Schleiermacher
evidently assumed the necessity of an oppositional
relation to something outside God himself. His speculative needs were not satisfied with the analysis of a
single figure, hence he was, as a matter of fact, more
speculative than the 'speculative' theologians who
flattered themselves that they had overthrown his
point of view. Schleiermacher is himself an example
that the type is not determined simply and solely by
intellectual dispositions. Between the intellectual, the
affective and the volitional dispositions there is a
constant play of action and reaction. In many natures,
i.e. the so-called 'mystics,' it is inner feeling rather than
any other element that leads to the conviction of the
inadequacy of all ideas to figure forth the highest ; it is
feeling again which sharpens our sense of the limitation
of all figures and all concepts, and draws attention to the
law of relativity, to the 'relativity' of all knowledge.
And in this way we get a certain spiritual kinship
between mystic and critic, even when these functions
are not united in one and the same person. Many of
the arguments which were employed by Carneades
against the dogmatism of the Stoics recur again in the
Neo-Platonist Plotinus, and in recent times the combination of mysticism with criticism is by no means rare ;
Schleiermacher is perhaps the best example, but these
two dispositions were also conjoined in Spinoza, Lessing
and Kant. Lively feeling and clear thinking play into
each other's hands much oftener than is commonly
supposed.

Within the group of intuitives we may distinguish
again between those in whom figures of sight predominate (the visuals), those in whom ideas of hearing
play the chief rôle (the auditives), those in whom idea-

tional life is chiefly determined by the general sensations corresponding to inner organic states (the vitalists), and those with whom ideas of movement have the most essential significance (the motorists).[130] Among New Testament authors the writer of the Gospel of St. John is certainly a visual. Although the antitheses between life and death and light and darkness are both favourite figures with him, yet the latter is always the determining one ; moreover, the opposition between the living and the dead is also presentable to the sense of sight, and the Johannine use of it witnesses to its visual origin. St. Paul is vital and motor. "Eye hath not seen nor ear heard " the things which belong to the nature of God, and his innermost need finds vent in "groanings which cannot be uttered"; he also possessed a great gift for speaking with tongues—a distinctly motor trait. Life and death were evidently figured forth from a state of inner conflict which made itself felt throughout the limbs. Pursuit and struggle, longing and hoping, flesh and spirit, are images and terms of speech familiar to all readers of the Pauline epistles. The capacity to entertain visions and hallucinations of hearing is sub-ordinated to the sense of life and motion. Jacob Boehme belonged to the group of visuals as well as to the vitalists. John Bunyan seems to have been predominantly motor, however clear his visions and hallucinations of hearing may have been. Martensen was distinctly visual.

Within the group of reflective natures we must distinguish between analytic and synthetic endowment. Analytic natures emphasise differences, qualities, *nuances*, sharp transitions ('leaps') and prominent individual traits ; synthetic natures seek after unity, coherence, gradation, continuous transition and common features. A complete opposition is here, of course, impossible, for we can only analyse that which is given connectedly and as a totality, and gather together that which is given as

different, manifold and isolated.   But significant differences in the whole tendency of the life of thought may
be determined according to the predominance of analysis
or synthesis in particular cases.   The first three evangelists
convey, on the whole, the impression of analysis, of
separate emphasis of individual features.   The Gospel
of St. John, on the other hand, testifies to a great and
powerful synthesis.   Pascal, Hamann, and Kierkegaard
are analytical (in Hamann's case with a paradoxical
insistence, sharpened by analysis, on totality as the true) ;
Augustine, Zwingli, and Schleiermacher are synthetic.[131]
The longing for unity and continuity is associated with
the expansive disposition and the continuous type, while
a sharp eye for differences generally denotes the discordant disposition and the affective type.

These intellectual differences (and whatever others
there may be) make themselves felt in all spiritual
activity—within the domain of science and art, as well
as in that of religion.   But they come out all the more
strongly, and with all the greater justification, the more,
as in the domain of religion, a purely objective standard
of measurement by which to determine the form and
validity of ideas is lacking.   For this reason it is more
important here than in other spheres that attention
should be drawn to personal differences and to the
understanding of these.

96. There are a group of differences which do not
spring from any one side of the life of consciousness,
but express themselves in the relation in which the
religious experience and religious faith of a man stands
to the rest of his personality, and also in the relation in
which, as an outcome of that personality, he feels himself
to his environment.   The need of sympathy and of
communion with his fellows will depend on these
relations.   The more the individual dispositions we
have been describing co-operate in any individual the

less his capacity and need for communion with others ; indeed, he will feel so far from others that only the most indirect communication will be possible. In character- istic contrast to the religious individualism which thus arises appears the disposition to live and work in common forms and images.

Within the *idiopathic* type, again, isolation may have been determined by different psychological causes.

In moments of rapture and of the sudden welling up of feeling a man is torn out of any definite connexion with the rest of his life, and hence it becomes impossible for him to maintain the connexion with and understanding of other men. During such moments no clear ideas can be formulated, and communication is impossible. At its height this state assumes the character of *religious Bacchantism*. In the primitive congregations this phenomenon frequently occurred (see § 60) ; and if this state aroused any scruples in the minds of the leaders, it was only on the grounds that, as it could not be com- municated to others, they could not be edified by it, not from any doubts as to its effects on the subject himself. On this subject Paul writes : " He that speaketh in an unknown tongue edifieth himself ; but he that prophesieth edifieth the church " (1 Cor. xiv. 4). No wonder that the Church instinctively, apart from any other causes which may have worked in the same direction, repressed these phenomena.

While here it is the degree of strength of the inner states which tend to isolation, this effect is produced in other cases by the *content and nature of what is experi- enced*. The individual may, owing to his affective disposition, make experiences which he cannot com- municate to others because they bear the stamp of singularity, unaccustomedness, or exception. He may be impressed with the view that his experience of life has left him different from other men. His explanations, his consolations, and his guiding thoughts will therefore be different from those of other men ; it will even seem to him as though he spoke a different language. The melancholic temperament is particularly open to this sort of isolation, especially when it is joined to robust powers of reflection ; for thus every formula which might serve as a bridge to facilitate communication is looked at from this side and that, till it comes to be regarded as a useless instrument. In Danish literature Sören Kierkegaard is a remarkable example of this type. In his *Posthumous Papers* we may study the isolating power of melancholy and restless reflection.

Here it is the relation between the life of feeling and that of ideas which brings about the isolation ; in other cases, however, it may be the form of the religious ideas, the *idiosyncrasy of the symbolisation*, which hinders communication. If we observe exactly, we shall see that there are hardly two men who form 'one and the same' idea in the same way and under the same form, and this must be especially true of the formation of religious ideas, in which so many different elements co-operate. Choice of symbols is often determined by analogies which only explain the special religious experience of the individual. In a state of inwardness or spiritual tenseness the most insignificant circumstance, the most personal event, may become the core of a system of symbols whose value is only patent to the individual himself. There is a sort of ideal fetishism in which the highest symbols that men can form recall the very lowest (cf. § 47). To the agitated mind the most insignificant thing may appear to be a symbol of the highest ; but the adoption as a symbol of any one particular thing in any particular case may depend on conditions never, perhaps, to recur. Thousands have seen burning bushes and felt a soft breath, and have had visions and hallucinations, but only to the prophetic spirit do these phenomena appear as revelations.[132]   It is not even as though the symbolising process always yielded a clear picture.   This only happens with great prophetic personalities, whose inner experience acquires exemplary significance, and whose symbolising faculty has all the vigour of their inner life.   But this is not the case with most men.   Symbolisation does not always yield a clear crystallisation; the individual himself is sensible of the unripeness and particularity of his form of faith, and hence forbears from communicating it.   The reserve which holds many men back from revealing their innermost experiences to other men is often bound up with this fact.

This reserve, however, may be a kind of *spiritual chastity* which makes it impossible, apart altogether from the particularity of the event and the crudity of its expression, for a man to pull out his innermost treasures even for his own inspection, still less for the inspection of others.   For under inspection the stamp of inwardness is apt to perish.   We must be silent over our interior life or it may cease to be interior.   There are flowers, often the most fragrant and beautiful, which only bloom in the shade.   Both orthodox and free thinkers are often guilty of spiritual violence, for they are apt to press their own views on others, regardless of the fact that there are places where a man must take off his shoes (*i.e.* his positive and negative dogmas), for the ground on which he stands is holy ground. Every individual is holy as a centre of value and as a centre of experience (§ 92).

But there are other natures who, though they cannot be spoken of as 'reserved,' are yet little suited to religious fellowship and feel very little want of it.   There are sharply cut personalities in whom that pliability is lacking which would enable them to join themselves to others and to seek out the common points which might very likely be discoverable. However clear they may be in their own minds, they do not care to give expression to this clearness in a form accessible to other men. They are often content to be regarded as enigmas, not because they seek to be peculiar, but because, being content with the clearness in their own minds, they think it best for other men to find it for themselves as they have done. The one special expression for their experiences which they have been led to adopt, and which does them good service in their spiritual economy, will be pertinaciously and doggedly maintained by them, whether or not it is comprehensible to others. In spite of all their sharpness, singularity, and inaccessibility, such natures are of great importance, because they so distinctly assert the principle of personality. They offer defiant resistance to the desire to interfere—an all too human trait within the religious sphere—and by so doing they benefit the reserved and chaste natures who do not always know how to defend themselves.

Within the *communicative type* also different motives may make themselves felt; but from the nature of the case it is impossible that there should be as many differences as in the idiopathic type.

Every personal development begins with a *childlike acceptance* of traditional ideas. Here, then, there may be many different degrees and *nuances* in the way in which each particular development either draws nourishment from the traditionary, or gradually cuts itself loose from it (cf. the implicit faith of § 42). Some individuals never remark any difference between their own experience and traditional symbols. Others remark a difference, but recoil before it; they are afraid of finding themselves in a region of pure subjectivity, where they will apparently be left to their own guidance, and hence, with greater or less personal truth and intellectual honesty, they rush back into the common forms. The feminine nature has always shown itself more prone than the masculine to unconditional acceptance of traditional forms, even when the tradition could not boast the venerableness of age ; women remained longer than men within Catholic and orthodox communions, while in the French Revolution they were more constant to the cult of Reason.[133]

There are special *ecclesiastical natures* with whom the life of feeling and idea is always involuntarily attuned to the great circle of common symbols into which they have been initiated. They live and work immediately in the traditional, and are always capable of finding both the beginning as well as the close of their experiences in the traditional forms. There is in their case, for the most part, an immediate unity of word and experience, of name and thing, and the word and the name seem to them plastic objects having an existence beyond the subjective use which is made of them. Such natures will be inclined to make the possibility of communion, of a Church, the criterion of the genuineness of experience and faith. Both Buddhism and Christianity have included faith in the Church as a special clause in their creed. The possibility of establishing a cultus and collecting a congregation is ·even for theologians of the most liberal tendency a sign of a true religion. "Only by the faculty of establishing a cult does true religion declare itself" (Tröltsch). It matters not what the individual experiences or expresses, but whether a congregation can gather, and a tradition form itself round definite facts and ideas (Kaftan).[134]

We cannot hope to get beyond the continual struggle and the continual action and reaction between the individual and the species in the religious sphere any more than in other spheres. But we must never forget that the species is made up of individuals and has its life

in them ; hence all that is great and real must originate
with these individuals.   Let us also remember that
'facts' are not more real or 'ideas' more true because
the number of those who believe in them is a large one.

(c) BUDDHA AND JESUS

97. The principle of personality is both elucidated
and confirmed by the fact that, at the source of the two
highest popular religions, stand two great personalities,
each with his own special qualities.   Buddha and Jesus
divide the world between them.   An attempt to discuss
their psychological characteristics is but natural in this
connexion, however difficult the task may be ; it will
bring before us the greatest examples of the typical
differences already discussed, which are so full of significance for the religious problem.

The difficulty depends mainly on two circumstances.
In the first place, myth, legend and dogma very early
surrounded these figures.   The brilliant light which
streamed from these personalities overpowered their
contemporaries and immediate successors, and made a
purely objective and historical account of their lives
impossible.   It is with them as with the angel who in
Dante's *Purgatorio* points the way up, while he himself
is hidden by the effulgence he emits.   Secondly, antiquity
did not possess that interest, so prominent a feeling of
modern times, in tracing step by step the development of
a personality from youth to maturity.   The great figures
of antiquity are exhibited to us in their perfection, and
we are not shown the stages and crises they passed
through on their way to that fixed form in which we
behold them.

I have already (§ 43) sketched the leading characteristics of Buddhism and Christianity.   A religion
must, of course, bear the stamp of its founder.   But we

shall not be repeating ourselves if we pause here for a moment to dwell on the personality of these founders. We may always discern a difference between the source and the stream. At the source we shall find the original dispositions in all their purity ; the stream will be determined by many other circumstances.

98. Buddha was the son of a king. In the midst of the brilliance and splendour of life his attention was drawn to suffering, decay and death. This caused him to meditate upon life, although in person he had had no experience of its seamy side. Neither by way of speculation nor of asceticism did he succeed in finding peace. He only attained this consummation when he learnt to regard the world as a great illusion, produced and fostered by lust, impulse and desire. From the desire to live arise sensuality, hatred, cruelty, besides all pain and all grief, and these only fade away when the desire is suspended. Buddha teaches that there are five fetters from which men must free themselves : selfishness, doubt, lust, asceticism (as an end) and hatred. They all have the same source. If a man can free himself from these he will reach the state of highest peace which is called Nirvana, and which can be qualified by no positive predicate because it is the opposite of every state known in human experience. Buddha is reported to have said of Nirvana, as he was on the point of leaving his palace to become a hermit, "When the fire of lust is extinct, that is Nirvana ; when the fires of hatred and infatuation are extinct, that is Nirvana ; when pride (false belief) and all other passions and torments are extinct, that is Nirvana." On a subsequent occasion he said to his disciples, 'Some ascetics and Brahmins bring false accusations against me, and say : He is a liar, he preaches destruction, annihilation, cessation of real life. What I am not and what I do not teach these dear ascetics and Brahmins assert that I am and that I teach.

There is only one thing I preach now as before, suffering and the annihilation of suffering." Neither virtue nor knowledge was for him the highest, but 'the immaterial, absolute extinction of all illusions.' Buddha waived all other metaphysical questions, for when a man is transfixed with an arrow the thing to do is to heal his wound ; it is a matter of indifference who shot the arrow and of what the bow and string are made.[185]

Buddha's teaching was in a certain sense nothing new. But, as passed through the crucible of his mind and his experience of life, tendencies which were already astir in the religious and philosophical development of India acquired a peculiar cohesion and concentration. The concept of Nirvana had already appeared in the Upanishads, on whose teaching Buddhism is indeed based in all essential points.[186] The chief characteristic of Buddha, and that which induced him to create a new form of life, is an inwardness and freedom, a practical and concentrated life of self-absorption. Neither cult nor myth, neither asceticism nor speculation are any longer regarded as of chief importance, but in their stead the quiet, inward perfection attained by rising above all that is material, *i.e.* all that is finite and mutable. All external distinctions, even that of caste, which was of such pre-eminent importance in India, are matters of indifference. Buddha does not come before us as a reformer of external conditions. He had no wish to overthrow Brahmanism. But he gave in his personality a living example of personal perfection, which pointed beyond everything that was already in existence. Entrance to the highest stood open to all, without regard to caste or race. The struggle for peace of soul and inner unity and freedom was for him the only thing that counted, and for this struggle he aroused an enthusiasm which found its consummation in the joy of having conquered the world.

Buddha's greatness consists in having exhibited unity
and freedom as an ideal of personality. Personality is
not absolutely bound up with this or that ; it is no stuff,
but a world of inwardness which, owing to its opposition
to all that is external, can never be positively expressed.

Psychologically speaking, he belongs to the class of
expansives, and with him meditation ranks before exertion.   His was a reflective, not an intuitive nature, and in
his reflection the synthesis which mastered all differences
preponderated over analysis.   His was—in spite of the
energy without which Nirvana cannot be attained—a
passive nature ; or perhaps his activities were absorbed
in the process of renunciation by which alone it is
possible to maintain a purely passive attitude towards
existence.   He conceived the unity of personality in contrast to the individual elements of personal life, but not
as being also the totality in which, as organised members
of a great complex whole, these elements could find their
place.   The concept of personality with Buddha is like
the den of lions to which all tracks lead but from which
none emerge.   In the Buddhist collection of poems
Dhammapadan (The Way to Truth) it is said, in the
spirit of Buddha : " Amongst the intolerant tolerant—
Amongst the violent extinct—Ungrasping among those
who grasp—Him do I call a Brahma." [137]

When Buddha had at length attained the perfection
from which the tempter (Mara, the Indian devil) had
in vain tried to withhold him, the latter made a last
attempt, begging him to keep the peace so hardly won
to himself, and not teach any one else how to attain it.
Buddha's answer is characteristic, " Whether the perfect
man tells or does not tell his disciples the truth, he is and
remains the same.   How is this possible ? Because the
perfect man has denied and cut out from the roots the illusion which defiles, which sows repeated existences, which
breeds pain, which produces life, old age and death." [138]

He preached the truth, then, because he had no reason for not doing so ; his attitude towards the alternative of preaching or not preaching was strictly neutral. This must always be the attitude of a man who has no longer any wishes. Hence the inner love to others which stamps the Buddhistic movement lacks a psychological basis. The perfection of the individual is distinctly opposed to the wish for the perfection of others. And yet sympathy for other men must have been one motive for Buddha's rupture with his princely life. He himself had not been smitten by the suffering he saw all around him ; what stirred his feeling was the general lot of men. Hence it can only be in virtue of a faulty analysis that he regards absence of hate as identical with love ; hatred was, as we have seen, one of the five fetters which had to be riven. But it is not enough to burst fetters ; we want the liberty of free movement. The breaking down of the barriers between men did not suffice to effect a positive union between them. Two masses of ice do not melt into one another because the partition wall between them is broken down ; warmth must be super-added. This warmth was, there is no doubt, present in Buddhism at its source ; but fear of the unrest of life, critical reflection, and the inclination to passivity were so predominant, that the sympathetic motive never became fully conscious of itself. For love is one with life and hope, and becomes impossible when wishes are regarded as inadmissible. A motive which played no small part in checking any positive and active sympathy in Buddha and his earliest disciples was the thought that a man exposes himself to greater possibilities of pain and sorrow when his love is attached to an object, than when his interests only embrace his own ego and its development. For a father bewailing the loss of a son Buddha had only the following consolation : " Yes, so it is, my father. What a man loves brings him woe and sorrow, suffering,

melancholy and despair." Hence feeling must be limited
so that it may not assume the form of pain. The
thought that a higher spiritual development may be attained through the sorrow and loss which love involves
than is possible where love is shunned or circumscribed
seems never to have dawned on Buddha. The father
turned from the Indian sage with an outraged heart, and
he was right in holding that a perfection won at such a
cost is not able to express the highest personal value.

Nevertheless the love of others had a positive basis
with Buddha and his disciples, for it was regarded as
a consequence of attained perfection, and so far was
antagonistic to the pure neutrality with which Buddha
confronted Mara. Looked at more closely, we may find
two motivations, the one purely psychological, the other
more metaphysical. Love is a kind of out-streaming or
out-raying of the inner life on other men. This conception is in accordance with Buddha's expansive nature ;
it was, strictly speaking, illogical that this expansion
should be checked by Nirvana. In the introduction
to the book *Jakata*, love to others (which has been
Englished as 'goodwill') is given as the ninth perfection, and is described as follows :

> As water cleanseth all alike,
> The righteous and the wicked too,
> From dust and dirt of every kind,
> And with refreshing coolness fills—
>
> So likewise thou both friend and foe
> Alike with thy goodwill refresh,
> And when the Ninth Perfection's gained,
> A Buddha's wisdom shall be thine.

But it is not only by such an involuntary outpouring
that a certain connexion is established between personal perfection and surrender to others,[139] but also by
the fact that when all the distinctions and barriers erected

by illusion fall away, the individual recognises himself in all other beings. In one of Buddha's sermons he says of him who has attained the true peace, "In his loving, sympathising, joyful and steadfast mind he will recognise himself in all things, and will shed warmth and light on the world in all directions out of his great, deep, unbounded heart, purged from all anger and scorn." Here then it is plainly stated that a positive recognition and not merely a negation of barriers takes place, and liberation from hate appears here only as the negative condition of positive expansion, which is made possible by recognition (*i.e.* the knowledge of the unity of all things).[140]

How self-perfection and love—being as totality in itself and being as member of a greater totality—are to be united, is the great problem at the solution of which mankind are unceasingly labouring. In the solution presented by Buddha in the sixth century B.C., self-perfection distinctly predominates. It follows as a corollary from this, as well as from his tendency to passivity and the predominance of reflection over intuition, that he founded not a church but a monastic order. Buddhism became a popular religion only by means of the legends which wove themselves round the figure of Buddha, by the forms of worship which were adopted from the older religion of India, and, not least, by the strong emphasis of active love to man. The sect of the Mahayana regarded Buddha as the god of gods, and his birth as man as an event which occupied gods and devils. Buddhism spread over Eastern Asia, clad in a flowing garment of mythological and liturgical forms. As a modern Buddhist has put it, it "softened Asia." But for the most part its effect has been damping, lulling, restraining, except where—as in the case of the Japanese[141]—it has encountered and been transformed by active forward-pressing racial tendency, and by the influence of an earlier religion (Shintoism) which had especially developed the feelings of individuality and of nationality.

99. Jesus of Nazareth, the carpenter's son, lived in the midst of his people, shared their memories and their hopes, wished with them and suffered with them. He did not, like the Indian prince, look down from the raised platform of a spectator on the life which he observed; he stood in the midst of life, in the midst of a wishing world. He wanted to purify and idealise men's wishes, not to do away with them. And even though wishing and the struggle for the realisation of wishes involve pain, yet he is not prepared to give them up, for pain is not always an effect the cause of which ought to be removed; it may also be an occasion for the testing of strength, a means of purification, a way to holiness. The faith of Jesus in the conservation of value was shown by his conviction that values must be won and held by means of struggle and suffering, in contradistinction to the thought that the whole sphere in which wishes, struggle and suffering have their home must be exposed and destroyed as the great illusion that it is. Contrasts are here given their full value: the character of Jesus does not fall under the expansive type; it is rather one of conflicting opposites. And he is a man of strong will; he does not retire that he may find rest, but seeks to determine the fate of his people by leading them to higher things. He is, at any rate as compared with Buddha, an emotional man. His spirit is violently stirred; he is moved to his inmost depths; his soul can be shaken and deeply troubled; he can be angry. Jesus' love is no mere gentle and involuntary outpouring; it is a restlessly seeking and struggling love; his is an enduring not a resigned surrender. There is no fear here that love may bring grief, for our weal and woe are bound up with a far wider circle of interests than that comprised in the isolated self-assertion of the individual. We here find a deep confidence in

the power of love and a sense of its capacity for widening the mind which leave no room for narrow scruples. And this love strives by means of the idea of a kingdom in which every individual has a place to find its consummation in a higher justice.

Jesus was born into a different race and a different culture from Buddha. Moreover, five hundred years lie between them, and the Jewish founder of religion lived among far more unquiet and complex historical conditions than did the Indian. But common to them both is this, that their greatness does not rest on any particular idea or institution that they originated, but on the wonderful concentration with which they gathered up all the most significant elements in the life of their respective nations, on the inwardness and depth with which they realised the thoughts of preceding ages, and on the magnetism with which their personalities were invested and which streamed forth from them over the world.

Jesus of Nazareth is the man of intuition, of metaphor, of prophetic countenance. His reflection is of the analytic type; he draws great distinctions, sets up barriers, and points out oppositions. He aimed at leading us *by means of* the great contrasts of life, not *round* them.

Buddha rejected all metaphors and thoughts as inadequate to express the Highest, and here we see his intellectual energy. Jesus has no such scruples, but he nowhere indicated the limits of the metaphorical, and this fact has given rise to most of the grave doubts and conflicts which have arisen within the Church which he founded. All are agreed that certain expressions were only meant to be interpreted symbolically. But how far does the symbolical extend? The fact that this question was left unsettled follows from the intellectual character of the founder.

In the idea of the kingdom of God, as enunciated by

Jesus, lay, as already said, the possibility that individual personalities might attain the Highest without the wiping out of all distinctions. Hence the group of peculiar personalities which formed the apostolic circle is characteristic. Buddha's disciples lack this stamp of individuality. This fact is bound up with the racial differences between the Indians and the Jews. It has even been asserted that India is the land of types and that the Indian people is denied the power of producing strong individualities. At any rate this difference is strongly marked in the personalities of the Masters. Jesus led his disciples in a great historical movement, in a struggle for the ideal against the opposition of the world, and only in such a struggle can personality develop in all its idiosyncrasy. And yet there is one point in which the attitude of Jesus towards history is analogous with that of Buddha. He does indeed lay great weight on development towards a future goal, but at the same time he maintains that this goal cannot be reached in positive fashion by working under temporal conditions; it can only be attained through a supernatural crisis for which men must hold themselves in readiness. And since this crisis will soon occur, an attitude of tense expectation, unceasing watching and prayerfulness is essential for those who are awaiting it. Here again, as with Buddha (cf. § 14), we are left unenlightened as to what significance we are to attach to the development and many-sided culture thus so suddenly interrupted.

The great importance attached to the life of expectation and striving was, however, of deep significance. Jesus' prophetic countenance, as well as the apocalyptic character of his ideas, taught men by means of great figures to look towards great aims—aims which are to be reached through time, and not through the overthrow of time. By means of transformations and adaptations this contribution to spiritual life has been preserved to the

continued life of the race, even though the narrow frame
within which the contribution was originally presented
has been destroyed. The struggling human will has
found, in the great metaphors of Jesus, symbols it could
adopt as its own. But for Buddha's ideas such a
transformation and adaptation was not so easy; he
offered sedatives not motives; hence his positive
influence on spiritual life and on the stream of culture
was necessarily more restricted. Buddha's thoughts are
like the grains of corn which, neither destroyed nor
fulfilled, still lie within Egyptian graves as they were
laid centuries ago. But the thoughts of Jesus have
proved their fruitfulness, for, perishing in their original
form, they have in virtue of this dissolution risen again,
to grow and work under new conditions throughout a
succession of historical adaptations. Buddha 'softened'
Asia, but Jesus taught Europe a great Excelsior.

(*d*) Is the Principle of Personality a Principle of Growth or of Dissolution?

100. Growth and dissolution are not mutually exclusive, for the seed-corn must perish if it is to sprout;
but there may be processes of dissolution which lead to
no fresh growth. It is often asserted that the principle
of personality is purely negative and disintegrating.
For it seems to put differences in the place of unity and
of that which is common to all. In a word, it isolates
individuals. Must it not therefore be in opposition to
every world-conception which seeks for unity behind
differences, as all thought and all faith more or less tend
to do?

Temporarily, perhaps, the disintegrating effects of
the principle of personality are preponderant. But there
is a great deal within the religious sphere which ought
to and must be disintegrated if it is to have any future

at all. Such, for instance, is the hierarchical character,
governed by tradition, which religions up to the present
time have generally exhibited, and which is often very
little in accordance with the personal character of their
founders.   There are also direct as well as indirect
coercions of conscience which must be done away with,
and in this process fellowship in feeling and idea must
necessarily suffer.   This will entail suffering on many, not
merely on such as are unable to stand alone, and on those
natures we have called 'ecclesiastical' (§ 96), but also
on those whose need of communion with others persists in spite of differences.   Moreover, the principle of
personality, like all great thoughts, may be misunderstood and misapplied.   A man may think he is realising
it when he withdraws himself from the influence of all
examples and all instruction through tradition and the
experience of other men, but in this way he only ends
by being "a fool of his own making."

In contrast to Catholicism, Protestantism emphasises
the principle of personality.   This is at once its strength
and its weakness.   It is its weakness because it prevents
authority taking the place that it occupies in the Catholic
Church.   The Protestant Church does not command
the respect of all its individual members as the source
of all instruction, and it is wanting in solidarity in
its struggle with the powerful and increasingly cen-
tralised organisation of Catholicism.   On the other
hand, this will be an increasing source of strength
to it if the future belongs to freedom and personal
truth—when indeed it will have to labour more
seriously than it has hitherto done in the cause of the
principle to which it owes its existence.   Catholicism
has been able in the nineteenth century to do what
Protestantism never has been able to do and never will
do, *i.e.* create new dogmas.   But if Protestantism could
produce new personalities, would not that be of even

more value? From the Catholic side the difference between orthodoxy and free religious views has lately been described as follows : " Does truth exist except in the hearts of the faithful? Does it correspond to an objective reality? Does it impinge upon us from without? Has it wandered down to us from the other world? Or, on the other hand, does it exist as a product of personal conscience, as a resultant of individual religiosity, as the expression and translation of inner piety in the breast of every individual ; is it, in one word, subjective? . . . Does religious truth come to us from God, or is it worked out in every detail by us? In the former case it is, in the latter it is to be."[142] To which we may add that if religious truth depends upon experience and can only be won through its teaching, it is emphatically to be, and that within each individual. But that does not prevent it from corresponding to a reality, viz. to the relation of value to reality. What other relation can religious truth express but this ? and where else but in individual personalities does this relation come to light? If we suppose it to extend beyond the limits of human life, we can only do so by the help of poetry and analogy ; as long as personal life exists, so long new relations between value and reality, and hence new truths may arise. If we understand by 'God' something which is not only 'without' us but is also active in all reality, in all values—that is to say, precisely in the relation between value and reality and in the personalities which experience this relation—it is a false dilemma to suppose that we must say *either* a truth comes from God *or* it is worked out by each one of us.

Protestantism, as A. Sabatier has so strikingly remarked, is a method, and this method can be none other than that which is given with the principle of personality, with the recognition of individual personalities as centres of value and experience. The Reformers of course did not perceive all this. They dissolved the existing Church, but arrived at no logical principle which could supply a basis for a new one.

Catholicism was vanquished by ecclesiastical Protestantism as the Ptolemaic astronomy by the Copernican. Just as little as Copernicus foresaw that, when once he had displaced the earth from the centre of the world, the disappearance of any fixed central point must necessarily follow, so little, within the religious sphere, did the Reformers perceive that, the Pope once expelled from his throne, history could no longer find a place for an absolute authority. If a man demands authority, he ought logically to abandon Protestantism and return to the Church which has most completely realised it in principle.

101. There is no doubt that we live in an age which must be described as 'critical,' not organising. But this is not an admission that the only forces in operation are disintegrating forces. There is nothing to prevent smaller groups of persons forming round a common tendency of thought and spirit, or a common symbol. And such a union is often deeper and freer than one in which traditional authority is the uniting bond. Moreover the principle of personality, itself the expression of a great truth, may be regarded as one of the highest spiritual values. Whatever faith a man has or will have, the fact that he puts his whole soul into it, and that in the discovery and appropriation of that which he believes his individuality finds scope to develop, invests it with a value which not even the best guaranteed ready-made system could ever command. This is a point at which all men may arrive at mutual understanding, however widely they may differ in respect to the content of their faith. As the appreciation of personal *nuances* increases, the personal accent will be less and less sacrificed to the integrity of positive or negative dogmas. Here we catch a glimpse of an extension of the spiritual

world which is certainly no less important than was the extension of the material world in its time. The finest flower of all culture blossoms in the sympathetic understanding of the personalities of other men, and it may perhaps follow, as a result of these personalities, that they will regard essential questions from a point of view very different from that which we ourselves occupy. Up to the present, few steps have been taken along this path. But the principle of personality is a positive and fertile principle, precisely because it points us to this path, and in so doing opens up the possibility of a feeling of solidarity deeper than any which is conditioned by adhesion to the same dogmas.

Within the realms of philosophy, the more the principle of personality is realised in particulars, the more it testifies to the richness and fulness of existence. The history of philosophy shows us that this has been specially recognised and valued by those thinkers who emphasise unity (*e.g.* Montaigne, Spinoza, and Fichte). The principle of the unity of existence must be the more powerful and its working must exhibit a deeper and more inward character the more and the stronger the differences exhibited by individuals. It is easy enough to believe in a unity when we rub out or underestimate the differences. Religious contemplation reveals to the man whose faith in the unity is less abstract in character how differently the universal life may appear in different beings. This does not shake his faith; on the contrary it strengthens it. His doubt is directed towards that superficial faith in the unity which conceives it either as entirely abstract or as entirely external; but this doubt arises out of a still deeper faith (*alte dubitat qui altius credit*). In the ethical sphere the same may be said. The kingdom of personalities which all ethical systems labour more or less eagerly to construct will be the more perfect the greater the number of different personalities in mutual harmony it embraces. The criterion for the value of a human society consists not only in the prevailing unity and the prevailing law, but also in the multiplicity of qualities, of different centres of value and experience which it is able to combine. The same may be said within the purely psychological sphere. The validity of the principle of personality involves comparative psychology in problems of greater range and greater depth than could have been contained within the framework of the older psychology. This is especially true of religious psychology. The history of religion has hitherto occupied itself exclusively with those views which have been held in common within the religious sphere. But there might perhaps be a good deal more to learn from the history of individual views of life, and since we are all 'individual' and not man in general, instruction in the latter, when once it can rightly be given, will perhaps prove the more valuable of the two.

A principle which discloses such wide horizons and gives rise to such grave problems can be no merely disintegrating one. It is one of the most fertile principles which has ever been able to establish itself.

(e) LEARNED AND LAY

102. According to the principle of personality, the religious convictions of each individual must be acquired from his experience of values, of reality, and of the mutual relation between these. From this there follows a spiritual and universal priesthood. But self-dependence and self-activity are developed best in reciprocal action, not only with real life, but also with other personalities who take life independently, and to whom it is granted to know the world of value as well as that of reality more thoroughly and comprehensively than is possible for the individual just entering upon life. Hence the principle

of personality does not exclude examples and teachers. The distinction between learned and lay does not disappear. On the contrary,—the farther the principle of personality penetrates, the better will the unlearned understand that they need the learned, and the more will they be able to make use of what they can learn from them. They will recognise the significance of the work of the learned, viz. to enlighten us about the great interconnected system of existence and the riches it contains, and to replace dreams and dogmas by clear knowledge. And yet they will know that in the last resort thought can only find a clue to the riddle of life in individual experience and individual belief, and not through any new enlightenment or old dogmatism. When every individual makes up his spiritual account on the basis of his own experiences and of his own intellectual development, there will be an enrichment of the spiritual life. Scientifically regarded, personality is the last—perhaps insoluble—riddle, the concluding point dimly discerned in the distance. For scientific thought is itself a spiritual activity which can only be exercised by a person—and the last riddle would remain unsolved even if science could explain everything else, so long as it did not explain its own ultimate presupposition. I have tried to explain this more clearly in my *Psychology,* and I concluded a later edition of that work with the words : " The thought which explains everything else will be its own last and insoluble problem." But in life personality is the first ; it is that which supports all—even science, and which impresses its seal on all things. From the instinctive impulses of life, in which personality is always revealing itself on new sides, up to the ultimate results of scientific thinking, there is a long series of transitions ; but when life, as well as science, rightly understands itself, no interruption or leap will be found at any point.

103. The matter appears in a very different light when

regarded from the standpoint of the principle of authority. Within the Christian Church, after the expiration of the age in which revelation was immediately continued, through "the testimony of spirit and of power," in the inspiration of individuals, and after personal experiences began to be checked by the authority of the Church (cf. § 60), the difference between learned and lay soon became more marked with regard to religious questions than it was on scientific questions. Whether the Church refers the layman to an infallible Pope chosen by herself or to a book guaranteed by the Church, after due selection and rejection, as infallible, he must in either case assume a receptive attitude. His faith becomes an implicit faith (cf. § 42).

And yet a time came when churchmen themselves felt in the position of laymen. This happened when the validity of tradition, and more especially of the genuineness of the Bible, was called in question. The principle of authority naturally leads to the study of the history of authorities. But who shall decide which historical view of the development of authority is the true one? On scientific grounds the matter is not open to doubt. The origin and the development of all traditions and of all books can only be scientifically investigated by means of philology and historical criticism. But since preachers and theologians are often as innocent of philology and history as is the ordinary layman, the authority has finally passed from the hands of churchmen to those of the scholar. But all this was steadily ignored. In the Tridentine Council it was declared not only that the authority of the Bible is based on the Church and that the Church alone has to decide what is to be received as the true tradition, but also that the Latin translation of the Bible (the Vulgate), which had been used for centuries in the Church, was to be the basis of all sermons and all discussion. The members of that council had no idea of

allowing "grammarians and pedants" to rank above
bishops and theologians, or even of admitting that an
expert in Greek or Hebrew was qualified to pass judgment
on a heretic.[143]   In the Protestant world an analogous
situation has arisen which in quite recent times has
assumed large dimensions.   Protestant orthodoxy led to
the rule of theologians, since only theologians well versed
in the Bible were qualified to decide what was the true
doctrine.   The reaction of the laity against this state of
things was mainly responsible for the spread of pietism
and rationalism ; they wanted to overthrow the many little
popes who had taken the place of the one great one.
But when rationalism organised itself into a doctrinal
system, a new movement of the laity arose against it.
Many circles drew nourishment from the old writings
and traditions which they failed to find in the new
rationalistic theology ; moreover, rationalism demanded
a reinterpretation of the Bible and of tradition, as
well as a critical attitude towards both, while the laity
preferred to hold to the sacred words as they stood.
Nowadays faith in the latter is a democratic principle.
It has recently once more been asserted, as it was
formerly at Tridentum, that "the belief of the unlearned cannot be dependent on the testimony of the
learned "(Grundtvig).[144]

Scholars, however, did not give up investigation,
least of all investigation of the inner and outer connexion of the biblical writings with the age which
produced them.   Religious ideas were discussed from
the standpoint of general philosophy, which also penetrated with more or less consistency into the region of
theology itself.   Hence arose an opposition between
the Church and theology, which is one of the most
remarkable signs of the present day.   Theology, which
has been so often regarded as the antipode of science,
is coming more and more to be recognised as one of its

advanced guards. Or, as a modern theologian has expressed it, it stands as a buffer between the Church and
scientific thought—as a buffer which both sides make use
of as it suits them.

For the principle of authority makes war on both
sides : on the one hand against the free, personal life of
the laity, who are told to subject themselves to the forms
of the Church ; on the other, against science when it
attempts to test the origin and value of these forms.
But the most peculiar feature of the case is the increasing
adherence to the principle of authority within lay circles
in the course of the nineteenth century. This principle
has proved itself democratic ; to those whose circumstances, inner and outer, do not permit of independent
research, with its labours, dangers and crises, it offers
a refuge, certainty and support. The firm grip which
Catholicism has over the masses is becoming clearer
every day ; and in Protestant churches an increasing
number of laymen and lay preachers bear rule in the
religious life. Within the Protestant churches it is the
laity far more than any church authorities who control
the orthodoxy of the preachers. This influence even
extends to theology, since the preachers, who are themselves controlled by laymen, expect to be consulted
as to the appointment of theological professors. The
Church, as it has been remarked, can neither do with
nor without theology.[145]

104. When the Church steps in between science and
the personal life of the individual and attempts to keep
them apart it offends two spiritual powers at once.
Such an act does not go unpunished.

The intellectual brilliancy which at one time centred
in the great ones of the Church, and from thence
illuminated the whole life of the Church, has passed
away. Real, serious, concentrated religious thinking
becomes increasingly rarer. Men only ask anxiously

whether they have satisfied the traditional dogmas. In the Catholic Church men live in the thirteenth, in the Protestant in the seventeenth century. In addition to the predominance of tradition there is, however, another feature, more worthy of recognition, which is peculiar to the Church of to-day ; I refer to the great philanthropic work she has organised. The type of St. Vincent de Paul is again amongst us. But the advantage which philanthropy gains by spending neither time nor strength in thought cannot in the long run make up for the disadvantage to which spiritual life is exposed, from the fact that independence is shackled by dread of free discussion of the most important questions in life.

The two spiritual forces which the Church is striving to keep apart will some day discover one another. Looked at more closely we see that the modern development of the Church, characterised as it is by conscious adherence to the principle of authority in larger circles than before, is yet in harmony with the principle of personality. The movement among the laity may for a time seem to have a retarding effect inimical to science, but in and for itself it is a sign that the somnolent faith in the letter is replaced by a living one, and between these two kinds of faith the principle of personality leaves us in no doubt which to choose. Owing to the stress laid on the salvation of every individual soul many more men are aroused to personal life than was previously the case, and, once aroused, this life will not be checked in its work of reshaping the old forms, and even of reaching out beyond them. The most important advances within the spiritual sphere often come from the most unexpected quarters. New values very often spring not from the world of criticism and analysis, but from circles in which men have lived with depth and fervour in the old values. History does not always pursue a straight course.

IV. ETHICAL PHILOSOPHY OF RELIGION

A. RELIGION AS THE BASIS OF ETHICS

So wie die Völker sich bessern, bessern sich auch ihre Götter.
LICHTENBERG.

Mit ihren Gemeinden wachsen die Götter.
ERWIN ROHDE.

105. As in its classical epochs religion gave man his whole conception and all his understanding of existence, so too it gave him his ethics, *i.e.* it indicated the highest ends of willing and thinking, set up patterns, laid down rules and laws. And as its explanation of nature was based on the intervention of supernatural powers, so its ethics are based on the revelation of the dependence of man on supernatural forces which direct his fate in this and perhaps also in another world. Ethics, then, is here based on a supernatural history. It depends on the relation in which a man stands to the supernatural world whether he can live rightly in the natural world. Nor was this illogical, for during the classical ages of religion men knew more about the supernatural than the natural world, and life in this world was nothing but a means to life in the other.

The relation, however, is more complex than might be thought at first sight. I have only spoken of religion in its classical ages. But the nature of the relation between religion and ethics, as it appears at such times, had a long previous history. And if we study the relation between religion and ethics in its historical

development, we shall find a constant process of action
and reaction going on between them, so that not only
does religion influence ethics, but, conversely, the ethical
development of man reacts on the character and content
of his religion.   Moreover, when we come to speak of
basis and justification, we shall find that, in the long run,
it is religion which is based upon ethical ideas, and not—
even in the classical ages of religion—*vice versa*.   The
value and significance which are attributed to religion
have, as their logical presupposition, certain ethical ideas,
to the precise formulation of which the religious consciousness does not feel itself impelled.   We must now
examine, both from the logical and historical points of
view, the state of the case when religion claims to be the
basis of ethics.

106. In the lowest forms of it with which we are
acquainted religion cannot be said to have any ethical
significance.   The gods appear as powers on which man
is dependent, but not as patterns of conduct or administrators of an ethical world - order.   Underlying the
concept of God, however, as we have already seen (cf.
§§ 45-55), is a long process of development, which is
essentially determined by the influence of the life of feeling on the manner and forms of thought.   The processes
which enter into the development of myths, legends, and
dogmas, are not of an exclusively intellectual nature ;
feeling is constantly operative, selecting and rejecting,
reinforcing and restraining.   And the life of feeling in
its turn is, of course, determined by human life and its
conditions.   Ethical feeling develops in the struggle for
life; in the struggle of the individual, but more especially
in the struggle of the family, of the clan, and of the
nation for existence.   In the course of this struggle men
discover the value of justice and of love.   This experience
cannot fail to exert an influence on religious ideas.   Even
if these ideas were originally formed without the co-opera-

tion of ethical motives, they will henceforward develop in harmony with ethical ideas. From purely natural forces which could be defied or evaded, the gods became ethical powers whom men neither could nor wished to defy. Not till men have discovered ethical problems in practical life and have developed an ethical feeling (which in its first inception may not be strong enough to confront other feelings independently), not till then can the figures of the gods assume an ethical character. The great aims of human life become now—on a larger scale and in an idealised form—the aims of the gods. The gods stand forth as the champions and defenders of the highest values with which men have become acquainted in their struggle for existence. What other aims and qualities could man attribute to his gods, or conceive as divine, but those which he has learnt from his own experience to recognise as the highest? Man grows with the growth of his aims, and with his growth grow the gods. It is a psychological impossibility that man should be able to conceive divine capacities and wishes which he himself has never experienced in any degree. This is true not only of his idea of god, but also of his idea of immortality. At the lowest stages the idea of immortality is as void of any proper ethical significance as is that of the gods. At this stage it comes natural to believe that men do not die. Do not the images of memory and of dreams witness to the fact that the dead can still affect us? From the standpoint of animism (§ 46), belief in immortality forms a part of the natural philosophy of man, but does not necessarily possess any ethical significance. The continuance of life after death is, in and for itself, just as indifferent as the fact whether we live in this world a few years more or less. Only when the conception of judgment, of reward and punishment, is united with the belief in immortality can an ethical moment be included within it.

The transition from nature religions to ethical religions has rightly been called the most important transition in the history of religion.[146] It is far more significant than that from polytheism to monotheism, to which too great importance has often been attached.

107. And yet even nature religions have their ethic, for they make definite claims on man. He must show respect and obedience to the divine powers who demand ceremonies and sacrifice in their honour. Men have thus to pass through a course of obedience and self-control ; they learn to subordinate themselves, while at the same time their lives acquire a wider horizon. Since the worship of the family, of the clan, or of the nation is shared in by all, it helps to nourish a feeling of solidarity which may acquire ethical significance. And as the forms of worship are handed down from generation to generation, and their fulfilment is regarded as a sacred duty, the idea of a historical connexion which must be carried on is inculcated and fostered. The consciousness of continuity is developed by inner dependence on ' the gods of our fathers.' Even here, then, at the stage of nature religions, we find religion exercising a disciplinary power,—a work of preparation which may afterwards acquire no small significance for ethical development.

Between nature religions and ethical religion we find a mass of intermediate forms. Even when the gods are conceived as administrators of the ethically good, it is not necessarily supposed that they themselves obey the laws which they impose. They often represent the good without being good themselves. This opposition sometimes comes out very naïvely in popular religions. It does not occur to a man to demand the same from his gods that he does from himself or from other men. Moreover, different stages of ethical development are often at war with each other within one and the same popular religion, for such religions are conservative in character, and cling to old forms even after they have accepted new ideas.   If in former times the gods demanded bloody, perhaps even human, sacrifices, they were, after all, only acting in accordance with the barbarous ethic of the race.   At a higher stage of development men themselves turn away from the committal of such bloody deeds, and thus an allegorical interpretation is given to the old command, or else a symbolical representation of the bloody actions is deemed sufficient.   It may even be denied that God ever demanded a bloody sacrifice (so the prophet Jeremiah, vii. 22-23).   We get here a characteristic transition from ritual to ethic, analogous to the transition already referred to in another connexion (cf. §§ 53, 71) from liturgy to religious speculation.   The religious ceremonial of purification (*e.g.* in the Persian and Jewish religions and in the Orphic rites of the Greeks) was afterwards explained as symbolic of the purification of the soul.   The teaching of the Vedanta (in the Upanishads) is a consistent, symbolic interpretation of the old Brahminic customs ; and just as the Vedantic philosophers explain the old Brahminical customs, so Plato explains the Orphic mysteries.   Martensen expounds the Mosaic command to sow a field with two kinds of seed and to wear clothes made of two kinds of cloth, as a device for impressing the great distinction between the holy and unholy, as a kind of exercise in ethical distinctions.

Sometimes the struggle between lower and higher ethical ideas which have arisen in the minds of the people may be traced in ethical contrasts within the world of the gods.[147]   We find a characteristic example of this in the Babylonian mythology.   The god Bel had brought a flood on the human race.   The god Ea, however, had warned a pious man, who saved himself and his family in a boat.   This caused Bel to fly into a rage, especially as he had not been invited by the rescued to their sacrificial feast. High words arose between Bel and Ea ; the latter maintained that it was unjust to make the good perish with the bad, and Bel was finally forced to admit that Ea was right. We get a mono-theistic version of the same feature when Jahve regrets having sent the flood, and declares he will not do it again. In northern mythology, ' Aegir's feast ' presents an example both of ethical contrasts within the world of the gods and of ethical criticism of one god by another. From conceptions such as these a natural transition leads to the idea that the evil in the world—hitherto, like the good, supposed to proceed from the gods—must now be attributed to gods of lower rank or to beings which are the antitheses of the gods. The older forms of faith were not familiar with any very sharply drawn distinction between good and evil. Oldenberg [148] remarks on this point *à propos* of the Indians : " The religious documents of old India reveal, with the completeness and transparency which characterises them, how an embodiment of the dis-tinction between good and evil (such as that which afterwards appeared in the opposition between Buddha and Mara) is alien to the oldest forms of belief, and must be alien to them, although in the course of a slow development it becomes more and more accentuated. The faith of the Rigveda . . . is still near to the pre-ethical period of religious development. For the most part good and gracious, yet the Vedic gods are still far from being exalted above evil and malice. The deepening of the inner life, the progressive moralisation of religion, must always increasingly make for the resolution of this old indecision, for the partition of the positive and negative between the great powers of existence." In Parseeism, as is well known, this con-trast is sharply emphasised. Among the Greeks, Plato, as far as may be gathered from his last work, saw in

the assumption of an evil principle, existing side by side
with the good, the only possible way of maintaining the
goodness of the deity in the face of the experience of
the discords of this world.

This great difference between nature religions and
ethical religions may even be traced in high-flying, philosophical and theological speculations. For it is, in
fact, an opposition between power and goodness, and
every attempt to establish a concept of God has to
reckon with the difficulties to which this opposition gives
rise. This is already evident in the question discussed
by Plato (in the *Euthyphron*), *i.e.* if good is good
because God (or the gods) wills it, or if God (or the
gods) wills the good because it is good. In the Middle
Ages this opposition was fined down to the struggle
between the two scholasticisms, Thomas Aquinas teaching that God willed the good because it was good,
while Duns Scotus said the good was only good because
God willed it. With the former, power is determined
by goodness ; with the latter, goodness by power.

The path thus followed by the religious life, under
the influence of ethical feeling and ethical ideas, naturally
led to the recognition of the independence of ethics over
against religion. If God wills the good because it is
good, there must be some criterion of good and evil
which is independent of the divine will, and men must
be able to discover this criterion, since without it they
could not know that that which God wills is good. And
if the good is good because God wills it, then men must
ask themselves why they call that which God wills
'good,' instead of merely saying, God wills what he
will. Religious faith, when it has become clear as to
its own nature and has attained its zenith, assumes an
independent human ethic, which has, as a matter of fact,
developed historically under the practical influence of
the ethical feeling of men.

108. Religious and ethical motives need not stand in a relation of complete opposition to one another, for religious motives may include ethical within themselves. This will be the case, for example, when nature religions have begun to develop in the direction of ethical religion. Religious motives may have every variety of colouring, according to the relation in which the ethical motives they contain stand to other elements, such as fear, hope, admiration, etc. It may be as difficult for the subject himself as it is for others to decide which is the predominant element. Often the religious motive is the form in which a man becomes aware of the utterance of his consciousness, because he knows no other form of idea, no other language in which he could clothe his self-knowledge. Schopenhauer has drawn attention to this in a striking passage.[149] " In good actions, the doer of which appeals to dogmas, we must always distinguish whether these dogmas were the real motive of the act, or whether they are not really the apparent justification by which he endeavours to satisfy his own reason concerning a good deed which proceeds from quite another source, which he performs because it is good, but which he cannot properly explain because he is no philosopher and yet ponders over the matter. But the distinction is very difficult to find, because it lies deep within the heart."

He who is just because the God in whom he believes is just, must attribute value to justice itself. Here religion has its logical premiss in an independent ethic, whether or no it consciously posits it. The logical premisses of our thinkings and doings can only be elucidated by means of express attention and analysis, which cannot develop until the stage of critical self-consciousness has been reached. When the question arises why these particular predicates are predicated of the deity, self-reflection leads back, through a greater or

smaller number of intermediate links, to independent evaluation and thought, for without these every predicate must
in the end appear meaningless to reflection.   Religious
consciousness, when confronted by the ethical principle,
experiences what Descartes experienced when he sought
to find a basis for the conception of the law-abidingness
of nature.   Descartes deduced this obedience to law
from the unchangeableness of God; but he established
the belief in the unchangeableness of God by means of
the law of causality.   But the whole meaning of the
axiom of causality is that nature is law-abiding.   Hence
the *détour* through the concept of God is, from the
logical point of view, superfluous.   The religious
motivation of the value of ethical qualities is also a
détour, for this value was already acknowledged at the
moment when these qualities were predicated of
God.

Values must be discovered and produced in the world
of experience before they can be conceived or assumed
to exist in a higher world.   The other world must
always be derived from this world; it can never be a
primary concept.   It changes with the changes of this
world.   Now it is a continuation, now an intensification
of this life; sometimes it is conceived as in all things its
opposite.   The content of religion always points back
to life in the world of experience, and without a knowledge of this life would be incomprehensible.   Discussion
is always led back by implacable logic to the conceptual
priority of ethics over religion.

This logical relation is in accordance with what we
learn from historical development (§§ 106-107).   It also
agrees with our psychological analysis of the essence
of religion, which led us to regard religious values as
secondary (§ 31) in comparison with those which are
immediately determined by the impulse alike to self-
preservation and to self-surrender.

But there is yet another, and that the most essential, side from which religion points back to ethics. If we inquire as to the value of the faith in the conservation of value, the answer cannot be given by religion only. For it is always possible that such a faith might be unnecessary or even inimical to the effort to discover and produce values in the world of experience. Were this so, the effect of religion would be to diminish energy and waste time. The necessary condition for the justification of religion, then, is that neither force nor time be withdrawn from ethical work. On the other hand, religion will gain in positive value if it can be seen to be a condition which enables us to produce and discover values within the world of experience.

The result at which we have now arrived is that religion in its historical development, as well as in its motives, its content, and its value points back to ethical presuppositions, even when it has all the appearance of serving as a basis for ethics.

B. RELIGION AS A FORM OF SPIRITUAL CULTURE

'Εὰν μὴ ἔλπεαι, ἀνέλπιστον οὐχ ἐξευρήσει.
HERACLITUS.

There are cases where faith creates its own verification.
WILLIAM JAMES.

109. It is characteristic of the way in which the religious problem is stated in modern times that the discussion turns more and more on the value of religion, rather than on the truth of any particular doctrines. The underlying assumption in this case is that the essence of religion does not consist in any solution offered by its teachings of the problems of life and of the universe, but in its practical influence on human life, on the significance which it possesses as a peculiar form of spiritual culture.

In the violent religious polemics of the eighteenth century the battle raged between dogmatism on one side and the hierarchy on the other.   It was the Church in its capacity of civil authority that men wanted to overthrow and destroy.   There was a general disposition to regard dogmas either as capriciously produced or as instruments employed by the clergy to get power over men's thoughts and thus over men themselves.   The polemics of Voltaire, Diderot, and Holbach are all based on this conception.   In the nineteenth century—which may be said, philosophically, to have begun with Rousseau, Lessing, and Kant—men started from the intellectual expression and external organisation of religion and went back to its inner creative and moving forces.   A distinction was drawn between these original forces and the products through which, at a given time and at given places, they expressed themselves.   But this distinction could not fail to suggest the question whether the intellectual forms and external organisations under which religion had hitherto always appeared in history might not disappear and be succeeded by other forms and organisations, without any loss accruing to the essential elements of religion.   The idea of 'a third kingdom' was adopted and developed in various ways, for a conception of life lying beyond the opposites which had hitherto so uncompromisingly confronted each other now began to be possible.   I have discussed this tendency at greater length in an article entitled " The Conflict between the Old and the New " (*International Journal of Ethics*, vi.).

The criterion of the value of religion and of its significance as an expression of spiritual culture must ultimately be an ethical one.   If we start with a sufficiently wide conception of ethics, we may say that the task of estimating all forms of spiritual development falls to the share of ethics.   There is a free republic of culture in which the work of material as well as of æsthetic, intellectual and religious enlightenment and philanthropic work are fully recognised, a society which occupies an all-important place side by side with the family and the State, and which works in reciprocal action with them. It is one of the functions of ethics to elucidate the value of spiritual and material culture. In this connexion religion itself, although not the final basis of ethics, acquires ethical significance.

All culture imposes tasks on human will and human activities, and we have next to inquire how far and in what way the nature of man is developed by his labour in the fulfilment of these tasks. But culture also brings goods, supplies needs, and affords satisfactions, and we must, therefore, investigate the relation between these goods and satisfactions and the development of human life. The value of religion must be examined from both these sides.

Our inquiry will be partly psychological and partly sociological. For religion is not altogether the individual's affair. More than any other form of spiritual culture it makes for solidarity. It has produced the need of communion and has thereby developed social feeling.

(*a*) Psychological Inquiry

110. We have seen that religion is in the last resort dependent on ethics for its criterion of value. Religion commends itself to the conscience of man, and in so doing presupposes that, consciously or unconsciously, he possesses a criterion by which he can estimate the values which religion seeks to maintain. But this does not exclude the possibility of religion being of the greatest importance as a *motive for action*, *i.e.* when it is a question of procuring for recognised values, at particular

moments and in particular situations, the mastery over
the will.

The distinction between motives of value and
motives of action is, in my view, of the greatest ethical
importance. The motive of valuation determines the content of ethics, those principles and rules which form the
basis of our valuations and of our strivings. The motive
of action, the moving force which impels us, in particular
cases and within particular spheres, to willing and doing
need not coincide with the underlying motive of
evaluation. There are many different motives of action
which may all lead in the direction required by the
motive of evaluation. Hence the motive of evaluation
need not be realised on every occasion ; we have only to
discover or search for it in doubtful cases, or when
psychological interests prompt us to investigate the
whole tendency of the life of the will ; it may even be a
sign of perfection that the motive of evaluation is not
the immediate motive to action, or, in plain words, it
is sometimes a bad sign if a man has always to consult
his conscience before acting. The more specialised
motives are generally the healthiest and the best.
Such specialised motives are family-feeling, friendship,
patriotism, pleasure in work, artistic and scientific
enthusiasm. These motives are tested and recognised
by the original motive of evaluation ('the conscience '),[150]
but it cannot take their place, unless indeed life is to be
robbed of its living and manifold content. It may be
taken as a test of perfection of character how far the
motive of valuation is concealed or potential and does
not intervene at every moment between the motives of
action which are necessary to the fulfilment of special
tasks. The distinction between motive of evaluation
and motive of action makes the ethical significance
of religious motives possible, even though the sovereign
decision as to what is right and good, *i.e.* the deter-

mination of the content of ethics, must not be sought in religion. Where religious motives are present their presence must sometimes be recognised. Possibly they could not be replaced by any other motives, and attempts to destroy them might result in replacing strength and harmony by uncertainty and weakness. Every man must be taken as he stands, and the question is how much farther he can grow from the point at which he now is. The burden of proof here lies, of course, with him who intervenes in the inner life of another man in order to change his motives. Let him beware above all things lest he check the forces which have hitherto been at work, for he may not find it so easy to supply others in their place. Only too often criticism has deprived men of the capacity and the courage to dare, to endure and to suffer. Religious motives which enable this capacity and this courage to develop have in this their justification and provide in this their own verification.

Often, if not generally, however, religious motives have only temporary and educational significance. They then have the significance, which is associated in general with the recognition of authorities and exemplars, of drawing attention to a matter which can only thus acquire direct and immediate value. In the course of human development countless re-adjustments of motives take place, and motives which can themselves possess no direct and immediate value may acquire value as intermediary links in development. Everything which, directly or indirectly, serves to make life wide, secure, and rich in content has its value, and ethics must not copy dogmatism and ask too anxiously after a man's creed.

111. The investigation of the religious motives to action must be undertaken from a purely ethical standpoint. And if it should prove that religious motives are very different in colouring (§ 108), it follows that they

will be very different in value. Where, *e.g.* the thought
of reward or punishment awarded by the deity in this
or in another life is of preponderating importance, we
find ourselves confronted by a low motive, even when
the tendency which it produces in certain cases is
deserving in other respects. When faith stands higher
than love, or when faith and love are at variance with
one another, there is, as a rule, a struggle between
religion and ethics. When it is not blind, 'goodwill'
works immediately towards the goal adopted by human
ethics, while faith may very possibly work in an opposite
direction. Faith separates, 'goodwill' unites. Among
the differences which this 'goodwill' encounters and has
to overcome are differences of creed. Since, as we
have seen, religion and ethics are related in essence, the
peculiar character of a religious as well as of an ethical
standpoint may be due to the relation between self-
assertion and self-surrender. Faith is the expression of
self-assertion ; love, of self-surrender. Hence a doctrinal
point of view which crushes down love at important
points tends more or less decidedly towards egoism. Is
a man entirely self-seeking in his religion, is the only
matter of importance for him to gain safety, peace, and
healing for his own ego, regardless of the fate of the rest
of existence ? or does he seek a great harmony, a
kingdom of values, such that the fate of his own ego
will depend entirely on the laws and conditions of this
kingdom ? The religious motives assume different
forms according to the answer given to these questions.
It is not without significance that the Church has for the
most part thought it dangerous to emphasise too strongly
an unconditional surrender, involving complete suppres-
sion of all consideration for self. Fénélon, for instance,
was obliged by the Church to recall his teaching on the
'disinterested love of God.' When the self-regarding
element is maintained in its independence and predomin-

ance, then the result will be a supernatural egoism, an 'other-worldliness.' Ethically considered, we cannot refuse our sympathy to the Saracen woman of whom Joinville, in his biography of St. Louis, relates that with a pan of fire in one hand and a jug of water in the other, she was seen to walk down the street of Damascus. On being asked by a monk what she intended to do with these things, she replied, "Burn up Paradise and put out the fires of hell, so that men may do good for the love of God." The Church has fostered the egoistic element in religious feeling for educational reasons. It may possibly be indispensable in many cases (cf. § 94), but there is no justification for attributing to it any special value while some of the noblest of human efforts are condemned as 'brilliant vices.' Similar educational considerations induced the Lutheran Church to maintain that the threat of the law's severity and of God's anger produces consciousness of sin and anxiety for the soul's salvation, and thus prepares the mind to appeal to God's mercy. Another conception had indeed been brought forward before the time of the Reformation, viz. that true repentance might perhaps be aroused if the ideal, in all its splendour, were revealed to the conscience of men, to excite in them, not fear of judgment, but the hope of attaining to the ideal. Such a conception, it is true, presupposes that the gospel was promulgated before the law. Luther and Melanchthon would have none of it, however. They rejected it on the ground that they must adapt themselves to the capacities of the 'people,' of the 'ignorant,' and could not stop to 'split hairs'![151] From the ethical point of view, there is no doubt that the attraction of the ideal and the cheerful glance of hope are healthier and more justifiable motives than the fear which the promulgation of the law is supposed to excite.

But apart from any particular colouring of the

Z

religious motives, we must remember that they can none of them possess ethical value unless the influence they exert on the mind is spontaneous; they must not be imposed from without, or consciously adopted or postulated. Voltaire said that if God had not existed, men would have had to invent him. But such an artificial God would be no good, even for the police duty which Voltaire had in mind. Religious feeling represents a real spiritual capital only when it springs up involuntarily from the inner needs of the heart. Like all immediate and natural feeling, it can only be produced and determined indirectly. When the sense of personal idiosyncrasy has sufficiently developed, we may hope that delicacy will take the place of the spiritual coarseness with which the matter is now so often treated.

Closely connected with the demand for personal integrity is the demand for intellectual honesty.[152] It is not sufficient justification of a religious motive that it is an expression of a man's personality; we must also be assured that the individual has done all that his capacities and his circumstances of life permit him to do to test the validity of the religious ideas which are incorporated in religious motives. Motives which can only flourish at the cost of love of truth can have no ethical value. And yet we may read nowadays eulogies of religious motives and of their social value, where not a word is said as to the duty of intellectual honesty; and this fact involves many natures in a tragic conflict. There are men especially fitted by their deep love to their fellows and their untrammelled sense of the needs and requirements of the personal life to be the ethical and religious teachers of their nation, but they are debarred from entering on this calling by the forms, congealed and dogmatic, which national life within the Church has assumed. While there are others, intellectually thick-skinned and emotionally superficial, who, unhindered by this dogmatic form, are

only too ready to publish themselves far and wide as
dignitaries of the Church. In the age of rationalism
and romanticism it was considered both justifiable and
necessary for any man who entered the service of the
Church as a teacher to adhere personally to the idealistic
and symbolical view of religious dogmas, although in
his sermons he made no distinction between symbolical
and literal truth. Men like Fichte and Schleiermacher
expressly taught this, and the latter put it into practice.
In our day such a view comes more and more into conflict
with the demands of personal integrity and intellectual
honesty. But the Church will find her relation with
intellectual culture become increasingly involved if she
persists in retaining a dogmatism which makes conflicts
of the kind we have been describing possible.[153]

112. Apart from its influence on particular actions,
that religious conception which holds fast to the conservation of value in existence must always be of great
significance, for it opens up a bright and wide horizon
for human strivings and workings. I am not here
thinking of the special forms under which such an
ethical idealism might appear. It is not the duty of
the philosophy of religion to construct a religion, but
to test the significance of that which is fundamental in
all religion.

Faith in the conservation of value leaves us, since we
are not able to trace out in detail the metamorphoses
values undergo, with the conception of existence as a
great system of potential values, to be transformed,
partly by means of human action, into actual values.
The ethical consciousness is rooted in the profound
conviction that there is a value which must be maintained as the highest, hence at this point the ethical and
religious consciousness unite. Religion can here appeal
to the fact that, however existence in its innermost
nature and its immeasurable interconnexion may be

constituted in other respects, it must at any rate contain within itself the necessary conditions for the existence of those values which men have learnt to recognise or have been able to produce. No one can ever prove that the genesis of the valuable in the world is due to an accident. It may be that the innermost essence of existence only reveals itself at the points at which value appears, although such a view involves the difficulty of reconciling these points with others at which we find the very opposite of anything to which we could apply the term valuable. If we explain these revelations of value as symptoms that the great evolutionary process of the universe is a divine work, we may conceive our work as a part of this divine work, as a part which is determined in quality as well as in quantity by our own nature and by our position in the universe. This throws a new light on our field of labour. We now recognise the limits of our capacity and of our strivings to be the limits within which the work we have to do lies— in so far as they are real limits and not mere obstacles, the destruction of which affords exercise for our striving. We may thus see ourselves at once as independent and personal beings, and as members of the all-embracing and interconnected order of things.

Such a belief possesses within the sphere of ethics the same significance as that possessed by ideas, anticipations, and hypotheses within the theoretical sphere. A too anxious adherence to experience is apt to dull our sight and blunt our instinct for new possibilities; this holds good in the practical as well as in the theoretical sphere. Heart and courage make many things possible which would otherwise never be realised, at any rate in the case of some individuals. Here, again, W. James's thesis that there are cases where faith creates its own verification holds good.

Belief and wish are near akin. The belief which can

not be proved is a wish that what we believe may be true. This wish may even lead to the discovery of the truth. The wish is of great importance in our spiritual economy, because it is a form of holding fast to something that has value even though this value can be realised neither at once nor some time hence, nor even within any measurable time. Such a wish may have negative as well as positive significance. It may exclude aims and actions which would be inimical to the value which lives in the wish. And it may sharpen the attention so that no possibility of taking a step in the direction of the realisation of the valuable escapes our notice. More values are likely to be redeemed, discovered, and produced when we hold fast to the content of our wishes than when a resignation devoid of wishes has set in, still less a state of satiety.

113. The significance of a mood such as we have been describing has often been emphasised from the philosophical side, in the full consciousness that it determines a choice of motives which may endue us with force and power in the battle of life, especially in the battle for the higher development of life.

According to Spinoza, all feelings which are bound up with limitation and weakness are of subordinate value or even altogether worthless. Not through pain or fear but by fixing his eye directly on the valuable and the good, and by striving with the clearest possible understanding to attain this, does a man attain to the highest perfection. The free man, by which Spinoza understands the man who is guided by clear understanding, thinks least of all about death; his aim is activity, life, reasonable self-assertion; his wisdom the meditation of life not of death.

Immanuel Kant (in his introduction to the *Critique of Judgment*) discusses the question of the significance of wish and longing for the spiritual life, and his conclusion is

summed up in the following passage: "Did we never exert
our powers except in the assurance that the realisation
of the desired object lay within our capability, they
would for the most part remain inactive." In the same
work he appeals to the beauty of nature, to genius
and to organic life, as witnesses that existence, working
according to its own laws, tends to produce that which
has value for man. And he takes this opportunity to
express his belief that the force at work in the great
inter-related system of nature is not alien to that which
leads men to the discovery and assertion of values. He
intimates that the distinction which we make between
scientific explanation and practical evaluation, between a
mechanical and a teleological conception, depends in
reality on the form of our knowledge, and does not
denote a dualism in the innermost essence of existence.
However much Kant is inclined in his ethics to lay
formal stress on the contrasts, discords, and catastrophes
within existence, yet his last look at it is hopeful, and
he assigns as the foundation of his hope the facts of life
and of beauty.

Stuart Mill (in his posthumous *Essays on Religion*)
asserts that imagination has its rights no less than
critical reflection, and that the former is within these rights
when it dwells by preference on cheerful possibilities, not
only because these afford us immediate satisfaction, but
also because they encourage us in our striving. To
dwell without necessity on the evil of life is a useless
expenditure of nervous power. It is not so important to
give definite form to hope as to extend the scale of
feeling as far as possible, so that the higher tendencies
should never be checked by the thought that life is
without meaning. This philosopher's line of thought
has recently been adopted by one of the most prominent
representatives of literary realism. In a speech made
to a French students' club in 1893, Emile Zola said, " I

confess that in literature we have curtailed our horizon unnecessarily. I for my part have often regretted my sectarian demand that art should not go beyond proved truths. Recent authors have extended the horizon, for they have reconquered the unknown and the mysterious, and in so doing they have done well. What is the ideal but the unexplained, those forces of the invisible world in whose stream we bathe, although we do not recognise them?" Zola only fears *empty* dreams. But he recommends faith in work, and belief in work—coupled with the emphasis on an extended horizon—must indicate a belief in the interconnexion of the power to work and the results it produces with the innermost essence of existence, faith, in fact, in the conservation of value.

114. These considerations find their more special application in our feeling for our own personality, for that part of existence with which we are indissolubly united. The underlying fundamentum of our personality was not produced by ourselves, and yet everything which we are afterwards able to produce, even by our utmost exertions, is determined by this underlying disposition. The route is determined at the starting-point, but it differs widely, in quality as well as in quantity, in different cases. Our individuality is a datum which is determined by the inter-relation of the species and, in the last resort, by the great inter-relation of the whole of nature. Our coming into existence may be compared to a budding from a great stem. Here we get at a special ground for the feeling of dependence which is such an essential element in religious feeling. This feeling of dependence holds good here of our innermost ego, of the very source of our strivings as well as of the original direction of our strivings.

The whole gamut of the moods evoked by our estimations of value may here find place. Here is the possibility of hope or fear, of cheerful resignation or

of passive bitterness, or of a self-scorn which, fixing its
gaze on the dark spots which are always to be found,
ends in the crippling of all power to will.   Here, too, in
Spinoza's words, we must direct our thoughts to life and
not to death, *i.e.* letting go the valueless, we must devote
ourselves to finding those values which can be preserved
or redeemed.   Faith in the conservation of value will
inspire us with courage not to give up things too easily
for lost, but to continue our search for value, for hidden
sources, until we discover how even " the least maintains
its place in the garland of life."

115. But our knowledge not only of individual but
also of cosmological possibilities—of existence as a whole,
as well as of our own innermost nature—is imperfect,
and in our efforts to comprehend it we are often
confronted by insuperable barriers.   Moreover, it may
be said, in a certain sense, that existence becomes
more mysterious with the progress of knowledge, since
every important advance opens out new regions to our
view.

In the second part of his *Aanden i Naturen* (Spirit
of Nature) H. C. Örsted has the following beautiful
passage : " Our wishes ought not to determine what we
shall accept as truth.   Must we not always take shame
to ourselves when we catch ourselves wishing for a truth
other than the actual one ? . . . No, let us give all
honour to truth : for with truth goodness is inseparably
united.   Perfect truth always brings consolation with it."

In his zeal to incite to fearless inquiry on the one
hand and administer comfort on the other, Örsted here
says more than he can prove.   That perfect truth will
always be consolatory can only be known when it is
found—but when will it be found ?   The element of
truth contained in Örsted's words is that we never have
the right to halt at a pessimistic dogma *because* we have
discovered a want of harmony between our experience

and our faith in the conservation of value. It is very possible that our experiences are incomplete and that extended experience would cancel the inharmonious relation to the conservation of value. Our present experiences sometimes lead to logical contradictions : but we do not therefore abandon the validity of our logical principles ; on the contrary, we believe that our experience is imperfect, and when we succeed in completing it we find the contradiction vanishes. We may similarly attempt to extend our experience when it conflicts with the conservation of value. And this extension can often only be attained by our own exertions, by a change in natural or social conditions, by intervention in the development of human character—more especially of our own. If we do not admit the possibility of such changes, *i.e.* that values may be redeemed and discovered, we shall, of course, not attempt these exertions. Thus the belief in the conservation of value may, in isolated cases, be a necessary condition for the exhibition of the conservation of value. No special ' consolation ' therefore is required.

Speaking generally, it is a dangerous principle that we must be consoled at any price. We may learn much here from the old mystics. The author of the *De Imitatione* says again and again that a man must love Jesus for Jesus' sake and not for his own consolation (*propria consolatio*) ; they who are always searching for consolation are hirelings. And when Suso asked a holy monk, who revealed himself to him in a vision after his death, what exercise was at once the most painful and the most efficacious, he was told that no discipline is so painful, and at the same time so searching, as to be forsaken by God, for then a man gives up his own will and submits for the sake of the will of God to be robbed of his God. Where self-consolation is the ultimate goal, piety passes over into egoism.

There can be no doubt, then, that faith in the conservation of value itself possesses value when it appears as a practical belief which, through the attempt to verify itself, incites to action. It also contains an element of consolation, for it raises our minds above the limited and finite. But the fact that religion is becoming increasingly significant as a means of consolation and that this point of view is so strongly emphasised are signs of its altered position in the spiritual life. Religion was once the pillar of fire which went before the human race in its great march through history, showing it the way. Now it is fast assuming the rôle of the ambulance which follows in the rear and picks up the exhausted and wounded. But this, too, is a great work. It is, however, not sufficient; and when religion has disburdened herself of all her dead values, she will once more, in intimate association with ethics, rise to be a power which leads men forward.

116. When we speak of the ethical significance of religion, we must include not only her motive power and her capacity to raise and extend men's view, but also, and not least, the co-operation and concentration of all the spiritual forces which she partly presupposes, partly effects. In my sketch of the great founders of religion (§§ 98-99), I tried to show that their originality exhibited itself not in any new ideas that they brought forward but in the deep and inner concentration of all the spiritual forces. And this concentration, as I have tried to show above (§§ 26-44), is connected with the psychological nature of religion. In religious feeling and belief, æsthetic, ethical, and intellectual elements co-operate with man's fundamental impulse to self-preservation. It is by means of their religious experience that men unconsciously balance their central account. All sides and tendencies of life are concentrated in the experience of single moments, and their total result

appears as a prevailing disposition, which in its turn gathers from all sides and tendencies of the psychical life in its search after form and expression. It is on this account that, in her classical periods, religion becomes a form of unity in which imagination and thought, self-assertion and surrender, conscious and unconscious strivings co-operate ; for religion alone offers a field for the play of all capacities and impulses. This concentration, of course, assumes different characters throughout the two different classical epochs which a great religion may pass through (§ 1). In the period of inception all interests other than the religious disappear ; all faculties and impulses work together in a passionate endeavour to hold fast to the object of faith and to be lost in it. In the periods of organisation the religious interest does not stand alone, but it decides how all other interests shall be satisfied ; work done within special spheres is so done that the object of faith directly determines the tendency and attitude towards any particular questions.

The religious problem arises with the division of labour, which involves a separation of the different psychical capacities and impulses. Concentration is at such times only too likely to be replaced by one-sidedness, division and want of harmony. It is no longer easy to find a point of union in which all efforts can focus. Religion itself in its traditional form can no longer satisfy the need of spiritual concentration, for she has developed a system of dogmas and ceremonies which stand outside life, instead of expressing the whole of life. Hence it is idle to hope to cure this division by a return to orthodox dogmatism. We must return to the spiritual needs of primitive Christianity and of the Middle Ages, if we are to have the old harmony together with the old dogmas. To think that the one can be separated from the other shows a remarkable blindness to the conditions of spiritual life.   But there are also many free-thinkers whose attitude to the religious problem proves how little sense they have of the deepest human needs.   They think that a form of life, such as was religion in her golden ages, involving the concentrated interplay of all faculties and impulses, can be deleted from life without any loss to the latter.   The whole spiritual life would suffer were such a form of it to perish.

We cannot live on residues.   Protestantism is a residue, and this is even truer of Pietism and Rationalism. But neither can we live on substitutes.   We must have equivalents.   And the great question here is whether equivalents are possible.

If we hold fast to the axiom of the conservation of value, we must also hold fast to the possibility of new forms of concentration arising within the sphere of spiritual life, in which the gains which division of labour has effected will not be sacrificed.   It is possible to entertain this hope.   History shows us a rhythm of critical and organising periods, but those who live in a critical age are inclined to believe that an organising period will never recur.   It is conceivable, however, that the division and dispersal of forces may lead to a higher concentration than any we have previously known.   The 'higher unity,' of which Hegel speaks so much, and the discovery of which he undertook so light-heartedly, may be the object of our faith and of our expectation, although we are not able to demonstrate its necessity or construct its fabric.

117.   In irreconcilable strife with ethics are all religions which render men weak and passive and leave them immersed in feelings and imaginings which are out of touch with real life; whether these pictures of the imagination are cheerful, such as the expectation of the millennium and the ecstasies of the world beyond, or gloomy, as are the mania of consciousness of sin, brooding

remorse and fear of hell.   For in these cases marrow
and force are taken from work and life in this world.
Men are so much engaged in looking either forward or
backward that they miss what is straight in front of them,
and it is that which gives life its tasks and its happiness.
Our conception of life must neither be based on a past
which cannot be changed nor on a future which only
comes at the end of the day ; neither on the death which
precedes our life nor on that which follows after it.   The
really religious battle-cry here is, "Let the dead bury
their dead ; take no thought for the morrow!"   Our
conception of life must be an exploration of life, a search
after such practical values as can be found or produced
in the present life, and the conservation of which is worth
believing in and fighting for.   We live in realities—not
in empty possibilities, still less in impossibilities.

As we have already seen (§§ 88, 115) faith in the
conservation of value has a tendency towards self-
verification, for it induces us to try by extended experiences to resolve the discords.   Even though it is often
impossible to refute a man who finds life worthless, *e.g.*
the suicide who thinks all roads are barred, yet we are not
really powerless.   We must set to work so to modify
physical, physiological, psychological and racial conditions that the melancholy, the relaxation of mind, the
want of courage to live which so often underlie a depreciatory judgment of the value of life, will disappear, or
at any rate will no longer be able to overspread and overwhelm a man's entire inner life.   Perhaps the suicide only
found all roads barred because his own spirit was fettered.
To open men's minds to the real values which already
exist or may be produced often costs a hard struggle.
For their motive of estimation—that which determines
all their judgments of value—must be changed.   Judgments of value can often only be refuted by changing the
principle on which they are based.   Conscious life may

be changed through changes of the unconscious and involuntary life, when perhaps direct influence on the clearly conscious life would be unavailing. We must work by means of a *vis a tergo*. In such cases the conservation of value is maintained by removing the causes which deprived life of all apparent value.

Different as is the conception of life here indicated from that of the old religions, yet it preserves its continuity with them. Beneath a sharp opposition we may trace a spiritual relationship. Religion has not lost its significance because it has become evident that it, no more than science, can solve the great riddles. Its fundamental element consists in the inner experience of the relation between value and reality, in conjunction with the need for an emotional and imaginative expression of the content of this experience. There will always be room for a poetry of life in which the great experiences of human life can find utterance, and of such a poetry humanity is always in need. It is this which constitutes for us the most important element of the old religions. Great poets (Æschylus, Dante, Shakespeare, Goethe) are able to endue this poetry of life with form, and every new and great epoch in the history of the art of poetry will bring us new forms of the poetry of life. The literature of the present day is not able to satisfy this need; its significance does not lie at this point. But though for the present we are obliged—unless we live with the great ones of past ages—to be content to murmur to ourselves the melody which the experience of life awakens in us, we need not therefore relinquish the hope that the old forces will eventually produce new forms.

(*b*) SOCIOLOGICAL CONSIDERATIONS

118. The significance of the Church, from the social point of view, must be recognised, before all else, in the

fact that in her best forms she represented a noble idealism,
—and does to a certain extent still represent it,—in the
midst of this finite, prosaic, and burdened world ; many
men have only been enabled to lift up their eyes and
see the stars by her help.   She has opened the world of
thought and of poetry to great multitudes, and without
her these multitudes would have perished in the battle
of life, or gone through life dully without having come
in contact with ideal powers.   The concentrated and
concentrating force of religion has enabled the Church
to work more widely and deeply than any other society
has been able to do.   Thought and poetry here went
hand-in-hand with high seriousness and the greatest
ethical decisions.   I am speaking here of the Christian
Church, for that is the Church nearest to us, whose
influence we have most opportunities of tracing.

How the Church could become a society of cultured
men is shown us by its attitude towards Greek learning,
the only independent and matured intellectual force
which confronted Christianity during the first fifteen
hundred years of its existence.   The Church employed
Greek thought for the formulation of her dogmas.   But
the form necessarily drew a part of the content after it.
One of the greatest representatives of the Church has even
gone so far as to say that it was through the Church that
Plato's doctrine became generally known.   Augustine
says, Plato would hardly have believed that his doctrines
would be taught to all nations and that through the
agency of Christianity.   The points which Augustine
admired in Plato were his ideal conception of inquiry
and of truth, his discovery of the relationship between
the soul of man and the highest truth, and the emphasis
he lays on the great opposition between the higher and
lower within the human soul.   Augustine even thought
that were Plato and his disciples to return to the earth
now they would join the Christian Church, for to do this

they would only have to alter a few words and opinions (*paucis mutatis verbis atque sententiis*)! [154] This reminds us of Gretchen's remark on Faust's confession of faith : " Ungefähr sagt das der Pfarrer auch, nur mit ein bischen andern Worten " [The parson says almost the same thing, only in rather different words.] In his old age, it is true, Augustine thought he had ranked the philosophers far too near the Evangelists. The attitude of the Church to Plato's, and afterwards to Aristotle's, philosophy is however a classical example of the work the Church might do as an organ for sowing and disseminating ideas in the soil of human life. As she adapted herself to Greek philosophy, so she has also—but slowly, for she takes only a short step at a time—adopted other ideas.   After a decent show of opposition there always comes a day when the Church announces herself to be in complete harmony with 'true' science.   In this way thoughts become absorbed either into the doctrines or into the practice and preaching of the Church, and are disseminated among large circles who would otherwise have remained in ignorance of them.   The future alone can show how great the elasticity of the Church is and if it will stretch still further in the future.

This whole process of adaptation would be impossible but for a certain consciousness within the Church that the essence of religion is not contained in the dogmas which have been formulated once and for ever.   These may be put aside.   It is not necessary to cancel them formally ; such a proceeding would be dangerous from the standpoint of Church politics or pedagogics, but attention is focussed on the central content of life which forms the background to these doctrines.   The Church stands as the bearer of a great tradition, of a group of figures in which countless generations, under the influence of, and in adherence to, the great example in whom the Church took its rise, have deposited their deepest experiences of life—everything that they have felt, thought and suffered under the buffetings of fate in small things as well as in great. In the Church's hymns more especially we hear, as it were, a cry in which thousands have expressed their fear and hope, their cares and thankfulness, their fall and their restoration, throughout the long life of the race. The individual feels that he has here before him great memories, common to all, of experiences within the sphere of the inner life. He finds in them fundamental thoughts which help him to understand himself and his own experience. In the Church's worship the great drama of the race is figured, and a wide horizon is here revealed to the individual, in the light of which he views and estimates his own life. As he participates in the Church's ritual he lives through in ideal fashion the great primeval contrasts of life, and his feelings become purified and idealised as they become associated with the thoughts of the typical events, the memory of which the Church celebrates.

The Church presses art into her service in her worship, as she does thought in her dogma. In this way the æsthetic needs are satisfied, not in isolation, but in closest union with the deep need of edification and of peace which is one side of the religious need. No spiritual faculty works here in isolation ; and how great is the significance of the Church for art may be seen from the fact that the periods of great art have so often coincided with the great organising periods of religion.

A social organisation which, in its noblest forms, has shown itself able to work with such concentration and such resourcefulness, and to influence such large circles, stands alone of its kind. At present no other social form of ideal culture is capable of undertaking the functions the Church has hitherto discharged.

2 A

119. The Church, as a society, finds its special strength in the fact that it originated in a spiritual movement, which diffused light all around, and not merely in an association of individuals, each one of which had developed in his own way.   The feeling of solidarity was present at its inception, not merely in its results.   The many feel that they are collectively confronted by one and the same power which claims their recognition.   And, after a period of conflict between a narrower and a wider tendency, this power showed itself capable of founding an international society.   The Church,—apart altogether from her old hospitality which did not lead to any enduring solidarity,—may be said to be the first international society, the first social form in which national limitations lost their significance.   The actual course of events, and the philosophical reflections to which these had given rise, had indeed, in the last centuries before the appearance of Christianity, brought about the theoretical and practical recognition of the solidarity of mankind, and the love of one's fellows (*caritas generis humani*) was known before it was inculcated by the Church.   But to construct a society on this basis was reserved for Christianity.   In Eastern Asia the development of Buddhism offers a parallel to that of the Church at many points.

Within the boundaries of individual nations the Church has, in quite recent days, been active in philanthropic endeavours on a large scale.   She is only too apt to take refuge in this when her intellectual sins are brought home to her,—and with a certain right, for charity covers a multitude of sins.   It does honour to the Church that she has led the way for modern philanthropy, and that she still to a great extent leads the van. Vincent de Paul, Pascal's contemporary, was familiar with the thoughts, premisses and points of view from which modern philanthropy still starts, even though they are no longer developed, expressed and applied in the spirit of the Church. In the Protestant world Johann Heinrich Wichern, founder of the ' Rauhen Hauses,' may be quoted as a worthy counterpart.[155]

The philanthropy of the Church has made great strides in the nineteenth century, more especially within the Catholic communion. Monasteries were dissolved in France at the time of the Revolution, but the monastic life developed itself anew on its own initiative, and at the end of the nineteenth century there were 25,000 monks and 142,000 nuns devoted exclusively to dangerous and thankless tasks, to the benefit not only of individual sufferers but also of public life.[156] A spiritual tendency which can produce such results is not dead. A keen-sighted observer says of the Americans of to-day, " They are a religious people. The importance which they still, though less than formerly, attach to dogmatic propositions does not prevent them from feeling the moral side of their theology. Christianity influences conduct, not indeed half so much as it ought, but probably more than it does in any other modern country, and far more than it did in the so-called ages of faith." [157]

I have tried to indicate briefly all that stands on the credit side of the Church's account in its relation to the spiritual life of man. But there is also a debit side to the account, and this we must now pass on to consider.

120. The fact that love to man has become an essential element in the ethics of a great popular religion is one of the utmost significance. From an ethical stand-point, however, we must demur at the limitations that have been assigned to this love. Amongst the Greeks love to man was kept within national limits, and in Christianity it was kept within the limits of dogma, for faith was made the condition and limit of love. Only where faith was, was love to be forthcoming, and the people to be loved are believers or those who can be turned into believers. In both these cases, in respect not

only of psychological basis but also of range, love is
denied perfect liberty of action. Throughout the whole
history of the Church we may trace this oppositional
relation between faith and love, and it is often difficult to realise that we have before us a Church which
is supposed to represent pre-eminently the religion of love.

When Jesus says "Whatsoever ye have done unto
one of the least of these my brethren, ye have done it
unto me," it might seem as if we had here the principle
of unconditional love to our fellows, since the person
doing the work of love did not know that he did it to
Jesus. But if we take into consideration the whole
context in which this passage occurs, the orthodox interpretation is probably right in its contention that these
words were addressed to believers, and that "the least
of these my brethren" is intended also to refer to
believers. We are not told what to think of the man
who feeds the hungry and helps the suffering from pure
love to his fellows, without inquiring whether they are
believers,—perhaps even in the absence of faith on his
own part. On this head there is much to object to in
the Church's philanthropy.[158] Hers is not the spirit of
the good Samaritan, but, generally speaking, of the
propagandist; at any rate, she very often demands the
outward signs of faith, by which means she frequently
excludes the honest and encourages hypocrites. However admirable her devotion and organisation, yet she
is too apt to sin against the holy spirit of brotherly love.

And if this is the fate of the brotherly love which the
Church itself proclaims, other qualities, which the Church
has never placed in the first rank, will hardly come off
better. Towards men who, either on intellectual or on
ethical grounds have deviated from orthodoxy, the
Church adopts an attitude little short of barbarian. She
can recognise no other point of view than that of an evil
will. Bishop Martensen once declared that the only

explanation of the defection of men like Kant and Jacobi, Schiller and Goethe, from the doctrine of the Church, was that in the depths of their hearts they entertained an antipathy towards the holiness of the Godhead. Not until the barbarous psychology which is concealed under such a judgment is corrected, can there be any hope of understanding and sympathy. The Church must, in all these respects, attain to a higher level of spiritual culture than that which she at present occupies.[159]

Moreover, the importance which, notwithstanding all historical, philosophical and ethical criticism, the Church persists in attaching to dogma brings her into opposition with herself in her mission as a great educational and philanthropical spiritual force. For it is an illusion to believe that she can maintain any lasting predominance over the masses when once the true state of the case as to the basis of the development and the practical significance of dogmas has become a matter of general knowledge. It often looks to a spectator as though the Church was staking her all in a game which is already and obviously lost. The intellectual discord brought about by dogmatic beliefs is making itself felt in increasingly larger circles. That to which Hobbes looked forward with hope is already coming to pass; the laity are gradually becoming enlightened (*paulatim eruditur vulgus*). It is true, as we have already seen (§ 103), that the conservative or reactionary tendency of the Church is supported by the laity. Still, signs of an opposing tendency are not wanting, and there are many things which indicate that variations of religious experience and the need of positive expression for these will develop in wider circles than hitherto.

There is here only one natural solution, a solution which is implied in the principle of personality, and which has also been brought forward within the Church, viz. absolute freedom of teaching, so that personal

integrity and intellectual honesty may come by their
rights. The laity will then have to choose for themselves and will divide on the lines of this choice.
Freedom of teaching, the right of which is at present
only admitted by the highest scientific institutions, must
be extended to all places and to all institutions where
men are addressed on spiritual matters. What we
want is opportunity to see with our own eyes, and to
make our own personal experiences. But how is this to
be attained if such opportunity is not even afforded to
the teacher ?

121. The list of valuable characteristics (virtues)
framed by philosophical ethics does not tally with that
drawn up by theological ethics. The opposition underlying these two valuations comes out more especially at
two points which are intimately connected, *i.e.* the place
assigned to self-assertion and to justice. In any closer
discussion of these two points we must distinguish
between the ethics of the Greeks and modern ethics.[160]

Greek ethic is occupied with the task of reconciling
the different elements of the life of the soul. Self-
assertion here occupies the first place. A man cannot
rise to be his best self in the absence of inner harmony ;
an inner order must be established so that no one
element shall encroach on any other, but every element
function rightly in the great harmony of the soul's life.
And that individual who is able to place himself in
an harmonious relation to the human society in which
he lives, similar to that in which the single elements
within his own soul stand to the whole—that is to say,
that individual who is able to subordinate himself to the
larger totality as a particular member of it—is leading
the right life.

In Christian ethics obedience, the obedience of faith,
is the cardinal virtue,—a natural consequence, this, of the
principle of authority. As compared with obedience love

is subordinate. Pride is the greatest sin, for it refuses
obedience. Egoistic self-assertion is condemned rather
because it is opposed to obedience than to love. The
demand for obedience is a demand for unconditional
subjection to an infinite power—an oriental trait which
reminds us that the great religions originated in the land
of the rising sun. The upright attitude, even during
prayer, of the free Greeks represents the contrary
attitude to this orientalism, which has also left its mark
in the feeling of sinfulness, differentiating it from the
ethical feeling of repentance. Love, it is true, presses
forward again and again within Christian ethics, but
always with a tendency to present itself in ascetic
opposition to self-assertion, both the self-assertion of
other men as well as that of the subject himself. The
Greek doctrine of harmony appears as sinful egoism.

Modern ethics is a readoption and extension of the
Greek. Self-assertion appears as magnanimity, and
occupies the first place. But it is more active in form
than it was among the Greeks. Its antithesis is not
so much the conflict between the different elements as
the indolence which opposes itself to extension and
development. Self-assertion is no longer exhibited as the
opposite of love. For magnanimity possesses strength
enough to support not only the individual's own life,
but also the life of other men. And the highest virtue is
justice, in which both self-surrender and self-assertion are
included. The ideal is a kingdom of personalities, in
which each individual unfolds his personality in such a
manner that in this very act he helps others to unfold
their own. This conception offers free scope to all
those ethical elements fostered by Christianity which are
of lasting value. But as long as obedience is regarded
as the cardinal virtue, and so long as 'goodwill,' both
psychologically and sociologically (*i.e.* both in motive
and in content), is limited by dogmatic conditions, so

long will there be continual war between philosophical and theological ethics.

C. PRIMITIVE AND MODERN CHRISTIANITY

But the greatest of these is charity.
ST. PAUL.

122. Christian ethics are not the same at all times. This fact constitutes a difficulty when the relation between religion and ethics comes up for discussion. In such discussions our thoughts turn naturally to Christianity, for that is the popular religion to which we have easiest access. Buddhism, the other great popular religion, could only be discussed from this point of view by an inquirer who had himself participated in the culture of Eastern Asia. If, therefore, we restrict ourselves to Christianity, we must at any rate inquire how the relation between religion and ethics varied during the different leading periods of the history of Christianity; for this relation varied with the varying relations in which religion stood to culture. If, then, we are to attempt to estimate the value of Christianity and to establish the elements of permanent value which it contains, we must make a preliminary study of the different conceptions of life which have been brought forward at different periods within the history of Christianity.

There are three great periods or leading forms of Christianity : primitive Christianity, Catholicism, and Protestantism. It is not difficult to compare these forms in respect of dogma. But it is difficult to compare the conceptions of life which correspond to the differences in dogma, for a conception of life is not always formulated in definite words; we must look for it rather in the general attitude towards goods and duties, and in its practical relation to the course of culture and of history.

123. The ethic of primitive Christianity was determined

by the lively expectation of the speedy second coming of
Jesus. In the belief that he was soon coming to found
a supernatural Messianic kingdom, in which the history
of the world would end, the Apostles and their immediate
successors overcame the difficulty presented by the fact
that Jesus, the Messiah, had had to suffer and to die.
The national expectation of the Messiah afforded a form
and framework for this belief; it also enabled the
Apostles to find witnesses to it in the ancient scriptures.

The result was that men turned from the consideration of earthly and human relations. Culture and all
work under temporal conditions, life in the family and in
the state, in art and in science, could acquire no immediate
value and no positive significance. Inert but tense
expectation was the prevailing mood. 'The kingdom
of God' was not to be realised by a long labour in time
on the firm ground of nature and human life, by the
discovery and production of values. The only thing of
importance was to be prepared to receive it when—still
in 'this generation'—it should appear supernaturally in
the heavens. This preparation was all that mattered,
hence: No change in existing circumstances! It is
best for men to abstain from marriage and to forbear
from giving their daughters in marriage; nor let the
slave try to get free. Such things deserve the smallest
possible attention, for they belong to the order which is
about to vanish away. When the men of that day prayed
'thy kingdom come' they thought, not of any vague participation in spiritual goods, but of the definite and supernatural coming of the Messianic kingdom ; the prayer was
a fervent wish that this coming might soon take place.
But the life based on this expectation was not a life of
suffering and trembling, nor of asceticism in the sense of
self-torment. It was no funeral march, but a pæan of
victory, for this vivid expectation set all the forces of
the spirit in motion. Great pictures presented themselves

to the imagination, and feeling at times became so overwhelming that words failed and men spoke 'with tongues,'
when the speaker was not able to explain even to himself
what it was which had stirred him.   Revelation was not
concluded with the death of Jesus, but was carried on in
the breasts of individuals through the motions of the
supernatural spirit.   If the belief in the speedy coming
of the millenary kingdom was the first essential trait of
primitive Christianity, enthusiasm was the second.   Men
were so carried away by enthusiasm that no elaborate
ecclesiastical organisation was either possible or necessary, any more than was any positive participation in
culture and social life.

Cultural tasks and points of view did not exist for
the primitive Christian conscience, which was swept
along in a single direction by no common forces.   The
virtues and duties inculcated by the ethic of primitive
Christianity were therefore essentially such as were
determinable by expectation and enthusiasm.   And the
great exemplary and symbolical significance of this
ethic is due to this fact.   All human life that has any
value is lived in expectation, and may draw instruction
from the heroic age of Christianity.   And without
enthusiasm nothing great is ever done.   Absorption in
the thought of life as a pilgrimage and the conception
of life of primitive Christian days may contribute to the
extension of the soul's horizon.   The positive, actual
tasks and goods which are determined by the progress
of human enlightenment, and for which our present
ethical points of view hold good, are, however, to be
sought in vain in the ethic of primitive Christianity.
For this ethic was content to leave everything as it was
so long as it did not distract thought from the expectation
of the advent of the future life.

Of course by means of adroit exegesis it is possible
to find all sorts of things in the New Testament, even

indications as to how we are to conduct ourselves under
circumstances from which it was the aim of New Testament ethics to distract attention.   It is possible, for
instance, to find hints as to the treatment of the social
question, the woman question, political tasks, etc.   The
Church very soon fell into these interpretations, which
often led to results exactly contrary to the clear and
distinct pronouncements of the New Testament, *e.g.*
with regard to the taking of an oath.   'The kingdom of
God' was gradually incorporated in the structure of
human culture, whereas originally it represented the
whole edifice, and looked to borrow nothing from 'this
world.'   And an expression such as 'the proof of the
spirit and of power' gradually evaporated until men
forgot that it originally referred to the manifestation of
the supernatural in the inner and outer worlds by means
of enthusiastic and prophetic speech and miracles, such as
Origen relates were performed by his contemporaries.[161]
Such an extension or, if that word be preferred, such an
idealisation has its great justification historically ; but we
must always remember that underlying this new interpretation was an adaptation within the sphere of interests
and of ideals.   Comparative ethics has to bring out as
sharply as possible the differences between standpoints
and conceptions of life, even when these seem to speak
the same language.   It is impossible to discover a distinct exhortation to any positive work of culture within
the New Testament, for the thought of an immeasurable
process of development in time, in the course of which
human life was slowly to develop its capacities and forces,
was foreign to the conception of life it represented.   It is
only in virtue of a modern re-interpretation (to borrow an
expression from B. Weiss's *Neutestamentlichen Theologie*)
that the metaphors of leaven and of seed-corn can be
appealed to, as they so often are, to prove that it was
part of the scheme of primitive Christianity to leaven the

history of human culture, and to develop itself within it. Let a man read for himself the tenth chapter of St. Matthew's Gospel, the seventh and fourteenth chapters of the Epistle to the Corinthians, as well as the whole of the Sermon on the Mount, forgetful of the ordinary edifying interpretation, and he will get a correct impression of the standpoint of primitive Christianity in all its historical peculiarity.[162]

The primitive standpoint held its ground in all essential points during the first two centuries after Christ. The post-apostolic period exhibited undiminished the characteristic belief in the speedy coming of the millennium and the quality of enthusiasm,[163] while Tertullian and Origen testify that at the end of the second century these traits still persisted. In the course of time they were superseded by the speculative development of dogma and the elaborated organisation of the Church (cf. § 60). With the waning both of ecstatic expectations and of individual enthusiasm a more positive relation to culture gradually became possible. But even Augustine felt as though he were living in the old age of the world rather than in a new period of culture. He is inclined to regard the description given in the Revelation of St. John of the twelve sitting on seats of judgment in the kingdom of the millennium as fulfilled in the prelates of his own age (*praepositi intelligendi sunt, per quos ecclesia nunc gubernatur*).[164] A characteristic example this of the way in which the Church transformed the notions of primitive Christianity ! As the opponent of an earthly state and of a purely human ethic, however, he preached the kingdom to come—and to come supernaturally—as the only right aim of life. Hence he sees no objection to the spread of asceticism nor to the gradual extinction of the human race by increased adoption of the celibate life. If we find in Augustine an oscillation between the transformation of and adherence to early Christian ideas, it is

owing to the inner struggle between two different types
of religious faith to which I have already (§ 43, cf. § 61)
alluded.   The opposition between the changeable and
the unchangeable is distinctly in the foreground with
Augustine, and tends to take the place of that between
the present and the supernatural future.   The influence of
Platonism may here be traced, together with the decadence of enthusiastic expectation.   Augustine's leading
thought is not so much that all present goods sink into
insignificance in comparison with future ones, but that all
finite goods fade into insignificance in comparison with
the eternal and infinite good which is one with God.
This latter contrast is the constantly underlying thought
of the *Confessions.*

124.   The unsolved problem which primitive Christianity bequeathed to the later Church was solved by
Catholicism in a manner which testifies to the strong
historical instinct of the leaders of the Church.   As
Harnack remarks in his *History of Dogma,*[165] we can
hardly conceive amid the Protestantism of our day the
influence exercised over men's minds by asceticism in
the fourth and fifth centuries, and the extent to which it
governed the imagination, the thoughts and the whole
sphere of life.   It threatened to break the Church in
pieces.   On the other hand, multitudes of fresh converts
from other nations were pressing into the Church, and
she found herself obliged to take up the work of an
educative, civilising and organising power.   Hence she
was obliged to adopt a broader view than any which
could have found acceptance in the early days of enthusiasm ; she had to endure much which she was unable
to hinder, and to incorporate elements which, in and for
themselves, lay outside her proper ideal.   A place within
the pale had to be found both for the 'perfect,' who still
took as their criterion the ideal of primitive Christianity,
and the imperfect, who wanted consolation and a norm

of life, but were not prepared to abandon ordinary human
existence.   Union with the ideal of primitive Christianity,
as well as with the realities of the present, had to be
maintained.   The problem was how to break with and
how rule the world at one and the same time.

The solution offered by Catholicism was the recognition of different grades of perfection.   The monk, the
priest and the layman each represented his degree or
form of Christianity, and the Church recognised them all.
The same psychological and pedagogical instinct which
had led the Church to recognise 'implicit faith' (§ 42) led
her here to the distinction between merit and duty.

The monk corresponds to the primitive Christian
type.   In answer to the question : Where is the ideal of
the first great days of Christianity ? Catholicism could
point to its monks and nuns who, filled by the desire after
the one thing needful, had broken the strongest bonds
which rivet men's souls to this world.   The monk and
nun do more than duty requires of men ; they fulfil not
only the general commandment but also the counsel of
perfection of the Apostle (1 Cor. vii.).   The priest
represents a middle form between the monk and the
layman.   By giving up family life he has followed one of
the Apostle's counsels, while for the rest he takes his
part in the human world, offering help and consolation to
those living within it.   The layman lives the human life
on all its different sides, but strives with the Church's
help to avoid losing himself in it.

This is the finest solution which, up to the present,
has been offered of the problem of maintaining the
primitive Christian ideal and at the same time working
on the side of culture and enlightenment in a world
whose continued existence was neither foreseen nor presupposed when the ideal was constructed.   This solution
rightly takes for granted that if the New Testament is to
continue to be regarded as presenting the highest rule of

life for men, we must assume that the conditions of life it
presupposed will be continuous. So we find Cardinal
Newman saying, "If the present distress of which St.
Paul speaks does not denote the ordinary state of the
Christian Church, the New Testament is scarcely written
for us, but must be remodelled before it can be made to
apply." This was a leading consideration for Newman
even in his Protestant days. But he looked in vain in
Protestantism for any satisfactory answer to the question :
What have we done for Christ ? His thoughts moved in
a direction similar to that of St. Theresa when she says :
"Wilt thou know what lent the words of the Apostles
their divine fire ? It was that they held in abhorrence
this present life and trod the honour of the world under
foot. They dared all for God." And in a vision she
heard the Saviour say : "What would become of the
world if there were no monks."[166]

And yet this solution is based on a compromise.
S. Kierkegaard has rightly remarked that the instinct of
Christianity failed when it established different classes of
Christians, for it thus opened a new way of escape from
the ideal which not a few availed themselves of.

The distinction between duty and merit cannot be
valid ethically, however, except on very superficial
grounds. For have I the capacity and the possibility of
'earning merit,' i.e. of doing something which exceeds
that which is ordinarily expected of man, it is evidently
my duty to do it. Ethically regarded, my duty is always
proportionate to my capacity ; it is individually proportionate. In ethics there must always be progressive
taxation.

"Ein jeder wird besteuert nach Vermögen," says Tell
when Hedwig complains of the large demands that were
made on him.[167] Moreover experience has shown that
those who feel that the highest is demanded from them
are not conscious that these demands outrun their duty.

They are natures who are more alive to the ideal and who recognise its operation in a wider range than do their fellows. " It is dangerous," says St. Theresa, "to rest content with a moderate effort where eternity is concerned." Catholic teachers of moral theology, after they have set forth the distinction between duty and merit, sometimes advise their hearers to make no use of the distinction. Their advice is more moral than their distinction.

125. Protestantism did not at first fully realise the great problem presented by its relation to primitive Christianity. It was a movement called into existence by the need of asserting the rights of freedom of conscience. Since much was found in the New Testament which Catholicism, owing to its hierarchical system and its involved relation to the world, could neither acknowledge nor allow to operate freely, it was not unnaturally believed that primitive Christianity was returning. Protestantism, however, soon came to signify not only an emancipation of the religious life and an attempt to go back to the source of Christianity, but also, more or less consciously, the emancipation of life in general from the authority of the Church. Life in the world was no longer regarded as lower than life in the cloister. The highest is to be attained, not by artificially induced asceticism, but by the inner surrender of the heart to God and by confidence in him. Worldly life was not merely to be endured, but to be fostered and developed ; and the individual could and should find his vocation in assisting in this development.

Their relation to the ideals and expectations of primitive Christianity was therefore left undetermined by the reformers. No definite guidance, *e.g.*, as to how the precepts of the Sermon on the Mount were to be fulfilled under the conditions and among the tasks of modern human life, was given. Later on, the High Church and

speculative theological party within the Protestant
Church conceived the matter as follows : primitive
Christianity is the ideal leaven which permeates, by
means of a long process of development in time, the life
of the world ; it produces the life of the Christian family
and Christian state, produces also Christian art and
science, and in this way conduces to the development
of the 'kingdom of God.' The primitive conceptions
of the second coming and the last judgment are now
relegated to a distant and twilight background, where
they appear like blue mountains on a distant horizon.
Since men have by this time learnt and experienced
much which was unknown to the New Testament
authors, it has become evident that these authors were
in error in expecting the 'second coming' so soon.
This error, however, when it is not explained away, is
regarded as immaterial. Like Catholicism, Protestantism
believes itself to stand in a relation of ethical continuity
with primitive Christianity. It will not admit that it has
only retained those elements of primitive Christianity
which can be realised under conditions of modern
culture, or rather under the new relations to culture
which it has attempted to adopt. People believe they
are conforming to the ethics of the New Testament because they clothe their ethical principles in
biblical formulæ. They forget that their relation to
culture is radically different from that of primitive
Christianity.

126. In quite recent times, however, Protestant
theology has begun to exhibit this relation with greater
clearness. Thorough-going historical studies and a
sharper understanding of ethical and cultural relations
have led a number of theological inquirers beyond the
standpoint usually adopted by the leaders of ecclesiastical
Protestantism on this question. Amongst the foremost
of these we may mention Albrecht Ritschl (in his

Geschichte des Pietismus) and Adolf Harnack (in his *Lehrbuch der Dogmengeschichte*).

In Ritschl's opinion the peculiar characteristic of Protestantism is that it represents Christians as those who, trusting in God, are to rule the world; they must not withdraw themselves from it, as the ascetics of the old Church, the mystics of the Middle Ages, and the modern pietists demanded. According to Ritschl, pietism blocked the way to the complete development of the Protestant programme—chiefly because it (more especially reformed pietism) aimed at restoring primitive Christianity. In Ritschl's opinion the principles of Lutheran Protestantism are supposed to be in harmony with the New Testament, while the converse does not hold good; belief in the validity of all the conceptions of the New Testament is not considered necessary to salvation. And amongst the biblical conceptions in which it is not necessary to believe, Ritschl especially mentions "the hopes of primitive Christianity in their particularity."

In Harnack's view primitive Christianity contained something more and something other than the 'gospel' proper, and not till this 'more' and this 'other' has been separated out can the 'gospel' appear in all its purity. Luther prepared the way for this; but as he failed to thrash out the speculative dogmas developed by the Fathers of the Church, so he failed to thrash out the primitive expectation of a speedy coming again, in which retirement from the world had its origin. The distinguished historian of dogma is perfectly well aware that the ethics of primitive Christianity were determined by the expectation of the last day, hence he maintains that the 'gospel,' especially as stated in the eighth chapter of the Epistle to the Romans and the thirteenth chapter of the first Epistle to the Corinthians, must be completed by a humane ethic. "If, in science as well as in the life of feeling, we could succeed in uniting the piety, inwardness and depth of Augustine with the openness, the quiet and energetic work and the bright, clear mood of the ancients, we should attain the highest. Goethe, indeed, did, in his best period, maintain this ideal to be his own, and the significance of the reformed evangelical Christianity (if indeed it is really something different from Catholicism) is included within this ideal." [168]

It is evident that a conception of life which adopts essential elements from the Greeks and from Goethe must differ widely from that of primitive Christianity. Goethe is, properly speaking, the first herald of the full gospel. Complete clearness cannot be reached from the standpoint of Ritschl and Harnack. But the great merit of these two thinkers, in addition to the wealth of learning which they bring to their research, is that they state the crucial problem clearly and sharply, and tear aside the veil of ambiguity which in actual life clothes the relation both of Catholicism and of ecclesiastical Protestantism to culture and to humanity.

127. In opposition to all these different standpoints, I wish to adopt one which might be called the *ethico-historical*. According to this view Christianity is a spiritual power which has penetrated, and still penetrates, deep into human life. As with many of the greatest movements in human culture, many features of its inception and early development will probably remain psychological and historical riddles as long as our only ways and means of understanding them are those afforded by history and psychology. But these features are not the only psychological and historical riddles. The point which is of the greatest significance for us comes out clearly and distinctly enough, however, viz. that Christianity bears the stamp of the actual historical conditions under which it arose. Christianity is an oriental movement; it bears a strong impress of its Jewish origin, modified, perhaps, by Persian

influences; in the course of its subsequent dogmatic
development it was determined by Greek thought, or, at
any rate, by Greek conceptual forms. Its later development took place under the influence (intellectual, æsthetic,
ethic and social) of conditions of culture which it had not
itself produced, and which were not presupposed at its
birth.   On this account it is impossible to take it, as
it stands, as the basis at all times of our conception
and our conduct of life.   It can no more afford us this
basis than can the ethic of the Greeks.   But this does
not rob it of its great significance.   It remains a spring
of life from which later ages draw those elements which
can serve them under existing conditions.   This is
the relation in which Catholicism and the different
Protestant movements have actually stood towards it,
but they have all alike thrown a cloak of silence over
this process of choosing and rejecting.   That which each
has taken each has regarded as essential.   And this is
the attitude also of humane ethics towards Christianity.
It acknowledges the influence it has exercised in deepening and intensifying the spiritual life, and the significance
which accrues to it in virtue of its having through its
great exemplar spread abroad the doctrine of brotherly
love through the whole earth.

We take from the New Testament, as from all
spiritual works, whatever we can best make use of in
our spiritual economy.   It contains thoughts, moods
and examples which will always accompany the human
race on its pilgrimage.   But *what* we use and *how* we
use it will be determined by our own independent experience of life and by our environment; and these impose
tasks upon us and show us goods which could not have
crossed the horizon in the age of primitive Christianity,
partly because they were not known, partly because they
were irreconcilable with the then only known aim of
life.   The Bible no more gives us an ethic than it

teaches us astronomy or natural history, although it contains many important elements which every ethic can and must include within itself.

We have before us the Christian and the Greek conceptions of life. And if we must choose between them, there is no doubt that our conception of life is more nearly related to the Greek conception than to that of primitive Christianity. For our aim is to discover and produce in the world of reality the values in the preservation of which we believe ; the task of ethics is to unfold and harmonise human life, both within the individual and within society. This task was recognised by the Greeks. Christianity made it possible for this task to be carried on at a much deeper level.

But it is not the gospel which has been amplified by Greek thought (§ 126), but Greek thought—reflections on life which may be said to be the first-fruits of the spiritual life in Europe—which has been deepened and extended by that which Christianity brought into the world. And not only by Christianity, for a third element or group of elements must be considered in addition to Hellenism and Christianity, *i.e.* the empirical science of recent centuries and the whole structure of modern idealistic and material culture. It is for ethics, not for the philosophy of religion, to discuss more closely the interconnexion of all these elements which enter into the spiritual life of man as this is and must now be lived.

D. WE LIVE BY REALITIES

Homo liber de nulla re minus quam de morte cogitat, et ejus sapientia non mortis sed vitae meditatio est.

SPINOZA.

(The free man thinks of nothing less than of death, and his wisdom is a meditation of life not of death.)

128. As a result of our inquiry the relation between religion and ethics is seen to be a very simple one ;

religion is faith in the preservation of value, and ethics investigates the principles according to which the discovery and production of values takes place. This view brings out clearly at once the difference and the connexion between religion and ethics.

The question as to what values are believed in, and how we are to know that what has been discovered and produced is valuable, refers us back from religion to ethics. The history of religion shows us very clearly that the most important of all oppositions is that between nature religions and ethical religion. The specific nature of a religion, therefore, will depend on the ethical standpoint. I must refer my readers to my *Ethik* for a full discussion of this point, and will only pause here to discuss a few points of view which are of special significance for the philosophy of religion.

According to my own ethical view, life must take the form of a personal work of art, for individual capacities and impulses must be harmonised within individual men, while at the same time individual personalities—precisely by means of the individual harmony within each individual—must be brought into harmony with one another. The problem here is how the self-development of the individual can assist the self-development of other men, or, in other words, how the fact that the individual is an end in himself can be a means to the attainment of the ends of others. This point of view embraces all work in the furtherance of culture which is more than a mere mechanical or restless working. All spiritual and material culture, all individual and social striving, finds its place in the ideal here indicated. The Greek, the Christian, and the modern spiritual development have each contributed to the establishment of this idea. A wide horizon here opens before us ; we look back to the spiritual struggles of the past, but we also look forward to spiritual and material labour for the deepening and progressive development of what has been already won. In its work at the shaping and applying of this idea, ethics itself becomes religion, for it is here working for the all-holiest, and everything which men call and have called holy must finally be estimated by means of the criterion which this idea supplies.

The concept of the holiest reflects in its different applications the degrees of religious development. In the most elementary sense, that is holy which can only be produced by an exalted power. It may be the earth or the fruits of the earth or man himself. But that which is regarded as the work of an exalted power and under its protection, gradually becomes identical, after the transition from nature religions to ethical religion has taken place, with that which is demanded by the highest ethical ideas which man is able to form. Hence religion and ethics ultimately meet in the concept of the holiest, and so we reach Goethe's definition :

> Was ist das Heiligste?—Das, was heut' und ewig die Geister,
> Tiefer und tiefer gefühlt, immer nur einiger macht.

That which is capable of the innermost appropriation by the individual and at the same time is able to establish the deepest fellowship between individuals—that is the Holiest. We are beckoned on,—beyond the externalities of life, beyond all that tends to divide,—to the highest values. The utmost difference and fulness is here found in combination with the highest degree of unity.

With regard to the application of this idea in detail many grave questions arise. But from the point of view of the philosophy of religion it is of special importance that an ideal such as Goethe's lines express was at any rate able to establish itself and to gain recognition. In spite of all its discords, existence has held room for a development in this direction. This is one of the realities which we must try to hold fast and to extend,

one of the things which make it possible for our wisdom
to be a meditation of life, not of death.

129. But what will the end be ? Whence comes the
valuable and whither goes it ? What is the nature of
the connexion between that for which we struggle and
that which makes us able to struggle on the one side and
the innermost essence of existence on the other?

There is a parting of the ways here—not only
because different people have given different answers to
these questions, but also in virtue of the differing degree
of importance which has been attached to the question
of arriving at an answer at all. I for my part see no
reason why we should demand at all costs an answer
which shall take us beyond what science can teach us
by means of its latest hypotheses. Above all, I see no
reason why we should fetter reason for the sake of presumptive solutions which only give us back our riddles
in still larger dimensions, complicated perhaps by logical
and ethical objections.

Such answers to these questions as transcend the
latest scientific hypotheses can only have a poetical
character; but there is nothing in this to prevent their
possessing great religious significance as the most vital
expressions which can be found for the relation between
value and reality as experienced by us. Properly
speaking, it is false to speak of their 'only' having
poetical value (cf. § 70). For it may be that poetry is a
more perfect expression of the highest than any scientific
concept could ever be. By poetry I do not here mean
vague moods and imaginings, but the spontaneous and
living form in which that which has been actually lived
through in moments of violent excitement clothes itself.
Some such process as this underlies all myths and
legends, all dogmas and symbols, taken at the moment
of birth (*in statu nascendi*). There is a poetry of life
which springs up while we are at work, a spark which

only kindles when there is an encounter between the
will and the hard flint of reality.   I have already touched
on this in my critique of S. Kierkegaard's conception of
the opposition between the æsthetic and poetical and
the ethical and religious conception of life.[169]   This
is a poetry which is opposed neither to will nor to
thought, even though it is most apt to arise when
thought and will touch their limits, and only repeated
trials can decide whether these limits denote an obstruc-
tion which can and must be overcome, or whether
they indicate the firm banks between which the stream
of life must always flow.   All great art presupposes
such poetry of life and is its transformation into clear
forms.   If in the present day it encounters especially
unfavourable conditions of life, there can be no doubt that
this must be ascribed to ancient dogmas rather than to
modern doubt.

The philosophy of religion concludes with the reference to this source, the preservation and disengaging
of which constitute the most important condition for
the future of the spiritual life.   Our epistemological,
psychological and ethical investigations arrive here at the
same result (cf. §§ 20-22 ; 70 ; 117).   On the other hand,
it is not the task of the philosophy of religion to construct a special circle of symbols and declare them to be
the only right ones.   The philosophy of religion interests
itself in working forces rather than in the fixed forms
which are thrown off and harden while such forces are
in operation.   But the comparative study of forms still
retains its significance ; it helps us to assign the different
forces to their proper species.   The philosophy of
religion interests itself less in any particular symbols or
dogmas than in the personal need, the interior feeling,
the authentic experience which finds expression in them
and which determines both the choice of symbols and the
degree of literalness with which they are interpreted.

When a great religion, such as Christianity, arises, the philosophy of religion recognises it as a witness to the fact that love, inwardness and purity are vital forces in human nature.

Whenever these inner forces seem to have disappeared, we may be sure it is because trust in the forming and symbolising capacity has become weakened under the rule of dogmatism and scepticism, a sovereignty which has generally been based on force. The careful observer notices that these forces are hidden, they move within the holy places of personality which are closed alike to importunate propagandists and to profane scoffers.

We are living in an age of transition. There is a want of harmony between our faith on the one hand and our knowledge and our life on the other. The task of harmonising free knowledge and free development of life with that which is, for us, of the highest value cannot be evaded. Nor can it ever be executed by way of speculation and construction. A new type of life must be created which neither dreads criticism nor expresses its freedom by 'mocking its chains,' but with cheerful confidence expresses its deepest experiences in a 'psalm of life.' Until such a type of life has been developed, many men will suffer injury to their souls. This may come about in many ways,—either because they cling with morbid extravagance to something which is out of harmony with their personal life or with the demands of intellectual honesty, because their own secret fear impels them to fanatical hatred of those whose faith is other than theirs, because they have become withered and dried up by higher criticism and satiety, or because they consume themselves in restless reflection. I do not say that those who suffer the most injury experience the greatest pain.

Life struggles upwards by means of the conflict between opposing forces, and the circumstances of the struggle are different for every individual soul. Hence

the art of living, like all other arts, must be one-sided
(cf. § 92). And for this reason each individual must
seek out his own place and must fight for that portion
of the truth which reveals itself to his sight. Only by
means of a firm grip can the 'higher unity' be reached,
but it will never be reached as easily as romantic
philosophy believed.

130. Every conception of life must in the long run
be determined by the values which are found or produced
in real life. Every conception of a future life, of a
higher world, is made up of elements which are taken
from *this* world. Life requires discipline and rules, but
the thoughts which underlie and determine the discipline
and the rules must in the last resort have been extracted
from this life. There is here a continuous circular
motion, which, however, does not exclude progress, for
even an imperfect ideal can make life more perfect than
it was before, and the more perfect life will then produce
still higher ideals. Even a step backwards may be a
transition towards—perhaps even a necessary means to
—an ascent, just as a spiral spring only recoils that it
may spring upwards again (*inclinata resurget*).

As Goethe defined the task of the poetic art to be
"clothing reality in a poetical form" and not "realising
the so-called poetical," so it is the task of religion to
make life ideal and harmonious, not to realise artificial
ideals imposed from without. Every ideal possessed of
significance will reveal itself as a great concentrated
expression of tendencies of life which must have been
moving spontaneously before they took on the form of
thought or imagery.

And here we must always find our greatest model
in the Greek way of life. Their conception of life
betrays a certain sadness, but they clearly and man-
fully fought for the rights of the life here below. In
the eternal dispute as to the meaning of life their

example must always be regarded as a document of such great weight as to throw, once and for all, the burden of proof on those who would make the value of this life dependent on what can be guessed of another. The spiritual healthiness of the Greeks is shown in the fact that they recognised the great task of life to be the discovery and creation here, amid the reality of this life, of such values as "the beautiful and the good." They did not borrow their criterion for this life from the conception of a life to come.

That Greek culture perished and that the oriental teaching of a future life conquered for a time, proves at the most that Greek culture stood in need of interiorisation. Orientalism has done much for the furtherance of spiritual life. Whether it was necessary in the sense that the same result could not have been reached by continuous development from the Greek standpoint, it is impossible to say ; our insight into the conditions of the historical development of culture is altogether too imperfect to enable us to decide. But orientalism has produced great evils of its own, and we can understand why Kant (in the notes he left behind) expressed a wish that we had been spared oriental wisdom.

This principle stands firm, and only he who has honestly and honourably laboured for the values which can be found and produced in *this* world is prepared for a future world—if there be a future world, a question which experience alone can decide. My dead friend, Johannes Fibigers, relates in his *Autobiography* that in a conversation on the question whether a future life awaits us, I remarked " It remains to be seen whether there is such a life." I do not remember having said this, but it expresses the results at which I have myself arrived. The horizon has not shut down upon me. But the more I have looked round on the world of thought and of reality, the more clearly it has been borne

in upon me that those who are still ready to preach
that were there no future life *this* life would lose all
its value, take a great responsibility upon themselves.
Those to whom the belief in a future life is a necessity
of life will have already become aware of this need ; but
they have no right to appeal to their experience unless
they have made a serious attempt to find and produce
value in *this* life.   And when will they be in a position
to say they have done enough in this direction ?   Up to
the present no evidence has been brought forward to
show that the lack of such a faith necessarily involves
the exclusion of some valuable personal quality.   The
views which individuals have formed, in accordance with
their own personality, of that which lies beyond the
world of experience must not be taken as a general
criterion of the value of personal life.[170]

Ethically considered, the command is : ' Make life, the
life thou knowest, as valuable as possible.'   Whether the
striving to fulfil this command necessarily presupposes
a belief in the conservation of value in a certain definite
form is a question which will receive different answers
from different persons, according to their differing experiences.   He who can find or produce nothing valuable
except it be suffused with the glow of eternity, stands
no whit higher than he who works with power and
inwardness in the service of the valuable, although this
value is, in his opinion, subject to the law of perishable-
ness.   He, however, who can dispense with the belief
in the conservation of value has on his side no right to
look down on him who sees in whatever value he may
have found or produced a single link in a great chain
of values which stretches away into the invisible.   It is
possible to hold such a belief without coming into conflict
either with the theory of knowledge or with ethics.   The
last word here must lie with the principle of personality
(92-93 ; 100-101).   Ethics has only to take care that in

their anxiety to save the values of life men should not forget life itself.

131. In a work entitled *Om Intolerance* [On Intolerance] (1878), and written with some warmth, S. Heegaard takes occasion to emphasise the significance of the statement, "we live by possibilities." In so doing he was guided by the thought that since science can neither dispute nor attest the validity of the religious ideas, their possibility must be always admitted in defiance of every criticism. He was thinking more particularly of the idea of personal immortality. His view was that we must base our life on the possibility of the validity of this idea.[171] In opposition to this view, I wish to bring forward the assertion I have put at the head of the chapter : We live by realities. We base every possibility on a reality ; we conclude to the possible from the real. Hence in the last resort we live entirely by reality, however great may be the significance that possibilities may acquire for us. Only when reality exhibits the good and the beautiful can the possible contain them. We live by values which reality produces, and these values do not necessarily fade, because their fate in time and in eternity does not lie open before us. In so far as we are able to form any opinion as to their fate, we base this opinion on our experience of reality : such views are unconscious or clearly conscious projections, generalisations, or idealisations.

We may discover what men's thoughts about this world have been from all that they have thought about a future world. Up to the present moment no description of heaven or of hell has been given the individual features of which have not been borrowed from terrestrial experience. This is as true of the descriptions of the underworld of Homer and Virgil as of the Revelation of St. John and Dante's *Divina Commedia*. In Lavater's description of the advent of the Anti-Christ, Goethe recognised the entry of the Kurfürst into Frankfort for

the coronation of Joseph II. The religious consciousness moves in a world of poetry, and is becoming
increasingly aware of the fact. The more clearly it recognises the figurativeness and insufficiency of its ideas,
the better it will be able to comprehend a standpoint
which attaches no weight to the formation of fixed and
exclusive ideas of the object of religion.

And how far are we to pursue possibilities? A
conclusion is unthinkable. We can always ask, "What
then?" A highest stage of life which would exclude
all possibilities of development would—according to all
known psychological laws—end in numbness and death.
Human thought soon discovered this. The ancient Indians
early perceived that the uninterrupted continuance of one
and the same state can afford no joy, and the Sankhya
philosophers maintained that he who gained admission
into the heavenly world would soon discover that there
are still higher stages than that which he has attained,
so that even heavenly joys contain an element of
unrest.[172] Some thousands of years later (in a letter to
Christian Wolff) Leibniz asserted that if blessedness
did not consist in progress, the blessed would end in a
state of stupefaction (*nisi beatitudo in progressu con-
sisteret, stuperent beati*).

If we really lived by possibilities, our life would be sacrificed to an unknown life. But the philosophy of religion
can here appeal to an idea which since Rousseau's time
has been the fundamental idea of modern pedagogics.
Every period of life has, or ought to have, its own proper
significance, and must not merely be regarded as a
preparation or introduction to one that is coming. As
childhood is an independent period of life having its value
and its end in and for itself, and is more than a mere
preparation for adult life, so, too, human life in its totality
has its independent value, and all the more since experience teaches us nothing about a continuation of it.

How a single personal life is bound up with the laws and values of the whole of existence is an insoluble problem. But if there be an inner connexion between it and them, so that our noblest and highest striving contains something which cannot die (whatever may be the form under which it is preserved), this value only arises when we take *this* life, the life which is known to us, as an independent task and attribute to it independent value.

If we assume that value will be preserved, and if we call the principle of the conservation of value by the name of God, then it will be clear that this principle can nowhere be so immediately present and operative as in our strivings to find and produce values. In order that values can continue to exist they must first come into existence. If we hold fast to this idea, our conception of life will no longer be a tantalising pursuit of the unattainable ; nor shall we end in any empty agnosticism (see §§ 18-22) ; on the contrary, the poet's words hold good—

> In that thou seek'st thou hast the treasure found,
> Close with thy question is the answer bound.

The eternal is in the present, in every valuable moment, "in each ray of sunshine," in the striving which takes 'Excelsior' as its motto. To live eternal life in the midst of time, that is the true immortality, whether or not there is any other immortality. The distinction between end and means falls away in such moments and in such strivings, as indeed it always disappears wherever there is any true personal life. And with this vanishes also the distinction between religion and ethics, for the ethical includes the religious (cf. § 89).

We end here in ideas which appear more or less clearly in every higher form of religion : in the Upanishads as well as in Christianity ; with Buddha as well as

with Spinoza and Schleiermacher.   If any one thought is
to be the last thought of mankind, it must be that of the
continuity of all forces and values, an idea which is our
theoretical and practical criterion, although it cannot be
established and formulated as a perfectly rounded-off
scientific concept (cf. §§ 22, 115-116).

The purely philosophical interest of the point of view
which I have been trying to establish in the inquiry
which here draws to its close lies in the fact that it endeavours to assert the continuity of spiritual development.
This fact discloses an analogy between the religious
problem and all other philosophical problems, and in
the last resort the decisive point for philosophers is not
whether or not a problem admits of solution, but whether
it has been rightly stated, *i.e.* stated in the manner
demanded by the nature of the human spirit and its
place in existence.   In the long run it will be seen that
the philosophical interest is one with the human interest,
and this the more the more they both become clear as to
their own nature.   Hence it is sufficient for the philosopher if he has done his best to define and to shed
light on the problem, and to state the conditions for its
solution.   He does not lose confidence in the significance
of his work, even though few are willing to admit its
validity and its value.

No one can do more towards settling his spiritual
account than make use of everything which he has learnt
in the school of life and of inquiry.   But if this is
honestly done, it may perhaps not be without significance
for others as well as for himself.

2 C

NOTES

¹ P. 8.—WHEN, a few years ago, BRUNETIÈRE, a French author, proclaimed in a declamatory work and to the great joy of many men, the "bankruptcy of the sciences," he thought, naïvely enough, that all he had to do was to abide by the distinction between faith and knowledge. But he drew upon himself a reprimand from the Archbishop of Paris, who instructed him that though faith is without doubt a free spiritual gift, yet before a man can believe in any doctrine (*e.g.* the Trinity, the divinity of Christ, immortality) he must be assured that it is taught by God, and he can only discover this by way of reason. The Archbishop added that M. Brunetière might have learnt this from any tyro in theology. According to THOMAS AQUINAS (*Summa theologica*, Pars X. Quaestio 2, Art. 2) "Faith presupposes natural knowledge, although that which in and for itself can be proved and known may also be an object of faith to those who cannot understand the proof." In the 19th century a decree of the Church was issued against a number of Catholic thinkers (Lamennais, Hermes, Bautain, the Traditionalists, Günther, Frohschammer) who had overstepped the line drawn by the Church with regard to knowledge and faith. A Papal decree of June 11, 1855, declared that "Rational conclusions can prove with certainty the existence of God, the spiritual nature of the soul and the freedom of the will." It was added that since faith presupposes a revelation it cannot be appealed to in discussions with naturalists and atheists. In a decree dated December 8, 1864 (the so-called "Syllabus"), the scholastic method is pronounced to be in accord with the requirements and progress of science. Modern Catholic scholasticism attacks the absolute faith according to authority which was defended by De Maistre and still more by Bonald, both of whom were traditionalists.

² P. 8.—See on this point my article entitled "The Conflict between the Old and the New" (*Journal of Ethics*, 1896).

³ P. 13.—Kant speaks more frequently of ends than of values. But it is evident (although Kant never sufficiently recognised this either in his psychology or in his ethics) that the concept of end *presupposes* the concept of value, since I can only adopt as my end that of which I have experienced the value. When Kant speaks of the "kingdom of ends" in contradistinction to the causal order of nature, he means by

this what later philosophers have called "the kingdom of values." Fries, for example, who was a disciple of Kant, takes the concept of value as his starting-point (*System der Philosophie*, Leipzig, 1804, §§ 238, 255, 330. *Neue Kritik der Vernunft*, Heidelberg, 1807, iii. p. 14). But HERBART and LOTZE are the men who have done most to procure acceptance of the concept of value in wider circles. After Lotze it was taken up by the theologian ALBRECHT RITSCHL and his followers. In Platonism and scholasticism, on the other hand, we find the confusion between explanation and estimation flourishing bravely. (Hume and Kant were the first to break away on this point.)

[4] P. 13—With regard to the different problems of philosophy see the Introduction to my *History of Modern Philosophy*.

[5] P. 17.—In a storm in the North Sea about thirty fishermen from the village of Harboöre lost their lives. In the official *Berlingske Tidende* of November 29, 1893, the Danish Meteorological Institute gives an explanation of this sad catastrophe. The Institute specially emphasises three points: (1) After a calm a storm often comes up from the direction opposite to that from whence the wind was blowing before the calm, upon which the sea, owing precisely to the fact of the calm, becomes very rough. (2) The water on the west coast of Jutland was low, while storms from the west had driven the sea northwards on to the Norwegian coast, from which it flowed down, as though on an inclined plane, with a strong current towards the coast of Jutland. (3) It concurred with high water on the latter coast. The same issue contains the funeral sermon of the preacher in which, *inter alia*, he said to the mourners: "The Lord has used this as a means to your conversion. . . . If this does not take effect, what other means can He use?" The preacher probably did not know that he was here following the same line of thought as Bossuet took in his funeral oration over Henriette d'Orleans, only that Bossuet exemplified it by the English Revolution, and the preacher by a spring-tide. No one will deny that this example is a typical one. Its Biblical analogy may be found in the explanation given by Deutero-Isaiah of the conquest of Babylon by Cyrus. It was Jahve's intention to use it as a means to save the people of Israel, and to awake their faith in the God announced by the prophet (Isaiah xlv.).

[6] P. 29.—In the Church Statutes of Denmark at the close of the fifteenth century we find: "We forbid any man under pain of excommunication to say that miracles take place in this diocese, either speaking generally or with special reference, without inquiry and ratification by an apostolic and ordained authority." *Dania*, iii. p. 348. In recent times so many miracles have taken place in the Catholic world, especially in France, that the authorities have had to exercise great acuteness (and subtle diplomacy) in distinguishing between true and false miracles—and, among the former, between those produced by God and those produced by the devil. Cf. LASSERRE: *Notre dame de Lourdes*, Livre 4. PESQUIDOUX: *La renaissance catholique*

en France, Paris, 1899, p. 52. According to Thomas Aquinas miracles —by which he understands something which transcends the capacities of nature—serve to reveal something supernatural. Cf. TESSEN-WESIERSKI : *Die Grundlagen des Wunderbegriffes nach Thomas von Aquino*, Paderborn, 1899, p. 41. But if a revelation (sanctioned by the Church) is now demanded before we can be sure that something supernatural has been revealed, and if the said revelation is itself a miracle, how can this circular movement ever come to an end, and how is entrance into the circle to be effected?

⁷ P. 31.—Cf. my lecture on *Vitalism* (1898). See also BOUTROUX : *De l'idée de la loi naturelle dans la science et la philosophie contemporaines*, Paris, 1895.

⁸ P. 33.—The fundamental concept on which I have here built is taken from Spinoza's treatise *On the Amendment of the Understanding*, which gives the epistemological basis of his constructive *Ethic*. It appeared again in the works of Kant's youth (see my article on " Die Kontinuität im philosophischen Entwickelungsgange Kants " in the *Archiv für Geschichte der Philosophie*, vii.), and, more recently, in Lotze. I took the opportunity to refer to this view when investigating the concept of cause in my *Psychology* (v. D.).

⁹ P. 34.—Although LEIBNITZ leant towards a pluralism, yet he pointed out clearly that the concept of law is primary as compared with the concepts of force and of individuality. *Force* is that which conditions a future change of state. It is presupposed that a connexion, according to law, holds between present and future. *Individuality* denotes the law according to which changes in the state of a being take place. The question is whether the law which governs the changes of an individual being can be understood apart from those which govern the changes of other beings. Leibnitz denies that this is possible, although, properly speaking, according to his own radical doctrine of multiplicity, he ought to assert its possibility. See my *History of Modern Philosophy*, i. pp. 344-45, 350-53.

¹⁰ P. 35.—ARISTOTLE : *Metaphysica*, i. b (p. 994 a); xii. 6-7 (pp. 1071-73). THOMAS AQUINAS : *Summa theologica*, Pars i. Qu. 2. Art. 3. EUGEN ROLFFS (*Die Gottesbeweise bei Thomas von Aquin und Aristoteles*, Köln, 1898) goes much further than earlier Catholic theologians in his recognition of the indebtedness of Aquinas to Aristotle. As a matter of fact, this important line of thought occurs in Aristotle ; Aquinas only adapted it to theological purposes, amplifying it on sundry special points.

¹¹ P. 38.—MARTENSEN : *Jakob Boehme*, pp. 100-105. Cf. THOMAS AQUINAS : *Summa theologica*, Pars i. Qu. 3, Art. 2 *Deus est actus purus, non habens aliquid de potentialitate.* If Martensen thought the higher concept of God which he defended was especially Christian he laboured under a strange illusion. It was indicated by Aristotle (and even as far back as the Eleatics and Plato) and came *via* Scholasticism to Descartes and Spinoza, while later still it was adopted

by Hegel. It is a concept in which speculative philosophers of all ages have found an (illusory) conclusion for thought.

[12] P. 42.—Cf. with regard to the Aristotelio-mediæval world-scheme my *History of Philosophy*, i. pp. 78-82.

[13] P. 43.—Cf. BERNHARD WEISS: *Lehrbuch der biblischen Theologie des Neuen Testaments*, 6th ed. p. 500.

[14] P. 45.—A. HARNACK: *Lehrbuch der Dogmengeschichte*, 3rd ed. 1894, ii. p. 75. Cf. also p. 472, on the Coptic monks who held fast to anthropomorphism, revelled in apocalyptic imagery, and defended their corporeal god with cudgels. Even Augustine (*Confessiones*, vi. 3) has told us himself that before his acquaintance with Ambrosius he believed that the Catholic Church taught a God who had human shape.

[15] P. 46.—*Confessiones*, iii. 11-12; vi. 4; vii. 16. The expression *totus ubique* reminds us of the ὅλον πανταχοῦ of PLOTINUS (*Ennead.* iii. 9, 3; v. 5, 9). Cf. with this SPINOZA's expression: "That which is in the part as well as in the whole" (*Ethica*, ii. 37-38; 44). It is possible that Spinoza may have borrowed the concept from Bruno, who was here influenced by Plotinus, see *Opere italiane*, especially p. 239, etc., 242; 315 (ed. Lagarde). Bruno uses the same figure (p. 242) for "that which is whole in the whole" as Plotinus, viz. that of a voice audible in all parts of a room. (In Bruno's Latin works we also find the expression: *Anima tota in toto et qualibet totius parte.* See my *History of Modern Philosophy*, i. pp. 132-33.

[16] P. 46.—*Heinrich Susos Leben und Schriften.* Edited by Diepenbrock, Regensburg, 1829, p. 212 ff.

[17] P. 47.—LIEBNER: *Hugo von St. Victoire und die theologischen Richtungen seiner Zeit*, Leipzig, 1832, pp. 292, 483. PETRI ABAELARDI *Dialogus inter philosophum, judaeum et christianum*, ed. Rheinwald, Berolini, 1831, p. 101 ff.

[18] P. 48. — *Sechzig Upanishads des Veda*, translated from the Sanskrit by PAUL DEUSSEN, Leipzig, 1897, p. 626. PLATO: *Republic*, Books ii. and iii. H. RELANDUS: *De religone Muhamedanica*, Trajecti ad Rhenum, 1717, p. 202 ff.

[19] P. 49.—Cf. the chapters in vol. i. of my *History of Modern Philosophy* on Nicholas Cusanus, Copernicus, and Bruno.

[20] P. 50.—NEWMAN: *Apologia pro vita sua*, London, 1879, p. 105. A. SÉGALA: *Le Purgatoire.* Trad. par F. de Bénéjac, Paris, 1880, pp. 8-15, 46. THOMAS AQUINAS teaches with regard to hell that it is probably situated under the earth and that its fire is of the same kind as terrestrial fire, an *ignis corporeus. Summa theol.* Suppl. Pars iii. Qu. 97, Arts. 5-7.

[21] P. 51.—MARTENSEN: *Jakob Boehme*, p. 239 and ff. I at first understood this expression to mean that Martensen regarded the visible ascension as a vision granted to one of the disciples. An auditor of my lectures on the philosophy of religion, however, drew my attention to Martensen's real opinion. I had taken him to be more

intelligent than he really is. For a supernatural vision would after all, even from Martensen's own standpoint, be a more ideal conception than one which involves one of the worst juggleries of the old rationalism—yet it is this which he supports.

[22] P. 53.—Cf. EDV. LEHMANN : *Zarathustra*, i. Copenhagen, 1899. OLDENBERG suggests that before the separation between the Iranians and Indians a Semitic or pre-Semitic influence might have been in operation. *Aus Indien und Iran*, Berlin, 1899, p. 71. If this be so, its after-effects must have developed differently under the influence of the different fates of these different peoples.

[23] P. 53.—ERIK STAVE (*Ueber den Einfluss des Parsismus auf das Judentum*, Haarlem, 1898, p. 175 ff.) believes that the Parsees exercised great influence on later Judaism and through this on the religions which developed out of it. Cheyne (*Jewish Religious Life after the Exile*) attributes great influence not only to the Persians but also to the Babylonians, and declares himself opposed to the view that seeks to explain the development of later Judaism through purely internal causes. This question is not so important for the history of philosophy as it is for the history of religion, although it would be of great psychological interest if it could be shown that the idea of the historical significance of life and of the conclusion of the course of this world in a final judgment had arisen independently among different peoples.

[24] P. 54.—R. WEISS : *Lehrbuch der neutestamentlichen Theologie*, p. 615 ff.

[25] P. 62.—Cf. my *History of Modern Philosophy*, i. pp. 315-19, ii. pp. 148-49. We should notice particularly the following utterances of Fichte's (*Appellation an das Publikum gegen die Anklage des Atheismus*, p. 77, Leipzig, 1799): "It is strange that this (Fichte's) philosophy should be accused of denying God, for what it really denies is the existence of the world in the sense in which dogmatism maintains it."

[26] P. 63.—Cf. my *Psychology* (v. D.), and my article entitled "La base psychologique des jugements logiques" (*Revue Philosophique*, 1901), chap. vi.

[27] P. 64.—Cf. A. LANG : *Myth, Ritual and Religion*, London, 1887, i. p. 163. "The difficulties of classification which beset the study of mythology have already been described. Nowhere are they more perplexing than when we try to classify what may be styled Cosmogonic Myths. The very word *cosmogonic* implies the pre-existence of the idea of a cosmos, an orderly universe, and this was exactly the last idea that could enter the mind of the myth-makers. There is no such thing as orderliness in their conceptions, and no such thing as a universe."

[28] P. 66.—Cf. GRANDGEORGE : *Saint Augustin et le Néoplatonisme*, Paris, 1896, pp. 101-105.

[29] P. 67.—Cf. my article : "Ueber die Kontinuität im philoso-

phischen Entwickelungsgange Kants " (*Archiv für Geschichte der Philosophie*, vii.), §16.

[30] P. 68.—See on Spencer my *History of Modern Philosophy*, ii. pp. 462-71; and on Sibbern my article: "Die Philosophie in Dänemark im 19. Jahrhundert" (*Archiv für Geschichte der Philosophie*, ii.)

[31] P. 68.—Cf. my *Psychology* (v. D. 5). Among other expositions of the law of relativity, I would draw special attention to the fundamental treatise of WILLIAM HAMILTON: *The Philosophy of the Unconditioned* (1829), (see also my *History of Modern Philosophy*, ii. pp. 385-90), and to CHARLES RENOUVIER'S article: "La loi de relativité" (*L'année philosophique*, 1898). FRANCIS BRADLEY in his important and stimulating work, *Appearance and Reality*, London, 1893, also builds on the law of relativity.

[32] P. 71.—Cf. also H. SIEBECK: "Die metaphysischen Systeme in ihrem gemeinsamen Verhältnisse zur Erfahrung" (*Vierteljahrsschrift für wissenschaftliche Philosophie*, ii.).

[33] P. 74.—For the whole problem of the relation between the spiritual and the material, see chaps. ii. and iii. of my *Psychology*.

[34] P. 78.—Cf. on this point my article "La base psychologique des jugements logiques " (*Revue Philosophique*, 1901), §§ 9-10.

[35] P. 78.—AUGUSTINUS: *De moribus ecclesiae Catholicae*, chap. xxvii. Cf. SCHLEIERMACHER: *Der christliche Glaube*, § 85. "To attribute mercy to God were more appropriate to a homiletic or poetic manner of speaking than to the dogmatic."

[36] P. 79.—*Upanishads*, DEUSSEN, pp. 68, 205, 799 ff.; 857 ff.

[37] P. 81.—DENIFLE has shown in his article, entitled: "Meister Eckhart's lateinische Schriften und die Grundanschauung seiner Lehre" (*Archiv für Litteratur- und Kirchengeschichte des Mittelalters*, ii.) —with the help of Eckhart's latest writings which he was the first to discover—that the German mystics were pupils of the scholastics, and themselves practised scholasticism. Still the difference remains that while the scholastics attempted to maintain the validity of analogy in respect of the concept of God the mystics rejected it. Throughout all the writings of the mystics we may trace the after-effects of neo-Platonism. Against the Christian representative of this tendency Thomas Aquinas, appealing sometimes to Aristotle sometimes to Paul, was never tired of polemicising. Cf. THOMAS AQUINAS, *Summa theol.* Pars i. Qu. 13, Art. 5. On the teaching of the mystics see LIEBNER: *Hugo de St. Victoire*, pp. 193-95; *Susos Leben und Schriften*, published by Diepenbrock, pp. 394, 410, 424 (on p. 394 we find: " Hence it is known to all well-instructed persons that the wisdomless being is also nameless; and hence Dionysius says God is a Not-Being or a Nothing "); *Deutsche Theologia*, chap. liii. If we study this mystical doctrine it will help us to understand the Buddhistic concept of Nirvana. For it was not of course the intention of the mystics that the rejection of all positive determinations should be taken to mean

that God is literally a Nothing (or is not). In the mystical concept of God, as well as in the Buddhistic concept of Nirvana, it is precisely the inexhaustible positivity which bursts through every conceptual form and makes every determination an impossibility.

[38] P. 83.—THOMAS AQUINAS: *Summa theol.* Pars i. Qu. 13, Art. 7: (cf. Qu. 45, Art. 3). Cf. *Hugo de St. Victoire* by LIEBNER, p. 195.

[39] P. 84.—Cf. with reference to the argument here developed my *Psychology* (v. B. 5).

[40] P. 87.—*Aus Schleiermachers Leben. In Briefen.* Berlin, 1858, ii. p. 344 and ff. Cf. with reference to the dispute between theism and pantheism my *History of Modern Philosophy*, i. pp. 315-17 ; 97 ff. ; 204 ff. ; 268 ; 517-20. EDUARD ZELLER (" Sendschreiben an J. H. Fichte," *Vierteljahrsschrift für wissenschaftliche Philosophie*, i.) asserts that the concept of pantheism connotes an immanent relation between God and the world only, and asserts nothing as to whether God has personality or not. That God cannot hope was taught by mediæval scholasticism, as we may see from ANDREAS SUNESEN'S *Hexaëmeron* (ed. Gertz, v. 3470 ff.) where it is said that the God-man could hope according to his human but not according to his divine nature, since the latter could not admit of increase :

> " Spem tamen admisit tantum substantia servi,
> Non natura dei, cui nil accrescere posset."

[41] P. 90.—TH. WAITZ : *Die Indianer Nordamerikas*, Leipzig, 1865, p. 126. J. M. MITCHELL : *Hinduism Past and Present*, London, 1885, p. 187. The Greek cultus of heroes rested on a similar tendency. Local heroes were nearer the inhabitants of a town or district than were the great national gods. See ERWIN ROHDE : *Psyche*, i. p. 191 ff. ; 197 ff.

[42] P. 91.—"What is dead, that is what is unchangeable. The Christian's God is the most living and hence the most changeable of beings." (From a letter to Wizenmann, Jacobi's orthodox friend, by a fellow-believer, on the possibility of receiving an answer to prayer.) GOLTZ : *Thomas Wizenmann. A contribution to the history of the inner struggle for belief in the minds of Christians in the second half of the eighteenth century*, Gotha, 1859, ii. p. 235. S. KIERKEGAARD, in his youth, drew from the orthodox doctrine of atonement the conclusion that a change must take place in God (*Efterladte Papirer* [Posthumous Papers] 1833-43, p. 26). He also says : "The thought that God is love in the sense that he is always the same, is so abstract that it is in reality a sceptical thought " (*ibid.* p. 413). He afterwards expressed himself in a different sense (*ibid.* 1844-46, p. 443 ff.).

[43] P. 93.—JULIUS LANGE : *Billedkunstens Fremstilling af Menne-skeskikkelsen*, i. p. 17 ff. ; 31 ff. ; ii. p. 56.

[44] P. 96.—For further discussion of this method I refer my readers

to the first chapter of my *Psychology*. I have given a short psychological characterisation of the religious feeling in my *Psychology* (vi. C. 8b). In my *Ethik* (chaps. xxxi.-xxxiii.), I proceeded to an investigation of religious phenomena from the ethical point of view, and I have studied the question from the same side in my smaller treatises. In my *History of Modern Philosophy*, I have dwelt with special emphasis on the significance of Hume, Schleiermacher and Feuerbach for the psychology of religion. In the last few years this branch of psychology has come more to the front. TH. RIBOT, in his *Psychologie des sentiments*, devotes a long chapter to the religious feeling. JAMES LEUBA: "A Study in the Psychology of Religious Phenomena" (*American Journal of Psychology*, April, 1896). E. RÉCÉJAC: *Essai sur les fondements de la connaissance mystique*, Paris, 1897. RAOUL DE LA GRASSERIE: *De la psychologie des religions*, Paris, 1899. E. D. STARBUCK: *The Psychology of Religion*, London, 1899. MURISIER: *Les maladies du sentiment religieux*, Paris, 1901.

[45] P. 100.—For the connexion between experience and the causal relation see my *Psychology*, (v. D. 1-2), and my article: "La base psychologique des jugements logiques" (*Revue Philos.*, 1901, chap. vi.).

[46] P. 102.—*Vie de Ste. Térèse écrite par elle-même*, chap. xxix. Cf. ALB. RITSCHL: *Geschichte des Pietismus*, ii. pp. 47, 228, 279.

[47] P. 102.—Examples occur in the material collected by LEUBA (see his *Study in the Psychology of Religious Phenomena*, quoted in note 44) of conversions both in ancient and modern times (see especially p. 350).

[48] P. 111.—J. ROYCE: *Studies of Good and Evil*, New York, 1898, p. 377.

[49] P. 118.—See on this point my *Psychology*, under the head of 'Faith' in the index. In quite recent times WILLIAM JAMES has laid great emphasis on the relationship of belief to will. See his *Prins. of Psychology*, ii. p. 321; 561 ff., and his work entitled *The Will to Believe and other Essays in Popular Philosophy* (1894).

[50] P. 122.—*Upanishads* by DEUSSEN, pp. 196, 317; St. Matthew's Gospel, xi. 28, 29. AUGUSTINUS: *Confessiones*, i. 1 (cf. iv. 18, and vi. 26). *Vie de Ste. Térèse par elle-même*, pp. 331, 591. S. KIERKEGAARD'S *Uvidenskabelig Efterskrift*, p. 370 (cf. my book *S. Kierkegaard som Filosof*, German translation in Frommann's *Klassiker der Philosophie*, Stuttgart, 1896, p. 118 and ff.; 158 f.).

[51] P. 123.—Cf. my *History of Modern Philosophy*, i. pp. 155-56, 399-400; 461 f. *J.-J. Rousseau og hans Filosofi*, German translation in Frommann's *Klassiker der Philosophie*, 1901, pp. 115-19. JOSEPH BUTLER: *Works*, Oxford, 1874, ii. p. 181 ff. *Life of F. D. Maurice*, London, 1884, i. 364 and passim.

[52] P. 124.—See my article, "Die Philosophie als Kunst" (*Ethische Kultur*, 1894).

[53] P. 125.—LUTHER, *Catechismus major* (Explanation of the first

commandment and the third article of faith).—*re* Zwingli see ED. ZELLER: *Das theologische System Zwinglis*, Tübingen, 1853, p. 22. Zwingli expressly defines *fides* by *fiducia* or, in his Swiss patois, *gloub* by *vertruwen*. Owing to the doctrine of predestination this element of unconditional faith comes out more prominently in the reformed than in the Lutheran teaching, cf. Zeller, *ibid.* p. 27. LUDW. FEUERBACH has pointed out with much emphasis how Luther's concept of faith distinguishes itself by this characteristic from earlier concepts of it. *Das Wesen des Glaubens im Sinne Luthers*, 2nd ed. Leipzig, 1855, pp. 16-21. This element was afterwards brought forward and illumined by ALBRECHT RITSCHL, especially in his posthumous work: *Fides implicita: eine Untersuchung über Köhlerglauben, Glauben und Wissen, Glauben und Kirche*, 1890, pp. 58-62. In his own teaching concerning faith Ritschl starts from the conception of religious faith as trust, and this enables him to thrash out the purely metaphysical element from the ecclesiastical dogma.

[54] P. 126.—In my *Psychology* (see under 'Resignation' in the index) I have described resignation as a mixed feeling which may appear with widely differing colouring. It is possible to understand by the word 'resignation' the negative and cool form of it which is lacking in the element of positive surrender. Here, as so often in psychology, we are obliged to modify the sense of current words—extending or limiting it. EHRENFELS (*Werttheorie*, i. p. 40) describes resignation as the form which arises when feeling is dulled by hopelessness.

[55] P. 127.—Cf. *S. Kierkegaard som Filosof*. German translation in Frommann's *Klassiker der Philosophie*, Stuttgart, 1896, pp. 116-72.

[56] P. 129.—Cf. ALB. RITSCHL: *Fides implicita*, pp. 1-8, 27, 44 ff. A. HARNACK: *Lehrbuch der Dogmengeschichte*, iii. p. 73 ff.; 534 ff.

[57] P. 132.—With reference to Nirvana see WARREN: *Buddhism in Translations*, p. 59 ff.; 283 ff.; 372. Cf. above, note 37. The Upanishads, by their distinct acknowledgment that all striving and all pain is connected with doubleness and with difference, prepared the way for Buddhism. See *Upanishads*, DEUSSEN, p. 393; 436 ff. That the *process* of deliverance after its conclusion must appear as an illusion, because the true good does not become, but is, was taught already in the Upanishads. See DEUSSEN: "Die Philosophie der Upanishads" (*Allg. Gesch. der Philos.* i. 2 pp. 318-22).

[58] P. 137.—TYLOR has developed the theory of animism in his excellent work, *Primitive Culture*, and later in his *Text-Book of Anthropology*. LUBBOCK and HERBERT SPENCER have also shed light on this theory.

[59] P. 138.—TIELE: *Elements of the Science of Religion*, i. pp. 68-77.

[60] P. 141.—H. USENER: *Götternamen: Versuch einer Lehre von der religiösen Begriffsbildung*, Bonn, 1896, p. 280. It seems to me that Usener overlooks the significance of tradition. Only the *first* time that the sheaf or St. John's wort is worshipped do we get a real momentary god. Afterwards there is at any rate so much of a

'generic concept' as is implied in the custom of previous years. The theory of momentary gods is only new in name and in the interesting examples of it that have lately been brought forward. Earlier writers had already distinguished between temporary and permanent fetiches. See CHANTÉPIE DE LA SAUSSAYE : *Lehrbuch der Religionsgeschichte*, i. p. 44. For the worship of artificial objects and stones among the Indians see A. LANG : *Myth, Ritual and Religion*, i. pp. 225, 275.

[61] P. 143.—A. LANG, i. pp. 30, 126. H. USENER : *Götternamen*, p. 75 ff. Cf. AUGUSTINUS : *De civitate dei*, iv. chaps. viii.-xi.

[62] P. 144.—KARL BUDDE : *Die Religion des Volkes Israel bis zur Verbannung*, Giessen, 1900, p. 65.

[63] P. 144.—See on this point my *Psychology*, v. B. 9b.

[64] P. 145.—See on this point my *Psychology*, v. B. 9 ; vi. C. ; vii. 6 ; E. 3.

[65] P. 147.—AUG. COMTE : *Cours de philosophie positive*, v. p. 71 ff. ; vi. p. 413. H. USENER : *Götternamen*, passim (especially pp. 73, 316 ff. ; 321 ; 334 ; 343).

[66] P. 148.—I was led to adopt this conclusion by my colleague, Professor WILHELM THOMSEN, who considers the first explanation to be the more probable. In that case there would be a relationship between the root of the word 'gott' (God) and 'giessen' (to pour) as also between the Greek χέειν, whose root χυ = the Sanskrit *hu*, from which comes *huta*, which means 'sacrificed' as well as "he to whom sacrifices are made."

[67] P. 152.—DEUSSEN : Die Philosophie des Upanishads (*Gesch. der Phil.* i. 2), p. 282 ff. Mitchell too (*Hinduism Past and Present*, pp. 51, 138) considers it probable that the belief in the transmigration of souls arose in the attempt to explain individual differences.

[68] P. 152.— *Brihadaranyaka Upanishad*, 4, 3, 9-16 (Deussen's translation, p. 468). Survivals of animism can also be traced in the doctrine of Zarathustra. H. OLDENBERG : *Aus Indien und Iran*, pp. 172-75. E. LEHMANN : *Zarathustra*, i. p. 79.

[69] P. 153.—RICHARD GARBE : *Die Sankhyaphilosophie*: *Eine Darstellung des indischen Rationalismus*, Leipzig, 1894, pp. 172-90.

[70] P. 154.—See on this point ERWIN ROHDE : *Psyche*, i. p. 211, 278 ff; ii. p. 38 ff; 62. GOMPERZ : *Griechische Denker*, i. pp. 101-10. OLDENBERG draws an interesting parallel between Indian and Greek development at this point, *Aus Indien und Iran*, pp. 75-85.

[71] P. 154.—LE PAGE RENOUF : *Lectures on the Origin and Growth of Religion as illustrated by the Religion of Ancient Egypt*, London, 1880, p. 182 ff.

[72] P. 156.—TIELE : *Elements of the Science of Religion*, i. p. 236.

[73] P. 170.—See my *Psychology*, v. B. 7a, and the literature there quoted, as also FRANCIS GALTON : *Inquiries into Human Faculty*, London, 1883, pp. 155-73. For Swedenborg's vision see EMANUEL SWEDENBORG : *Summaria expositio doctrinae Novae Ecclesiae*, Amstelodami, 1769, § 119. (Notice in this vision the delightful incident of the angels, when

they thought they had discovered that Swedenborg embraced the orthodox doctrine of the Trinity, threatening to shut him out of heaven, and how Swedenborg had to expressly beg them to look more closely and notice that he transformed the three divine persons into three attributes of one and the same person. Thus he taught the angels and kept them from acting too hastily.) For St. Vincent de Paul's vision see BROGLIE : *St. Vincent de Paul,* Paris, 1898, p. 123.

⁷⁴ P. 170.—See on this point ERWIN ROHDE : *Psyche,* passim. DIELS (in his edition of the *Parmenides*) speaks of "those highly-gifted conductors of the Delphic oracle, who from the fifth to the sixth century exercised the greatest possible influence on the religion and morals, the political and social relations of Greece and the neighbouring countries." Their names are almost unknown to us. It was due partly to the development of the enlightenment (sophistry), partly to the democracy that no hierarchy worthy of the name developed in Greece, in spite of the great part played by mysteries and prophecy. DIELS : *Parmenides Lehrgedicht,* pp. 12-13.

⁷⁵ P. 171.—Cf. CORNILL : *Der israelitische Prophetismus,* Strassburg, 1896, pp. 82-92. According to the traditional view, Judaism became a book religion much earlier.

⁷⁶ P. 174.— FR. NIELSEN : *Pavedömmet i det nittende Aarhundrede* [The Papacy during the Nineteenth Century], ii. pp. 216-23. For the earlier history of the Conceptio immaculata, see HARNACK'S *Lehrbuch der Dogmengeschichte,* iii. pp. 584-87. The attitude of the future Cardinal Newman to this new dogma is especially interesting. (HUTTON : *Cardinal Newman,* pp. 201 ff.).

⁷⁷ P. 174.— In an article in the *Nineteenth Century* (Feb. 1900) on the "Continuity of Catholicism" the Jesuit Father Clarke writes : "Before our Lord ascended into heaven, we are told in Holy Scripture that, during the forty days that intervened between His resurrection and His ascension into heaven, He appeared to His apostles 'speaking of the kingdom of God' (Acts i. 3). Now the kingdom of God is in the New Testament a synonym for the Church of Christ. . . . In this passage it has reference primarily to the Church on earth. It informs us that our Lord instructed His disciples on the nature of the Church which He had come to found on earth, its constitution, its government, its discipline, its sacraments, and, above all, in the sacred doctrines which it was commissioned to teach to mankind. . . . Every Decree of Councils, every infallible utterance of Popes, is but the unfolding of some further portion of this body of doctrine." As to the source of this knowledge of what Jesus said to His disciples during the forty days we are not enlightened. It is made a matter of faith that what was necessary to faith was imparted during this time. As is very well known, it is not only the Catholics who have used 'the forty days' to smuggle in what is not otherwise to be found in the New Testament.

⁷⁸ P. 175.—A. HARNACK : *Lehrbuch der Dogmengeschichte,* i. p. 16 ff.

[79] P. 176.—See in addition to *Conf.* x. (especially 6; 35-38; 65) also i. 1, where a difference is made between calling on God and knowing him); iii. 11 ("Deus est interior intimo meo et superior summo meo"); vi. 1. ("Quaerebam te foris a me, et non inveniebam deum cordis mei"), also, *De vera religione*, c. 39 (Note foras ire: in teipsum redi, in interiore homine habitat veritas).

[80] P. 177.—*Upanishads*, DEUSSEN, pp. 164-66; 395.

[81] P. 178.—LIEBNER: *Hugo de St. Victoire*, pp. 41, 271, 332. HAURÉAU: *Les œuvres de Hugues de St. Victoire*, Paris, 1886, p. 140 ff. The expression 'embrace' or 'touch' me ("venit ut tangat te, non ut videatur a te") recalls Plotinus (cf. *Ennead.* v. 3, 16, 17; ii. 7-36). We are reminded in spite of ourselves here of the story of Amor and Psyche. Greek as well as Hebrew erotics might have lent symbols to religious experience. ANGÈLE DE FOLIGNO: *Le livre des visions et instructions*, 3me éd. Paris, 1895, p. 67 ff. The agreement in the terminology of Hugo de St. Victoire and St. Theresa is worthy of note. Cf. *Vie de Ste. Térèse écrite par elle-même*, Paris, 1896, p. 181 and ff.; 209 and ff.; 275 and ff.

[82] P. 180.—*Susos Leben und Schriften*, published by Diepenbrock, Regensburg, 1829, p. viii. and ff. *Vie de Ste. Térèse*, pp. 280-382. It is recounted of St. Brigitta that before she gave her revelations to the world they were examined by an orthodox theologian that he might delete anything which came from the devil and not from God. See H. SCHÜCK: *Sveriges Litteratur till Frihetstidens början*, Stockholm, 1896, p. 95 ff.

[83] P. 180.—HAURÉAU: *Les œuvres de Hugues de St. Victoire*, p. 137. *Vie de Ste. Térèse*, p. 97 and ff.; 181. Cf. JULIUS LANGE: *Menneskefiguren i Kunstens Historie* [The human figure in the history of art], Copenhagen, 1899, p. 266.

[84] P. 182.—ED. ZELLER: *Das theologische System Zwinglis*, p. 31 ff.

[85] P. 183.—JULIUS LANGE: *Menneskefiguren i Kunstens Historie*, p. 299.

[86] P. 184.—AUGUSTINUS: *Confessiones*, vi. 6; xiii. 10, 13. MARTENSEN: *Meister Eckhart*, p. 103; my *History of Modern Philosophy*, ii. 189 and f.; 213; 376 and f. CHR. SCHREMPF: "Kierkegaard's Stellung zur Bibel und Dogma" (*Zeitschrift für Theologie und Kirche*, i., 1891). For examples from the ecclesiastical life of the present day, see STARBUCK: *Psychology of Religion*, chaps. xix.-xxiii., cf. *ibid.* p. 368.

[87] P. 188.—"La base psychologique des jugements logiques" (*Revue Philosophique*, 1901), § 27 (cf. § 22 and § 24).

[88] P. 189.—Cf. H. OLDENBERG's characterisation of the etymological school of religious knowledge in his work *Aus Indien und Iran*, pp. 44-55.

[89] P. 193.—The passages in Sabatier's work towards which this criticism is directed are pp. 268, 308, 388. Cf. also p. 347, where it is said that it is the task of theology to explain the religious

experiences made within the Christian Church. But Sabatier did not himself observe this restriction. He did not see that religious experience was indispensable to him, and that he could not get round it by means of concepts deduced from it. He here becomes a religious materialist, in so far as he is guilty of the same dogmatic faults as is materialism.

⁹⁰ P. 194.—In my *History of Modern Philosophy*, ii. p. 280, I have already made this criticism.

⁹¹ P. 196.—For the problem of personality in its relation to other problems see my *Psychology* (ii. 8d ; iii. 11 ; v. B. 5-6 ; vii. C. 3). The Conflict between the Old and the New (*Journal of Ethics*, 1896), pp. 335-37.

⁹² P. 200.—The concepts of myth and legend are not employed in this way by all historians and philosophers of religion. A. LANG does not differentiate between them (cf. *Myth, Ritual and Religion*, i. p. 164 and ff.). LE PAGE RENOUF understands by legend a further amplification of the myth, which was originally simple and limited (*Origin and Growth of Religion*, p. 106). In my application of the two concepts I follow RENAN (cf. SÉAILLES : *Ernest Renan*, pp. 115-25) and SIEBECK : *Religionsphilosophie*, p. 273.

⁹³ P. 201.—For a further discussion of this relation see my article " La base psychologique des jugements logiques " (*Revue Philosophique*, 1901), §§ 14, 15, 21.

⁹⁴ P. 203.—DILTHEY in the *Archiv für Geschichte der Philosophie*, vi. p. 96 and ff.

⁹⁵ P. 211.—Cf. USENER : *Götternamen*, p. 78 and ff. ; 177-87. TIELE: *Elements of the Science of Religion*, i. pp. 173-77; ii. p. 85 and ff.

⁹⁶ P. 212.—DEUSSEN, *Geschichte der Philosophie*, i. 1, pp. 239-82.

⁹⁷ P. 213.—ERIK STAVE, *Ueber den Einfluss des Parsismus auf das Judentum*, Haarlem, 1898, p. 185.

⁹⁸ P. 214.—For Kant's religio-philosophical standpoint see my *History of Modern Philosophy*, ii. p. 98 and ff. Among Kant's successors FRIES was the one to see most clearly that the logical consequence of the turning taken by Kant was that religious ideas could now only be supposed to have symbolic and poetic significance. See his youthful work, *Wissen, Glaube und Ahndung* (1804), pp. 252-57 ; (*Ueber die Dogmen der natürlichen Religion*, p. 158 ff. ; 260). He developed his views at greater length in his *Religionsphilosophie* (1832). We may notice particularly here the following passage : " The most beautiful that we are able to conceive seems (to religious faith) the truest picture of the eternal truth. . . . This religious conviction is not merely figurative, it works itself out in real poetry. Its truth is the truth concealed in the deep innermost seriousness of the poet." That expression ' truest ' may easily lead to dogmatism. The dogmatic tendency is more apparent in APELT, a pupil of Fries, than in Fries himself. See the former's *Religionsphilosophie* (1863), p. 163, where certain definite symbols are set up as necessary and true. Mr.

KNUD OBEL, who has assisted me in preparing this book for publication, made some remarks on my treatment of the symbolic concept which seem to me so interesting that I must beg leave to quote them here : " In the moment of formation of a symbol for a religious feeling an entirely new feeling arises. Since it is an intuitable symbol of a cosmical relation, a feeling is evoked which differs both from the feeling which is excited by the relation to be symbolised and from that which is aroused by the relation from which the symbol is borrowed—and the reason of this is that the two relations are brought together in consciousness. The cool universal receives warmth from the symbol and from everything connected with the feeling which comes from life's innermost springs : at the same time this workaday feeling acquires a new tone by the extension of the idea to great relations ; it is pitched in the key of sublimity." This is thought out in just the right spirit. The free formation of symbols within the religious sphere, however, has up till now been allowed far too little significance for there to be definite and decisive experiences of how the symbol reacts on feeling and on consciousness generally. We can only illuminate this point by the way in which ready-made dogma has reacted upon the religious consciousness. We may *e.g.* compare the ideas of Jesus current among the early Christians with the firmly established and limited Christology of orthodox religiosity, and the different manner in which the religious consciousness has shaped itself in the two cases. The reaction of the symbol will be analogous to that of dogma.

⁹⁹ P. 220.—Cf. my *Ethik* (2nd German ed.), pp. 262-65. EHRENFELS : *Allgemeine Werttheorie,* i. pp. 132-45.

¹⁰⁰ P. 224.—Cf. my *Ethik,* p. 266 and f.

¹⁰¹ P. 227.—Cf. the chapter on Schopenhauer in my *History of Modern Philosophy,* ii. The ethico-scientific side of Schopenhauer's conception of life is brought forward (and almost exclusively emphasised) by RICHARD BÖTTGER : *Das Grundproblem der Schopen-hauerschen Philosophie,* Greifswald, 1898. In the latest and most excellent exposition of Schopenhauer's philosophy (JOH. VOLKELT : *Arthur Schopenhauer,* Stuttgart, 1900), the limit of his pessimism is brought out clearly. The great and striking contradictions in Schopenhauer are closely connected with the fact that he himself never clearly and logically perceived the limit of his own pessimism. His indigna-tion against the traditional optimism and his own (especially in his early years) discordant spirit led him to express his pessimism with more violence than was logically consistent with the rest of his thought.

¹⁰² P. 231.—*Reden Gotamo Buddhos,* translated by Neumann, ii, p. 84. *Dhammapadan* (The Path of Truth), translated by Neumann, Leipzig, 1893 (v. 91 ff. ; 373 ff.) (Cf. Fausböll's Latin translation : *The Dhammpada,* 2nd ed., London, 1900.)

¹⁰³ P. 231.—AUGUSTINUS: *Confessiones,* xi. 13 ; xii. 18. MARTENSEN :

Meister Eckhart, p. 21. *History of Modern Philosophy* (chapters on Boehme and Spinoza).

[104] P. 233.—*Reden Gotamo Buddhos,* translated by Neumann, i. p. 515 ff.; ii. p. 90; 475 ff. WARREN: *Buddhism in Translations,* p. 437. *Dhammapadan,* v. 210 f. (Neumann's translation).

[105] P. 237.—The apostle Paul was no doubt thinking of the time when God should be 'all in all' (1 Cor. xv.); but from the whole context in which this expression occurs, it is doubtful whether we are justified in deducing from this the doctrine of Apocatastasis (the final salvation of all men). God will be made all in all by Christ giving over to him the mastery; but the mastery, which according to the orthodox doctrine Christ had exercised, did not consist in the destruction or conversion of all inimical powers, but in reducing them to a state of powerlessness and subjection to his will. Cf. B. WEISS: *Lehrbuch der biblischen Theologie des Neuen Testaments,* p. 405 and ff.

[106] P. 238.—AUGUSTINUS: *De vera religione,* Cap. 40-41; cf. *Retractationes,* i. 7; *De civitate dei,* xxi. 17.

[107] P. 239.—The conclusion that God could not be blessed was drawn by SCHOPENHAUER: *Aus Schopenhauers handschriftl. Nachlass.,* Leipzig, 1864, p. 441. S. KIERKEGAARD: *Efterladte Papirer* [Posthumous Papers], 1854-55, p. 169; and GUYAU: *L'irréligion de l'avenir,* p. 388. The conclusion that sympathy with the damned must render the blessedness of the redeemed an impossibility was drawn by Schleiermacher (*Der christliche Glaube,* § 163, Appendix). But these conclusions presuppose other primary concepts of value than those which were known to primitive Christianity, or to Augustinus and Thomas. THOMAS AQUINAS expressly asserts that the blessedness of the saved is experienced all the more keenly in contrast with the sufferings of the damned: "Quum contraria juxta se posita magis elucescant, beati in regno coelesti videbunt poenas damnatorum, ut beatitudo illis magis complaceat" (*Summa theol.* iii. suppl. 94, 1). Conversely, the sufferings of the damned are increased by the fact that they first (before the last judgment) see the joy of the blessed and later (after the last judgment) can remember this joy (*ibid.* 98, 9). That one man could be blessed even though no others are, is established by Aquinas as follows: "Homo habet totam plenitudinem suae perfectionis in deo. . . . Perfectio caritatis est essentialis beatitudini quantum ad dilectionem dei, non quantum ad dilectionem proximi. Unde si esset una sola anima fruens deo, beata esset, non habens proximum, quem diligeret" (*Summa theol.,* Pars ii. Quaestio 4, Art. 8). A brilliant psychological exposition of the doctrine of eternal punishment was given by St. George Mivart, Roman Catholic and man of science, in an article entitled: "Happiness in Hell" (*Nineteenth Century,* 1892-93). His aim was so to interpret this doctrine that it should not conflict with ethics. When the state of those in hell is described as torment, this may mean that the distance from the highest blessedness is so great that in virtue of this contrast the state

must be called torment, although in comparison with our state in this life it might not be torment at all. His explanation, we notice, involves a very different application of the law of contrast from that made by Augustine and Aquinas. The ethical standpoint has changed. The Catholic Church answered this psychological attempt of their one-time apologist by putting his works on the register of forbidden books. See St. George Mivart's retrospect of the dispute in his article: "Roman Congregation and Modern Thought" in *The North American Review*, April 1900.

[108] P. 239.—*Summa theol.* iii. suppl. 94, 3.

[109] P. 240.—AUGUSTINUS: *De Moribus Manichaeorum*, Cap. 4 ; *De natura boni*, Cap. 10. The doctrine of the creation is open to the same difficulties as attach to that of an emanation. Cf. note 28 above and the corresponding passage in the text.

[110] P. 240.—THOMAS AQUINAS: *Summa theol.*, Pars i. Qu. 19, Art. 31. "Quum nihil ei perfectionis ex aliis accrescat, sequitur, quod alia a se eum velle non sit necessarium absolute." Cf. above, note 40.

[111] P. 246.—It is interesting to remember that in his preparatory studies for the *Kritik der reinen Vernunft*, KANT first regarded the categories as anticipations (or ' presumptions '). This conception would have led him to a more correct result than did the more dogmatic conception at which he arrived when actually elaborating his chief work. Cf. my article on "Die Kontinuität im philosophischen Entwickelungsgange Kants" (*Archiv für Gesch. der Philos.* vii.), § 15.

[112] P. 248.—Cf. my *Ethik*, chaps. iii. and vii. (especially vii. 4) and FRANCIS BRADLEY: *Appearance and Reality*, chap. xxv.

[113] P. 258.—Cf. my *Psychology*, vi. E.

[114] P. 267.—Cf. my *History of Modern Philosophy*, the chapters on Boehme, Bayle, Leibniz, Butler, and Schelling.

[115] P. 272.—Cf. my *Psychology*, vi. D. (cf. ii. 5) ; *Ethik*, p. 107 ff. ; 131 ff.

[116] P. 273.—See on this point my *History of Modern Philosophy*, ii. p. 31.

[117] P. 274.—I have dwelt on this side of the religious problem in my *Ethik*, pp. 472-76.

[118] P. 276.—WALLACE : *Russland*, chap. x.

[119] P. 279.—For a fuller discussion of this point see my *Ethik*, pp. 162-70.

[120] P. 280.—The Jesuit, Father Clarke, wrote of the scientist, St. George Mivart, who had formerly, partly on theological and partly on biological grounds, been one of the most eager and most fanatical opponents of Darwin, but who afterwards criticised the doctrines of hell (see note 107) and the infallibility of the Pope, and also appeared as a supporter of the higher criticism—of this man Father Clarke wrote in the *Nineteenth Century* (Feb. 1900, p. 256), that his fault was that he never made an act of complete intellectual submission to the Church and never gave up his private judgment, but that on the contrary he

presumed to teach the Church instead of being willing to be instructed by her.

[121] P. 281.—JUL. LANGE: *Menneskefiguren i Kunstens Historie* (The human figure in the history of art), p. 334.

[122] P. 282.—*Reden über die Religion*, p. 91.

[123] P. 283.—Cf. DURCKHEIM: *La division du travail social*, pp. 172-77. AMOS: *The Science of Law*, p. 134.

[124] P. 285.—LEUBA: "A Study in the Psychology of Religious Phenomena" (*The American Journal of Psychology*, vii. p. 323 and ff.). STARBUCH (*The Psychology of Religion*, London, 1900, p. 85. Two types of conversion) has drawn a similar distinction.

[125] P. 286.—Cf. ROYCE's article "The Case of John Bunyan" (printed in *Studies of Good and Evil*, New York, 1898).

[126] P. 289.—Cf. my *History of Modern Philosophy*, ii. pp. 355-60. Comte wanted to limit his religious as well as his intellectual interest to "le domaine planétaire" (*Politique positive*, iv. p. 211). JOHN INGRAM, well-known as a writer on economics, has given a good and interesting exposition of Comte's conceptions both of the history as well as of the philosophy of religion in his *Outlines of the History of Religion*, London, 1900.

[127] P. 291.—Cf. on this point my *Psychology*, p. 144 and f., and S. E. SHARP: "Individual Psychology" (*American Journal of Psychology*, April 1899), p. 44 and ff.

[128] P. 291.—Cf. LEUBA: "The personifying passion in youth" (*The Monist*, July 1900).

[129] P. 292.—SCHLEIERMACHER: *Reden über die Religion*, p. 168 and ff. Cf. for Schleiermacher's theory of knowledge my *History of Modern Philosophy*, ii. p. 202 and ff. MARTENSEN: *Levned* (*Life*) i. p. 69 and ff.

[130] P. 294.—See on this point my *Psychology*, p. 144, and also L. W. STERN: *Ueber die Psychologie der individuellen Differenzen*, Leipzig, 1900, p. 47 and ff.

[131] P. 295.—For the contrast between these two types see my book *S. Kierkegaard som Filosof* (German translation in Frommann's *Klassiker der Philosophie*, Stuttgart, 1896), pp. 74-82.

[132] P. 298.—The purely individual side of symbol-making has been well described by RÉCÉJAC: *Essai sur les fondements de la connaissance mystique*, Paris, 1897. ("Un buisson ardent, un souffle de l'air ont donné aux prophètes l'apparition de Dieu: l'esprit peut donc prêter son infinité aux moindres lueurs de la conscience mystique," p. 263.)

[133] P. 300.—Cf. my *Ethik*, p. 315 and ff.

[134] P. 300.—TRÖLTSCH in the *Zeitschrift für Theologie und Kirche*, v. p. 426. KAFTAN, *ibid.* vi. p. 94.

[135] P. 303.—WARREN, *Buddhism in Translations*, p. 59. *Die Reden Gotamo Buddhos*, translated by NEUMANN, i. p. 232 and ff.; 244-48; ii. pp. 148-60. Cf. above, notes 37 and 57.

[136] P. 303.—DEUSSEN's translation of the *Upanishads*, pp. 476-79 (Deliverance from Karma, *i.e.* from desire). The name *Nirvana* occurs in

the later Upanishads (*ibid.* p. 695). Cf. for the general relation of the Upanishads to Buddhism, Deussen's remarks in his "Philosophie der Upanishads" (*Geschichte der Philosophie*, i. 2), S. V.

[137] P. 304.—*The Dhammapada*, ed. Fausböll, 2nd ed. London, 1900, p. 91.

[138] P. 304.—*Die Reden Gotamo Buddhos*, i. p. 516. According to another account (see *Die Reden Buddhos*, ii. p. 450 and ff.) it was the thought of the dulness and unreceptiveness of men, of their disinclination to accept any teaching which runs counter to the stream, which held Buddha back. But a god revealed to him that, notwithstanding this, there are many noble, clear-seeing, and intelligent men in the world, and his sympathy, too, caused him to abandon his first resolve. The conversation between Buddha and the sorrowing father mentioned below in the text occurs in the *Reden Buddhos*, ii. p. 475 and f. (See above, note 104.)

[139] P. 306.—Cf. in this connexion my *Ethik*, p. 175 and ff.

[140] P. 307.—WARREN : *Buddhism in Translations*, p. 28. *Die Reden Buddhos*, translated by Neumann, i. p. 447. A psychological riddle, however, still remains. For while love is mentioned as the ninth perfection, indifference is the tenth, and this is compared with the earth, which exhibits neither "hate nor friendliness" against "the sweet or sour" which is thrown upon it. And side by side with expansion, as conditioned by recognition, we find immovability !

[141] P. 307.—Cf. TOKIWO YOKOI : "The Ethical Life and Conceptions of the Japanese" (*Journal of Ethics*, vi.), p. 184 ; 190 and ff.

[142] P. 313.—GEORGES GOYAU : *L'Allemagne religieuse. Le Protestantisme*, Paris, 1898, p. 121. Cf. above, notes 77 and 120.

[143] P. 319.—SARPI : *Histoire du Concile de Trente.* Trad. franç. par Amelot de la Haussaye, Amsterdam, 1686, pp. 137-49.

[144] P. 319.—For the religious movement during the first decades of the nineteenth century in its relation to the immediately preceding time see my treatise on "Glauben und Wissen in ihrer geschichtlichen Entwickelung" (only in Danish).

[145] P. 320.—"The churches were neither able to support nor to do without theology. Theology clings to science, and yet is no science, but a utilisation of scientific culture for ecclesiastical ends. This cleavage within the nature of theology need not always be as painful as it has become for us in the last two centuries. But it must always remain." TRÖLTSCH : "Die Selbständigkeit der Religion" (*Zeitschr. für Theol. und Kirche*, vi. p. 109. The expression "buffer" occurs in the same passage.

[146] P. 325.—TIELE : *Elements of the Science of Religion*, i. pp. 63, 67.

[147] P. 326.—TIELE : *ibid.* i. pp. 105-109.

[148] P. 327.—*Aus Indien und Iran*, p. 101 and ff.

[149] P. 329.—*Welt als Wille und Vorstellung*, p. 436.

[150] P. 334.—On the difference between motive of estimation and motive of action see my *Ethik*, p. 33 and ff. ; 38 and ff. ; 66.

[151] P. 337.—Cf. Joh. Clausen: *Lov og Evangelium i Forhold til Christendomsforkyndelsen, forhandlet mellem Reformatorerne i Wittenberg og Agrikola fra Eisleben* (Law and Gospel in their relation to the preaching of Christianity as treated by the Wittenberg reformers and Agricola von Eisleben), Copenhagen, 1872, pp. 51-64. That Agricola displayed in the course of the dispute a want of self-control and a tendency to hair-splitting does not do away with the psychological and ethical justification of his first assertion, when the personal differences of the people who were to be influenced is sufficiently taken into consideration.

[152] P. 338.—For the distinction between honesty, personal truth, and intellectual uprightness see my *Ethik*, pp. 245-49.

[153] P. 339.—What conflicts the desire to preach under existing circumstances may involve on honest and intellectually upright natures may be learnt from the fate of Märklin and Schremff. Cf. D. F. Strauss: *Christian Märklin. Ein Lebens- und Characterbild aus der Gegenwart*, Mannheim, 1851. Chr. Schrempf: *Akten zu meiner Entlassung aus dem Württembergischen Kirchendienst*, Göttingen, 1891. Id.: *Eine Frage an die evangelische Landeskirche Württemberg*, Göttingen, 1892. Cf. also my *Ethik*, p. 491. Carlyle's *Life of Sterling* is also in this respect a document of great interest

[154] P. 352.—*De vera religione*, cap. 3, 4.

[155] P. 355.—E. de Broglie: *St. Vincent de Paul*, 4me éd., Paris, 1898. H. Krummacher: *Johannes Heinrich Wichern. Ein Lebensbild aus der Gegenwart*, Gotha, 1882.

[156] P. 355.—Taine: *Le régime moderne*, ii. pp. 105-13; cf. R. Davey in the *Fortnightly Review*, August 1900, p. 275.

[157] P. 355.—James Bryce: *The American Commonwealth*, iii. p. 55.

[158] P. 356.—See on this point my *Ethik*, pp. 504-506.

[159] P. 357.—Cf. my essay on "Faith and Knowledge."

[160] P. 358.—For further details see my *Ethik*, pp. 192-97; 267-71.

[161] P. 363.—Cf. Lessing's treatise: *Ueber den Beweis des Geistes und der Kraft*.

[162] P. 364.—The difference between the primitive Christian and the modern Christian conception of life is brought out from such different standpoints as are represented by Schopenhauer, L. Feuerbach, and Strauss on the one hand, and S. Kierkegaard on the other; not always, however, with a sufficient sense of historical conditions. Cf. the last chapter of my work, *Sören Kierkegaard som Filosof* (Frommann's *Klassiker*). Harnack, in his monumental *History of Dogma*, has discussed from the purely historical point of view the idiosyncrasies of primitive Christianity and its relation to the Christianity of the Church. In his critique of this work O. Pfleiderer has reproached Harnack for representing such a deep chasm between Apostolic and Catholic Christianity. Pfleiderer was of opinion that the early Christian expectation of a speedy second coming, and of a

kingdom of God on earth, had become untenable in face of the actual historical disappointment, and that it was absolutely inevitable that this should be replaced by a spiritualistic eschatology (*Die Entwickelung der protestantischen Theologie in Deutschland seit Kant*, Freiburg, 1891, p. 370 and ff.). But the very fact of the necessity of this substitution testifies to the existence of the 'chasm.' The chasm came into existence when the attitude towards culture changed, and it is Harnack's merit that he indicated it so sharply and clearly, and thus historically sharpened and hardened the difference between the conception of life held by the early Christians and that entertained by the later Church, which difference the thinkers above-named had already brought to light by means of an immediate comparison.

[163] P. 364.—Cf. H. WEINEL: *Die Wirkungen des Geistes und der Geister im nachapostolischen Zeitalter bis auf Irenäus*, Freiburg, 1899.

[164] P. 364.—*De civitate dei*, xx. 9.

[165] P. 365.—*Lehrbuch der Dogmengeschichte*, ii. p. 9.

[166] P. 367.—HUTTON : *Cardinal Newman*, pp. 110-119. *Vie de Ste. Térèse écrite par elle-même*, pp. 165, 177.

[167] P. 367.—Cf. *Ethik*, pp. 93-95.

[168] P. 371.—A. RITSCHL: *Geschichte des Pietismus*, ii. pp. 122-25, 308, 448. A. HARNACK: *Lehrbuch der Dogmengeschichte*, i. 72 ; iii. p. 101 and ff. Cf. an utterance of KARL HASE'S in the year 1831, quoted in BÜRCKNER'S *Karl von Hase*, Leipzig, 1900, p. 46. TRÖLTSCH expresses himself in a similar sense in his article " Die Selbständigkeit der Religion " (*Zeitschr. für Theologie und Kirche*, v.-vi.), and SABATIER in his *Philosophie de la Religion*, pp. 220, 230, 237 and f., 251 and f.

[169] P. 377.—*Sören Kierkegaard som Filosof* (German translation, Stuttgart, 1896, p. 115 and f.).

[170] P. 381.—According to the view of the Stoics, the value of life consisted in the knowledge of existence and the exercise of valuable qualities of character. A human life such as this did not, in their opinion, stand far behind that of the gods, the only difference being that the gods are immortal; this, however, in the Stoics' view, did not affect the real value of life ("vita beata, par et similis deorum, nulla alia re nisi immortalitate, quae nihil ad bene vivendum pertinet, cedens coelestibus "—CICERO : *De natura deorum*, ii. pp. 61, 153). Compare in modern times, in addition to Kant, SPINOZA (*Ethica*, v. 41), SCHLEIERMACHER (*Der christliche Glaube*, § 158), and, quite recently, characteristic utterances from FRANCIS BRADLEY (*Appearance and Reality*, pp. 501-10), and H. R. MARSHALL (*Journal of Ethics*, ix. p. 364 and ff.).

[171] P. 382.—Cf. my critique of Heegaard's work in the journal, *Nar og Fjern* ("Far and Near "), 1878.

[172] P. 383.—R. GARBE: *Die Sankhyaphilosophie*, a sketch of Indian Rationalism, Leipzig, 1894, p. 135. Cf. above, note 170.

INDEX

THE END